# Portuguese: A Linguistic Introduction

This accessible new book provides a comprehensive introduction to the linguistic structure of Portuguese. Clearly organized, it covers the central topics of syntax, phonology, morphology, semantics, and pragmatics, and explores the social and historical background of Portuguese, its development and spread in the world, and related sociolinguistic issues such as dialect variation and language planning. It also includes a chapter on Portuguese in Brazil, where approximately 80% of Portuguese speakers live. Assuming very little prior knowledge of linguistic terminology, *Portuguese: A Linguistic Introduction* is designed to help intermediate and advanced students of Portuguese understand how the language functions at all levels, and to give students of linguistics a useful starting point for work on the structure of Portuguese. Keeping formalism to a minimum, it focuses on presenting the linguistic facts in a systematic way, providing a useful global overview of the Portuguese language and its surrounding issues.

MILTON M. AZEVEDO is Professor of Hispanic Linguistics in the Department of Spanish and Portuguese, University of California, Berkeley. His previous books include *Passive Sentences in English and Portuguese* (1980), *A Contrastive Phonology of Portuguese and English* (1981), *Teaching Spanish: A Practical Guide* (second edition), coauthored with Wilga M. Rivers (main author) and William H. Heflin, Jr. (1988), *La parla i el text* (1996), *Introducción a la lingüística española* (1992), and *Vozes em Branco e Preto. A Representação Literária da Fala Não-Padrão* (2003). He has also written widely on the Spanish and Portuguese languages for a number of journals.

D1292934

# Portuguese: A Linguistic Introduction

Milton M. Azevedo

CAMBRIDGE
UNIVERSITY PRESS

CAMBRIDGE UNIVERSITY PRESS
Cambridge, New York, Melbourne, Madrid, Cape Town,
Singapore, São Paulo, Delhi, Tokyo, Mexico City

Cambridge University Press
The Edinburgh Building, Cambridge CB2 8RU, UK

Published in the United States of America by Cambridge University Press, New York

www.cambridge.org
Information on this title: www.cambridge.org/9780521805155

First published 2005

*A catalogue record for this publication is available from the British Library*

*Library of Congress Cataloguing in Publication data*
Azevedo, Milton Mariano, 1942–
Portuguese : a linguistic introduction / Milton M. Azevedo.
    p.  cm.
Includes bibliographical references and index.
ISBN 0-521-80126-5 (hbk.) – ISBN 0-521-80515-5 (pbk.)
1. Portuguese language. 1. Title.
PC5043.A94 2004
469 – dc22   2004049687

ISBN 978-0-521-80126-3 Hardback
ISBN 978-0-521-80515-5 Paperback

Gladly dedicated to
Blondie and Álvaro
for their steadfast friendship and good-humored encouragement

# Contents

# Maps

# Tables and figure

**Tables**

## Figure

# Acknowledgments

It would be difficult to properly recognize every individual who has made a contribution to this book and I apologize in advance to those inadvertently omitted. I begin by thanking those students who took the classes where the original materials were used, and whose comments helped shape ideas and refine the presentation. Colleagues who deserve specific recognition for having contributed invaluable insights and comments on portions of the manuscript include Ana Maria Carvalho (University of Arizona), Jerry R. Craddock (University of California, Berkeley), Regina Igel (University of Maryland), Sandi Michele de Oliveira (University of Copenhagen), Clea Rameh (Georgetown University), Lyris Wiedemann (Stanford University), Antonio Simões (University of Kansas), and Thomas Stephens (Rutgers University).

My gratitude is gladly extended to the following colleagues and friends, who generously contributed valuable information, data, bibliographic items, or comments:

> Deolinda Adão (University of California, Berkeley)
> Diniz Borges (Institute for Azorean-American Studies, College of
> the Sequoias, Visalia)
> Luiz Carlos Cagliari (Universidade de Campinas)
> Filomena Capucho (Universidade Católica Portuguesa, Viseu)
> Tito Cardoso e Cunha (Universidade Nova de Lisboa)
> Carmen Chaves Tesser (University of Georgia)
> Melissa Gomes Frosini (102 Studio, São Paulo)
> Ataliba Teixeira de Castilho (Universidade de São Paulo)
> J. Chrys Chrystello (University of Technology, Sydney)
> Geraldo Cintra (Universidade de São Paulo)
> Sofia Ferreira Goldar (Universidade Católica Portuguesa, Viseu)
> Waldemar Ferreira Neto (Universidade de São Paulo)
> Francisco Gomes de Matos (Universidade Federal de Pernambuco)
> Hildo Honório do Couto (Universidade de Brasília)
> Eduardo Mayone Dias (University of California, Los Angeles)
> Ramiro Dutra (journalist, Los Angeles)
> Brian King (University of California, Berkeley)

Alberto Lemos (former Editor, *Jornal Português*, California)
Armando Jorge Lopes (Universidade de Mozambique)
Maria C. Odom (Editor, *Portuguese American Chronicle*, California)
Urbana Pereira (Universidade de Aveiro)
Pepetela (Visiting Professor, University of California, Berkeley)
Maria Aparecida Torres (Universidade de São Paulo)

Special acknowledgment is due to Karen C. Sherwood Sotelino (University of California, Santa Cruz) for proofreading the manuscript professionally and contributing excellent stylistic suggestions. I thank Rakhel Villamil-Acera, doctoral candidate at the University of California, Berkeley, for her invaluable research assistance. I am particularly appreciative of the encouragement received at critical points from Frederick "Freddie" Renart, Esq. A sabbatical leave from the University of California, Berkeley, and support from the Committee on Research are also gratefully acknowledged. And in a very special way, I am grateful to Kate Brett, who initiated this project, and to Helen Barton, who saw it through most of the editorial process with patience and good humor. Any extant imperfections are, of course, *mea culpa*.

# Abbreviations and symbols

## Abbreviations

| | |
|---|---|
| AD | a date of the Christian Era (Lat *Anno Domini*) |
| adj. | adjective, adjectival |
| adv. | adverb(ial) |
| Ar | Arabic |
| art | article |
| BC | before Christ |
| BE | British English |
| BP | Brazilian Portuguese |
| cf. | compare (Lat *confer*) |
| coll. | colloquial |
| dial. | dialectal |
| Eng | English |
| EP | European Portuguese |
| f. | feminine |
| Fr | French |
| fut. | future |
| Gal | Galician |
| Ger | German |
| GP | Galician-Portuguese |
| Gr | Greek |
| H | high (variety) |
| Houaiss | Houaiss's Dictionary (Houaiss 2001) |
| imperf | imperfect |
| ind. | indicative |
| irreg. | irregular |
| It | Italian |
| Lat | Latin |
| lit. | literally |
| L | low (variety) |
| m. | masculine |

| mil. | military |
| mod. | modern |
| MP | Modern Portuguese |
| MoP | Mozambican Portuguese |
| n., N | noun |
| NP | noun phrase |
| nav. | navy, naval |
| obs. | obsolete |
| OP | Old or medieval Portuguese |
| orth. | orthography, orthographic |
| P1pl | first person plural 'we' |
| P1sg | first person singular 'I' |
| P2pl | second person plural 'you (pl.)' |
| P2sg | second person singular 'you (sg.)' |
| P3pl | third person plural 'they' |
| P3sg | third person singular 'he/she' |
| Pg | Portuguese |
| part | participle |
| perf | perfect |
| pl | plural |
| pluperf | pluperfect |
| pop. | popular, population |
| pos | possessive |
| Pr | Provençal |
| prep. | preposition |
| pres. | present |
| reg. | regular |
| S | sentence |
| sg | singular |
| st. | standard |
| sub | subjunctive |
| subj | subject |
| VBP | Vernacular (aka Popular) Brazilian Portuguese |
| VP | verb phrase |

### Symbols

| [ ] | phonetic transcription |
| / / | phonological (or phonemic) transcription |
| { } | morphemic transcription |
| ° | a Glossary entry |

| | |
|---|---|
| ' | placed before a vowel in phonetic transcription to show syllable stress |
| x < y | x originates from, results from y |
| x > y | x changes into, becomes, yields y |
| * | in the examples, indicates an ungrammatical or ill-formed word, phrase, or sentence; in diachronic linguistics alone, a hypothetical or unattested form; in the Glossary, a cross-reference to another entry |
| a → b | a originates b (or b is created from a) |
| a ~ b | a and b are equivalent |

# Introduction

This book grew out of an overview of Portuguese designed for undergraduate seniors and graduates with varying levels of familiarity with the language and little or no training in grammar or linguistics. Some of these students were native or semi-native speakers, while others had learned the language through formal study rather than residence in a Portuguese-speaking country. As a group, they were typical of students interested in studying language as a means of communication and literary expression rather than an end in itself, and curious to learn something about the structure and use of Portuguese without going too deep into its formal analysis under any one of the linguistic theories available. Presenting the language to those students in a systematic but interesting way turned out to be a challenging and rewarding experience. Patterned on that course, this book has been organized around several key topics seen from a linguistic viewpoint rather different from the prescriptive approach usually found in grammar manuals. Owing to its general character, *Portuguese: A Linguistic Introduction* introduces only a handful of the language's main aspects, leaving out several otherwise important topics and a number of details that should be taken up at a more advanced level.

This book is divided into eight chapters, the first of which, "Portuguese in the world," surveys the external history of the language, that is the facts surrounding its development and spread beyond its original territory. The next three chapters deal with select topics of its phonology or sound system (Chapter 2, "Sounds"), its morphology or the internal organization of words (Chapter 3, "Words"), and its syntax or sentence structure (Chapter 4, "Sentences"). Aspects of the internal history of the language, that is how it grew out of popular Latin, are presented in Chapter 5, "Portuguese in time." In continuation, Chapter 6, "The expansion of European Portuguese," overviews language variation in continental Portugal, its autonomous regions of Madeira and the Azores, and Africa, Asia, and America. Chapter 7, "Brazilian Portuguese," examines in some detail the variety of the language spoken by about 80% of its speakers. Finally, Chapter 8, "Sociolinguistic issues," analyzes select topics such as diglossia, styles and registers, forms of address, profane language, and communicative strategies.

The premise adopted is that a language is primarily an instrument of communication that operates in a social context and is marked by a certain degree of variation. Consequently, rather than refer to an idealized version of Portuguese, this book takes into account linguistic data such as obtain in actual language use. Whereas some of the data agree with the rules found in normative grammars based on literary usage, others clash with them. Learners need to get used to this situation and accept the fact that no living language can be reduced to a set of right-or-wrong rules such as are favored by language mavens. There are issues of usage about which speakers do not always agree, and for which objective analyses cannot offer a single "correct" solution. One reason for this is that we do not possess enough data concerning those issues. Although this situation is beginning to change with the emergence of linguistic corpora, we are not yet in a position to draw definitive conclusions, even assuming such a goal is viable. If anything, corpora of real speech show that Portuguese varies considerably. This is not surprising: a language geographically so far-flung, spoken by over two hundred million people in four continents, could not fail to show a great deal of variation.

I have made an effort to make this book user-friendly by organizing the material, particularly the examples, in a legible format and cross-referencing the chapters. Thus, an indication like (2.3.2) refers to material in Chapter 2, section 3, subsection 2. Formal analysis and terminology have been kept to a minimum, but even so a certain amount of it, particularly in the chapters on phonology, morphology, and syntax, is inevitable: you cannot talk about the motor of your car without naming its parts.

I have tried to explain technical terms in the text and have added a glossary of terms (indicated by a superscript °) that students seemed to find most troublesome. Readers should find linguistic dictionaries such as Matthews 1997 or Crystal 1994, to which I am indebted, particularly useful in resolving doubts about terminology.

While regional and social variation is taken into account, unless otherwise stated the examples represent the usage of educated adult speakers and reflect the kind of language college-trained foreign learners can reasonably expect to encounter in their contacts with educated speakers of Portuguese. Individual words are glossed for their most general meaning when used to illustrate pronunciation or morphology. Consequently a word like *pena* may be glossed simply as 'feather' even though it has other meanings, such as 'pen,' 'pity,' or the third person singular of the present indicative of the verb *penar* 'to suffer.' As learners soon find out, any third person singular verb form can be used not only with the Portuguese equivalents of *he* (*ele*) and *she* (*ela*) but also with three forms meaning *you*, namely *você*, *o senhor* (m.), and *a senhora* (f.). To avoid cumbersome glosses forms such as *critica* 'he/she/you (sg.) criticizes' or *criticam* 'they/you (pl.) criticize,' the persons of the discourse are signaled by abbreviations such as P3sg or P3pl (see Abbreviations). All glosses, rewrites of passages in non-standard Portuguese, and translations of citations are my own.

As is well known, the countries where Portuguese has official status have yet to agree on a common orthography. To be sure, some spelling differences reflect variations in pronunciation, as in Brazilian Portuguese (BP) *fato* 'fact' vs. European Portuguese (EP) *facto* 'fact' vs. *fato* 'suit of clothes' should be considered a separate word. Other differences, however, are purely visual, as in the case of the word for *linguistics*, which is written with an umlaut (*lingüística*) in BP and without it (*linguística*) in EP. There is really no good reason for such discrepancies, which are due less to language differences than to the stubbornness of those who make decisions on spelling matters, but one learns to live with them. Fortunately for learners, those spelling differences, puzzling as they can sometimes be, are really minor and do not interfere with comprehension. This book uses the current Brazilian orthography except in examples of European usage or in quoted passages and bibliographical items, which are given in their original spelling.

Such minor discrepancies are not a linguistic problem, for a language can exist with two or more partially overlapping spelling systems. Even variations in the lexicon and grammar do not necessarily compromise the integrity of the overall system, as is clearly demonstrated by the case of English, with two major international standards and other emerging regional ones (Burns and Coffin 2001; Trudgill and Hannah 2002). Whenever appropriate, I have compared the Brazilian and European varieties, which differ in various ways. For reasons discussed in Chapter 2, pronunciation can be a bit of problem for learners accustomed to BP when they are exposed to to EP, though the problem is lesser in the opposite direction. Lexical differences between BP and EP can be substantial, depending on the semantic area involved (Villar 1989, Prata 1984) but do not affect the structure of the language. Although the syntactic core is common to both varieties (as well as to the EP-related varieties spoken in Africa), there are clear contrasts in certain areas of sentence structure, such as the use (or, in the case of BP, non-use) of unstressed pronouns. There are also important contrasts in pragmatics, that is the norms of personal interaction and the strategies used to ask for something, to interrupt, to agree, to disagree, and so on. Unfortunately, little research has been carried out in the pragmatics of either variety, let alone in comparing them systematically, and consequently learners used to one variety have to feel their way around in communicating with speakers of the other. They can find solace, as well as encouragement, in the fact that native speakers face similar difficulties and usually overcome them, as demonstrated by the millions of Portuguese living in Brazil and thousands of Brazilians living in Portugal.

The often sharp differences between the educated and vernacular or popular varieties of Brazilian Portuguese can also be a source of puzzlement for learners. Those differences, however, are not unique and should not be blown out of proportion: popular speech in London, New York, Mexico City, Paris, or for that matter Lisbon can be just as impenetrable, initially at any rate, to outsiders. An American friend of mine who had studied Portuguese for over a year summed up this situation in a pithy message e-mailed a few weeks after arriving in Rio: "This language is going to kill me. I'm starting to hear things on TV and in conversation with educated people, but when it comes to the street, it's like they speak a different language." Nevertheless he survived, traveled around, met people, made friends, and is currently making plans to go back. His experience, which is that of many other people, simply underscores the fact that comprehension does not happen between languages or varieties of a language, but between people. A speaker of variety A who is dismayed or annoyed because speakers of variety B do not talk like the folks back home does not have a linguistic problem but a cultural one, which can only be solved if one is genuinely willing to work to develop the ability – which does not come naturally – to understand the other. It is a process that can be frustrating at times, but a dash of good humor certainly helps, and a bit of linguistics may be prove handy to sort out those differences and show they are not haphazard but systematic. It is hoped that this book will be of use to serious learners of Portuguese like my friend in coming to terms with this multifaceted language.

# 1    The Portuguese language in the world

On March 22, 2002, in Dili, the capital city of East Timor, a national constitution was enacted, whose Article 13 stated that "*O tétum e o português são as línguas oficiais da República Democrática de Timor-Leste*," meaning 'Tetum [a Southeast Asian language] and Portuguese are the official languages of the Democratic Republic of East Timor.' A significant detail is that all the names and most of the surnames of the parliamentarians who signed the new constitution are Portuguese (*Lourdes, Manuel, Maria, José, Luisa, Norberto, Costa, Martins, Silva, Alves*, and so on), even though reportedly only about 2% of the population of East Timor speak Portuguese (Ethnologue.com 2002).

Having a constitution was a major accomplishment for that small country. After becoming independent in 1975 from Portugal, whose colony it had been since the fifteenth century, Timor was occupied by Indonesia for the next twenty-five years, and had to secure its freedom again at a heavy toll in human lives. Historically, however, this is just one more occasion on which Portuguese has served not only as a vital link to the outside world but also as a common language for speakers of East Timor's nineteen other languages, some of which, like Adabe or Habu, have only about one thousand speakers each. Portuguese has often played the role of a lingua franca° (a topic to be taken up again in Chapter 6) since the fifteenth century, when it began to spread from its birthplace in the Iberian Peninsula to reach the four courners of the earth.

At the time of writing (2002), Portuguese has official status in eight countries, namely Angola, Brazil (Brasil), Cape Verde (Cabo Verde), Guinea-Bissau (Guiné-Bissau), Mozambique (Moçambique), Portugal, São Tomé and Príncipe (São Tomé e Príncipe), and East Timor (Timor Leste). Spoken by about a million people in 1500, it is now estimated to be the first language of some 176 million people, a figure that shoots up to 191 million if we include secondary speakers, that is people who have learned Portuguese as a second language (www.ethnologue.com). Though approximate, such figures put Portuguese in sixth place among the languages with the largest number of speakers, after Mandarin Chinese, English, Spanish, Hindi, and Arabic (Crystal 1997:289). In what follows we will review the main points of the external history of Portuguese, identify its geographic distribution to facilitate visualizing its extension on a map, and highlight other aspects of the language's situation in the world.

## 1.1    The growth of Portuguese

Portuguese is a Romance° language, like Catalan, French, Galician, Italian, Rumanian, Romansh, and Spanish (to mention only those with official status and leaving out others such as Corsican, Piedmontese, and Sardinian). Perhaps disappointingly, the word "Romance" in this context has nothing to do with Latin lovers; rather, it comes from the Latin adverb *romanice* 'in the Roman way,' which was used in the Middle Ages to designate the new speech that grew out of the popular Latin spoken in the Western Roman Empire. From the last centuries of the Empire until the emergence of Portugal as a sovereign state in the twelfth century, the language now called Portuguese gradually took shape as a spoken tongue, largely overshadowed by the universality of medieval Latin as the medium of written communication.

### 1.1.1    Roman Hispania

So far as we know, the earliest inhabitants of the Iberian Peninsula included the ancestors of the Basques in the north, the Tartesians in the south, the Iberians (a name linked to that of the Ebro River) in the east and, after about 1000 BC, the Celts, who came from northern Europe and mixed with the Iberians. Trade on the Mediterranean led to the establishment of colonies by the Phoenicians (Málaga and Cádiz), by the Carthaginians, themselves of Phoenician origin but established in Carthage, near present-day Tunis (Cartagena and Mahon, on the island of Menorca), and by the Greeks (Ampurias, on today's Costa Brava).

The Romans arrived in the Iberian Peninsula in 218 BC and colonized it in two centuries, except for a northeastern strip in today's Basque Country. They called the peninsula *Hispania* – according to a charming legend, after a Phoenician name, *i-shepham-im* or 'land of rabbits' (Eslava-Galán 1995:13) – and divided it into provinces (Map 1.1). They also provided effective administrators and troops to keep the *pax romana* 'Roman peace.' The northwestern corner of the peninsula became a province called *Gallaecia*, after its early inhabitants, the Gallaeci, a name that persists in the toponym 'Galicia' (Pg, Gal *Galiza*), which is one of contemporary Spain's autonomous regions, bounded to the east by two other autonomous regions, Asturias and Castilla-León, and to the south by the Minho River, its natural border with Portugal.

To the south and to the east of Gallaecia lay another Roman province, named *Lusitania*, after a mythical demi-god, Luso (Lat *Lusus*), a son of Bacchus and the legendary founder of Portugal. That name survives in the prefix *Luso-* 'Portuguese,' used in expressions like *estudos luso-brasileiros* 'Luso-Brazilian

Map 1.1 Schematic location of the provinces of Roman Hispania

studies' or *lusófono* 'lusophone,' that is, 'Portuguese-speaking.' It also appears in *lusofonia* 'lusophony,' a somewhat protean designation, referring loosely to the Portuguese-speaking peoples and/or regions, which was coined in the late twentieth century based on the French word *francophonie* 'francophony,' or 'French-speaking.' When the Romans defeated the Carthagenians in the second Punic War (202 BC), Lusitania was part of the Roman province of Hispania Ulterior, and its administrative center was located in what is now Mérida, in Spanish Extremadura. Nevertheless, most of Lusitania's territory from the left bank of the Minho to the Algarve region in the south makes up today's Portugal. This country's name, in turn, goes back to the Latin toponym PORTU CALE, an erstwhile Roman military installation named *Cale* which overlooked a port on the Douro river, near the site of today's city of Porto (Eng *Oporto*, so called because of the Portuguese habit of referring to "o Porto"). Over the centuries, the Latin spoken in Gallaecia would change into a Romance speech which in turn gave origin to two closely related languages, namely Galician, still spoken in that region, and Portuguese, which spread southward in the wake of conquest and settlement.

According to the Roman Empire's colonizing policy, land was provided as a bonus for retired soldiers, many of whom had served in the legions stationed in the peninsula. Soldiers, settlers, and administrators all spoke Latin, and although Rome did not care what language subjected peoples actually spoke – learning Latin was considered a privilege rather than a duty – the prestige of Roman civilization, manifested by an impressive network of paved roads, bridges, aqueducts, temples, theaters, public baths, circuses, and an administrative organization unparalleled in the ancient world, led the original inhabitants of Hispania to adopt the language and customs of the Romans. After a period of bilingualism, the languages spoken before the Romans' arrival – with the exception of Basque – were eventually replaced by the settlers' popular Latin, which coexisted with the more cultivated variety used by officials and an educated elite. Eventually, some cities in Hispania – Tarragona, Córdoba, Mérida – emulated Rome in beauty and quality of life, and in the first century of our era a number of Hispanic Romans – such as the philosophers Seneca the Elder, his son Seneca the Younger, the poets Lucan and Martial, and the rhetorician Quintilian – made major contributions to Latin letters.

### 1.1.2   Visigothic Hispania

The collapse of the Western Roman Empire, whose last emperor, Romulus Augustulus, was deposed in 476 AD, brought about the breakdown of administrative cohesiveness and communication among Hispania's various regions. The ensuing isolation led to increasing regional differentiation in the Latin spoken in Hispania and elsewhere. Beginning in the first decade of the fifth century, a series of invasions by Germanic tribes such as the Suevi, the Vandals, and the Alans culminated, in the early sixth century, with the arrival of the Visigoths. These either enslaved, killed off or drove away their predecessors, with the exception of the Suevi, who maintained a small kingdom in Gallaecia until about 585, when they too were conquered by the Visigoths. Being quite romanized, thanks to an early sojourn in Roman Gaul, the Visigoths adopted Roman Hispania's language, customs, and religion. By the end of the sixth century the Visigothic kingdom, which had Toledo as its capital, extended all over the peninsula, though its suzerainty over the Basque Country remained nominal, as the Roman domination had been – a factor that permitted survival of the Basque language until our days.

Even in the heyday of the Roman Empire the speech of the inhabitants of the peninsula was essentially popular Latin, which differed noticeably from the literary Latin we learn at school. By the end of the sixth century, however, that speech had changed even further, into something considerably different from Latin as it was still spoken and written, as a learned language, by a literate minority associated primarily with clerical life. This new way of speaking, whether or not people realized that it derived from Latin, became known as *fabulare romanice*, that is 'to speak Romance.' Eventually the adverb *romanice*,

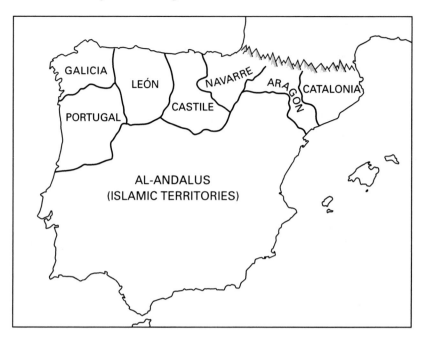

Map 1.2 Schematic location of Christian dominions and Islamic holdings in Hispania in the early tenth century

shortened to *romance*, was reinterpreted as a noun designating the local speech. In other words, everyone spoke Romance, and a few, usually members of the clergy, also learned to speak and write medieval Latin. (The verb *fabulare*, originally meaning 'to spin a yarn,' was the source of Pg *falar*, Sp *hablar* 'to talk.') Since most people were illiterate, and all writing was done in Latin, written signs reflecting a Romance speech were slow to appear, and its growth and expansion are closely linked to those of the Christian kingdoms that emerged from what had been Roman Hispania.

### 1.1.3 Islamic Hispania

In 711, the Iberian peninsula was invaded by an Islamic army made up of Berbers and Arabs, collectively called Moors° (after Lat *Mauri*, the name of the inhabitants of Mauritania in Roman North Africa). The invaders crossed the Strait of Gibraltar (from *gebel-al-Tarik* 'Tarik's hill,' a toponym that preserves the invaders' leader's name) and in a short time overwhelmed the Visigothic kingdom. By 718 the peninsula had been divided (Map 1.2) into a southern Islamic area, Al-Andalus (a name that recalls the ferocious Vandals and is preserved today in the place-name Andalusia), and a northern fringe under

Christian domination. The latter area, which included a few strongholds in the mountains of Asturias, the Basque region, and a string of fortifications called the Spanish March, set up by Charlemagne (742–814) along the Pyrenees, would eventually be divided into several Christian kingdoms and counties which, for the next seven centuries, fought to reconquer the territory lost to the invaders. Also in 718, the Christians holding out in the mountains of Asturias achieved a small victory over a detachment of Moors in a skirmish celebrated in legend as the battle of Covadonga, traditionally held to be the beginning of the reconquest which culminated in the fall of Granada to the Catholic Monarchs Ferdinand and Isabella in 1492.

## 1.2    The formation and expansion of Portuguese

A fundamental linguistic consequence of the Arab conquest of the Iberian Peninsula was that in each of the small northern territories the Romance vernacular° developed features that differentiated it from the speech of neighboring regions. The speech of Christians in Al-Andalus itself, known as Mozarabic° (from Ar *musta'rib* 'Arab-like'), was eventually absorbed by the northern Romances as these expanded into territory conquered from Islam. In the Christian area, starting at the Mediterranean end of the Pyrenees, in the region around Barcelona, there arose Catalan, which was carried to Valencia, Alicante, and the Balearic Islands in the first half or the thirteenth century by military conquest. Immediately to the west a group of closely related vernaculars known to linguists as Navarro-Aragonese developed. In an initially small area around and north of Burgos, there was another Romance known as Castilian, which in time would extend over most of the peninsula and develop into modern Spanish. To the west of Castilian there developed a Romance speech known as Leonese, or Asturian-Leonese, parent of the various *bables*, as the vernaculars spoken in Asturias are still called. Finally, in the northwest corner of the peninsula, in the former Roman province of Gallaecia, was born the vernacular which linguists refer to as Galician-Portuguese, the parent of modern Galician as well as of Portuguese.

By the eleventh century the kingdom of Castile (Sp *Castilla*) had acquired hegemony over Leon and Galicia and was leading the reconquest of Muslim Spain. Its policy of establishing alliances with the Franks beyond the Pyrenees entailed an infusion of French culture, such as the creation of monasteries linked to Cluny Abbey in Burgundy, and the substitution of Roman liturgy for the ancient Hispanic (often called "Mozarabic") liturgy inherited from the Visigothic kingdom. Another consequence was the presence of French noblemen who came to seek fortune in frequent campaigns waged against the Muslim states of Al-Andalus.

One of these French adventurers, Count Raymond of Burgundy, a region in central eastern France, in 1087 married Urraca (a charming name meaning

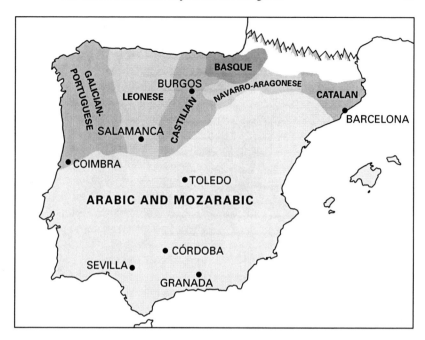

Map 1.3 Schematic location of the language areas in the Iberian Peninsula (ca. tenth century)

'magpie'), a daughter of King Alfonso VI of Leon and Castile, who granted the newlyweds the county of Galicia. In 1093, another daughter of Alfonso VI, Teresa, married Raymond's cousin, Henry of Burgundy, who received the county of Portucale, stretching southward as far as the region of Coimbra, which had been taken from the Arabs in 1064. After Count Henry's death (ca. 1112), his son Afonso Henriques (the ending -*es* is a patronymic° signifying 'son of') assumed the title of king, secured Portugal's independence from Castile and Leon through a combination of military strength and diplomacy, and proceeded to conquer territory to the south. After several major victories and setbacks, the drive southward was completed by Afonso III, the fifth Portuguese king, who conquered the Algarve in 1249. These historical events – Portugal's independence and the establishment of her borders – contributed powerfully to the gradual differentiation of Portuguese and Galician in the later Middle Ages. Portuguese independence also blocked the expansion of Castilian into the southwest of the Iberian Peninsula, notwithstanding the union of the Portuguese and Spanish crowns from 1580 to 1640, which had no linguistic sequels.

From the late twelfth century to the early fourteenth, Galician-Portuguese – a convenient term limited to the period when the two languages had not yet become clearly differentiated – was used in a poetic style which imitated, in form as well as content, the lyric poetry cultivated in the courts of Provence. As regards prose, although the first document in a language recognizable as Portuguese is dated from about 1214 or 1216 (5.6.1), systematic use of Portuguese in place of Latin in royal documents began only in 1255, under Afonso III (who reigned 1248–1279). This preference was made mandatory in 1279 by his successor, Dinis, himself a renowned poet in the Galician-Portuguese tradition. By the time King Dinis died in 1325, however, Portuguese and Galician had drifted apart enough to preclude writing poetry in Galician-Portuguese (Vázquez-Cuesta and Mendes da Luz 1987:204).

Between 1255 and 1335, Portuguese was used extensively in private documents, letters, municipal ordinances (*foros* and *forais*), royal decrees (*Leis Gerais*, or General Laws), reports from the royal chancery (*Inquirições*), translations of Castilian legal documents, and a variety of other writings which provided a training ground for the first literary texts that began to appear in the fourteenth century. These include didactic works like King João I's *Livro da Montaria* (a hunting treatise) and King Duarte's *Leal Conselheiro* ('Loyal Counselor'), as well as historical works like the Count of Barcelos's vast *Crónica Geral de 1344* ('General Chronicle of 1344'), and the single-reign histories of Fernão Lopes (?1378/1383–?1460) such as the *Crónica de El Rei D. João I* ('Chronicle of King João I'), *Chronica do senhor rei D. Pedro I* ('Chronicle of King Pedro I'), and so on.

The end of the fifteenth century and the first half of the sixteenth was a period of intense change. In 1492 Columbus arrived in America and Antonio de Nebrija, an Andalusian, published his *Gramática de la lengua castellana,* the first formal grammar of a Romance language. A major political event was the end of Muslim sovereignty in Spain with the capture of the kingdom of Granada by the Catholic Monarchs, Ferdinand and Isabella, in 1492. In the same year these monarchs promulgated the expulsion of all Jews who would not convert to Catholicism, some sixty thousand of whom sought refuge in Portugal, where they soon had again to choose between conversion or expulsion. In 1517 Luther reportedly nailed his ninety-five theses onto the door of the Castle Church in Wittenberg, thus launching the Reformation.

In 1516 Garcia de Resende (1470–1536) published the *Cancioneiro Geral,* a compilation of courtly poetry. His contemporary Gil Vicente (1460/1470–?1536), working virtually single-handed between 1502 and 1536, created Portuguese theater in a medieval tone still noticeable in his last play, *Floresta de enganos* ('Forest of Errors'), produced in the year of his death. Change, however, was in motion for both the culture and the language of Portugal. In 1527 Francisco de Sá de Miranda (?1495–1558), a nobleman who had studied law at the University of Coimbra, returned from a sojourn in Italy and began to disseminate the literary ideas of the Renaissance, although with a slight delay in relation to the rest of Europe, since Petrarch and Boccacio had been dead for nearly a century. There was enough change in the air to attract the Inquisition, introduced in 1531 to protect souls by burning unrepentant bodies and heretical books, for which an underground market was made possible by the movable type press, developed by Gutenberg in 1468. Among books unwelcome in the peninsular kingdoms were those by the great humanist thinker Erasmus (?1466–1536).

In 1536 Fernão de Oliveira published his *Grammatica da lingoagem portuguesa*, the first of its kind, followed in 1540 by João de Barros's own *Gramática da língoa portuguesa*. In 1572 Luiz Vaz de Camões (?1525–1580) celebrated Vasco da Gama's discovery of the sea route to India in his epic poem *Os Lusíadas*. The prevailing eagerness for new things clamored for a renovated language, and as it adjusted to new cultural realities, Portuguese shaped a modern image for itself. Linguistic features considered too close to Galician were eschewed (6.2), and southern Portuguese, loosely identified with the speech of the Coimbra–Lisbon area, provided the new frame of reference for the language.

After Portuguese and Galician split, their paths diverged substantially. Whereas Portuguese acquired full autonomy by becoming the official language of an independent state, Galician found itself limited to oral communication at the local level and excluded from an official role in public administration, education, and the higher forms of literary expression. Such limitations caused Galician to be not only subordinated to Spanish but also progressively infiltrated by it, particularly in the lexicon and morphosyntax. Since becoming coofficial with Spanish in Galicia, as allowed by Spain's 1978 Constitution, Galician has been able to recover much lost ground through use in public administration, education, and the public media. Even so, and despite an increase in the number of books published in Galician, its presence in the privately owned media is still limited, and indications that the number of native speakers may actually be decreasing (Fernández Rodríguez *et al.* 1996) are not encouraging. All in all, the task of normalizing and unifying local varieties, described by Teyssier (1985:48) as essential to forge a modern Galician language, is still unfinished.

Back in the sixteenth century, Portuguese seafarers were busy exploring the coast of Africa. Following the conquest of Ceuta in 1415, they reached Madeira and the Azores between 1419 and 1427, and in 1445 set up the first *feitoria*, or trading post, in the region of Arguin, in today's Mauritania. In 1457 the Cape Verde archipelago was discovered, and in 1482 the fort of São João da Mina, which would play a major role in the slave traffic, was built in territory of today's Ghana. In 1497–1498 Vasco da Gama arrived in Calicut, on the west coast of India; in 1500 Pedro Álvares Cabral landed in Brazil; and by 1515 the Portuguese had reached Goa in India, Malacca in Malaysia, and Hormuz at the mouth of the Persian Gulf. A Portuguese trading expedition arrived in China in 1514, and in 1518 a Portuguese fort was built in Colombo, Ceylon (today's Sri Lanka). Japan was reached in 1543, and in 1549 a trading post was set up in

Macao (Pg Macau). In 1606 the Portuguese reached the New Hebrides (today's Vanuatu), the last of a series of maritime enterprises that opened the path to a world larger than Europe and provided riches undreamed of: by the end of the fifteenth century gold trading in Africa surpassed other sources of the royal income (Saraiva 1997:39).

This gold coin, however, had a negative flip side: since everyone wanted to share in the colonial enterprise, fields lay fallow and unemployed peasants swelled Lisbon's population. Inflation was rampant, and the Crown had neither the people nor the means to run such a far-flung empire. To make things worse, from the end of the sixteenth century it faced increasingly strong competition from the Netherlands and England. Furthermore, when Portugal was ruled by Spanish kings for dynastic reasons between 1580 and 1640, Portuguese ships and colonies became a legal target for those competing nations, then at war with Spain. As a result, by the middle of the seventeenth century the Portuguese possessions were fast being lost to the Dutch and the British. After Portuguese sovereignty was restored in 1640 and peace was made with Britain and the Netherlands, Portugal's remaining colonial empire included Angola, Mozambique, Portuguese Guinea (now Guinea-Bissau), Cape Verde, and São Tomé and Príncipe in Africa; Goa, Damão and Diu, in India; East Timor in South-East Asia; and Macao in China. There was also Brazil, where gold was discovered in 1690. By the end of the eighteenth century it is estimated the Crown had received between one and three thousand tons of gold and over two million carats in diamonds (Saraiva 1997:75). Most of those riches reportedly went to English bankers, but Portugal, though impoverished and sorely taxed by the effort, had succeeded in opening up the oceans and making Portuguese an international language.

## 1.3    Portuguese pidgins and creoles: A thumbnail sketch

A linguistic consequence of the spread of Portuguese in Africa and Asia was the creation of Portuguese-based languages of the pidgin° and creole° category, about which we will say more in section 6.5.1. A pidgin is a grammatically simplified hybrid language, with words from two or more languages, created through continuing interaction of people who do not have a language in common. Pidginized versions of Portuguese have supposedly been used since the fifteenth century in the Mediterranean and along the coast of Africa, where Portuguese sailors and traders came into contact with speakers of African languages. Eventually, pidgin Portuguese became a ° lingua franca for European traders and navigators, as well as for Africans and Asians. Although a pidgin is nobody's native language, when the offspring of pidgin speakers acquire their parents' language, it becomes a creole. Thus a creole may become the primary language of a formerly pidgin-speaking community.

Places where Portuguese-based pidgins developed included the region around Fort São João da Mina, which was a trading post serving an area including today's Senegal, Sierra Leone, Liberia, Ivory Coast, and the Gold Coast as far as the Niger Delta. A similar process took place further south in today's Guinea-Bissau, where slaves were sent from the trading post in Cacheu to Cape Verde, and thence to America. There was another trading zone in the Gulf of Guinea, connected with the island of São Tomé, also used in the slave traffic. In due time several creoles developed that are still spoken in Guinea-Bissau and the islands of Cape Verde, São Tomé and Príncipe, and Annobón, which is part of Equatorial Guinea (a Spanish colony between 1778 and 1968).

One of the consequences of intermarriage between Portuguese settlers and natives of Africa and Asia was the development of several Portuguese-based creoles, some of which are still spoken. A group of creoles known as Indo-Portuguese developed in the colonies of Goa, Damão, and Diu, which were taken over by India in 1961. In Ceylon (today's Sri Lanka), a Portuguese creole was still spoken by small communities in the 1970s, when its chances of survival were described as "bleak" (Smith 1978:32). In the Malay peninsula and the Indonesian archipelago the growth of Malayo-Portuguese creoles came in the wake of trading posts, which were lost to the Dutch in the seventeenth century; the sole exception was Macao, which remained Portuguese until it was turned over to China in December 1999. In Malacca (today a state of Malaysia), West African Pidgin Portuguese was used and eventually conditioned the development of a creole called Papia Kristang ('Christian talk') that still had some 1000 speakers in the early 1980s (Baxter 1988:1). Other Portuguese creoles used to be spoken in Indonesia (Java and Timor), Macao, Hong Kong, and Singapore, but at the end of the twentieth century they were reduced to "small communities isolated from each other" (Teyssier 1985:48).

## 1.4     The spread of Portuguese

The national language of Portugal (pop. 10,266,053, area 92,080 square kilometers or 35,552 square miles – slightly larger than Maine, 33,265 square miles), Portuguese is spoken natively by almost the entire population, with the exception of recent immigrants and bilingual minorities in areas in the north and the northeast along the border with Spain, where Galician and Leonese dialects are spoken (6.3). Portugal's territory includes the Atlantic archipelagos of Madeira (two islands) and the Azores (nine islands), both of which enjoy autonomous administrative status.

In 1822 Portugal lost Brazil, and in the twentieth century, all of its remaining colonies. In Asia, Portuguese is an official language only in East Timor (pop. 750,000, area 14,609 square kilometers or 5640 square miles, slightly bigger than Connecticut, 5018 square miles). It is still spoken by a fast-shrinking minority in the former colonies of Goa, Damão, and Diu (India) and Macao (turned over to China in 1999).

In Africa, Portuguese is the official language of five countries which became independent from Portugal in the mid-1970s, collectively called PALOP (*Países Africanos de Língua Oficial Portuguesa* 'African Countries Where Portuguese is the Official Language'). On the east coast there is Mozambique (pop. 19,371,057, area 801,590 square kilometers or 309,494 square miles, somewhat larger than the combined area of Texas and Tennessee, 308,951 square miles), and on the west coast lie two others, Angola (pop. 10,366,031, area 1,246,700 square kilometers or 481,352 square miles, a little over three times the area of California, 158,706 square miles) and Guinea-Bissau (pop. 1,315,822, area 36,120 square kilometers or 13,943 square miles, slightly more than the combined area of Massachusetts and Connecticut, 13,302 square miles). Off the west coast of Africa lie the two small island countries, Cape Verde (pop. 405,163, area 4,033 square kilometers or 1556 square miles, a bit larger than Rhode Island), and São Tomé and Príncipe (pop. 165,034, area 1001 square kilometers or 371 square miles, 5.5 times larger than the area of Washington, DC). In these countries, however, despite its official status, Portuguese is the native language of only a minority, and outside the larger cities relatively few people speak it fluently as a second language (6.5). As we will see in Chapter 6, the coexistence of creoles and African languages spoken by different ethnic groups poses a unique situation for the future of Portuguese in these regions.

## 1.5     Immigrant communities

Portuguese is spoken by communities of immigrants and their descendants in several countries. The presence of Portuguese speakers in European countries (e.g. France, ca. 750,000; Germany, ca. 78,000), is the outcome of twentieth-century immigration in search of work. A group of self-exiled Portuguese Jews from Brazil landed in New Amsterdam (today's New York) in 1654 (Pap 1949:3), but most people of Portuguese descent in the United States trace their ancestry to immigrants in the late nineteenth and twentieth century (6.7).

Immigration with substantial linguistic consequences, however, started in the early nineteenth century, when whalers from the Azores – soon followed by others from Cape Verde, mostly creole speakers – began to settle in New England (Newport, New Bedford, Cape Cod) and Rhode Island. Immigrants from continental Portugal established communities in Connecticut, New York, New Jersey, and Pennsylvania. It was Azoreans who made up most of the Portuguese community in California, although there were also immigrants from Madeira and continental Portugal. Although the current generation of Portuguese Americans is largely bilingual, language maintenance is strong enough to support some newspapers and a small but thriving Portuguese American literature (Almeida

2001, Stephens 1989, Vaz 2001). Figures for 1997 showed 515,000 Portuguese immigrants living in Canada and 55,339 in Australia (Rocha-Trindade 2000a:21). As in the United States, a sizeable body of Portuguese-language literature exists in Canada (Joel 2000).

## 1.6  Portuguese in Brazil

Portuguese is one of the most widely spoken languages of the world largely on account of Brazil, a nation of continental dimensions with a vast population. The country extends over 3,286,475 square miles (slightly over the 3,126,793 square miles of the forty-eight contiguous US states, or over six times the combined area of Germany, France, and Spain). Brazil's population, which reached 175 million in 2002 and was estimated at 178,103,554 in January 2004 (www.ibge.gov.br), makes it the sixth most populous country after China, India, the United States, Indonesia, and the Russian Federation (Embassy of Brazil, London, www.brazil.org). These figures mean that about 80% of the world's speakers of Portuguese live in Brazil, and even if the language were spoken nowhere else, it would still be placed seventh (instead of sixth) among the world's languages with most speakers. The city of São Paulo alone, with 10,405,867 inhabitants, has a slightly larger population than Portugal's 10,066,253. Together, East Timor and the five African countries where Portuguese is the official language have about 32,373,107 inhabitants; if we add to these the 4,806,353 Portuguese immigrants all over the world (site *Imigração Portuguesa*, www.imigrantes.no.sapo.pt in 2002), we would have a total of 37,189,460 – only slightly above the population of the state of São Paulo (36,969,476).

Settlement of colonial Brazil began with the foundation of a village named São Vicente ('St. Vincent') on the northern coast of today's state of São Paulo. At first the colony was divided into fifteen *Capitanias* ('Captaincies'), vast territories awarded on a hereditary basis to individuals charged with exploiting them. Because the captaincies failed (with the exception of those of São Vicente and Pernambuco, the latter in the northeast), in 1548 the Crown switched to a system of appointed governors who reported directly to the king. As colonization expanded, the territory was further divided and more governors appointed, but by the beginning of the nineteenth century the colonial enterprise was exhausted (Prado Junior 1942:5–6) and resentment against its exploitative practices intensified. In January 1808, French troops invaded Portugal in retaliation for its refusal to abide by Napoleon's ban on trade with Great Britain. Acting as Regent due to Queen Maria's illness, Prince João (later King João VI) ordered the royal court and some 10,000 followers to leave for Brazil, under the protection of a British fleet, to resettle in Rio de Janeiro.

After Napoleon's defeat in 1814, the Congress of Vienna decided to recognize only Lisbon as the seat of the Portuguese government. To get around that decision, in 1815 Prince João signed a decree elevating Brazil to the category of a kingdom united to Portugal and the Algarve, a measure that enabled him to stay in Brazil even after becoming king on Queen Maria's death (1816). When the court finally returned to Portugal in 1821, King João left his son, Prince Pedro, as Regent of Brazil. At this point, Brazilian nationalistic feelings, exacerbated by the Portuguese Parliament's humiliating decision to return Brazil to colony status, led the Regent in 1822 to declare Brazil an independent Empire and to assume the title of Pedro I. Except for some bloodshed in the provinces of Grão-Pará (today's states of Pará and Bahia), the independence process was much less violent in Brazil than in either the United States or Spanish America.

Since becoming independent, Brazil has followed a totally separate path, politically as well as culturally, from the other Portuguese-speaking lands, a circumstance that has contributed to the specific character of Brazilian Portuguese. Whereas in the African countries Portuguese is the native speech only of a minority, in Brazil it has been for generations the native language of a majority of the population. Also, contact with the languages spoken by the indigenous inhabitants, by African slaves, and by immigrants, as well as the influence of exogenous cultures – French, British, American – have had substantially different results in Brazil than in Africa or Asia. According to Article 13 of the Brazilian Constitution, Portuguese is the only official language. The approximately 170 indigenous languages (a flexible figure, since there is no consensus as to how to separate "languages" from "dialects") have only about 330,000 speakers, primarily in the Amazon region. In late 2002 the city council of São Gabriel da Cachoeira, a municipality covering about 112,000 square kilometers in the State of Amazonas, passed an ordinance (Municipal Ordinance 145/2002) making the indigenous languages Nheengatu, Tukano, and Baniwa coofficial with Portuguese (Oliveira 2003). It is, however, too early to speculate on the possible impact, if any, that such measures might have on Portuguese.

Immigration, once a factor of some language diversity, has decreased since the middle of the twentieth century, and the number of speakers of heritage languages (the most numerous being Italian, German, Polish, and Japanese) falls short of 1% of the total population. Since education must be in Portuguese (bilingual schools are few and cater to an affluent minority), immigrants' descendants tend to be Portuguese-dominant, even when they speak their heritage language.

## 1.7     The Community of Portuguese Language Countries

A little over a quarter century ago, the late French philologist Paul Teyssier assessed the situation of Portuguese as being supported primarily by only Portugal and Brazil. In both countries, Portuguese is a truly *national* language:

besides being the native tongue of most people, it fulfills all roles in public and private communication, government, education, and the media, without competition from any other language. In Teyssier's view, in the African countries (and one might add, in East Timor as well) the future of Portuguese would depend on its relationship to local indigenous languages and creoles, a situation he considered comparable to "the situation of English and French in other [African] regions" (1985:47).

The overall situation of Portuguese as an international language may in the long run be helped by the creation, in November 1989, of the *Comunidade dos Países de Língua Portuguesa* – CPLP ("Community of Portuguese Language Countries"), made up of the seven countries where Portuguese is official plus East Timor with the status of "Guest Observer" at the time of writing. Defining itself as an organization based on the commonality of the Portuguese language, the CPLP proposes to undertake joint action in cultural, economic, and educational fields. One of its projects includes the establishment of an International Institute of the Portuguese Language. It would be premature to speculate about the extent to which such activities may influence the learning of Portuguese as a second language in those countries where, its official status notwithstanding, it is actually a minority language.

## 1.8    Varieties of Portuguese

The English language taken to America in the seventeenth century has since changed substantially, giving rise to an American English standard that partially diverges from British English, particularly in pronunciation and vocabulary, less so in syntax. Elsewhere, largely due to its global role as the first and second language of millions of new speakers, English has changed enough to give rise to the concept of "new Englishes" and new standard varieties (Crystal 1997:130; Trudgill and Hannah 2002).

Likewise, Portuguese in Brazil has changed in a variety of ways since the sixteenth century, and today a standard for Brazilian Portuguese (BP), partially different from the standard for European Portuguese (EP), is clearly distinguishable. This is hardly surprising, for a language can only remain relatively homogeneous if it is used by a speech community small enough to allow continuous feedback among its members, and isolated enough to prevent influence from other languages. That is definitely not the case of either English or Portuguese, which are spoken by millions of people over a vast territory.

Whether BP and EP are still "the same language," or whether BP has changed enough to justify being classified as a "different language," is a debated topic that has received varying solutions – none definitive – from linguists. Some scholars have written about "the existence of two cultivated and sovereign norms – one Portuguese, the other Brazilian – within the single linguistic system of the

Portuguese language" (Vázquez-Cuesta and Mendes da Luz 1987:129). Others have claimed that the language spoken in Brazil (though not its written variety) is a language different from that spoken in Portugal (Perini 1997). This book adopts the viewpoint that, while substantial differences exist between BP and EP, they are outweighed by the similarities, and consequently BP and EP are varieties of the same language. Our presentation will concentrate on what is common to both varieties and focus on contrasts whenever appropriate. Learners of Portuguese make their individual choice on the basis of personal preferences or practical reasons – such as an intention to travel, work, or live in one country or the other – but soon find out that learning to use one variety does not preclude understanding the other.

Since most of the press in Portugal or Brazil uses a standardized language, educated persons familiar with either variety encounter little difficulty in reading most articles in a newspaper or news magazine written in the other. Copy written in a more colloquial language – by definition a local feature – is bound to present difficulties of the kind an American would find in a British publication or a Briton in an American one. Clearly, difficulties due to lack of familiarity with national or local events, or to references to specific institutions or persons – like the puzzlement experienced by an American trying to figure out a news item on cricket or that felt by a Briton trying to read an article on baseball – are cultural and circumstantial rather than linguistic.

Differences in speech are more intensely felt, and familiarity with one variety does not ensure immediate comprehension of the other. Pronunciation plays a major role in this. Like Spanish or Italian, Brazilian Portuguese articulates vowels rather clearly. In contrast, in European Portuguese unstressed vowels tend to be weakly articulated or altogether eliminated, and even a short utterance includes sequences of consonants that do not occur in Brazilian Portuguese (2.9). Consequently, while speakers of European Portuguese find it relatively easy to figure out Brazilian pronunciation, those familiar with the latter alone may require major adjustments to become comfortable with European Portuguese. (Learners need not feel embarrassed about this, since Brazilians visiting Portugal often find themselves in the same predicament.)

Comprehension, however, is a relative matter: educated speakers of BP and EP talking about a topic with which they are both familiar should experience minimal difficulty in understanding each other. On the other hand, either might have a hard time following a heated argument in very colloquial style in the other variety. The ultimate test, if you are a soccer fan, may well be listening to a radio broadcast of a match: if you can follow you should have no difficulty with other language styles. As regards the media, EP speakers are more exposed to BP than the other way round: whereas the presence of Portuguese programs on television in Brazil is minimal, it has been reported recently that as many as seven programs from the Brazilian TV network Globo were being broadcast in Portugal on a single day (Brittos 2001:24).

Whereas in the late nineteenth century J. Leite de Vasconcellos, the founder of Portuguese dialectology, could go unchallenged in classifying Portuguese as spoken in Brazil as an "overseas dialect" (1970:132–133; Head 1994), over a century later, such classification is untenable, given the vast body of linguistic evidence that Brazil has its own linguistic norm. Perception of this situation is evidenced by the indication "translated from the Brazilian" or "translated from Brazilian Portuguese" in European translations of some Brazilian novels (such as Rosa 1987, 1990, 1991). Furthermore, some European universities offer separate courses in European Portuguese and Brazilian Portuguese (Endruschat 2001).

Whilst European Portuguese continues to provide a linguistic frame of reference for the African countries, the development of local standards is currently a topic of debate among African linguists (6.5). Brazilian Portuguese, in turn, may be expected to serve as the model of choice for Portuguese as a second language in neighboring regions such as the Southern Cone, where Brazilians increasingly interact with Argentinians, Chileans, Uruguayans, and Paraguayans. In the United States, consistently with faculty research interests and of most college students' academic or travel goals, Brazilian Portuguese provides the contents of most textbooks published since the 1970s, such as Ellison *et al.* 1971; Abreu and Rameh 1972, 1973; Tolman *et al.* 1988, 1989; and Perini 2002a, 2004.

As this brief overview suggests, Portuguese is a richly diverse language, sporting as much variation as other languages which, like English or Spanish, have spread themselves far and wide over the globe. In projecting itself beyond its original territory, Portuguese has served a variety of communicative purposes, as the native language not only of immigrants and settlers but also of communities only remotely connected with their European roots. It has been a contact language for individuals who depended on it for communication, trade, or even survival. It is the heritage language of communities which, while proud of their Portuguese descent, have shifted to another primary language. It has even served as a foundation for new pidgin and creole languages, some of which are still spoken. We would be pursuing a chimera if we thought something so variegated could ever remain immutable through time and space, and present the same facies everywhere. The only way to come to terms with Portuguese – as with English – is to accept it as a plural linguistic entity.

Once the basic vocabulary and structures have been acquired, learners venture beyond the artificial predictability of classroom practices and instruction manuals to be confronted with a remarkable degree of variation, manifested in surprising departures from standard morphological details and syntactic arrangements. As their horizon expands, learners find out that attaining proficiency involves

Table 1.1 *Speakers of Portuguese in the world**

|  | Population* | % of Pg-speaking | Number of languages** | Literacy rate* |
|---|---|---|---|---|
| Angola | 10,776,471 | 42 | 41[+] | 42% |
| Brazil | 182,032,604 | 99 | 192[#] | 86.4% |
| Cape Verde | 412,137 | 10 | 2[***] | 76.6% |
| Guinea-Bissau | 1,360,827 | 0.03[c] | 21[***] | 42.4% |
| Mozambique | 17,479,266 | 47[l] | 39[+] | 47.8% |
| Portugal | 10,102,022 | 99+ | 4+ [##] | 79.3% |
| São Tomé and Príncipe | 175,883 | 2.12 | 4[***] | 79.3% |
| East Timor | 997,853 | 2 | 19[+] | 48% |

* Data from the CIA World Factbook (www.cia.gov).
** Including Portuguese.
*** Including creole varieties.
[c] Couto 1991:116.
[l] Lopes 2002c:51.
[+] Approximate figure; some scholars count as languages what others count as dialects.
[#] www.ethnologue.com mentions 192 living languages; Portuguese is official; others include Indian languages and immigrant languages such as Spanish, German, Italian, Japanese, Korean, etc.
[##] Portuguese official; Mirandese has official local status; others include Galician, creole varieties, and recent immigrant languages such as Bulgarian.

the challenge of acquiring a specific code – Brazilian Portuguese or European Portuguese, as the case may be – for active use, while striving to be able to understand other codes so as to expand their communicative ability. Learners would do well to keep in mind that, for all its importance, the grammar of a language is only one element in a complex system that functions as both a cognitive tool and a means of interaction in socially defined contexts. Once some of the grammar is more or less in place (a phrase that aptly describes most learners' proficiency even after years of practice), we must continuously refine our sense of the pragmatics of interaction in order to be successful in communication.

The view of the language as a variable system is at odds with notions expressed in traditional grammars and adopted by teachers who insist that there is only one "correct" way to speak the language. Such an attitude is particularly damaging in coming to terms with Brazilian Portuguese, where there is marked divergence between popular speech and educated speech, on the one hand, and between speech and writing on the other. Another misconception to be avoided is that the written language is somehow superior to speech, or that any departures from the written norm, such as occur in spontaneous speech, are to be regarded as deviations from an ideal of correctness. Though unsupported by any scientific evidence, such notions are propagated by a host of self-appointed language arbiters who proffer inept advice on matters of correctness and find errors where a bona fide language specialist would find none. Perhaps the most important thing to keep in mind, in approaching Portuguese, is that a flexible attitude towards diversity will go a long way towards understanding its various manifestations, all of them legitimate means of individual and cultural expression for millions of people around the world.

# 2    Sounds

The primary medium of Portuguese, like that of any other language, is phones,°
that is articulated sounds made by the organs of speech (Figure 2.1, p. 26).
Although used for talking, those organs are primarily involved in breathing
and eating. Furthermore, not all sounds produced by them are actually used in
speech. Heavy breathing, Bronx cheers, catcalls, or whistles of various kinds,
loaded with meaning as they may be, are not phones.

Phones occur in speech in sequences called *syllables* (2.6). Although the exact
nature of syllables is a matter of debate among linguists, you can develop a feel
for them simply by humming a song while keeping the beat by tapping your
foot. In Portuguese as in English, in every word of two or more syllables there
is one that is pronounced louder than the others. That extra degree of loudness
is known as lexical *stress* (2.9). As the following series of words illustrates, the
position of the stressed syllable is crucial to identify the meaning of a word:

| | | |
|---|---|---|
| *sabiá* | *sa-bi-á* (a kind of thrush) | stressed on the last |
| *sabia* | *sa-bi-a* 'P3sg knew' | stressed on next to last |
| *sábia* | *sá-bi-a* 'learned (f. adj.)' | stressed on the third from last |

Individual phones, their arrangement in syllables, and the placement of stress
along syllable sequences are three basic elements of speech.

## 2.1    The representation of phones

Some phrase books coach pronunciation by transcribing words in a way that
approximates English phones, separating syllables with hyphens, and showing
stressed syllables in capitals: *Muito obrigado* **MWIN-too oh-bree-GAH-doo**
'thank you.' Though useful for getting along in basic communication, such
representation is not precise enough for analyzing speech. Nor is ordinary writing, which represents speech in a conventional, almost stylized manner. The
Portuguese alphabet has twenty-three letters (*a, b, c, d, e, f, g, h, i, j, l, m, n, o,
p, q, r, s, t, u, v, x, z*), to which *k, y, w* are added to write words from other languages. A few letter combinations, or *digraphs*°, stand each for a single phone,
as in

**ch** *chato* 'boring,' *achar* 'to find'      **rr** *carro* 'car,' *barro* 'mud'
**nh** *acanhado* 'shy,' *ganhar* 'to win'      **lh** *falha* 'flaw,' *palha* 'straw'

The letters *gu* and *qu* may function as digraphs or as two sounds:

Digraph (*qu* = hard *g*; *qu* = hard *k*)      Two sounds

*guitarra* 'guitar,' *guerra* 'war'      *água* 'water,' *égua* 'mare'
*quente* 'hot,' *quiabo* 'okra'      *aquático* 'aquatic'

In addition, some letters may be modified by diacritics° such as the cedilla (*ç*) or the various accents placed on vowels, viz.:

*acute* accent   *lá* 'there,' *pé* 'foot,' *rio* 'river,' *só* 'only,' *açúcar* 'sugar'
*grave* accent   *à* 'to the' as in *vou à piscina,* 'I'm going to the pool'
*circumflex*   *relevância* 'relevance,' *bebê* 'baby,' *avô* 'grandfather'
*tilde*   *irmã* 'sister,' *relações* 'relations'
*umlaut*   *lingüista* 'linguist' (currently used in BP but not in EP)

Books published up to the early twentieth century show other consonant combinations that have since been abolished, such as *ph* (*pharmacia,* mod. *farmácia* 'pharmacy') or a few double letters (*commercio,* mod. *comércio* 'commerce'). EP spelling retains *nn* in *connosco* 'with us,' written *conosco* in BP.

An additional inconvenience is that the same phone may be represented by more than one letter:

**g, j**      *gente* 'people,' *jornal* 'newspaper'
***ch, x***      *chá* 'tea,' *xadrez* 'chess'
**s, ss, c, ç, z**      *só* 'only,' *massa* 'mass,' *cedo* 'early,' *caça* 'hunting,'
                 *voz* 'voice'
**z, s, x**      *zebra* 'zebra,' *casa* 'house,' *exame* 'exam'

Conversely, a letter may stand for different phones:

**c**      *capa* 'cloak,' *cego* 'blind'
**g**      *gato* 'cat,' *gênio* 'genius'
**x**      *paixão* 'passion,' *táxi* 'taxi,' *exato* 'exact'

Different letter combinations may also stand for the same phone, as **am, ão** (*falaram,* 'they spoke,' *falarão* 'they will speak'). Unlike in standard English, the letter **h** before a vowel normally represents no phone, as in *homem* 'man' (an exception is the conventional representation of laughter: *hahaha*). Regional variation further distances writing from speech: although **ch** in words like *chama* 'flame,' *chato* 'flat' stands for the sound of *sh,* as in *ship,* in areas in northern

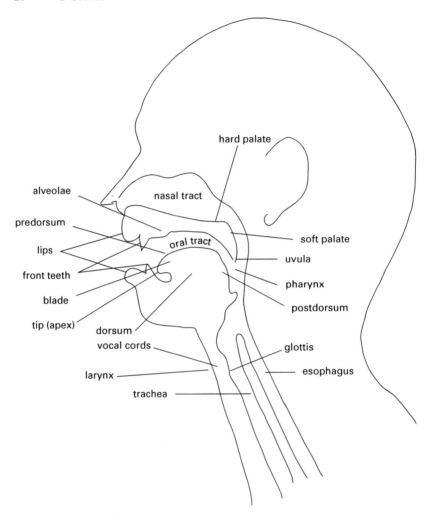

Figure 2.1 The organs of speech

Portugal or central Brazil such words are pronounced with a *tch*-like sound (like *ch* in *chat, cheap*).

To overcome the inconsistencies of ordinary spelling linguists use systems of phonetic transcription. The most widespread of these is the International Phonetic Alphabet (IPA 1999). Phonetic transcriptions are enclosed in square brackets [ ], with the symbol ' placed before a stressed syllable, as in *aqui* [a'ki] 'here,' *capa* ['kapɐ] 'toad,' *barracão* [baha'kẽw] 'shack.' The phonetic symbols used in this book are shown in Tables 2.1 and 2.2 (under "allophones" – a concept explained in section 2.3). Examples are intended to illustrate specific phones, although in many cases other pronunciations for the same words are possible. Unless otherwise indicated, the pronunciation depicted reflects educated usage in Brazilian Portuguese (BP) as heard in the southeast of Brazil (states of Minas Gerais, São Paulo, and Rio de Janeiro). For European Portuguese (EP), the accent of reference is that of educated speakers from the city of Lisbon. Certain pronunciation variations heard in regional or social accents will be mentioned in later chapters.

Transcriptions, unless otherwise indicated, reflect the pronunciation that corresponds basically to the consultative style described in Joos 1967. It is the relatively unmonitored pronunciation used by educated speakers in situations that entail neither disdain for correctness nor concern for elegance, and in which they aim at sounding neither too distant nor too chummy. References to formal pronunciation, in turn, should be understood as being used in styles aiming for maximum clarity and involving a degree of self-monitoring, as when we try to clarify an utterance: *Eu disse comprimento, não cumprimento* 'I said length, not greeting.' Finally, casual pronunciation (a label adopted here to cover Joos's informal and intimate styles) veers towards unconcern for form and uses more emphatic or emotional language, with virtually no self-monitoring.

In the following sections we will analyze Portuguese phones from two complementary viewpoints, namely how they are articulated, which is the purview of *articulatory phonetics* (2.2), and the way phones work together in a system, which is the area of *phonology* (2.3).

## 2.2    Articulatory phonetics

Phones are articulated by the organs of speech, which are made up by the respiratory apparatus and the vocal tract (Figure 2.1). Breathing involves the lungs, the bronchi, the trachea (or windpipe), and the larynx. In the larynx, right behind the Adam's apple, there are two muscular bands, called *vocal cords* (or *vocal folds*), which can move close together or wide apart to control the passage of air. Above the larynx and beginning with the pharynx, we distinguish the *oral tract* and the *nasal tract*, which together constitute the *vocal tract*, where most of the articulation process takes place. The oral tract includes the mouth and its organs, such as the tongue, the teeth, the lips, the alveolar ridge, the hard palate, the soft palate or velum, and the uvula. For descriptive purposes the tongue is divided in several areas, namely the *tip*, the *blade* (which extends about half an inch behind the tip), and the *dorsum*, each of which participates in the formation of specific phones.

The space between the vocal cords constitutes the *glottis*, a triangular opening leading into the pharynx. As the vocal cords tense up and the glottis narrows, the pressure of egressive air causes them to vibrate. This vibration propagates

harmonically through the air, like that of the strings of an acoustic guitar in the body of the instrument, imparting to phones a feature known as *voicing*.°
You can feel this vibration by lightly touching the area of your Adam's apple while humming continuously a series of phones like *ee-ee-eye-eye-ow*. You can also feel the contrast between voiced and voiceless phones by pronouncing continuous phones like *vvvv-ffff-vvvv-ffff* or *zzzz-ssss-zzzz-ssss*, or **th** as in *that* and *th* as in *think*: **ththth**-*ththth*-**ththth**-*ththth*. You will develop a much sounder grasp of practical phonetics if you do similar experiments as we go along, so as to get a feel for the position and movement of the speech organs as they articulate each phone. It will also help to systematically relate the articulation of each phone to the respective phonetic terminology, as the terms reflect very closely what goes on in your speech apparatus.

Most phones are formed as air exits through the oral tract, while the nasal tract is blocked off by the tip of the velum touching the pharynx wall. Such sounds are called *oral*. If, however, the tip of the velum is lowered, blocking the oral tract, air goes out through the nasal tract, causing a resonance known as *nasality*. Nasal phones are represented in English by **m, n** (*money*) and in Portuguese by **m, n, nh** (*maninha* 'little sister,' *campo* 'field,' *santo* 'saint') or by a tilde over **ã** or **õ** (*lã* 'wool,' *põe* 'P3sg puts'), or by a mute consonant after a vowel as in *som* 'sound.'

Despite their variety, the phones of all languages can be sorted, in terms of their articulatory features, into three categories, namely *vowels, glides*, and *consonants*. In what follows, let us keep in mind that we are talking about phones, not letters.

### 2.2.1    *Vowels, glides, and diphthongs*

To have an idea of what a vowel is, try to pronounce a long, uninterrupted sound like *eeeeeeeee* (that is, the *ee* or *ea* in *see* or *tea*) and feel how air flows out freely. This kind of phone has the fundamental characteristic of vowels, of being articulated without any obstruction to the passage of air (Table 2.1).

Now to get a feel for how vowels vary, repeat the experiment, alternating the vowels of words like *see, ah, low*, do: *eeee-aaaah-ooooh-oooo*. You will notice that the specific quality, or timbre, of this long vocalic sound is modulated by factors like the position of the tongue, or the shape of the lips. According to the relative height of the tongue, vowels are classified as *high, mid*, or *low*. Depending on the degree of horizontal fronting or backing of the tongue, they are classified as *front, central*, or *back*. These terms refer to the position of articulation of a given vowel in relation to the other vowels, rather than to any precise location inside the oral tract (Ladefoged 2001:71). Back vowels (Table 2.3) are formed with a degree of lip-rounding that gives them a labial articulation that is missing in non-back (that is, front and central) vowels.

Like vowels, glides are phones formed without any obstacle to the passage of air (Table 2.1). Unlike a vowel, however, a glide cannot be the center of a syllable, nor can it be pronounced in isolation (2.6). Rather, a glide is always articulated next to a vowel, either before it (*onglide*) or after it (*offglide*). In either case the vowel and glide together form a *diphthong*°, as in *ai* [aj] 'ouch' or Eng *I* [ɑj]. Another difference is that whereas in the articulation of a vowel the tongue remains in a given position (as when you say *aaaaaaah* at your doctor's request), a glide is formed while the tongue is moving. Since the tongue can only move so far without encountering an obstacle (such as the palate, for example), the possible duration of a glide is minimal.

In forming an offglide, the tongue moves *away* from the position of a vowel. The resulting sequence of *vowel + glide* constitutes a *falling* diphthong:

| **vowel + front offglide** | **vowel + back offglide** |
|---|---|
| *pai* [aj] 'father' | *mau* [maw] 'bad' |
| *lei* [lej] 'law' | *eu* [ew] 'I' |
| *méis* [mɛjs] 'honeys' | *céu* [sɛw] 'sky' |
| *boi* [boj] 'ox' | *dou* [dow] 'I give' |
| *sóis* [sɔjs] 'suns' | *sol* [sɔw] 'sun' (in BP only) |

When, conversely, the tongue moves *towards* the position of a vowel, forming a sequence of *onglide + vowel*, the result is a *rising* diphthong:

**back onglide + vowel**
*quatro* ['kwatɾu] 'four'
*água* ['agwɐ] 'water'
*quota* ['kwɔtɐ] 'quota'
*lingüista* [l ĩ'gwistɐ] 'linguist'

Articulatorily, then, to form the front glide [j] the tongue moves towards or away from the position of articulation of the vowel [i] near the front section of the palate. Conversely, the back glide [w] is formed as the tongue moves towards or away from the position of articulation of the vowel [u] near the velum.

Portuguese sequences of [j] + vowel or [w] + vowel are unstable and tend to be pronounced as [i] + vowel or [u] + vowel, respectively. Thus depending on pronunciation style we may have either a diphthong or a hiatus,° that is as two contiguous vowels in separate syllables:

| | **dipthong** onglide + vowel | **hiatus** vowels in contiguous syllables |
|---|---|---|
| *pátria* 'fatherland' | *pá-tria* ['pa-tɾjɐ] | *pá-tri-a* ['pa-tɾi-ɐ] |
| *quieto* 'quiet' | *quie-to* ['kj ɛ-tu] | *qui-e-to* [ki-'ɛ-tu] |

Table 2.1 *Portuguese vowel and glide phonemes and their main allophones*

| Phonemes | Allophones | | |
|---|---|---|---|
| **Oral vowels** | | | |
| /i/ | [i] | high front | *li* 'I read [past]' |
| /e/ | [e] | medium front | *lê* 'he reads' |
| /ɛ/ | [ɛ] | low-medium front | *pé* 'foot' |
| /a/ | [a] | low central | *lá* 'there' |
| /ɔ/ | [ɔ] | low-medium back | *nó* 'knot' |
| /o/ | [o] | medium back | *avô* 'grandfather' |
| /u/ | [u] | high back | *nu* 'nude' |
| **Glides** | | | |
| /j/ | [j] | high front (palatal) | |
| /w/ | [w] | high back (velar) | |

**Oral diphthongs**

**Falling**

| | | | |
|---|---|---|---|
| /iw/ [iw] *riu* 'P3sg laughed' | /uj/ [uj] *fui* 'I was' | | |
| /ew/ [ew] *meu* 'my' | /ej/ [ej] *rei* 'king' | | |
| /ɛw/ [ɛw] *céu* 'sky' | /ɛj/ [ɛj] *papéis* 'papers' | | |
| /aw/ [aw] *mau* 'bad' | /aj/ [aj] *mais* 'more' | | |
| /ow/ [ow]* *sou* 'I am' | /oj/ [oj] *dois* 'two' | | |
| /ɔw/ [ɔw]* *sol* [sɔw] 'sun' | /ɔj/ [ɔj] *sóis* 'suns' | | |
| /uw/ [uw]* *culpa* ['kuwpɐ] 'guilt' | /uj/ [uj] *fui* 'I went' | | |

**Rising**

| | | | |
|---|---|---|---|
| /je/+ [je] *série* 'series' | /we/ [we] *lingüeta* 'latch' | | |
| /jɛ/+ [jɛ] *dieta* 'diet' | /wɛ/ [wɛ]+ *cueca* 'shorts' | | |
| /ja/+ [ja] *quiabo* 'okra' | /wa/ [wa] *quarto* 'room' | | |
| /jo/+ [jo] *biologia* 'biology' | /wo/ [wo] *vácuo* 'vacuum' | | |
| /jɔ/ [jɔ] *maior* 'bigger' | /wɔ/ [wɔ] *quota* 'quota' | | |
| /ju/+ [ju] *viuvez* 'widowhood' | | | |

# Nasal vowels#

/in/ [ĩ] *fim* [fĩ] 'end,' *cinto* ['sĩ tu] 'belt'
/en/ [ẽ] *dentro* ['dẽ tru] 'inside'
/en/ [ɛ̃] *lã* [lɛ̃] 'wool,' *canto* ['kɛ̃ tu] 'corner'
/on/ [õ] *som* [sõ] 'sound,' *conto* ['kõ tu] 'tale'
/un/ [ũ] *um* [ũ] 'one,' *mundo* ['mũ du] 'world'

# Nasal diphthongs

## Falling

/enj/ [ẽĩ] *em* 'in'
/ɛnj/ [ɛ̃ĩ] *mãe* 'mother'
/onj/ [õĩ] *ações* 'actions'
/unj/ [ũĩ] *muito* 'much,' BP *ruim* 'bad'
/ũnw/ [ẽw̃] *pão* 'bread'

## Rising

/wan/ [wɛ̃] *quanto* 'how much'
/wen/ [wẽ] *freqüência* 'frequency'
/win/ [wĩ] *qüinquagenário* 'fifty years old'
/jan/## [jɛ̃] *amianto* 'asbestos'
/jen/## [jẽ] *arreliento* 'annoying'
/jon/## [jõ] *biombo* 'partition'

* Post-vocalic /l/ pronounced as [w] in BP only. See section 2.5.
** BP /ow/ is normally pronounced [o] in unmonitored speech.
+ These rising diphthongs alternate with two-vowel sequences: *cue-ca* / *cu-e-ca, quia-bo* / *qui-a-bo, bio-lo-gi-a* / *bi-o-lo-gi-a*, etc.
# Nasal vowels are interpreted phonologically here as a sequence of vowel + nasal.
## These diphthongs may alternate with sequences of vowel + nasal consonant: *biom-bo* / *bi-om-bo*.

Finally, a vowel between two glides forms a triphthong: *Uruguai* [uɾuˈgwaj], *Paraguai* [paɾaˈgwaj]. (See Table 2.1 for a list of Portuguese diphthongs.)

### 2.2.2    Nasal vowels and diphthongs

A peculiarity of Portuguese (shared with only French among the Romance languages) is nasal vowels (Table 2.1) which contrast with their oral counterparts:

*cito* [ˈsitu] 'I cite' / *cinto* [ˈsĩtu] 'belt'    *juta* [ˈʒutɐ] 'jute' / *junta* [ˈʒũtɐ] 'junta'
*teta* [ˈtetɐ] 'teat' / *tenta* [ˈtẽ tɐ] 'P3sg    *popa* [ˈpopɐ] 'stern' / *pompa* [ˈpõpɐ] tries'    'pomp'
                                                   *lá* 'there' [la] / *lã* [lɐ̃]

Diphthongs and triphthongs may also be nasal, as in *pão* [pɐ̃w̃] 'bread,' *cem* [sẽj] 'hundred,' *quão* [kwɐ̃w̃] 'how much.' *Muito(s)* [ˈmũjtu] 'very, many' (as well as its obsolete clipped variant *mui*) is the only instance of nasal [ũj] in all varieties of Portuguese, although in BP *ruim* 'bad' tends to be pronounced [ˈhũj] rather than [huˈĩ] as in EP, and the same goes for derived forms such as *ruindade* 'cruelty,' *ruinzão* 'cruel,' *ruinzinho* 'shabby.' Although these phones are either vowels or diphthongs phonetically, their pronunciation may involve a weak constriction like a nasal palatal consonant (see section 2.2.3) which links up with a following vowel, as in *tem amigo* [ˈtẽjⁿ aˈmigu] 'has a friend' instead of [ˈtẽjaˈmigu], or *cem anos* [ˈsẽjˈⁿɐnus] 'a hundred years' instead of [ˈsẽjˈɐnus]. The nasal vowel [õ] in final position may be diphthongized: *dom* 'gift' [dõ] ~ [dõw̃], *som* 'sound' [sõ] ~ [sõw̃].

### 2.2.3    Consonants

As we have seen, when vowels and glides are articulated, no obstacle interferes with air leaving the oral cavity. Consonants, on the contrary, are always formed when there is an obstacle blocking, wholly or partially, the passage of air (Table 2.2). Three criteria are used for classifying consonants. One is *voicing*: if the vocal cords vibrate (see the examples in section 2.2), consonants are voiced, as **b d g** [b d g] in *bodega* [boˈdɛgɐ] 'tavern,' and if they do not vibrate, consonants are voiceless, as **p t c** [p t k] in *peteca* [peˈtɛkɐ] 'shuttlecock.'

The second criterion, *manner of articulation*, based on how the obstacle is made, comprises the following seven categories: *stop* (or *occlusive*), *fricative*, *affricate*, *lateral*, *vibrant*, *retroflex*, and *nasal*.

*Stop* (*occlusive*): The vocal tract is momentarily stopped, shutting off the flow of air, and then reopened, letting air burst out, hence the alternate name of *plosive*. In [p] (*pai* 'father') or [b] (*boi* 'ox') the obstacle is created by the lips coming together. Consonants other than stops involve a partial obstacle.

*Fricative*: The opening is narrow enough to create friction as air goes through, as in [s] *só* 'alone,' [z] *zum* 'zoom,' [ʒ] *já* 'already,' [ʃ] *chá* 'tea,' [f] *fé* 'faith,' or [v] *vi* 'I saw.'

*Affricate*: As in stops, there is an initial closure, which is then partially released, producing friction as in fricatives. Examples are the voiceless affricate [ʧ] of Eng *chip* and its voiced counterpart [ʤ] or Eng *jeep*. The affricate [ʧ] occurs in the Brazilian leave-taking expression *tchau* (< It *ciao*), and in the BP pronunciation of **t** and **d** before the sound [i] as in *tio* ['ʧiu] *tio* 'uncle,' *este* ['esʧi] or *dia* [ʤiɐ] 'day,' *ode* ['ɔʤi] 'ode.'

*Lateral*: The tongue creates an obstacle in the central area of the vocal tract, letting air out laterally, on one side alone or on both sides, as [l] in *lei* 'law' or [ʎ] as in *ilha* ['iʎɐ] 'island.'

*Vibrant*: An articulator, such as the tip of the tongue, moves quickly once or several times. Only one vibration is involved for the voiced *flap* [ɾ] of *caro* ['kaɾu] 'dear,' and two or more vibrations participate in the formation of the voiced *trill* [r] of *carro* ['karu] 'car' or *rei* [rej] 'king.' In EP the uvular vibrant [ʀ] is the usual phonetic value of **r** or **rr** in words like *rato* 'rat,' *carro* 'car,' *honra* 'honor.' Laterals and vibrants are grouped under the generic label *liquids*. (In BP the alveolar trill [r] has largely been displaced by a glottal (see below) fricative transcribed as [h].)

*Retroflex*: The tip of the tongue is raised and turned backwards towards the pre-palatal region, as in the pronunciaton of **r** in American English. A retroflexed sound, transcribed [ɹ], occurs in the interior of the states of São Paulo and Minas Gerais (7.3.1.2).

*Nasal*: As mentioned earlier, the velum is lowered, letting air through the nasal tract, where it resonates, as in [m] *meu* 'my,' [n] *nós* 'we,' [ɲ] *pinho* 'pine.'

The third criterion, *place of articulation*, concerns the location of the obstacle, and provides the following categories: *bilabial, labiodental, (linguo)interdental, (linguo)dental, (linguo)alveolar, (linguo)palatal, (linguo)velar, uvular*, and *glottal*.

*Bilabial*: The lips come together, as in [p] *pai* 'father,' *boi* 'ox,' *mar* 'sea.'

*Labiodental*: The lower lip touches the upper front teeth, as in [f] *fala* 'speech' or [v] *vala* 'ditch.'

*Interdental*: The tip of the tongue comes under the upper front teeth, as in English [θ] *thin* or [ð] *that*.

*Dental* and *alveolar*: For dental phones, the tongue touches the inner surface of the front teeth, and for alveolar phones it touches the alveolar ridge. The stops [t] and [d] tend to be dentoalveolar in Portuguese (*tu* 'you,' *dois* 'two'), whereas they are fully alveolar in English (*too, dual*). Other alveolar consonants

Table 2.2 Portuguese consonant phonemes and their main allophones

| Phonemes | Allophones | Voicing | Area of articulation | Manner of articulation | Active articulator | Passive articulator | |
|---|---|---|---|---|---|---|---|
| /p/ | [p] | unvoiced | bilabial | occlusive | lower lip | upper lip | pato /pato/ ['patu] 'duck' |
| /b/ | [b] | voiced | bilabial | occlusive | lower lip | upper lip | bala /bala/ ['baɫɐ] 'bullet' |
| | [β]¹ | voiced | bilabial | fricative | lower lip | upper lip | aba /'aba/ ['aβɐ]¹ 'brim' |
| /t/ | [t] | unvoiced | laminoalveolar | occlusive | blade | front teeth | tapa /'tapa/ ['tapɐ] 'slap' |
| /d/ | [d] | voiced | laminoalveolar | occlusive | blade | front teeth | dado /'dado/ ['daduɪ] 'die' |
| | [ð]¹ | voiced | interdental | fricative | blade | front teeth | dado /dado/ ['daðuɪ]¹ 'die' |
| /k/ | [k] | unvoiced | dorsovelar | occlusive | dorsum | soft palate | coco /'koko/ ['koku] 'coconut' |
| /g/ | [g] | voiced | dorsovelar | occlusive | dorsum | soft palate | gato /'gato/ ['gatu] 'cat' |
| | [ɣ]¹ | voiced | dorsovelar | fricative | dorsum | soft palate | chaga /'ʃaga/ ['ʃaɣɐ]¹ 'wound' |
| /f/ | [f] | unvoiced | labiodental | fricative | lower lip | front teeth | café /ka'fe/ [ka'fɛ] 'coffee' |
| /v/ | [v] | voiced | labiodental | fricative | lower lip | front teeth | vaca /'vaka/ ['vakɐ] 'cow' |
| /s/ | [s] | unvoiced | predorsoalveolar | fricative | predorsum | alveolae | sopa /'sopa/ ['sopɐ] 'soup' |
| /z/ | [z] | voiced | predorsoalveolar | fricative | predorsum | alveolae | zebra /'zebra/ ['zebɾɐ] 'zebra' |
| /ʃ/ | [ʃ] | unvoiced | dorsopalatal | fricative | dorsum | hard palate | chato /'ʃato/ ['ʃatu] 'flat' |
| /ʒ/ | [ʒ] | voiced | dorsopalatal | fricative | dorsum | hard palate | jato /'ʒato/ ['ʒatu] 'jet' |
| /l/ | [l] | voiced | dorsoalveolar | lateral | apex | alveolae | lado /'lado/ ['ladu] 'side' |
| /ʎ/ | [ʎ] | voiced | dorsopalatal | lateral | dorsum | hard palate | palha /'paʎa/ ['paʎɐ] 'straw' |
| /r/ | [ɾ] | voiced | apicoalveolar | tap | apex | alveolae | caro /'karo/ ['karu] 'expensive' |
| /ʀ/² | [h] | unvoiced | glottal | fricative | see footnote 2 | | ['kahu] |
| | [ʀ] | voiced | uvular | trill | dorsum | velum | carro /'karo/ ['kaʀu] 'car' |
| | [r] | voiced | apicoalveolar | trill | apex | alveolae | ['karu] |
| | [x] | unvoiced | dorsovelar | fricative | dorsum | hard palate | ['kaxu] |
| /m/ | [m] | voiced | bilabial | nasal | lower lip | upper lip | mapa /'mapa/ ['mapɐ] 'map' |
| /n/ | [n] | voiced | laminoalveolar | nasal | apex | alveolae | pano /'pano/ ['panu] 'cloth' |
| /ɲ/ | [ɲ] | voiced | dorsopalatal | nasal | dorsum | soft palate | banha /'baɲa/ ['baɲɐ] 'lard' |

¹ In some varieties of EP.
² /ʀ/ used here as a generic symbol. In BP the allophones [ʀ r x h] may occur in the same region, although one of the most widespread renderings is the fricative [h], formed when egressive air causes friction in glottis and pharynx.

include the fricative [s] (*sim* 'yes'), the lateral [l] (*lá* 'there'), and the vibrant [ɾ] (*cara* 'face').

*Palatal*: The tongue blade touches the palate, as in the fricatives [ʃ] (*chá* 'tea') and [ʒ] (*já* 'already'), the affricates [ʧ] (*cheap*), [ʤ] (*jet*), or the voiced lateral [ʎ] (*alho* 'garlic').

*Velar*: The tongue dorsum touches the velum, as in the stops [g] (*gago* 'stammerer') and [k] (*coco* 'coconut').

*Uvular*: The uvula vibrates, as in the voiced trill [ʀ], or it may be the place where a constriction of the vocal tract articulates a fricative, voiceless [x] or voiced [ʁ]. These phones are possible pronunciations of initial **r** (*rápido* 'fast') or intervocalic **rr** (*carro* 'car').

*Glottal*: The articulation is made in the glottis by a movement of the vocal cords. For the voiceless glottal fricative [h] the glottis narrows, causing friction as air rushes out, as in Eng *he, home*, BP *rápido* ['hapidu] 'fast,' BP *carro* ['kahu] 'car.' This sound is the most common pronunciation of initial **r** (*rei* 'king') and intervocalic **rr** (*torre* ['tohi] 'tower') in BP (Perini 2004:26).

The glottis may close momentarily, creating an occlusion responsible for the *glottal stop* [ʔ] that occurs marginally in English between vowels, in interjections conventionally written *ah-ah* or *oh-oh*.


## 2.3    Phonology

The phonetic description of phones is complemented by phonology, which analyzes how they work together as a system in a given language. In this case we refer to them as *phonemes*°. The basic property of phonemes is that they signal differences in meaning. Thus the words *mama* 'teat,' *mana* 'sister,' and *manha* 'guile' form minimal pairs° that contrast in meaning owing to the nasal consonants [m], [n], [ɲ]. This meaningful contrast allows us to postulate the Portuguese phonemes /m/, /n/, and /ɲ/. It is conventional to transcribe phonemes between slashes to differentiate them from phonetic transcriptions.

Whereas the phones of the world's languages are virtually infinite, each language has a finite set of phonemes. Phones with similar articulation may correspond to separate phonemes in one language and variants of the same phoneme in another. Such variants are traditionally known as allophones°. For example, both Portuguese and English have the stops [t], [d] and the affricates [ʧ], [ʤ]. Since these phones appear in minimal pairs such as *tip/chip* or *dig/jig*, we classify /t/, /d/, /ʧ/, /ʤ/ as separate phonemes in English. In BP, however, pairs like *tipo* ['tipu] ~ ['ʧipu] 'type' or *digo* ['digu] ~ ['ʤigu] 'I say' are simply pronunciation variants of the same word. Likewise, minimal pairs like *sheep/cheap* or *cash/catch* serve to identify /ʃ/ and /ʧ/ as English phonemes. In

Portuguese, on the contrary, [ʧ] is just a regional variant of [ʃ], and we say that both [ʧ] and [ʃ] are allophones of the phoneme /ʃ/.

The symbols for the phonemes of Portuguese and their allophones are shown in Tables 2.1 and 2.2.

### 2.3.1    *Phonological processes*

One way to account for the various pronunciations of the same word is to consider them different phonetic realizations of the same basic phonological representation. Thus *tipo, digo* would have the phonological representations /tipu/, /digu/, and as many phonetic representations as there are ways of pronouncing them. The actual phonetic articulation in BP of /t/ as [ʧ] or of /d/ as [ʤ] before [i] results from a process called *palatalization*, which causes the tongue blade to move towards the palatal region. In other varieties of the language, where phonological process is not operative, such as EP, /d/ and /t/ are always pronounced as a dental (or dentoalveolar) [d] or [t].

Phonological processes act on the phonemes in a word's phonological representation so as to ultimately yield the allophones present in its phonetic representation(s). A phonological process is either categorical or variable. A categorical process applies whenever the required conditions are fulfilled, as in the case of the voicing of the Portuguese phoneme /s/ in word-final position before a word beginning with a vowel: *os amigos* [uza'migus] 'the friends.' A variable process, on the contrary, may or may not apply, depending on a variety of factors. For example, the conjunction *e*, phonologically /i/, if unstressed after a vowel, as in *sala e quarto* 'living room and bedroom,' may be pronounced as the vowel [i] in slow speech ['sa-lɐ-i-'kwaʀ-tu], or as the glide [j] in fast speech ['sa-lɐj-'kwaʀ-tu].

Phonological processes operate in four basic ways, as follows:
(1) They may change a feature of a phoneme, as when voiceless /s/ becomes voiced before a vowel or a voiced consonant, yielding [z]: *os amigos* [uza'migus] 'the friends,' *os dois* [uz'dojs] 'the two of them.'
(2) Conversely, they may add a new feature, as when /d/ or /t/ become palatalized respectively as [ʤ] or [ʧ]. Both these cases of feature change or addition illustrate assimilation°, a process whereby a phoneme becomes more like a neighboring phoneme.
(3) In addition, phonological process may eliminate a full phoneme, as in the loss of the final /r/ of infinitives in BP: *falar* > [fa'la] 'to speak,' *comer* [ku'me] 'to eat,' *partir* [paf'ʧi] 'to leave.'
(4) Finally, phonological processes may add a whole phoneme, as when an initial /i/ is added to a foreign word beginning with s + consonant to adapt it to BP pronunciation, as in Eng *stress* > BP *estresse*, Eng *stereo* > BP *estéreo*.

## 2.4    Portuguese phonemes

The phonological inventory of Portuguese (Tables 2.1 and 2.2) may be described as including the seven vowels /a e ɛ i o ɔ u/, the two glides /j w/, and the nineteen consonants /p b t d k g f v s z ʃ ʒ m n ɲ l ʎ ɾ ʀ/. The vowel inventory of EP includes also the vowels /ɐ/ and /ɨ /, which are responsible for certain contrasts that do not occur in BP (2.4.2).

### 2.4.1    Nasalization

While the phonetic nature of nasal vowels is well understood, linguists have interpreted their phonological status in several ways. For Portuguese nasal vowels, there are two basic options. Interpretation (A) below postulates five independent nasal phonemes / ã ẽ ĩ õ ũ/, which yield the phonetic nasal vowels [ɐ̃ ẽ ĩ õ ũ]. Interpretation (B) postulates phonological sequences of a vowel plus a nasal consonant that may be represented as /n/, thus: /an en in on un/. Each such sequence undergoes two phonological processes, namely vowel nasalization followed by loss of the nasal consonant (/an/ → /ãn/ → [ɐ̃]). Thus a word like *lã* 'wool' derives from a phonological representation like /lan/, with nasalization yielding /lãn/ → [lɐ̃] and loss of the nasal consonant yielding the phonetic form [lɐ̃]. Whichever theoretical interpretation one chooses, it is crucial for learners to acquire control of the nasalization mechanism to avoid pronouncing an [m] or [n] in words spelled with **m** or **n** after a vowel in final position or before a consonant, such as *com* 'with,' *campo* 'field,' *canto* 'corner.'

|  | **Intepretation A** | | **Interpretation B** | |
|---|---|---|---|---|
|  | phonological representation | phonetic transcription | phonological representation | phonetic transcription |
| *lã* 'wool' | /lã/ → | [lɐ̃] | /lan/ → /lãn/ | → [lɐ̃] |
| *tenda* 'tent' | /tẽda/ → | ['tẽdɐ] | /tenda/ → /tẽnda/ | → ['tẽdɐ] |
| *sim* 'yes' | /sĩ/ → | [sĩ] | /sin/ → /sĩn/ | → [sĩ] |
| *onda* 'wave' | /õda/ → | ['õdɐ] | /onda/ → /õnda/ | → ['õdɐ] |
| *um* 'one' | /ũ/ → | [ũ] | /un/ → /ũn/ | → [ũ] |

The contrasts /e/ : / ɛ / (*este* 'this' : *este* 'East') and /o/ : /ɔ / (*forma* 'mould' : *forma* 'form') hold in stressed position only. Whereas in BP only /e/ and /o/ occur before a nasal consonant, EP allows any of these vowels in that position, as we can see in the following examples:

|  | **EP** | **BP** |
|---|---|---|
| *lema* 'motto' | ['lemɐ] | ['lemɐ] |
| *ténis* 'tennis' | ['tɛniʃ] | ['tenis] |
| *tomo* 'tome' | ['tomu] | ['tomu] |
| *bónus* 'bonus' | ['bɔnuʃ] | ['bonus] |

In BP a nasal consonant in syllable-initial position tends to impart a degree of nasalization to the preceding vowel. Consequently, words like *cama* 'bed,' *tenho* 'I have,' *fino* 'fine,' *ponho* 'I put,' *punho* 'fist' have a slightly nasalized stressed vowel. Such pronunciation differences are responsible for differences in spelling, as in EP *ténis, bónus* vs. BP *tênis, bônus.*

This process of phonetic nasalization by assimilation varies not only regionally but also from one speaker to another. The vowel /a/ in particular tends to become nasalized, changing from [a] to a mid-central nasalized [ɐ̃], as in *cama* ['kɐ̃mɐ] 'bed,' *cano* ['kɐ̃nu] 'pipe,' *banho* ['bɐ̃ɲu] 'bath.' The contrasts /e/ : / ɛ/ and /o/ : / ɔ/ tend to be neutralized before a nasal consonant and a high-mid [e] or [o] is the norm in BP (*tênis* [tenis] 'tennis,' *tônico* ['toniku] 'tonic'). However, a few words have alternate pronunciations with either vowel, as in *fome* ['fomi] ~ ['fɔmi] 'hunger,' *Antônio* [ɐ̃'toniu] ~ *António* [ɐ̃'tɔniu]. Likewise, either [e] ~ [ɛ] or [o] ~ [ɔ] may occur in specific forms of the verbs *tomar* 'to take,' *comer* 'to eat,' *fechar* 'to close,' and *frear* 'to brake':

*toma* 'P3sg takes' ['tomɐ] ~ ['tɔmɐ]     *tomam* 'P3pl take' ['tomɐ̃w̃] ~ ['tɔmɐ̃w̃]
*come* 'P3sg' [komi] ~ ['kɔmi]     *comem* 'P3pl eat' ['kom ẽj̃] ~ ['kɔm ẽj̃]
*fecho* 'I close' ['feʃu] ~ ['fɛʃu]     *fecha* 'P3sg closes' ['feʃɐ] ~ ['fɛʃɐ]
*freia* 'P3sg brakes' ['frejɐ] ~ ['frɛjɐ]

### 2.4.2    Stressed vowels

Since stress affects vowel quality, we will take up stressed and unstressed vowels separately. In stressed position, both BP and EP show a seven-way contrast among the phonemes /i e ɛ a ɔ o u/:

/i/ *bico* 'a bird's beak'     /u/ *suco* 'juice'
/e/ *beco* 'alley'     /o/ *soco* 'a punch'
/ɛ/ *seco* 'dry'     /ɔ/ *soco* 'I punch'
/a/ *saco* 'bag'

Although in EP syllable-final /a/ is usually pronounced [ɐ] before a nasal consonant (*pano* ['pɐnu] 'cloth'), stressed [ɐ] and [a] contrast in the first person plural of *-ar* verbs, distinguishing the present ending *-amos* ['ɐmuʃ] from the preterit -*ámos* ['amuʃ], as in example 1a. This contrast does not occur naturally in BP where both endings are pronounced [ɐ] and written alike, as in 1b:

(1)     a. EP *Trabalhamos* [ɐ] *hoje porque não trabalhámos* [a] *ontem.*
        b. BP Trabalhamos [ɐ] *hoje porque não trabalhamos* [ɐ] *ontem*
           'We work today because we did not work yesterday.'

### 2.4.3 Unstressed vowels

The pronunciation of unstressed vowels varies according to their position in relation to the stressed syllable. An unstressed vowel may be either *final* or *non-final*, and in the latter case it may be *pre-stressed* or *post-stressed*. In EP unstressed vowels tend to be shortened, compressed, or eliminated altogether, which imparts an overall consonantal character to pronunciation. This is a major difference from BP, which mostly pronounces unstressed vowels rather clearly, although there are exceptions, such as Mineiro°, which tends to slur and eliminate those vowels in word-final position.

*2.4.3.1 Unstressed final position*    In BP unstressed final /a/ (spelled **a**) is either a weak [a] or a mid central vowel [ɐ]: *bala* ['balɐ] 'bullet.' The phonological contrasts /i/ : /e/ and /u/ : /o/ are neutralized, which explains why [i] corresponds to orthographic **i, e** and [u] to orthographic **o, u**. Thus the final vowels in *xale* ['ʃali] 'shawl' and *galo* ['galu] 'rooster' are the same as the final vowel in *cáqui* ['kaki] 'khaki' and *bônus* ['bonus] 'bonus,' respectively. The unstressed vowels [e], [o] in final position (corresponding to the letters **e, o**) reflect a pronunciation that survives in areas in the southern state of Rio Grande do Sul and in some rural areas of the state of São Paulo (Rodrigues 1974:186ff.), where one can hear alternations like *pobre* ['pɔbri] ~ ['pɔbre] 'poor' or *do gado* [du'gadu] ~ [do'gado] 'of the cattle.'

In EP unstressed final /a/ is pronounced as a central mid vowel [ɐ] (*casa* ['kazɐ] 'house'), while unstressed final /e/, spelled **e**, yields a higher central vowel, transcribed [ə]. The vowels [i] and [u] also occur in final unstressed position, which means that EP has a four-way contrast, compared with the three-way contrast of BP, as shown below. As mentioned above, however, unstressed vowels, particularly in final position, are systematically weakened and tend to be dropped in fast pronunciation (*casa* ['kaz], *hoje* ['oʒ] 'today').

| **BP** | | | **EP** |
|---|---|---|---|
| /i/ | [i] | táxi ['taksi] 'taxi' | [i] táxi ['taksi] ~ ['taks] |
| /e/ | [i] | taxe ['taʃi] 'P3sg may tax' | [ə] taxe ['taʃə] ~ ['taʃ] |
| /a/ | [ɐ] | taxa ['taʃɐ] 'tax,' 'P3sg taxes' | [ɐ] taxa ['taʃ] ~ ['taʃ] |
| /u/ | [u] | tacho ['taʃu] 'cauldron' | [u] tacho ['taʃu] ~ ['taʃ] |

*2.4.3.2 Pre-stressed position*    In BP the phonemes /i e a o u/ occur in pre-stressed position with the respective phonetic values [i e a o u], and generally corresponding to written **i e a o u,** as in *pirata* 'pirate,' *cutelo* 'cleaver,' *pecado* 'sin,' *covarde* 'coward,' *pagar* 'pay.'

Certain broad generalizations distinguish northern speech, characterized by open pre-tonic vowels [ɛ] and [ɔ], from southern speech, characterized by closed pre-tonic vowels [e] and [o] in words like *sereno* 'dew,' *veneno* 'poison,' *moreno* 'swarthy,' *colega* 'colleague' (Leite and Callou 2002). Since these differences are purely phonetic and entail no meaningful contrasts, they need not concern us further.

The contrasts /e/ : /i/ and /o/ : /u/ are unstable in pre-stressed position, and consequently words with orthographic **e, o** tend to be pronounced with [i], [u], as in *moleque* [mu'lɛki] 'street boy,' *pequeno* [pi'kenu] 'small.' Due to a phonological process called vowel harmony°, the high vowels [i], [u] are likely to occur if a stressed high vowel follows, as in

*menino* [mi'ninu] 'boy'          *moringa* [mu'rĩgɐ] 'jug'
*seguro* [si'guɾu] 'insurance'     *coturno* [ku'tuhnu] 'military boot'

In word-initial position, orthographic **e,** and to a lesser extent **o,** in pre-stressed position likewise tend to be pronounced respectively as [i] or [u]:

*emenda* [i'mēdɐ] 'amendment'       *entrega* [ĩtɾ'ɛgɐ] 'delivery'
*operação* [upeɾa'sẽ w̃] 'operation'  *horizonte* [uɾi'zõʃi] 'horizon'
*boneca* [bu'nɛkɐ] 'doll'           *comércio* [kum'ɛhsiu] 'commerce'

If the stressed vowel is high, vowel harmony reinforces this trend:

*ferido* [fi'ridu] 'wounded'       *serviço* [sih'visu] 'service'
*formiga* [fuh'migɐ] 'ant'         *coluna* [ku'lunɐ] 'column'

In most cases, [e], [o] can occur in monitored pronunciation if clarification is required: *boneca* [bo'nɛ kɐ] 'doll,' *emenda* [e'mēdɐ] 'correction,' *perdiz* [peh'dis] 'partridge,' *formiga* [foh'migɐ].

In both BP and EP, although the phonological contrast /e/ : /ɛ/ does not occur in unstressed position, the low-mid vowels [ɔ], [ɛ] are retained in certain derived words. These include adverbs in *-mente* (*certo* 'certain' ['sɛh tu] > *certamente* 'certainly,' BP [sɛhtɐ'mēʃi], EP [sɛɾt'mēt]; or *somente* 'only,' BP [sɔ'mēʃi], EP [sɔ'mēt], and words formed with the superlative suffix *-íssimo/a*: *perto* 'near' > *pertíssimo* 'very near' [pɛh'tisimu].

In BP [ɛ] and [ɔ] may be either kept or replaced respectively by [e] or [o] in derived words formed with the diminutive suffixes *-inho/a, -zinho/a*. In some accents, such as Mineiro, [i], [u] are common in such words:

|  | **BP in general** | **Mineiro** |
|---|---|---|
|  | [ɛ] ~ [e] and [ɔ] ~ [o] | [ɛ] ~ [e] ~ [i] ~ [ĩ] |
|  |  | [ɔ] ~ [o] ~ [u] ~ [ũ] |
| *velho* 'old' > *velhinho* | [vɛ'ʎiɲu] ~ [ve'ʎiɲu] | [vi'ʎiɲu] ~ [vi'ʎ ĩ] |
| *Zé* > *Zezinho* (from the name 'José') | [zɛ'ziɲu] ~ [ze'ziɲu] | [zi'ziɲu] ~ [zi'z ĩ] |
| *pé* 'foot' > *pezinho* 'little foot' | [pɛ'ziɲu] ~ [pe'ziɲu] | [pi'ziɲu] ~ [pi'z ĩ] |
| *só* 'alone' > *sozinho* 'quite alone' | [sɔ'ziɲu] ~ [so'ziɲu] | [su'ziɲu] ~ [su'z ĩ] |

In EP pre-stressed vowels regularly undergo a phonological process called raising⁰, which causes them to be articulated one level higher on the scale in Table 2.1: /o/ (spelled **o**) yields [u] (*pomar* 'orchard' [pu'maɾ], *provocar* 'to provoke' [pɾuvu'kaɾ]); /e/ (spelled **e**) is raised and centered, and pronounced [ə], as in *pegar* [pə'gaɾ] 'to grab,' *depois* [də'pojʃ] 'after,' whereas /a/ corresponds to [ɐ], as in *pagar* [pɐ'gaɾ] 'to pay,' *catar* [kɐ'taɾ] 'to pick up.' The presence of a syllable-final /l/, phonetically a velar lateral [ɫ], however, contributes to have /a/, /e/, /o/ pronounced respectively as [a], [ə], [o], as in *palmar* [paɫ'maɾ] 'palm tree grove,' *selvático* [səɫ'vatiku] 'savage,' *colcha* ['koɫʃɐ] 'bedspread.'

*2.4.3.3 Post-stressed non-final position*    Post-stressed non-final vowels occur only in words stressed on the third syllable from the last. In BP all five phonemes /i e a o u/ may occur in this position. The phoneme /a/ is articulated as a weak [a] or [ɐ]: *cágado* ['kagɐdu] 'turtle,' *pênalti* ['penɐwtʃi] 'penalty (sports).' As in other unstressed positions, the contrast /e/ : /i/ is weakened, so that orthographic **e** may correspond to either [e] or [i], as in the following examples, where the second member of each pronunciation pair rhymes with *código* ['kɔʤigu] 'code':

| *córrego* ['kɔhegu] | ~ | ['kɔhigu] 'creek' |
|---|---|---|
| *pêssego* ['pesegu] | ~ | ['pesigu] 'peach' |
| *cônego* ['konegu] | ~ | ['konigu] 'canon' |
| *tráfego* ['tɾafegu] | ~ | ['tɾafigu] 'traffic' |

Written **o** likewise corresponds to either [o] or [u], as in *cômodo* [ 'komodu] ~ ['komudu] 'comfortable,' *diálogo* [ʤi'alogu] ~ [ʤi'alugu] 'dialog,' with the second member of each pair rhyming with *centrífugo* 'centrifugal.' Since post-stressed non-final vowels are naturally weak, they may be devoiced and shortened or even dropped in popular pronunciation, as in

Table 2.3 *Comparison of phonemes of Portuguese and English*

**Portuguese**

Consonants

| | bilabial | labio-dental | dento-alveolar | alveolar | palatal | velar | uvular |
|---|---|---|---|---|---|---|---|
| Stop | p b | | t d | | | k g | |
| Fricative | | f v | | s z | ʃ ʒ | | ʀ¹ |
| Affricate | | | | | | | |
| Lateral | | | | l | ʎ | | |
| Nasal | m | | | n | | ɲ | |
| Vibrant | | | | ɾ | | | |
| Glides | | | | | j | w | |

Vowels

| | front | central | back |
|---|---|---|---|
| High | i | ɨ² | u |
| Mid | e | ɐ³ | o |
| | ɛ | | ɔ |
| Low | | a | |

**English**

Consonants

| | bilabial dental | labio- | dental | alveolar | palatal | velar | glottal |
|---|---|---|---|---|---|---|---|
| Stop | p b | | | t d | | k g | |
| Fricative | | f v | θ ð | s z | ʃ ʒ | | h |
| Affricate | | | | | tʃ dʒ | | |
| Lateral | | | l | | | | |
| Nasal | m | | n | | | | |
| Vibrant | | | | | r | | |
| Glides | | | | | | j | w |

Vowels

| | front | back |
|---|---|---|
| High | ij | uw |
| | i | ʊ |
| Mid | e | o |
| | ɛ | ʌ ɔ |
| Low | æ | a |

¹ As in Table 2.2, /ʀ/ is used here as a generic symbol. The allophones [ʀ r x h] may occur in the same region, often in the speech of the same speaker, although [h] is the most widespread rendering.
² A phoneme in EP only: *pegar* [pi'gar] 'to grab' vs. *pagar* [pɐ'gar] 'to pay.'
³ A phoneme in EP only in the contrast *falamos* [fɐ'lɐmuʃ] 'we speak' vs. *falámos* [fɐ'lamuʃ] 'we spoke.'

*estômago* [isˈtomᵇgu]        pop. [isˈtomu] 'stomach'
*pêssego* [ˈpesⁱgu]           pop. [ˈpezgu] 'peach'
*córrego* [ˈkɔhⁱgu]           pop. [ˈkɔɹgu] 'creek'

## 2.5    Comparison with English

English-speaking learners of Portuguese may benefit from a comparison between the phonemes of the two languages (Table 2.3) and the articulation of their main allophones. Whereas Portuguese clearly distinguishes diphthongs from vowels, in English the articulation of / ij ej uw ow/ (/ow/ > [əw] in British English) includes a downglide typical of falling diphthongs. Despite some phonetic similarity, the offglides in [aj], [ɔj], [aw] are shorter in Portuguese than in English. Consequently, the diphthongs of Pg *mau* 'bad,' *pai* 'father,' *dói* '(it) hurts' are respectively shorter than those in Eng *cow, pie, boy*.

English vowels tend to be longer in open syllables than in syllables closed by a consonant. In the latter case the vowel tends to be shorter if the consonant is voiceless than if it is voiced. These differences can be noticed by comparing vowel length in triplets like *tea, steed, steep*. In BP, stressed vowels tend to be slightly longer than unstressed ones in monitored pronunciation; in casual pronunciation vowel length can vary considerably, depending on factors such as speech style or emphasis. In some accents, such as Mineiro, stressed vowels can be rather drawled out. Variation in vowel length is a major difference between BP and EP, which, as pointed out earlier, shortens or even eliminates unstressed vowels, thus creating a series of consonants strung together. Another difference is that EP phones tend to be articulated with the tongue a bit retracted and raised, conditioning a somewhat velarized resonance (Cruz-Ferreira 1999:126) that is lacking in BP.

Other differences relate to area of articulation. Pg /i/ and /u/ are a bit higher and more fronted than Eng /ij/, /uw/ (cf. Pg *si* 'B (musical note)' : *sea*, Pg *tu* 'you' : *too*). Likewise, Pg /ɛ/ is more fronted and shorter than Eng /ɛ/ (cf. Pg *sete*: Eng *set*), and Pg /a/ is less backed than Eng /ɒ/. The contrast between the vowels of *bait/bet* does not match that of Pg /e/ : /ɛ/ (*este* [ˈestʃi] 'this': este [ˈɛstʃi] 'east'), which learners tend to underdifferentiate.

If transferred to Portuguese, the articulation of English vowels not only causes a foreign accent but may interfere with comprehension by underdifferentiating the contrasts between the vowels /e u o ɔ/ and the diphthongs /ej uw ow ɔw/. The contrast Eng [ow] : [ɔ] does not match Pg [o] : [ɔ] (*avô : avó*), since Eng /ɔ/ in final position tends to be lengthened (*law* [l ɔː]) and even diphthongized, as in the case of some US southern varieties (cf. *law* [lɔw]).

Unstressed English vowels tend to undergo lenition°, a phonological process involving a softening of articulatory effort. They are thus reduced to either a central mid [ə] or a high central [ɨ] (Whitley 1986:58), as illustrated by the stressed/unstressed vowels in pairs like *Asia* [ej] / *Asiatic* [ə], *repetitive* [ɛ] / *repetition* [ə], *contemplate* [ɒ] / *contemplative* [ə], *Adam* [æ] / *adamic* [ə]. Since no such reduction occurs in BP, where even unstressed vowels retain a distinctive quality, English speakers' tendency to pronounce [ə] in unstressed position undermines important distinctions such as that between masculine and feminine endings, indicated by the contrast [u] : [ɐ], as in *menino* 'boy' vs. *menina* 'girl.'

Of the nineteen Portuguese consonant phonemes, fifteen / p b t d k g f v s z ʃ ʒ l m n/ have an approximate articulatory homologue in English, although the use of like symbols should not be mistaken for identical phonetic realizations.

*Stops* /p t k b d g/. The basic allophones of these phonemes are respectively the stops [p t k b d g]. In southern Portugal, lenition causes intervocalic / b d g / to be pronounced as the fricative allophones [β δ γ]: *cabra* ['kaβrɐ] 'goat,' *lado* ['laδu] 'side,' *figo* ['fiγu] 'fig.' (Phonetic similarity between [β] and [v] lies at the source of the erroneous notion that EP speakers "change their **b**'s for **v**'s.") As mentioned earlier, in BP there is a tendency to palatalize /t d/, yielding the affricates [tʃ dʒ] when followed by [i], spelled either **i** or unstressed **e**: *tio* ['tʃiu] 'uncle,' *sete* ['sɛtʃi] 'seven,' *sede* ['sedʒi] 'thirst.' Such palatalization, which apparently started in Carioca° speech, is currently slowly spreading out, but the older pronunciation of /t d/ as stops [t d] is still used. In accents such as Paulista, final unstressed vowels tend to be devoiced or even lost, and consequently such words end in an affricate: ['estʃ], ['sedʒ].

The voiceless stops corresponding to /p t k/ (spelled **p, t, k/qu**[e,i]) and /b g/ (spelled **b, g/ gu**[e,i]) share the same basic articulation in Portuguese as in English. Pg /t d/, however, have an alveodental articulation, whereas Eng /t d/ are fully alveolar, a minor difference which may cause a slight accent. English voiceless stops in syllable-initial position are released with a slight puff of air, called aspiration, which may be shown in transcription as a raised $^h$ [p$^h$ t$^h$ k$^h$]. Since there is no such aspiration in Portuguese, using it in words like *pata* 'paw,' *tapa* 'slap,' *capa* 'cloak' may result in an accent. Furthermore, since Eng /b d g/ are only partially voiced, unless preceded by a voiced segment, this aspiration reinforces the contrast between /b d g/ and the voiceless phonemes /p t k/. Thus absence of aspiration in Portuguese seemingly explains why English-speaking learners experience some difficulty distinguishing between Pg [p t k] and [b d g]. The American pronunciation of intervocalic /t d/ as an alveolar tap [ɾ] (*waiter/wader* ['wejɾəɹ]) has no correlate in Portuguese, where /r/ is a separate phoneme. Consequently, pronouncing /t d/ as [ɾ] is likely to cause miscomprehension, as in *pata* 'paw' or *cada* 'each' (cf. *para* 'for' ['parɐ], *cara* 'face' ['karɐ]).

*Fricatives* / f v s z ʃʒ /. The fricatives /f/ and /v/ (spelled **f, v**) are articulated like Eng [f] (*fogo* 'fire' ['fogu]) or [v] (*vila* 'village' ['vilɐ]). Articulation of Pg /ʃ/, /ʒ/ and pre-vocalic /s/, /z/ is also close to English. The phoneme /z/ has a voiced alveolar allophone [z], spelled either **z** (*zebra*), **x** (*êxito* 'success'), or **s** between vowels (*casa* 'house'), or before a voiced consonant (*asno* 'donkey,' *rasgo* 'tear,' *israelense* 'Israeli'). /s/ is a voiceless alveolar fricative [s], spelled **ss** or **ç** between vowels (*cassa* 'muslin,' *caça* 'hunting') or **s** in other positions (*sal* 'salt'); in word-final position /s/ becomes voiced by assimilation to a following vowel or voiced consonant, as in *os amigos* 'the friends' [uza'migus], *os doces* 'the sweets' [uz'dosis].

In both EP and Carioca, palatalization of post-vocalic /s/ yields the palatal fricative [ʃ] both finally or before a voiceless consonant (*custos* 'costs' ['kuʃtuʃ]). Before a voiced consonant, this fricative is voiced as [ʒ] (*os dois bois* 'the two oxen' [uʒ-'dojʒ-'bojʃ]), although before a vowel or a voiceless consonant it remains [ʃ]: *os amigos*, Carioca [uza'miguʃ], EP [uzɐ'miguʃ]. Although a hallmark of Carioca speech, which is a prestigious accent, this palatal [ʃ] is not readily imitated elsewhere in Brazil.

In EP syllable-final /s/ followed by another /s/ yields the sequence [ʃs] as in *ascender* [aʃ-s ẽ-'deɾ] 'ascend' (cf. *acender* 'to light' [a-s ẽ-'deɾ]), *os sapatos* [uʃ-sɐ-'pa-tuʃ] 'the shoes.' In BP, on the contrary, two contiguous /s/ assimilate into a single syllable-initial [s]: *ascender/acender* [a-'sẽ-deɾ], *os sapatos* [u-sa-'pa-tus]. Consequently, BP speakers have to learn by heart the spelling differences between word pairs like *ascético* 'ascetic'/*acético* 'acetic' or *ascender* 'to ascend'/*acender* 'to light,' whereas EP speakers easily correlate [ʃs] with **sc**.

The voiceless palatal fricative / ʃ / (spelled **ch, x**), as in *chato* ['ʃatu] 'flat,' *xerife* [ʃe'rifi] ~ [ʃi'rifi] 'sheriff,' and its voiced counterpart /ʒ/, spelled **j, g**<sup>e,i</sup>, as in *jato* ['ʒatu] 'jet,' *gelo* ['ʒelu] 'ice,' are similar in articulation to Eng *shape* and *azure*, respectively.

*Nasals* /m n/. The nasal phonemes /m/ and /n/ (spelled **m, n**) are articulated like Eng /m n/ in pre-vocalic position (*minuto* 'minute'), with the minor difference that Eng [n] is alveolar, while Pg [n] is dental. Since written post-vocalic **m** and **n** do not stand for consonants but rather indicate that the preceding vowel is nasal (*sim* 'yes' [sĩ], *com* 'with' [kõw]), learners should avoid pronouncing them, particularly between words: *com alguém* 'with someone' [kõwawgẽj] rather than *[kõwmawgẽj].

*Liquids* / l ʎ ɾ ʀ/ and nasal /ɲ/. Pre-vocalic /l/ is pronounced in BP as a voiced dental lateral [l] (*lapela* 'lapel'), whereas Eng /l/ has an alveolar articulation. In EP, though not in BP, a slight degree of velarization is noticeable. In EP syllable-final position /l/ is a strongly velarized lateral [ɫ], as in *mel* [mɛɫ] 'honey,' not unlike Eng *Mel*. In BP this velarized pronunciation used to be considered standard until the middle of the twentieth century, and can be heard in recordings from the 1940s and 1950s. (Mascherpe [1970:41] listed it as the normal realization of post-vocalic /l/.) It is still heard regionally (as in in the extreme south) and among older speakers elsewhere, but it is in the process of being replaced by a velar glide [w] that forms a diphthong with the preceding vowel (Demasi 1995, Leite and Callou 2002:47–48) in sequences like *-al, -el, -il, -ol, -ul,* as in *mil* [miw] 'thousand,' *sul* [suw] 'south,' *mel* [mɛw] 'honey,' *sol* [sɔw] 'sun,' *sal* [saw] 'salt.'

By neutralizing the contrast /l/ : /w/, this diphthongization process creates homonyms (that is, like-sounding words) such as *mal* 'evil' / *mau* 'bad,' or rhymes such as *papel* 'paper' / *céu* 'sky,' or *vil* 'vile'/ *viu* 'P3sg saw,' neither of which exists in EP.

Neither the palatals /ʎ/, /ɲ/ nor the vibrants /ɾ, ʀ/ have counterparts in English. The voiced lateral palatal /ʎ/, spelled **lh**, is articulated with the tongue blade against the palate (*filho* 'son' ['fiʎu]). It occurs initially in only a few words (*lhama* 'llama,' *lhano* 'unpretentious'), of which the only relatively frequent one is the pronoun *lhe* 'to him/her/you.' English speakers tend to substitute the sequence [li] or [lj], pronouncing words like *malha* 'knit sweater' or *molho* 'sauce' as *['ma-li-ɐ], *['ma-ljɐ], *[ 'mow-li-u], *['mow-lju].

The nasal palatal /ɲ/, spelled **nh**, is articulated very much like /ʎ/ but with the velum lowered to let air escape through the nasal tract. It occurs initially in some fifty words (mostly borrowings from indigenous languages such as *nhandu* 'emu,' *nhenhenhém* 'babble') as well as medially (*senhora* 'lady' [si'ɲɔrɐ]). Like [ʎ], [ɲ] does not come easily to English speakers, who tend to substitute [ni] or [nj], *senhor* *[sini'or] or *Senhora* *[si'njɔrɐ].

Despite being spelled with the same letter **r**, the phonetic outputs of Pg /ɾ/ and /ʀ/ are very different from Eng /r/, which is a central alveolar glide-like retroflexed consonant. A phonetic [ɾ] occurs in American English as the pronunciation of intervocalic **t, d** (*waiter, wader*), and also in the tapped Scottish **r** (Ladefoged 2001:151). Portuguese /ɾ/ is phonetically a tap [ɾ] artic-ulated by the tongue touching the alveolar ridge once, as in *cara* ['kaɾɐ] 'face.'

The phoneme /ʀ/ has several phonetic realizations, the oldest of which is an alveolar trill formed by the tongue tip touching the alveolar ridge a couple of times, as in *carro* ['karu] 'car.' Once considered standard in Brazil, this pronunciation can be heard in songs recorded in the 1940s and 1950s, but it seems to be giving way to a range of articulations which include, among other possibilities, a voiceless uvular trill, voiceless [ʀ] or voiced [ʁ], a velar voiceless fricative [x], and the widespread glottal fricative transcribed [h]. Consequently, a word like *barro* 'mud' may be pronounced variously as ['baru], ['baʀu], ['baxu], or ['bahu]. As mentioned above, it is not unusual for two or more allophones to occur in the speech of the same speaker.

The contrast /ɾ/ : /ʀ/ however, only holds between vowels (*caro/carro*). Only /ʀ/ occurs initially (*rádio, Roberto*) or after syllable-final /l/, /s/, or orthographic **n** (*palrar* 'to babble,' *transreceptor* 'transceiver,' *enredo* 'plot'). In syllable-final position EP tends to have /ɾ/, often weakened, whereas in BP either /ɾ/ or /ʀ/ occurs. In word-final position the contrast /ɾ/: /ʀ/ is neutralized: EP tends to have a light tap [ɾ] whereas in BP any of the alternatives described above are possible. Except in monitored pronunciation, BP tends to eliminate final /ɾ/ in infinitives, so that *fala(r)* [fa'la] 'to speak,' *come(r)* [ku'me] 'to eat,' *parti(r)* [par'ti] 'to leave' rhyme with *lá* 'there,' *você* 'you,' *aqui* 'here.'

## 2.6    Syllables

Syllables are short phone sequences organized according to language-specific phonotactics°, that is rules specifying the position in which a given phone can occur, which phones can or cannot occur next to each other, and so on. Every syllable has a *nucleus* (N), which in Portuguese must be a vowel or a diphthong. (In English certain consonants may be a syllable nucleus, as /n/ in *mutton* ['mʌt-n] or /l/ in *little* ['lɪt-ɫ].) Monosyllables have only the nucleus: *há* [a] 'there is,' *é* [ɛ] 'is,' *eu* [ew] 'I,' *oi* 'hi.' Consonants coming before the nucleus constitute the *onset* (O), as [p] in *pá* 'shovel,' or [s] in *só* 'only.' Consonants following the nucleus form the *coda*, like [s] in *voz* 'voice.' The nucleus and the coda, if there is one, make up the *rhyme* (R). Portuguese syllable types may be represented as in Table 2.4.

The onset may have a single consonant (C) or a cluster of two specific consonants, $C_1 C_2$. As shown in Table 2.4, $C_1$ is either a stop /p b t d k g/ or a labiodental fricative /f v/ and $C_2$ must be a liquid /l ɾ/. Since Portuguese phonotactics exclude the cluster /dl/, the sequence /d/ + /l/ splits between contiguous syllables, and only occurs in items of specific groups, such as:

– words derived from foreign words with /dl/: *adleriano* (< name 'Adler') – *ad-le-ria-no*
– scientific nouns: *adlúmia* '*Adlumia fungosa*,' *adlumina* 'adlumine' – *ad-lú-mi-a, ad-lu-mina*
– learned compounds: *adligar-se* 'to attach itself to another (of a plant)' – *ad-li-gar-se*

In unmonitored speech those consonants are separated by introducing a vowel, as in the brand name *Revlon*, pronounced [hɛ-vi-'lõ]. The cluster /tl/ occurs initially in the onomatopoeic word *tlim* [tlĩ] ~ [ti'lĩ] 'ringing' and medially in fewer than fifty words, such as *atlas* 'atlas' or *atlético* 'athletic'; /vl/ and /vr/ occur initially only in the name *Vladimir* and its popular variant *Vradimir*.

No clusters occur in the coda, where possible phonemes include /l/, /s/; in addition, since the contrast between /ɾ/ and /ʀ/ is neutralized, words spelled with a final -r can be pronounced with [ɾ] or one of the allophones of /ʀ/ ([ʀ], [ʁ ], [x], or [h]), as in the following examples. A consonant following one of these phonemes begins a new syllable:

| coda position: only /l ɾ ʀ s/ | /l ɾ ʀ s/ + consonant |
|---|---|
| *cal* /kal/ [kaw], [kaɫ] 'lime' | *al-ma* ['aw-mɐ], ['aɫmɐ] 'soul' |
| *par* /paɾ/ [paɾ], [pah] 'pair' | *ar-ma* ['aɾ-mɐ], ['ahmɐ] 'weapon' |
| *paz* /pas/ [pas] 'peace' | *cas-ta* ['kas-tɐ] 'caste' |

The nasal /n/ occurs in the coda only if we choose to represent nasals as sequences of vowel + /n/. Phonetically, however, such a sequence is simply a nasal vowel. If we choose to include nasal vowels in the phonological representation, words like *lã* 'wool' or *transpor* 'transpose' would be /lɐ̃/, /trẽs'por/, following the pattern CV and CCVC.

Phonotactic divergences between BP and EP account for minor differences in syllable structure. In EP consonant clusters other than those shown in Table 2.4 may occur at the onset of a syllable, either initially or medially:

| initial position | medial position | |
|---|---|---|
| *psi-quiatria* | *a-bso-lu-to* | *ma-gno* |
| *pneu-monia* | *a-dvo-ga-do* | *a-gnós-ti-co* |
| *gnóstico* | *pers-pe-cti-va* | *a-dsor-ção* |

If there are three or more consonants, the second one is always /s/ in syllable-final position: $C_1 C_2 - C_3$ (*abs-ter* 'to abstain') or $C_1 C_2 - C_3 C_4$ (*abs-trair* 'to abstract', *ads-trin-gen-te* 'astringent'). In BP this syllabification may occur in monitored pronunciation, but in spontaneous speech consonant sequences other than those clusters are broken up by inserting the vowel /i/ (or /e/ in some accents). The same goes for word-initial non-cluster sequences of the type $C_1 C_2 V$, such as *pneu, pneumonia, psiquiatra, gnomo*, which become $C_1 V - C_2 V$, as in the examples below:

| | monitored pronunciation $VC_1 C_2 - C_3 (C_4)$ | spontaneous pronunciation $VC_1 - [i]C_2 - C_3 C_4$ |
|---|---|---|
| *absoluto* | [ab-so-'lu-tu] | [a-bi-su-'lu-tu] |
| *agnóstico* | [ag-'nɔs-ti-ku] | [a-gi-'nɔs-ʧi-ku] |
| *absurdo* | [ab-'suh-du] | [a-bi-'suh-du] |
| *advogado* | [ad-vo-'ga-du] | [a-ʤi-vo-'ga-du] ∼ [a-de-vo-'ga-du] |
| *perspectiva* | [pehs-pek-'ʧi-vɐ] | [pehs-pe-ki-'ʧi-vɐ] |
| *magno* | ['mag-nu] | ['ma-gi-nu] |

|  | $C_1 - C_2V$ | $C_1$ [i] $- C_2V$ |
|---|---|---|
| *pneu* | [pnew] | [pi-'new] |
| *psiquiatra* | [psi-ki-'a-tɐ] | [pi-si-ki-'a-tɐ] |
| *pneumonia* | [pnew-mu-'ni-ɐ] | [pi-new-mu-'ni-ɐ] |
| *gnomo* | ['gno-mu] | [gi'no-mu] |

When Portuguese borrows a foreign word ending in a consonant other than /r s l/, its pronunciation is adjusted according to Portuguese phonotactics: Eng *modem* > Pg *modem* ['modẽj], Eng *short* 'shorts' > BP ['ʃɔhʧi] (cf. EP *shorts* [ʃɔrts], Eng *bang bang* > BP *bangue-bangue* ['bẽgi'bẽgi] 'Western [movie]', Eng *VIP (lounge)* > BP *(sala) VIP* ['vipi], *far West* > *faroeste* [faro'ɛsʧi] 'a Western (movie).'

## 2.7    Resyllabification

Several phonological phenomena may take place over a word boundary, that is between contiguous words, changing their syllable structure. A word-final consonant forms a new syllable by linking with the initial vowel of the following word. In consequence, a sequence like *os amigos americanos* 'the American friends is resyllabified as *o-sa-mi-go-sa-me-ri-ca-nos* [u-za-'mi-gu-za-me-ɾi-'kɐ-nus].

In EP final /r/ links with a following vowel, thus becoming syllable-initial (*falar alto* 'to speak loudly' [fᵊ-'la-'ɾał-tu]). In BP the contrast between /r/ and /ʀ/ is neutralized in this position, and furthermore in unmonitored pronunciation this /r/ tends to be dropped in verb infinitives. Consequently a sequence like *comer alface* 'to eat lettuce' is likely to be [ku-'me-aw-'fa-si] in unmonitored pronunciation. In monitored pronunciation, however, a linking vibrant is possible, as in [ku-'me-ɾaw-'fa-si].

Likewise in EP word-final /l/, phonetically a velarized lateral [ł], links with a following vowel, becoming syllable-initial, as in *papel amarelo* 'yellow paper' [pɐ'pɛ-łɐ-mɐ-'ɾɛ-lu]. In BP, syllable-final /l/ is usually a velar glide [w], which forms a diphthong with the preceding vowel, [pa'pɛw], and may link with a following vowel: [pa'-pɛw-a-ma-'ɾɛ-lu] or [pa-pɛ-'wa-ma-'ɾɛ-lu]. Nevertheless, an [l] may occur in this position, in the speech of the same person: [pa-'pɛ-lɐ-mɐ-'ɾɛ-lu] ∼ [pa-'pɛ-wɐ-mɐ-'ɾɛ-lu]. Word-final /s/ followed by a vowel is pronounced [z], voiced and syllable-initial: *dois atos* 'two acts' [doj-'za-tus], *coisas americanas* 'American things' ['koj-zɐ-za-me-ɾi-'kɐ-nɐs].

The occurrence of two vowels over a word boundary may have different results (Bisol 1992, 1996). We will consider only a few cases. Identical unstressed vowels may be pronounced in separate syllables or fused into a single syllable:

Table 2.4 *Portuguese syllable structures, types, consonant groups, and consonant sequences*

**Syllable types:**

| V | *é* 'is' | CV | *pó* 'dust' | $C_1C_2$ V | *crê* 'P3sg believes' |
|---|---|---|---|---|---|
| VG | *oi* 'hi' | CVG | *boi* 'ox' | $C_1C_2$ VC | *três* 'three' |
| VC | *ar* 'air' | CVGC | *dois* 'two' | $C_1C_2$ VG | *frei* 'friar' |
| VGC | *eis* 'here is' | CVC | *voz* 'voice' | $C_1C_2$ VGC | *freis* 'friars' |
| $C_1C_2$VCC | *trans-* [*] | CVCC | *perspirar* 'to perspire' | | |

**Clusters (indivisible and always before the nucleus):**

| /pl/ *plano* 'plan' | /pr/ *preço* 'price' | /kl/ *claro* 'clear' | /kr/ *cruz* 'cross' |
|---|---|---|---|
| /bl/ *bloco* 'block' | /br/ *bravo* 'brave' | /gl/ *glosa* 'gloss' | /gr/ *gruta* 'grotto' |
| /tl/ *tlim* 'tlin' | /tr/ *trio* 'trio' | /dl/ – | /dr/ *draga* 'dredger' |
| /vl/ *Vladimir* | /vr/ *Vradimir* | /fl/ *flor* 'flower' | /fr/ *fração* 'fraction' |

**Non-cluster consonant sequences after the nucleus (divisible sequences):**
$VC_1$ – $C_2$ *es-te* 'this', *al-to* 'high', *hor-ta* 'vegetable garden'

**Examples of syllable division:**

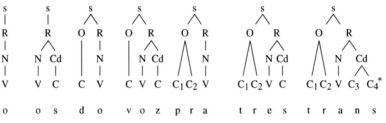

[*]Assuming /trans/ as a phonological representation S = syllable; R = rhyme; N = nucleus; O = onset; Cd = Coda; V = vowel; C = consonant; G = glide; $C_1$, $C_2$ = different consonants.

*casa agradável* 'pleasant house' ['ka-zɐ-a-gɾa -'da-vew] ~ ['ka-za-gɾa-'da-vew]

*osso humano* 'human bone' ['o-su-u-'mɐ-nu] ~ ['o-su-mɐ-nu]

*esse irmão* 'this brother' ['e-si-ih-mẽw] ~ ['e-sih-mẽw].

If the second vowel is either unstressed /i/ or /u/, the vowels may be in separate syllables or combine to form a diphthong, or the first vowel may be elided:

*essa história* 'this story' ['ɛ-sɐ-i s-'tɔ-ɾi-ɐ] ~ ['ɛ-sɐjs-'tɔ-ɾi-ɐ] ~ ['ɛ-sis-'tɔ-ɾi-ɐ]

*outra usina* 'another factory' ['o-tɾɐ-u-zi-nɐ] ~ ['o-tɾɐw-zi-nɐ] ~ ['o-tɾu-zi-nɐ].

## 2.8    Other phonological processes

*Lenition°* is also involved in the weakening and loss of unstressed vowels, as in BP *para > pra* [pra] 'for,' EP *pessoa > p'ssoa* [p'soɐ] 'person,' or of consonants, such as final /r/ in BP *falar > falá, comer > comê,* partir > parti.

*Devoicing°*, a process whereby a voiced phone becomes voiceless, accounts for voiceless final unstressed vowels in BP (*moro muito perto* 'I live rather close' ['mɔ-ru̥'mũj-t u̥'pɛh-t u̥]) and in EP (*é do Porto* 'it's from Oporto' ['ɛ-du̥-'poɾ-t u̥]).

*Monophthongization°* is a process that reduces a diphthong to a single vowel. In BP the diphthong /ow/, stressed or unstressed, is usually pronounced [o] although the glide [w] may be reinstated in monitored speech, as in *falou pouco* [fa'lo'poku] ∼ [fa'low'powku] 'P3sg spoke little.' Monophthongization does not affect, however, the diphthong [ow] originating from velarization of post-vocalic /l/ in BP, as in *soldado* 'soldier' /soldado/ → [sow'dadu], *voltamos* 'we came back'/voltamos/ → [vow'tɐmus], which contrasts with *votamos* [vo'tɐmus] 'we vote.'

The opposite process, *diphthongization°*, causes a vowel to be articulated as a diphthong. It occurs in BP when a stressed vowel is followed by word-final /s/, although in monitored pronunciation this syllabus nucleus may revert to a vowel:

|  | unmonitored pronunciation | monitored pronunciation |
|---|---|---|
| *mas* /mas/ 'but' (cf. *mais* 'more') | [majs] | [mas] |
| *pés* /pɛs/ 'feet' | [pɛjs] | [pɛs] |
| *vez* /ves/ 'time' | [vejs] | [ves] |
| *pôs* / pos/ 'P3sg put' | [pojs] | [pos] |
| *luz* / lus/ 'light' | [lujs] | [lus] |
| *português* /portu'ges/ 'Portuguese' | [pohtu'gejs] | [pohtu'ges] |
| *inglês* /in'gles/ 'English' | [ĩglejs] | [ĩ'gles] |

## 2.9    Prosody: Stress, pitch, and rhythm

The umbrella label "prosody" covers the interrelated phenomena of stress, pitch, and rhythm, usually referred to as "suprasegmentals," since they are perceived as being superimposed onto the segments that make up a phone sequence.

Stress, mentioned at the beginning of this chapter, is the phonetic correlate of shifts in articulatory and respiratory intensity, caused by increased muscular activity during the production of a given syllable relative to neighboring syllables. Monosyllables uttered in isolation cannot be said to have stress. Even though we tend to refer to stressed and unstressed vowels, auditorily stress involves the degree of loudness of the syllable as a whole, which is why some phoneticians prefer to put the stress mark ['] before the syllable, rather than on the vowel, in phonetic transcription.

A words is called an *oxytone*° if the stressed syllable is the last one (*aqui* 'here,' *você* 'you'), a *paroxytone*° if stressed on the second from last syllable or penult (*fala* 'speech,' *capa* 'cloak'), and a *proparoxytone*° if the stress falls on the third from last syllable or antepenult (*hipótese* 'hypothesis,' *tentáculo* 'tentacle'). There are also cases of stress on the fourth syllable from the last. In BP, this includes words with a consonant sequence such as **pt** or **tn**, which, as noted earlier (2.6), is broken up by a vowel, as in *críptico* ['kri-pi-tʃi-ku] 'cryptic' or *étnico* ['ɛ-tʃi-ni-ku] 'ethnic.' Another case, found regularly in EP, though not so commonly in BP, involves proparoxytone verb forms with an unstressed object pronoun (3.4, 5.2) placed after the verb, such as *estudávamo-lo* 'we studied it' or *comprávamo-los* 'we used to buy them.'

Each Portuguese word carries lexical stress in a given position (only a few, like *projétil/projetil* 'projectile' or *réptil/reptil* 'reptile,' admit two possibilities). As mentioned earlier, given two otherwise identical phoneme sequences, stress position is phonologically contrastive, as in *cara* 'face' vs. *cará* 'a kind of yam.' Contrasts based on stress position differentiate past perfect forms (3.5.2.2) from future forms, as in *andara* 'P3sg had walked' / *andará* 'P3sg will walk.'

Phonetically, a syllable is either stressed or unstressed (Cagliari 1999:39). Phonologically, however, a secondary degree of stress has been described in BP forms derived from words with stressed [ɔ] or [ɛ] and bearing endings such as *-eiro, -inho, -zinho, -zal,* or *-mente*:

| | |
|---|---|
| *copo* [kɔ'pu] 'drinking glass' | > *copinho* [kɔ'piɲu] |
| *café* [ka'fɛ] 'coffee' | > *cafezinho* [kafɛ'ziɲu] 'a demitasse of coffee' |
| *café* [ka'fɛ] 'coffee' | > *cafezal* [kafɛ'zaw] ~ [kafe'zaw] 'coffee plantation' |
| *só* [sɔ] 'alone' | > *sozinho* [sɔ'ziɲu] 'alone' |

Although this secondary stress holds when such words are uttered in isolation, in normal speech the apparent prominence of these syllables seems to owe more to the retention of the open vowel than to an actual increase in stress. The secondary stress in words like *rapidamente* 'rapidly' or *tristemente* 'sadly' (on *-ra* and *-tris*, respectively) results from the fact that such adverbs are compounds rather than derived words (3.6). Such secondary stress is variable and more likely to occur when emphasis is intended.

A group of words pronounced in the same breath group constitutes a phonological phrase°, in which there is only one strong phrase stress, usually coinciding with the last word stress. Thus an utterance like *Eu chamei três táxis* 'I called three taxis' would likely be *Eu chamei três TÁXIS* at its most generic rendering, and the stress in the words *eu, chamei,* and *três* would be lower in relation to the stressed syllable of *táxis,* although stronger than the unstressed syllables. Such stress variation makes possible subtle contrasts like the following:

| | |
|---|---|
| *feroz cidade* 'wild city' | vs. *ferocidade* 'ferocity' |
| *voraz cidade* 'voracious city' | vs. *voracidade* 'voracity' |
| *veloz cidade* 'fast city' | vs. *velocidade* 'velocity' |
| | (Oliveira 1976). |

Pitch is the auditory correlate of the frequency of vibration of the vocal cords, and physiologically, it relates to the degree of tension of the cords as they vibrate. Pitch is measured in hertz (Hz, a unit of frequency equal to one cycle per second) and varies in range, depending on factors such as the speaker's sex or age, from between 80 and 200 Hz for males, between 180 and 400 Hz for females. In Portuguese as in English, pitch variation plays a distinctive role at sentence level, combining with stress to create melodic contours, referred to as *intonation,* which signal whether an utterance is a statement, a question, or a command.

Intonation also conveys information about speakers' attitudes, such as hesitation, annoyance, or cooperativeness, and consequently a good grasp of it is essential for capturing the full intent of an utterance. Unfortunately, of all the aspects of prosody, it is the least amenable to verbal description, and full control of intonation in a foreign language can only be acquired by carefully listening to and imitating appropriate models. A few generalizations, however, can be made.

Pitch variations in Portuguese have traditionally been described in terms of three levels, labeled low (1), mid (2), and high (3) (Staub 1956, Rameh 1962, Ellison and Gomes de Matos 1987, Azevedo 1981a). An extra high (4) level is associated with emphasis. Arrows are used to show rising ⬈, falling ⬊, or sustained ➔ pitch at the end of phonological phrases, signaling the direction of pitch that forms terminal contours.

If a sentence like *Ela vem amanhã* 'She is coming tomorrow' is uttered as a statement, pitch stays at level 2 beginning at the first stressed syllable (*el*) and drops to level 1 at the last stressed syllable, which usually carries phrase stress. The result of that drop will be a falling terminal pitch (*Ela$^2$ vem$^2$ amanhã$^1$* ⬊). Questions introduced by an interrogative word (*quando* 'when,' *quem* 'who,' and so on) usually have falling terminal pitch when intended simply to elicit information (*Quando$^2$ é que a Maria$^1$ vem$^1$?* ⬊ 'When is it that Maria is coming?'). Rising terminal pitch is possible, however, when conveying an element of surprise or doubt, or a request for confirmation (*Quando$^2$ é que a Maria$^2$ vem$^3$?* ⬈).

Yes/no questions, on the other hand, typically have rising terminal pitch (*Ela²
já² chegou³?* ✔ 'Has she already arrived?') Sustained pitch (*Ela chegou ontem*
➥ 'She arrived yesterday') suggests an unfinished utterance, leading a listener
to expect additional information, such as *e vai embora amanhã* ↘ 'and will
leave tomorrow.'

Rhythm, the third element of prosody, has to do with variations in tempo
related to our perception of recurring patterns of speech units. In English tempo
patterns involve the alternation of stressed and unstressed syllables. Other languages use different units, such as short vs. long syllables as in Classical Latin,
or high and low pitches as in some Asian languages, or syllables as in Italian
or Spanish. Languages used to be classified as having either syllable-timed
rhythm (like Italian or Spanish) or stress-timed rhythm (like English or Dutch).
Some phoneticians, however, have pointed out that language comparison fails to
support such a dichotomy. Nooteboom (1997:663) and Ladefoged (2001:231)
suggested that whether a language has variable or fixed stress is more important
as far as characterizing rhythm is concerned.

The traditional view of syllable-timed rhythm has to do with a relatively
even distribution of stressed and unstressed syllables of approximately the
same duration. Stress-timed rhythm, in turn, involves distribution of stressed
syllables along even intervals, with the unstressed syllables clustered between
two stresses. While consensus has yet to be reached, scholars agree that EP
belongs to the stress-timed type (Cruz-Ferreira 1999:129). Others point out
that some speakers of BP have stress-time rhythm, while others have syllable-
timed rhythm (Cagliari & Abaurre 1986, Massini-Cagliari 1992).

Whilst a comparison of sufficiently large samples of the two varieties of
Portuguese has yet to be carried out, it is apparent that striking differences in
rhythm patterns obtain between them. In BP differences in duration between
stressed and unstressed syllables seem linked to emphasis. In EP, on the contrary, unstressed vowels are systematically shorter than stressed ones and may
be deleted in unmonitored speech, causing rhythm to be stress-timed. Thus an
utterance such as *uma linha de pensamento partilhada pela maioria* 'a line of
thought shared by the majority,' which in BP would be something like (3a), in
EP would be more like (3b), where a raised sign indicates a weakened vowel.

(3)     a. BP [umɐ'liɲɐdipẽsa'mẽtupahti'ʎadɐpelɐmajo'riɐ]
        b. EP [umᵉ' liɲᵉdpẽ sᵉ' mẽ tᵘ pᵉ'ti'ʎadᵉplᵉmᵉju'riᵉ]
        *uma linha de pensamento partilhada pela maioria*

In themselves, phones have no meaning. How meaning-bearing phone
sequences are organized is the subject of morphology, which will occupy us in
the next chapter.

# 3 Words

Even if Polonius found Hamlet's reply "Words, words, words" a trifle odd, he had no reason to question what it meant – after all, the prince was holding a book, which is where anyone would expect to find words. Like Polonius, most of the time we act as if we knew what a word is, and feel no urge to question the status of words like *chuva* 'rain,' *filhinho* 'sonny,' *ponta* 'point,' *guarda* 'guard,' *pé* 'foot,' or *papai* 'daddy.' But what about forms like *pontapé* 'kick,' *guarda-chuva* 'umbrella,' *filhinho-de-papai* 'mamma's boy'? Are they single words or combinations of two or three words? And what should we say of word combinations that function like a meaning unit, such as *bico-de-papagaio*, *rabo-de-arara*, *parece-mas-não-é* or *planta-de-Natal*, which despite their literal meanings (respectively 'parrot's beak,' 'macaw's tail,' 'it-seems-but-it-isn't,' 'Christmas plant') are simple regional Brazilian names for the *Euphorbia pulcherrima*, the *poinsétia* 'poinsettia' of Yuletide fame? In this chapter we will look into *morphology*, itself made up of two Greek words, *morphē* 'form' + *logos* 'study,' that is, the study of the form of words.

## 3.1    Words and morphemes

Despite their variety, words have a definite internal structure. In words like *carros* or *senhores*, we recognize two formants. One is the stem° (*carr-*, *senhor*), which bears the lexical° meaning of an extralinguistic referent°, such as things, persons, ideas, and so on. The other is a suffix° (*-s*, *-es*), attached to the stem and carrying the meaning 'plural.' This kind of meaning has no extralinguistic referent; rather, it is strictly grammatical, that is, it has to do with the structure of the language. In *carro* we likewise recognize two formants, namely the stem *carr-* (which occurs in related words like *carreta* 'cart') and the suffix *-o*, which is a noun-forming element that also appears in words like *livro, menino*. Formants like *senhor, carr-, -s, -es, -o* (phonologically /seɲoɾ/, /kaʀ/, /s/, /es/, /o/), which cannot be further subdivided without losing their meaning, constitute word-building blocks called morphemes°. Like a phoneme, a morpheme is an abstract concept and each of its actual manifestations is called an allomorph°. The morpheme **plural**, for instance, has the allomorph **-s** in *casas, carros* and the allomorph **-es** in *rapazes, mulheres*. (We will use boldface to distinguis morphemes from words as necessary.) Morphemes like **-s, -es**, which are always linked to other morphemes, are *bound forms*, whereas morphemes like **táxi, senhor**, which may occur alone in an utterance (*Senhor! Táxi?*), are *free forms*.

Like morphemes, words are either *grammatical* or *lexical*. Grammatical words (also called structural, or function words) signal structural relationships between words, like *de* in *cadeira de rodas* 'wheelchair,' *com* in *café com leite* 'coffee and milk,' or *e* in *bom e barato* 'good and cheap.' Lexical words (also called content words), in contrast, have extra-linguistic referents: nouns refer to beings, things, concepts; adjectives refer to qualities; and verbs refer to actions, states, or processes.

| Nouns (beings, things, concepts) | Adjectives (qualities) | Verbs (actions, states, processes) |
|---|---|---|
| mulher 'woman' (being) | alegre 'merry' | andar 'to walk' (action) |
| apartamento 'apartment' (thing) | colorida 'colorful' | ficar 'to remain' (state) |
| amizade 'friendship' (concept) | agradável 'pleasant' | morrer 'to die' (process) |

The traditional classification of words in parts of speech (*nouns, adjectives, pronouns, verbs, adverbs, prepositions,* and *conjunctions*), which goes back to ancient Greek and Roman grammarians, can be useful, as long as we do not think of them as rigid categories but rather as labels for certain roles which words perform in an utterance. Thus, *saber* may be a verb (*quero saber o nome dela* 'I want to know her name') or a noun (*o saber não ocupa lugar* 'knowledge does not take up space'), or an invariable formant in the expression *a saber* 'to wit,' 'viz.'

### 3.1.1     Morphological variation: inflection

Inflection is a morphological process that modifies certain grammatical features of a word by means of inflectional suffixes°, without changing its lexical meaning. Some such changes include making nouns and adjectives plural, as in *orquídea negra* > *orquídeas negras* 'black orchid/s,' or making an adjective masculine or feminine, as in *homem gordo* 'fat man' vs. *mulher gorda* 'fat woman' (3.2). Inflection also changes verb endings to show person, as in *trabalhamos* 'we work' vs. *trabalhas* 'you work,' or tense, as in *trabalhei ontem* 'I worked yesterday' vs. *trabalharei amanhã* 'I will work tomorrow' (3.5).

### 3.2     Nouns and adjectives

Nouns are lexical words that have extralinguistic referents such as animate beings (*cachorro* 'dog,' *Sandra*), things (*comida* 'food'), or abstract concepts (*liberdade* 'freedom'). A noun may consist of a lexical morpheme, either alone (*boi* 'ox,' *pau* 'stick') or together with a noun-forming grammatical morpheme, called the *theme vowel°*, as in *livr-* + *-o* > *livro, cas-* + *-a* > *casa, gent-* + *-e* > *gente* 'people.' Adjectives have a lexical stem that refers to qualities of nouns and grammatical suffixes, as in

| lexical stem | grammatical suffix | |
| --- | --- | --- |
| *alegr-* | *e* | *alegre* 'merry (m./f.)' |
| *fei-* | *a* | *feia* 'ugly (f.)' |
| *ocult-* | *o* | *oculto* 'hidden (m.)' |

### 3.2.1    Gender

Gender is a purely grammatical category whereby every Portuguese noun is classified as either *masculine* or *feminine*. For most nouns, this classification relates to no identifiable feature of the noun's referent, as shown by the fact that the same object may be designated by nouns of either gender, as in *o bastão/a bengala* 'walking stick,' or *o impermeável/a capa (de chuva)* 'raincoat.'

All the same, most nouns in *-o* are masculine (*o momento* 'moment,' *o assunto* 'subject') and nouns in *-a* are usually feminine (*a fazenda* 'farm,' *a mala* 'suitcase'). An occasional feminine noun in *-o* such as *a virago* 'mannish woman' is a rare exception, but there are a few nouns in *-a* that are masculine:

| | |
| --- | --- |
| *o lama* 'lama' | cf. *a lama* 'mud' |
| *o grama* 'gram' | cf. *a grama* 'grass' |
| *o coma* 'coma' | cf. *a coma* 'mane' |

Nouns with other endings, as in the following examples, belong to either gender. Consequently, a learner's only safe guideline is to learn every noun with its article.

| | |
| --- | --- |
| *a ponte* 'bridge' | *o pente* 'comb' |
| *a cal* 'lime' | *o mal* 'evil' |
| *a voz* 'voice' | *o arroz* 'rice' |
| *a bílis* 'bile' | *o lápis* 'pencil' |

For a subset of nouns referring to humans and certain animals, however, gender is linked to the referent's biological sex. The gender of nouns referring to humans usually correlates with biological sex, and masculine nouns in *-o* or *-e* usually have a feminine counterpart in *-a*:

| | |
| --- | --- |
| *o menino* 'boy' | *a menina* 'girl' |
| *o monge* 'monk' | *a monja* 'nun' |

These are not cases of gender inflection but rather of replacement of the noun-forming suffix -*o by -a*, or simply of adding -*a* to a masculine form to create a feminine noun:

| | |
|---|---|
| *o engenheiro > a engenheira* 'engineer' | *o arquiteto > a arquiteta* 'architect' |
| *o advogado > a advogada* 'lawyer' | *o agrônomo > a agrônoma* 'agronomist' |
| *o juiz > a juíza* 'judge' | *o monitor > a monitora* 'monitor' |

Some nouns in -*e*, however, may be of either gender (*o/a agente* 'agent,' *o/a tenente* 'lieutenant') and a few have also a variant in -*a* with a different meaning (*o/a governante* 'the governing official' vs. *a governanta* 'the housekeeper').

Nouns (among them a few derogatory slang terms) designating a condition or activity which, for biological or social reasons, is exclusive to or typical of individuals of one sex or the other, belong to only one gender:

| | |
|---|---|
| *o eunuco* 'eunuch' | *a meretriz* 'prostitute' |
| *o jesuíta* 'jesuit' | *a parturiente* 'woman in labor' |
| *o castrado* 'castrato' | *a mocréia* (sl.) 'ugly woman' |
| *o cardeal* 'cardinal' | *a madame* (sl.) 'madam, brothel manager' |
| *o veado* (sl.) 'homosexual male' | *a menstruante* 'menstruating woman' |
| *o padre* 'priest' | *a madre* 'nun' |
| *o bispo* 'bishop' | *a gestante* 'pregnant woman' |

Some single-gender nouns denote persons of either sex, whereas other single-form nouns, including most nouns ending in -*ista*, may be masculine or feminine, as shown by the article:

| Single gender, either sex | Either gender, sex distinguished by article |
|---|---|
| *a pessoa* 'person' | *o/a estudante* 'student' |
| *a vítima* 'victim' | *o/a camarada* 'comrade' |
| *a testemunha* 'witness' | *o/a colega* 'colleague' |
| *o algoz* 'tormentor' | *o/a mártir* 'martyr' |
| *o indivíduo* 'individual' | *o/a assistent* 'assistant' |
| *o carrasco* 'executioner' | *o/a artista* 'artist' |
| *a criança* 'child' | *o/a feminista* 'feminist' |
| *o cônjuge* 'spouse' | *o/a pianista* 'pianist' |

In a small subset, however, variation in gender does not correlate with biological sex and the noun may refer to males or females:

| | |
|---|---|
| *o/a sentinela* 'sentry' | *o/a personagem* 'character (play, novel)' |
| *o/a ordenança* 'orderly (mil.)' | *o/a praça* 'private soldier (mil.)' |

Even though nouns referring to animals do not constitute a morphological category, they illustrate how varied gender representation is. For most names of animals, the words *macho* 'male' or *fêmea* 'female' are added to indicate biological sex (*a tartaruga macho* 'male turtle'/*a tartaruga fêmea* 'female turtle'). Gender is linked to final *–o* or *–a* for names of certain animals (*o gato/a gata* 'cat,' *o raposo/a raposa* 'fox' – in the latter, the feminine is the generic form). Finally, a third subset involves morphologically unrelated pairs: *o bode* 'he-goat'/*a cabra* 'she-goat,' just like *o homem* 'man'/*a mulher* 'woman' or *o pai* 'father'/*a mãe* 'mother.' Summing up:

| **macho/fêmea** | **final -o/-a** | **unrelated pairs** |
|---|---|---|
| *o jacaré macho/fêmea* 'alligator' | *o pato/a pata* 'duck' | *cavalo* 'horse'/*égua* 'mare' |
| *a girafa macho/fêmea* 'giraffe' | *o lobo/a loba* 'wolf' | *cão* 'dog'/*cadela* 'bitch' |
| *a cobra macho/fêmea* 'snake' | *o leão/a leoa* 'lion' | *burro/besta* 'donkey' |
| *a onça macho/fêmea* 'jaguar' | *o mulo/a mula* 'mule' | *bode* 'male goat'/ *cabra* 'female goat' |

Although intrinsically genderless, adjectives inflect to replicate the gender of an accompanying noun through a process called agreement°. Adjective gender inflection follows a few general rules, though there are exceptions. The general case covers adjectives in which the suffixes *-o/-a* function as masculine and feminine markers respectively: *bonito cravo* 'pretty carnation'/*bonita rosa* 'pretty rose.' Adjectives in *-a, -e, -r, -l, -z, -s*, or *-m* (corresponding to a nasal vowel), are usually invariable, wih the exception of gentile° adjectives (Table 3.1). Adjectives in *-or, -u*, and *-ês* add an *-a* (*lutador > lutadora* 'fighting,' *cru > crua* 'raw,' *inglês > inglesa* 'English').

Through a phonological process called metaphony°, some adjectives with stressed [o] in the masculine singular have [ɔ] in the feminine singular and in both plural forms. Since this change in vowel quality cannot be predicted, words of one type or another have to be learned individually.

**[o] > [ɔ] (metaphony)**

*gostoso > gostosa, gostosos, gostosas* 'tasty'
*formoso > formosa, formosos, formosas* 'attractive'
*grosso > grossa, grossos, grossas* 'thick'
*idoso > idosa, idosos, idosas* 'aged'
*charmoso > charmosa, charmosos, charmosas* 'charming'

**[o] = [o] (no metaphony)**

*moço > moça* 'young'
*fofo > fofa* 'soft'

*oco > oca* 'hollow'
*fosco > fosca* 'dark'
*tosco > tosca* 'rough'

Table 3.1 *Adjectives invariable in gender*

| Ending | |
|---|---|
| -*a* | *cosmopolita* 'cosmopolitan,' *indígena* 'indigenous,' *cipriota* 'Cypriot' |
| -*e* | *forte* 'strong,' *triste* 'sad,' *alegre* 'merry,' *berbere* 'Berber,' *bermudense* 'Bermudan' |
| -*l* | *cordial* 'cordial,' *fiel* 'faithful,' *azul* 'blue' |
| -*z* | *capaz* 'capable,' *soez* 'vile,' *feliz* 'happy,' *feroz* 'ferocious,' *motriz* 'motor,' *lapuz* 'coarse' |
| -*r* | *exemplar* 'exemplary,' *par* 'even (number),' *ímpar* 'odd (number),' *familiar* 'familiar' |
| -*or* | *indolor* 'painless,' *maior* 'bigger,' *menor* 'smaller,' *melhor* 'better,' *pior* 'worse' |
| -*m* | *comum* 'common,' *ruim* 'bad,' *afim* 'akin, willing,' *mirim* 'small,' *marrom* 'brown' |
| -*ês* | *cortês* 'courteous,' *pedrês* 'mottled' |

Exception: gentile° adjectives in
  -*l*, -*z*, -*ês*:

| | |
|---|---|
| *espanhol* (m.) > *espanhola* (f.) 'Spanish' | *andaluz* (m.) > *andaluza* (f.) 'Andalusian' |
| *inglês* (m.) > *inglesa* (f.) 'English' | *francês* (m.) > *francesa* (f.) 'French' |

For other endings, there are some general norms but exceptions exist. Table 3.2. shows the more frequent cases.

### 3.2.2   Number: Plural of nouns and adjectives

As in English, number in Portuguese involves a contrast between one and more than one. *Ambos* 'both' is a lone case of dual plural, and nouns referring to two or more items of a kind are morphologically singular, like *o par* 'the pair,' *o casal* 'the couple,' *a parelha* 'the team (of animals).' Like gender, number is a mandatory category: a noun is either singular or plural, and accompanying determinants and adjectives reflect this fact through number agreement.

The plural of nouns and adjectives is formed on the singular according to regular rules, with some exceptions. Nouns and adjectives ending in a vowel, stressed or unstressed, oral or nasal, form the plural by adding /-s/, spelled **s** (*caqui maduro* > *caquis maduros* 'ripe persimmon/s,' *carro verde* > *carros verdes* 'green car/s,' *irmã alemã* > *irmãs alemãs* 'German sister/s.' (Adjustments in spelling and accentuation may be required, as in *armazém* [ẽj] > *armazens* [ẽj] 'warehouse/s.')

The plural allomorph /es/, written **-es**, occurs with nouns in -*r* and -*z* (*bar* > *bares, cruz* > *cruzes*) as well as optionally in paroxytones ending in -*n*, where it signals a nasal diphthong in the singular but a full vowel in the plural: *abdômen* [ab'dom ẽj] > *abdomens* or *abdômenes* 'abdomen/s.' Nouns and adjectives

Table 3.2 *Feminine of adjectives*

| Ending | General rule | Variants (nc = no change) |
|---|---|---|
| -ês | *inglês* > *inglesa* 'English'<br>*português* > *portuguesa* 'Portuguese' | nc: *cortês* 'courteous' |
| -or | *encantador* >*encantadora* 'charming' | nc: *melhor* 'better,' *pior*<br>'worse,' *menor* 'smaller,'<br>*maior* 'bigger' |
| -u | *cru*> *crua* 'raw'<br>*nu* > *nua* 'naked' | nc: *zulu, hindu* |
| -éu [ɛw] | *ilhéu* > *ilhoa* | |
| -dor | *trabalhador* > *trabalhadora/trabalhadeira* 'diligent'<br>*gerador* > *geradora/geratriz* 'generating' | |
| -tor | *motor* > *motora/motriz* 'motive' (as in *força motriz*<br>'motive power') | |
| -ão | *são* > *sã* 'healthy'<br>*alemão* > *alemã* 'German'<br>*cristão* > *cristã* 'Christian'<br>*glutão* > *glutona* 'glutton'<br>*respondão* > *respondona* 'given to rude answers' | |

ending in /s/ are invariable if the last syllable is unstressed: *um pires simples* 'a plain saucer'/*dois pires simples* 'two plain saucers,' *um reles lápis* 'a worthless pencil'/*dois reles lápis* 'two worthless pencils.' Some linguists postulate for such invariable forms a plural allomorph without a phonological representation, shown as Ø (zero). Thus, *pires* + **plural** would be represented as *pires* + Ø. Table 3.3 shows other cases of pluralization.

For reasons related to the historical development of Portuguese morphology, nouns in *-ão* form the plural in three ways, exemplified by *mão* > *mãos* 'hand/s,' *pensão* > *pensões* 'boarding house/s,' *cão* > *cães* 'dog/s.' Although there is no overt indication of how a given noun in *-ão* will pluralize, a few general trends are apparent. Only the pattern *-ão* > *-ões* is productive, and it includes the following categories:

| | |
|---|---|
| loan words°: | *vagão* 'wagon' > *vagões* (< Eng *wagon*), BP<br>*caminhão* > *caminhões* / EP *camião* > *camiões*<br>'truck/s' (< Fr *camion*) |
| augmentatives<br>in *-ão*: | *amigão* > *amigões* 'good buddy/buddies,' *dedão* ><br>*dedões* 'big toe/s' |
| abstract nouns: | *sequidão* > *sequidões* 'dryness,' *sensação* ><br>*sensações* 'sensation/s' |
| all nouns in<br>*-são*: | *alusão* > *alusões* 'allusion/s,' *abusão* > *abusões*<br>'abuse' |
| all nouns in<br>*-ção*: | *obrigação* > *obrigações* 'obligation/s,' *vocação* ><br>*vocações* 'vocation/s' |

Table 3.3 *Noun and adjective plural endings*

| Ending | Nouns | Adjectives |
|---|---|---|
| oxytones in -s, -z<br>plural: add -es | *o ananás > os ananases*<br>'pineapple/s'<br>*a voz > vozes*<br>'voice/s'<br>*o deus > os deuses*<br>'god/s'<br>*a luz > as luzes*<br>'light/s' | *cortês > corteses*<br>'courteous'<br>*atroz > atrozes*<br>'atrocious'<br><br>*andaluz > andaluzes*<br>'Andalusian' |
| paroxytones in -s<br>plural: θ | *o pires > os pires*<br>'saucer/s'<br>*o ônibus > os ônibus*<br>'bus/es' | |
| -al, -el, -ol, -ul<br>plural: replace /i/ for /l/ + -s | *animal > animais*<br>'animal/s'<br>*papel > papéis*<br>'paper/s'<br>*lençol > lençóis*<br>'bedsheet/s'<br>(Exceptions: *mal > males*<br>'evil/s',<br>*cônsul > cônsules* 'consul/s' | *vital > vitais*<br>'vital'<br>*amável > amáveis*<br>'friendly'<br>*espanhol > espanhóis*<br>'Spanish' |
| stressed -il<br>plural: -l > Ø + -s | *fuzil > fuzis*<br>'rifle/s'<br>*projetil > projetis*<br>'projectile/s' | *febril > febris*<br>'feverish'<br>*senil > senis*<br>'senile' |
| unstressed -il<br>plural: -il > -ei + s | *fóssil > fósseis*<br>'fossil/s'<br>*réptil > répteis*<br>'reptile/s'<br>projétil > projéteis<br>'projectile/s' | *fácil > fáceis*<br>'easy'<br>*difícil > difíceis*<br>'difficult'<br>*erétil > eréteis*<br>'erectile' |
| stressed on the next<br>to last syllabe in -n<br>plural: -ns or -nes | *gérmen > gérmens, gérmenes*<br>'germ/s' | |

The other two types, *-ãos* and *-ães*, are closed sets that include a number of common nouns:

**-ão > -ães**

*pão > pães* 'bread/s'
*cão > cães* 'dog/s'
*capitão > capitães* 'captain/s'
*alemão > alemães* 'German/s'
*capelão > capelães* 'chaplain/s'

**-ão > -ãos**

*cristão > cristãos* 'Christian/s'
*chão > chãos* 'floor/s'
*cidadão > cidadãos* 'citizen/s'
*irmão > irmãos* 'brother/s'
*mão* 'hand' > *mãos* 'hand/s'

Nouns in -*ão* may be analyzed as having a phonological representation in -/n/, e.g. /patron/, /kan/, and /man/. This analysis is supported by the presence of /n/ in derived forms like *patrono* 'patron saint,' *canino* 'canine,' and *manual* 'manual.' Though absent in the singular, the theme vowel of such theoretical forms is either *e* (as in /patron + e/, /kan + e/) or *o* (as in /man + o/). The nasal consonant nasalizes the preceding vowel and assimilates to it completely, yielding /patrõ/, /kã/, and /mã/. In nouns with the theme vowel -*e*, the final nasal vowel, /õ/ or /ã/, originates the diphthong [ãw] in the singular ([patrãw, [pãw]). The theme vowel -*e* appears in the plural, forming the sequences /õe/ or /ãe/, which respectively yield diphthongized endings as in [patrõjs], [pãjs]. For nouns with the theme vowel -*o*, dipthongization° (/ão/ > [ãw]) yields singular forms like *mão*, to which the plural ending /s/ is added directly. Loan words in -*om* [õ] tend to appear in doublets, -*om* ~ -*ão*:

> *garçom*/*garção* 'waiter'          *guidom*/*guidão* 'handlebar'
> *acordeom*/*acordeão* 'accordion'    *odeom*/*odeão* 'music hall'

In nouns of the type /penson + e/, the nasal consonant /n/ disappears after nasalizing the preceding vowel, which forms a diphthong with the semivowel [j] originating from the unstressed theme vowel, *pensão* > *pensões*. In nouns of the type /man + o/ and /pan + e/ the nasalized vowel forms a diphthong with the unstressed theme vowel, which changes into a glide, either /o/ > [w] (*mão* > *mãos*) or /e/ > [j] (*pão* > *pães*). There is, however, some variation: some nouns in -*ão* have two or even three plurals. Grammar manuals prescribe one or another, but there is no definitive study on actual usage.

### Nouns in -ão with two or three plurals

> *refrão* >    *refrãos, refrães* 'refrain/s'
> *vulcão* >    *vulcões, vulcãos* 'volcano/es'
> *vilão* >     *vilãos, vilães, vilões* 'villain/s'
> *ancião* >    *anciãos, anciões, anciães* 'old man/men'

## 3.3    Determinants

Determinants (Table 3.4) include grammatical words such as articles, demonstratives and possessives, which have a noun-qualifying function. The definite article is usually anaphoric, i.e. it signals a noun that has occurred earlier in the discourse or that is supposed to refer to something known. Thus definite articles (*o, a, os, as* 'the') generally introduce a noun that conveys specific information (*O ajudante telefonou* 'the aide phoned') while indefinite articles (*um, uns* 'a, an,' *uma, umas* 'some') introduce a noun representing non-specific information (*Um ajudante telefonou* 'an aide phoned').

The definite article *o* also serves to nominalize° a word of any other class, that is, to make it into a noun, as in *o bom disso tudo é que ela sobreviveu* 'the good thing about all that is that she survived.' Singular definite and indefinite articles as well as plural definite articles are used to signal a noun used in a generic sense. Thus in 1a and 1b, respectively, the noun refers to all referents, male or female, of the categories *advogado* and *político*:

(1)     a. *O/um advogado deve conhecer a lei*
           'The/a lawyer must know the law.'
        b. *Os políticos deveriam pensar no povo.*
           'Politicians should think about the people.'

Unlike articles, demonstratives are primarily deictic° (from the Gr *deixis* 'signal, indication'), that is, they point to something situated in the extralinguistic world. The demonstratives (*est-, ess-, aquel-*) form a three-point system to signal what is near the speaker (*est-*), near the hearer (*ess-*), or distant from both (*aquel-*).

Demonstratives show gender by the endings *-e, -a* and have regular plural formation. The demonstratives *isto, isso, aquilo*, on the other hand, refer to an object or an aggregate that has been mentioned or that is apparent from the context. These demonstratives are masculine in gender, as shown by adjective agreement: *isso é feio, mas aquilo é grotesco* 'this is ugly but that is grotesque.' An anaphoric use of *este/aquele* corresponds respectively to *the latter/the former*, as in (2):

(2)     *O presidente e o ministro chegaram, este de carro e aquele de helicóptero.*
        'The president and the minister arrived, the latter by car and the former by helicopter.'

Two tendencies of BP should be noticed. One is the reduction of the system of demonstratives to two points only: *ess-/aquel-* and *isso/aquilo*. The other is an expansion of the system by combining demonstratives with the place adverbs *aqui* 'here,' *aí* 'there,' *ali* 'over there,' *lá* 'over there,' as in *esse livro aqui* 'this book,' *esse livro aí* 'that book,' *aquele livro ali/lá* 'that book over there.'

Possessives refer to the persons of discourse (3.4), namely the speaker or first person (P1), the hearer or second person (P2), and the so-called third person (P3), which refers to something or someone that is neither P1 nor P2. Possessives may be combined with a definite article or a demonstrative, and function as adjectives when directly qualifying a noun, as in *o meu relógio* 'my watch,' *aquele nosso amigo* 'that friend of ours.' They function as pronouns when qualified by an article or a demonstrative to refer to a noun that is understood from

Table 3.4 *Determinants*

| | Person | m. sg | m. pl. | f. sg. | f. pl | Generic* (aka "neuter") |
|---|---|---|---|---|---|---|
| Definite articles | | o | os | a | as | |
| Indefinite articles | | um | uns | uma | umas | |
| Demonstratives | | este | estes | esta | estas | isto |
| | | esse | esses | essa | essas | isso |
| | | aquele | aqueles | aquela | aquelas | aquilo |
| Possessives | P1sg | meu | meus | minha | minhas | |
| | P2sg | teu | teus | tua | tuas | |
| | P3sg, P3pl | seu | seus | sua | suas | |
| | P1pl | nosso | nossos | nossa | nossas | |
| | P2pl | vosso | vossos | vossa | vossas | |

* Formally masculine singular: *Isto é bonito.*

the context, as in 3a–3b. However, use of *seu/sua/seus/suas* can be ambiguous, since these possessives may be interpreted as referring to the hearer or to a third party, as in 3c. Such ambiguity can be prevented by use of *dele/dela/deles/delas* (formed by combining *de + ele*, etc.) as in 3d:

(3)  a. *O meu carro está na garagem, onde está o seu?*
    'My car is in the garage; where is yours?'
  b. *Aquele meu guarda-chuva velho sumiu. E aquele seu?*
    'That old umbrella of mine has vanished. What about that one of yours?'
  c. *A Mara me pediu para trazer o seu dicionário.*
    'Mara asked me to bring her dictionary/your dictionary.'
  d. *A Mara me pediu para trazer o dicionário dela.*
    'Mara asked me to bring her dictionary.'

## 3.4  Personal pronouns

Personal pronouns are grammatical words that refer directly to the persons of discourse. Table 3.5 shows their forms for the syntactic functions (4.2) of subject, direct object, indirect object, and prepositional object. This array covers all possibilities, but in actual usage it is restructured in ways that will be commented on in Chapter 7.

Third person pronouns, singular as well as plural, inflect for gender with both the subject and direct object, and for number alone with the indirect object. Though morphologically masculine, *eles* may refer generically to an aggregate of elements of both genders, as in 4a–4b:

Table 3.5 *Personal pronouns*

| | P1sg | P2sg | P3sg | P1pl | P2pl | P3pl |
|---|---|---|---|---|---|---|
| **Subject** | Speaker | Hearer | Neither P1 nor P2 | Speaker plus someone else | Hearer plus someone else | Neither P1 nor P2 |
| | eu | tu | ele (m.), ela (f.) | nós | vós | eles (m.) elas (f.) |
| | | | você o senhor (m.) a senhora (f.) | | vocês os senhores (m.) as senhoras (f.) | vocês os senhores (m.) as senhoras (f.) |
| **Prepositional** | mim comigo | ti contigo | si consigo | conosco (EP connosco) | convosco | si consigo |
| **Direct object** | me | te | o, lo, no (m.) a, la, na (f.) | | | os, los, nos (m.) as, las, nas (f.) |
| **Indirect object** | | | lhe | nos | vos | lhes |
| **Reflexive (DO/IO)** | | | se | | | se |

**Third person pronouns**

| subject | direct object | indirect object |
|---------|--------------|-----------------|
| *ele, ela* | *o, a* | *lhe* |
| *eles, elas* | *os, as* | *lhes* |

(4)   a. *A Mara e o Joaquim chegaram ontem.*
         'Mara and Joaquim arrived yesterday.'
         – *Eles ficam até quando?*
         'Until when are they staying?'
         – *Até o Natal.*
         'Until Christmas.'
      b. *Aquela professora americana e os alunos dela, quando é que eles chegam?*
         'That American teacher and her students, when are they arriving?'

Second person pronouns fall into two categories: *tu* (P2sg) and *vós* (P2pl) take specific second person verb forms: *tu falas* 'you speak,' *vós falais* 'you speak' (3.5). Informal *você/vocês* and deferential *o senhor/a senhora/os senhores/as senhoras* are lexicalized forms of address that function for all purposes like pronouns and combine with third person verb forms (8.4). Since *você/s* and *o/s senhor/es, a/s senhora/s* take third person object pronouns, a sentence like *Preciso vê-lo para lhe dar um recado* is ambiguous, as it may mean 'I need to see you (m. sg.) / him to give you/him/her a message.'

Direct and indirect object pronouns are clitics° (5.2), that is unstressed forms that are placed before or after a verb form as an extra syllable, as in 5a–5b:

(5)   a. *Ele o comprou/comprou-o ontem.*
         'He bought it yesterday.'
      b. *Ela me deu/deu-me um presente.*
         'She gave me a gift.'

Combinations of indirect object + direct object clitics (Table 3.6) occur in EP though not in BP, where prepositions (*para, a* 'for, to') are used to introduce an indirect object, as in example 6 below (for clitic deletion in BP, see 7.3.2.4).

(6)   a. EP *Ela entregou-mo* = BP *Ela o entregou para mim.*
         'She handed it to me.'
      b. EP *Eu entreguei-lhos* = BP *Eu os entreguei para ele/para ela/para você/para vocês/para eles/para elas.*
         'I handed them to him/her/you/them.'

Table 3.6 *Direct object (DO) and indirect object (IO) clitic combinations*

|  | IO | | | | |
| --- | --- | --- | --- | --- | --- |
| **DO** | **me** | **te** | **nos** | **vos** | **lhe/lhes** |
| **o** | mo | to | no-lo | vo-lo | lho |
| **a** | ma | ta | no-la | vo-la | lha |
| **os** | mos | tos | no-los | vo-los | lhos |
| **as** | mas | tas | no-las | vo-las | lhas |

### 3.5    Verbs

English speakers cannot be blamed if they find Portuguese verbs overwhelming. The most complex English verb has eight forms (*be am are is was were been being*), besides two relics (*art wert*) and a country cousin (*ain't*). Other verbs have five (*do does did done doing*), four (*come comes came coming*), three (*put puts putting*), two (*can could*) or just one (*ought must*). By contrast, most Portuguese verbs have several dozen forms, neatly arrayed in six-packs called *tenses*. Despite such morphological luxuriance, they are quite systematic and can be mastered with a bit of perseverance and time. In this section we will cover the main aspects of verb tense formation.

There are three verb classes called *conjugations*, each identified by a specific theme vowel° (or conjugation vowel), *-a, -e,* or *-i.* A verb is referred to and listed in dictionaries by its citation form, the *infinitive*, which shows the theme vowel followed by the infinitive marker *-r*, and so we refer to *-ar, -er,* and *-ir* verbs. The sole exception is *pôr* 'to put' (and its derivatives, such as *compor* 'to compose' or *depor* 'to depose'), which largely follows the *-er* conjugation, but has enough irregularities to be considered separately (Table 3.14). The historical reason for this is mentioned in section (5.3.4). Impersonal° and defective verbs (3.5.6) have fewer forms.

The endings of the *-er* and *-ir* conjugations overlap somewhat, and most irregular verbs have tenses that form regular subsets. Newly created verbs, like *faxar* 'to fax,' *escanear* 'to scan,' are always in *-ar* or *-ear*, and are fully regular. Our presentation shows all six persons of speech, including *tu* (P2sg), alive in EP and used regionally in BP, and *vós* (P2pl), which though archaic for most speakers, is still in use in parts of northern Portugal. It also leads a ghost existence in certain formal oratorical styles or as the prescribed epistolary form in the Brazilian military. Furthermore, familiarity with these forms helps one understand older literary texts.

Table 3.7 *Verbs: stem, theme vowel, and desinences*

|       | Future indicative | | | | Present indicative | | | |
|-------|------|-----|-----|-----|------|------|-----|-----|
|       | Stem | TV  | TMD | PND | Stem | TV   | TMD | PND |
| P1sg  | fal  | a   | re  | i   | fal  | (a) * | o   |     |
| P2sg  | fal  | a   | rá  | s   | fal  | a    |     | s   |
| P3sg  | fal  | a   | rá  |     | fal  | a    |     |     |
| P1pl  | fal  | a   | re  | mos | fal  | a    |     | mos |
| P2pl  | fal  | a   | re  | is  | fal  | a    |     | is  |
| P3pl  | fal  | a   | ra  | ão  | fal  | a    |     | m*  |
| P1sg  | com  | e   | re  | i   | com  | (e) * | o   |     |
| P2sg  | com  | e   | rá  | s   | com  | e    |     | s   |
| P3sg  | com  | e   | rá  |     | com  | e    |     |     |
| P1pl  | com  | e   | re  | mos | com  | e    |     | mos |
| P2pl  | com  | e   | re  | is  | com  | e    |     | is  |
| P3pl  | com  | e   | r   | ão  | com  | e    |     | m*  |
| P1sg  | part | i   | re  | i   | part | (i) * | o   |     |
| P2 g  | part | i   | rá  | s   | part | e    |     | s   |
| P3sg  | part | i   | rá  |     | part | e    |     |     |
| P1pl  | part | i   | re  | mos | part | i    |     | mos |
| P2pl  | part | i   | re  | is  | part | (i)  |     | is  |
| P3pl  | part | i   | r   | ão  | part | e    |     | m** |

* Parentheses signal the theme vowel is dropped when the person–number desinence begins with a vowel other than /i/.
** Orthographic **m** indicates a nasal diphthong -*am* [ɐ̃w̃], -em [ẽj̃].

## 3.5.1    Conjugations

Verb forms may be analyzed as combinations of morphemes following the general formula

*Theme + Tense–Mood Desinence + Person–Number Desinence.*

The theme (T) includes the stem, which carries the lexical meaning, plus one of the theme vowels *a, e, i*. The tense–mood desinence (TMD) identifies the tense and the mood, and the person–number desinence (PND) assigns a verb form to one of the persons of discourse. This is exemplified in Table 3.7, where the future indicative forms *falaremos* 'we will speak,' *comeremos* 'we will eat,' and *partiremos* 'we will leave,' show the stem (*fal-*, *com-*, *part-*), the theme vowel (*-a-, -e-, -i-*), the tense–mood desinence (*-re-*), and the person–number desinence of the first person plural (*-mos*). Some forms lack one or more of these formants, and a handful of high-frequency irregular verbs will be dealt with in 3.5.3.

Although tenses are used to refer to time, their actual chronological value is rather flexible, and names such as *present* or *future* should be regarded primarily as identificatory labels. Verb tenses are grouped into three categories called *moods*, namely *indicative, subjunctive,* and *imperative*. There are also three non-finite or uninflected tenses, viz.

| infinitive | gerund | participle |
|---|---|---|
| *falar* 'to speak' | *falando* 'speaking' | *falado* 'spoken' |
| *comer* 'to eat' | *comendo* 'eating' | *comido* 'eaten' |
| *partir* 'to leave' | *partindo* 'leaving' | *partido* 'left' |

### 3.5.2    Regular verb formation

In the formula *stem + TV + TMD + PND* the theme vowel comes right after the stem and before any suffixes. In verbs with the infinitive in *-ar*, the theme vowel (TV) is *-a* throughout, but in verbs with the infinitive in *-er* or *-ir*, the theme vowel is either *-e* or *-i*, depending on the specific tense. In *uninflected* forms the theme vowel remains constant (cf. infinitives *-ar, -er, -ir*, gerunds *-ando, -endo, -indo*, or participles *-ado, -ido*).

The gerund is invariable and the participle varies in gender and number in passive and passive-like constructions only (4.8.1). The infinitive is invariable, but it has an inflected counterpart (Table 3.8) which has endings for all persons except P1sg and P3sg (for use of the inflected infinitive, see section 4.13). For regular verbs, personal infinitive forms are identical to those of the future subjunctive (3.5.2; Table 3.12), whereas for irregular verbs the future subjunctive has a specific stem.

Table 3.8 *Inflected infinitive*

|  | *falar* | *comer* | *partir* |
|---|---|---|---|
| P1sg | fal-a-r | com-e-r | part-i-r |
| P2sg | fal-a-re-s | com-e-re-s | part-i-re-s |
| P3sg | fal-a-r | com-e-r | part-i-r |
| P1pl | fal-a-r-mos | com-e-r-mos | part-i-r-mos |
| P2pl | fal-a-r-des | com-e-r-des | part-i-r-des |
| P3pl | fal-a-r-em | com-e-r-em | part-i-r-em |

*3.5.2.1 Present tenses and the imperative*    The present indicative (Table 3.9) has a stem followed by a theme vowel and a person–number desinence. Exceptions are P1sg, where the theme vowel is replaced by the unique person–number desinence *-o*, and P3sg, which has no person–number

Table 3.9 *Present indicative, present subjunctive, and imperative*

|  | *falar* | | *comer* | | *partir* | |
|---|---|---|---|---|---|---|
|  | indicative | subjunctive | indicative | subjunctive | indicative | subjunctive |
| P1sg | fal-o | fal-e | com-o | com-a | part-o | part-a |
| P2sg | fal-a-s | fal-e-s | com-e-s | com-a-s | part-e-s | part-a-s |
| P3sg | fal-a | fal-e | com-e | com-a | part-e | part-a |
| P1pl | fal-a-mos | fal-e-mos | com-e-mos | com-a-mos | part-i-mos | part-a-mos |
| P2pl | fal-a-is | fal-e-is | com-e-is | com-a-is | part-is | part-a-is |
| P3pl | fal-a-m | fal-e-m | com-e-m | com-a-m | part-e-m | part-a-m |

|  | **imperative** | | | | | |
|---|---|---|---|---|---|---|
|  | *falar* | *comer* | *partir* | | | |
|  | *affirmative* | | | | *negative* | |
| P2sg (tu) | fal-a* | com-e* | part-e* | não fal-es | não com-as | não part-as |
| P2pl (vós) | fal-a-i | com-e-i | part-i | não fal-eis | não com-ais | não part-ais |
| *Same as the present subjunctive:* | | | | | | |
| P3sg (você) | fal-e | com-a | part-a | não fal-e | não com-a | não part-a |
| P3pl (vocês) | fal-em | com-am | part-am | não fal-em | não com-am | não part-am |

\* Also used with *você* in BP.

desinence. The contrast between indicative and subjunctive hinges on the alternation of the vowels *-a/-e* for *-ar* verbs and *-e/-a* for *-er* and *-ir* verbs. In P1sg, however, the contrast is between the vowels *-o/e* for verbs in *-ar* and *-o/-a* for verbs ins *-er* and *-ir*. The person–number desinence of P3pl forms, orthographically *-m*, may be interpreted phonologically as a nasal consonant /n/, which both diphthongizes and nasalizes the preceding vowel, so that *-am, -em* are phonetically nasal diphthongs (*falam* ['falẽw̃], *podem* ['pɔdẽj̃]). This analysis applies to P3pl in other tenses as well.

Imperative forms for *tu* and *vós* derive from corresponding present indicative forms minus the final *-s*. The imperative forms of *você(s)* are the corresponding forms of the present subjunctive. In negative commands, subjunctive forms are used for all persons (Table 3.9).

### 3.5.2.2 Past tenses: Imperfect, preterit, and past perfect (pluperfect)

*indicative*    In imperfect forms the stress falls systematically on the theme vowel (*-a* for verbs in *-ar* or *-i* for verbs in *-er, -ir*). The tense–mood desinence is *-va* (*-ve* in P2pl) for *-ar* verbs and *-a* (*-e* in P2pl) for *-er, -ir* verbs.

In the preterit P1sg and P3sg lack a theme vowel and each has a unique ending. P1sg has *-ei* for *-ar* verbs and stressed *-i* for *-er* and *-ir* verbs, while

Table 3.10 *Past tenses: Imperfect, preterit, and past perfect (pluperfect) indicative*

| | Imperfect | | | Preterit | | |
|---|---|---|---|---|---|---|
| | *falar* | *comer* | *partir* | *falar* | *comer* | *partir* |
| P1sg | fal-a-va | com-i-a | part-i-a | fal-ei | com-i | part-i |
| P2sg | fal-a-va-s | com-i-a-s | part-i-a-s | fal-a-ste | com-e-ste | part-i-ste |
| P3sg | fal-a-va | com-i-a | part-i-a | fal-ou | com-eu | part-iu |
| P1pl | fal-á-va-mos | com-í-a-mos | part-í-a-mos | fal-a-mos (*) | com-e-mos | part-i-mos |
| P2pl | fal-á-ve-is | com-í-e-is | part-í-e-is | fal-a-stes | com-e-stes | part-i-stes |
| P3pl | fal-a-va-m | com-i-a-m | part-i-a-m | fal-a-ram | com-e-ram | part-i-ram |
| **Past perfect (pluperfect)** | | | | | | |
| | *falar* | | *comer* | *partir* | | |
| P1sg | fal-a-ra | | com-e-ra | part-i-ra | | |
| P2sg | fal-a-ra-s | | com-e-ra-s | part-i-ra-s | | |
| P3sg | fal-a-ra | | com-e-ra | part-i-ra | | |
| P1pl | fal-á-ra-mos | | com-ê-ra-mos | part-í-ra-mos | | |
| P2pl | fal-á-re-is | | com-ê-re-is | part-í-re-is | | |
| P3pl | fal-a-ram | | com-e-ram | part-i-ram | | |

(*) EP falámos.

P3sg has -*ou* (pronounced [o] in BP except in monitored speech, which has [ow]) for -*ar* verbs, -*eu* for -*er* verbs, and -*iu* for -*ir* verbs. The morpheme -*ste*- may be considered a tense–mood desinence, but since P2sg lacks its usual -*s* ending and P2pl has -*s* instead of the usual -*is*, it makes sense to consider -*ste* and -*stes* specific endings for those persons.

In the past perfect the theme vowel is stressed throughout and the tense–mood desinence -*ra* (-*re* in P2pl) characterizes this tense, which in BP is largely replaced by the compound form, e.g., *tinha falado* (Table 3.10).

*3.5.2.3 Future and conditional*    These tenses are derived from the infinitive and characterized by a stressed tense–mood desinence. In the future, this desinence is -*ei* for P1sg, -*e*- for P1pl and P2pl, and -*a*- for P2sg, P3sg, and P3pl. In P3pl the vowel -*a*- combines with the person–number marker -*m*, signaling the nasal diphthong [ẽw̃]. Actually, the spelling distinction between the preterite (*falaram*) and the future (*falarão*) is relatively modern; until the beginning of the twentieth century it was common to see both forms written with -*ão*.

The tense–mood desinence in the conditional is stressed -*ia*- throughout except in P2pl, which has -*ie*-. In both tenses, vowel alternation has historical reasons. (In Brazilian grammars the future indicative and the conditional are respectively labeled "future of the present" and "future of the preterit.")

Table 3.11 *Future indicative and conditional*

| | Future indicative | | | Conditional | | |
|---|---|---|---|---|---|---|
| | *falar* | *comer* | *partir* | *falar* | *comer* | *partir* |
| P1sg | fal-a-r-ei | com-e-r-ei | part-i-r-e-i | fal-a-r-ia | com-e-r-ia | part-i-r-ia |
| P2sg | fal-a-r-á-s | com-e-r-ás | part-i-r-ás | fal-a-r-ia-s | com-e-r-ia-s | part-i-r-ia-s |
| P3sg | fal-a-r-á | com-e-rá | part-i-rá | fal-a-r-ia | com-e-r-ia | part-i-r-ia |
| P1pl | fal-a-r-e-mos | com-e-r-e-mos | part-i-r-e-mos | fal-a-r-ía-mos | com-e-r-ía-mos | part-i-r-ía-mos |
| P2pl | fal-a-r-e-is | com-e-r-e-is | part-i-r-e-is | fal-a-r-íe-is | com-e-r-íe-is | part-i-r-íe-is |
| P3pl | fal-a-r-ão | com-e-r-ão | part-i-r-ão | fal-a-r-ia-m | com-e-r-ia m | part-i-r-ia-m |

Table 3.12 *Past and future subjunctive*

| | Past subjunctive | | | Future subjunctive | | |
|---|---|---|---|---|---|---|
| | *falar* | *comer* | *partir* | *falar* | *comer* | *partir* |
| P1sg | fal-a-sse | com-e-sse | part-i-sse | fal-a-r | com-e-r | part-i-r |
| P2sg | fal-a-sse-s | com-e-sse-s | part-i-sse-s | fal-a-r-es | com-e-r-es | part-i-r-es |
| P3sg | fal-a-sse | com-e-sse | part-i-sse | fal-a-r | com-e-r | part-i-r |
| P1pl | fal-á-sse-mos | com-ê-sse-mos | part-í-sse-mos | fal-a-r-mos | com-e-r-mos | part-i-r-mos |
| P2pl | fal-á-sse-is | com-ê-sse-is | part-í-sse-is | fal-a-r-des | com-e-r-des | part-i-r-des |
| P3pl | fal-a-sse-m | com-e-sse-m | part-i-sse-m | fal-a-r-em | com-e-r-em | part-i-r-em |

*3.5.2.4 Past and future subjunctive*   In the past subjunctive the theme vowel is stressed throughout and is derived from the infinitive by insertion of the tense–mood desinence *-sse* /se/. This future subjunctive, which has the same endings as the inflected infinitive, is formed on the stem of the preterit indicative, e.g. *fiz* 'I did' > (*quando eu*) *fizer* 'when I [fut.] make', *vi* 'I saw' > (*quando eu*) *vir* 'when I [fut.] see.'

### 3.5.3   Irregular verbs

Irregular verbs involve changes in the stem or in the tense–mood or person–number desinences. Changes in the stem vowel in the present indicative (and derived tenses) involve alternation between a mid-high vowel [e] and a mid-low vowel [ɛ], spelled **e**, or between a mid-high vowel [o] and a mid-low vowel [ɔ], spelled **o**, in all persons.

For *-ar* verbs like *pegar* 'to grab,' *cegar* 'to blind,' *regar* 'to water (plants),' *levar* 'to take,' stressed orthographic **e** is normally pronounced [ɛ]: *eu pego* 'I grab.' A few verbs have [e] throughout, like *chegar* 'to arrive' (*eu chego*) and verbs in which stressed **e** is followed by a palatal consonant such as [ʒ], e.g., *desejar* 'to desire' (*eu desejo*), or by a nasal consonant such as [m] in *remar* 'row' (*eu remo*). In BP, however, a few verbs, like *fechar* 'to close' have [e] or [ɛ] (*eu fecho*) 'I close'.

Likewise, some verbs like *engordar* 'to put on weight,' *podar* 'to trim (plants),' *arrotar* 'to belch,' *coçar* 'to scratch,' which have an orthographic **o** in the stem, have [ɔ] throughout: *eu engordo, você engorda*. An exception are verbs with a radical in **o**, such as *doar* 'to donate,' *voar* 'to fly,' or *coar* 'to strain (a liquid),' which have [o]: *eu dôo, ele voa, eles coam*.

In *-er* verbs like *beber* 'to drink,' *ceder* 'to cede,' *dever* 'to owe,' *meter* 'to stick, to insert,' P1sg has [e] (*eu bebo, cedo, meto, devo*) and the other forms with stressed **e** have [ɛ]: *tu bebes, ele cede, eles devem*. Likewise, *-er* verbs like *mover* 'to move' and *correr* 'to run' have [o] in P1sg (*eu movo, eu corro*) and the other forms have [ɔ]: *tu moves, ele corre, eles movem*. *Poder* 'to be able' and *querer* 'to wish' have respectively [ɔ] or [ɛ] in all stem-stressed forms. Although the stem vowel tends to be closed when a nasal consonant follows, as in *comer*, BP has either [ɔ] or [o] in P2 *comes*, P3sg *come*, P3pl *comem*.

Some verbs in *-ir*, like *progredir* 'to progress,' *prevenir* 'to prevent,' and *agredir* 'to assault,' change **e** [e] into **i** [i] in stressed position: *este país progride pouco* 'this country progresses little.' A number of verbs in *-ir*, like *servir* 'to serve,' *prevenir* 'to prevent,' *agredir* 'to assault,' have [i] in P1sg. *eu não sirvo para isso* I'm no good that' and [ɛ] in the other persons: *esse lápis não serve* 'that pencil won't do.'

Other verbs in *-ir*, such as *dormir*, have stressed [u] in P1sg and [ɔ] in other persons: *eu durmo muito mal mas a minha mulher dorme* [ɔ] *maravilhosamente* 'I sleep very poorly but my wife sleeps wonderfully.' The spelling of verbs like *dormir* masks the fact that for most speakers (of both BP and EP) unstressed *o* is phonetically [u]. Consequently, there is alternation between stressed [ɔ] in P2sg, P3sg, P3pl and [u] in the other persons.

Whereas orthographic **o** normally appears in P1pl and P2pl (*dormimos, cobrimos, tossimos, conferimos, competimos*), the corresponding forms of *engolir* 'to swallow' are spelled with an **u**: *engulimos, engulis*. A similar situation obtains in *vestir* and the verbs of the first set (*pedir*, etc.), where unstressed written **e** is pronounced as [i] in BP and [ə] in EP (*pedimos*). The type represented by *fugir* 'to run away,' with stressed [u] in P1sg and [ɔ] in the other persons (*eu fujo, ele foge*), contrasts with the type represented by *iludir* 'to fool,' which has [u] throughout (*eu iludo, ele ilude*).

Another type of irregularity involves changes in the form of either the stem itself or the tense–mood or person–number desinences of the first and third persons singular of the present and preterit indicative. In some cases there are also variations in the future indicative or the participle. The most frequent among such irregular verbs are listed in Table 3.13.

Other stem variations shown in Table 3.13 have to do with an irregular form for P1sg in the present indicative (which, as noted, is the basis for the present subjunctive), alternating with a regular form for other persons. In *perder* 'to lose', *valer* 'to be worth', *ouvir* 'to hear', *pedir* 'to ask', *medir* 'to measure' that stem is respectively *perc-*, *v*[a]*lh-*, *ouç*, *p*[ɛ]*ç-*, *m*[ɛ]*ç-*.

The four verbs *dizer* 'to say', *trazer* 'to bring', *fazer* 'to make/do', *poder* 'can/may' have a special stem for P1sg in the present indicative (*digo, trago, faço, posso*) and another for the preterit (*disse, trouxe* ([trows-] or [tros-]), *fiz-*, *pude-*). This preterit stem naturally reappears in the past perfect, the past subjunctive, and the future subjunctive. However, whereas *poder* forms the future indicative and conditional regularly (*poderei, poderia*), *dizer, trazer*, and *fazer* have a special stem for these tenses (*dir-, trar-, far-*). In *ter* 'to have', *pôr* 'to put', and *vir* 'to come' the stem of the present indicative acquires a nasal consonant which appears as a palatal in P1sg (*tenh-, venh-, ponh-*) and disappears after nasalizing the stem vowel in the other persons (*tens, tem, temos, tendes, tem*). The imperfect stem has a nasal palatal consonant and a vowel rise: *e > i* (*tinh-, vinh-*), *o > u* (*punh-*). In addition, in these verbs the preterit has two radicals with vowel alternation: *tiv- / tev-, pus/pos, vim/vie*.

The four verbs *saber* 'to know', *querer* 'to want', *requerer* 'to require', *caber* 'to fit' share several irregularities without forming a uniform pattern. *Caber* and *requerer* have a diphthongized stem vowel in the first person of the present indicative and present subjunctive (*caibo > caiba, requeiro > requeira*). *Saber* and *querer* have both a diphthongized stem vowel in first person of the present subjunctive (*saiba, queira*), but *saber* has a different diphthong in the first person of the present indicative (*sei*), while *querer* is regular in the present indicative except for P3sg, which lacks the desinence -*e* (*eu quero, tu queres, ele quer*). Finally, *caber, saber*, and *querer* have a specific preterit radical (P1sg *coube, soube, quis*), whereas *requerer*, though historically related to *querer*, is regular (P1sg *requeri*, P2sg *requereste*, and so on).

The five verbs *dar* 'to give', *estar* 'to be', *haver* 'there to be', *ser* 'to be', and *ir* 'go' share certain features with each other as well as with other irregular verbs. In addition, each has a few unique features of its own. *Dar* changes the radical vowel in the preterit, to [e] in P1sg, P3sg, and P1pl (*dei, deu, demos*) and to [ɛ] in P2sg and P2pl (*deste, destes*). The radical in [ɛ] appears regularly in the past perfect (*dera*) and in the past and future subjunctive (*desse, der*). Like *estar, ser*, and *ir*, the verb *dar* has, in P1sg of the present indicative, an ending *ou*, usually pronounced [o] or, in monitored pronunciation, [ow]. *Estar* shows in the P1sg of the preterit indicative the same type of [i] ∼ [e] vowel alternation found in *ter* and *fazer* (*estive* ∼ *esteve, tive* ∼ *teve, fiz* ∼ *fez*), and

Table 3.13 *Irregular verbs*

| Infinitive | Present indicative | Preterit | Other irregularities |
|---|---|---|---|
| caber | P1sg **caibo** | P1sg **coube** | |
| | P3sg cabe | P3sg **coube** | |
| dizer | P1sg **digo** | P1sg **disse** | FutInd: **direi** |
| | P3sg diz | P3sg **disse** | Part: dito |
| fazer[1] | P1sg **faço** | P1sg **fiz** | FutInd: **farei** |
| | P3sg faz | P3sg **fez** | Part: feito |
| ler[2] | P1sg **leio** | | |
| | P3sg lê | | |
| odiar[3] | P1sg **odeio** | | |
| | P3sg odeia | | |
| ouvir | P1sg **ouço** | | |
| | P3sg ouve | | |
| pedir[4] | P1sg **peço** [ɛ] | | |
| | P3sg pede [ɛ] | | |
| perder | P1sg **perco** [e] | | |
| | P3sg perde [ɛ] | | |
| poder | P1sg **posso** [ɔ] | P1sg **pude** | |
| | P3sg pode [ɔ] | P3sg **pôde** | |
| querer | P1sg **quero** [ɛ] | P1sg **quis** | PresSubj: **queira** |
| | P3sg quer [ɛ] | P3sg **quis** | |
| requerer | P1sg re**queiro** | | |
| | P3sg requer [ɛ] | | |
| rir | P1sg **rio** | | |
| | P3sg ri | | |
| saber | P1sg **sei** | P1sg **soube** | PresSubj: **saiba** |
| | P3sg sabe | P3sg **soube** | |
| seduzir[5] | P1sg **seduzo** | | |
| | P3sg seduz | | |
| trazer | P1sg **trago** | P1sg **trouxe** | FutInd: **trarei** |
| | P3sg traz | P3sg **trouxe** | |
| valer | P1sg **valho** | | |
| | P3sg vale | | |
| ver | P1sg **vejo** | P1sg **vi** | Part: visto |
| | P3sg **vê** | P3sg **viu** | |

[1] Like *fazer*: *refazer* 'to redo, remake,' *satisfazer* 'to satisfy,' *desfazer* 'to undo.'
[2] Like *ler*: *reler* 'to reread,' *crer* 'to believe.'
[3] Like *odiar*: *ansiar* 'to yearn,' *incendiar* 'to set on fire.'
[4] Like *pedir*: *medir* 'to measure.'
[5] Like *seduzir*: *produzir* 'to produce,' *reduzir* 'to reduce,' *conduzir* 'to conduct.'

*haver* shows in the preterit indicative the *ou* diphthong (usually [o] except in careful pronunciation) in *caber, saber, trazer* (*houve, coube, soube, trouxe*). On the other hand, *ser* shows several radicals (*s-* ~ *so-* ~ *sej-, é-, fu* ~ *fo-*), some of which are shared with *ir*.

Finally, a handful of high frequency anomalous verbs show so many anomalies in some tenses that it is simpler to list them (Table 3.14).

### 3.5.4    Perfect and continuous tenses

In addition the simple tenses seen so far there are also constructions made up of an inflected auxiliary verb° followed by one or two non-finite forms (Table 3.15). *Perfect* tenses are made up of a conjugated form of *ter* (or *haver* in rather formal styles) and the participle of the main verb: *tenho trabalhado* 'I have worked,' *tens dormido* 'you have slept.' *Continuous* tenses are formed with *estar* and a gerund: *estou andando* 'I'm walking,' *estávamos dormindo* 'we were sleeping.'

Combining an inflected form of *ter* and the participle of *estar* plus the gerund of the main verb yields a *perfect continuous* tense: *tenho estado estudando* 'I have been studying.' These tenses are structurally very similar to their English counterparts given in the glosses, although there are some differences in usage.

### 3.5.5    Double participles

Besides the regular participles in *-ado* and *-ido*, a number of verbs have one or two irregular participles (Table 3.16). The regular form generally occurs in perfect tenses (3.5.4) while the irregular form occurs as adjectives or in passive constructions (4.8.1), but usage varies considerably.

### 3.5.6    Impersonal verbs

A few verbs lacking a subject occur only in the third person singular. A subset of these includes verbs having to do with weather phenomena such as *chover* 'to rain,' *relampaguear* (and its variants *relampejar, relampar, relampear*) 'to flash like lightning,' *trovejar* 'to thunder,' *nevar* 'to snow,' *ventar* 'to blow (the wind),' and a few others: *Ontem ventou, relampagueou e trovejou, mas não choveu* 'yesterday the wind blew, there was lightning and thunder, but it did not rain' (4.7).

## 3.6    Adverbs

Adverbs are words (or phrases° that function as a single lexical unit) that add circumstantial information to whole sentences or to a specific element of a

Table 3.14 *Anomalous verbs*

| Tense | Person | dar | estar | haver | ir | pôr | ser | ter | vir |
|---|---|---|---|---|---|---|---|---|---|
| PresInd | P1sg | dou | estou | hei | vou | ponho | sou | tenho | venho |
| | P2sg | dás | estás | hás | vais | pões | és | tens | vens |
| | P3sg | dá | está | há | vai | põe | é | tem | vem |
| | P1pl | damos | estamos | havemos | vamos | pomos | somos | temos | vimos[3] |
| | P2pl | dais | estais | haveis | ides | pondes | sois | tendes | vindes |
| | P3pl | dão | estão | hão | vão | põem | são | têm | vêm |
| ImperfInd | P1sg | dava | estava | havia | ia | punha | era | tinha | vinha |
| PretInd | P1sg | dei | estive | houve | fui | pus | fui | tive | vim |
| | P2sg | deste | estiveste | houveste | foste | puseste | foste | tiveste | vieste |
| | P3sg | deu | esteve | houve | foi | pôs | foi | teve | veio |
| | P1pl | demos | estivemos | houvemos | fomos | pusemos | fomos | tivemos | viemos |
| | P2pl | destes | estivestes | houvestes | fostes | pusestes | fostes | tivestes | viestes |
| | P3pl | deram | estiveram | houveram | foram | puseram | foram | tiveram | vieram |
| Pluperf | P1sg | dera | estivera | houvera | fora | pusera | fora | tivera | viera |
| FutureInd | P1sg | darei | estarei | haverá | irei | porei | serei | terei | virei |
| Conditional | P1sg | daria | estaria | haveria | iria | poria | seria | teria | viria |
| Imperative | P2sg | dá[4] | está | [há][2] | vai | põe | sê | tem | vem |
| | P3sg | dê | esteja | haja | vá | ponha | seja | tenha | venha |
| | P2pl | dai | estai | havei | ide | ponde | sede | tende | vinde |
| | P3pl | dêem | estejam | hajam | vão | ponham | sejam | tenham | venham |

|  |  | dar | estar | haver | ir | pôr | ser | ter | vir |
|---|---|---|---|---|---|---|---|---|---|
| PresSubj | P1sg | dê | esteja | haja | vá | ponha | seja | tenha | venha |
|  | P2sg | dês | estejas | hajas | vás | ponhas | sejas | tenhas | venhas |
|  | P3sg | dê | esteja | haja | vá | ponha | seja | tenha | venha |
|  | P1pl | demos | estejamos | hajamos | vamos | ponhamos | sejamos | tenhamos | venhamos |
|  | P2pl | deis | estejais | hajais | vades | ponhais | sejais | tenhais | venhais |
|  | P3pl | dêem | estejam | hajam | vão | ponham | sejam | tenham | venham |
| PastSubj | P1sg | desse¹ | estivesse | houvesse | fosse | pusesse | fosse | tivesse | viesse |
|  | P2sg | desses | estivesses | houvesses | fosses | pusesses | fosses | tivesses | viesses |
|  | P3sg | desse | estivesse | houvesse | fosse | pusesse | fosse | tivesse | viesse |
|  | P1pl | déssemos | estivéssemos | houvéssemos | fôssemos | puséssemos | fôssemos | tivéssemos | viéssemos |
|  | P2pl | désseis | estivésseis | houvésseis | fôsseis | pusésseis | fôsseis | tivésseis | viésseis |
|  | P3pl | déssem | estivessem | houvessem | fossem | pusessem | fossem | tivessem | viessem |
| FutSubj | P1sg | der | estiver | houver | for | puser | for | tiver | vier |
| Infinitive |  | dar | estar | haver | ir | pôr | ser | ter | vir |
| Gerund |  | dando | estando | havendo | indo | pondo | sendo | tendo | vindo |
| Participle |  | dado | estado | havido | ido | posto | sido | tido | vindo |

¹ Forms with a stressed **e** are pronounced [ε] (all irregular verbs).
² A theoretical form.
³ *Vimos* is replaced by PretInd P1pl *viemos* in colloquial BP, possibly to avoid homophony with *vimos* 'we saw' from *ver* 'to see.'
⁴ Imperative forms of *tu* are regularly used with *você* in colloquial BP.

Table 3.15 *Simple and compound (perfect, continuous, and perfect-continuous) tenses*

| Tense names | Simple and perfect tenses | Continuous and perfect continuous tenses |
| --- | --- | --- |
| Present | ando | estou andando |
| Present Perfect | tenho andado | tenho estado andando |
| Imperfect | andava | estava andando |
| Preterit | andei | estive andando |
| Past perfect | andara | estivera andando |
| Past perfect (comp.) | tinha andado | tinha estado andando |
| Future | andarei | estarei andando |
| Future Perfect | terei andado | terei estado andando |
| Conditional | andaria | estaria andando |
| Conditional Perfect | teria andado | teria estado andando |
| Pres Subj | ande | esteja andando |
| Pres Perf Subj | tenha andado | tenha estado andando |
| Past Subj | andasse | estivesse andando |
| Past Perf Subj | tivesse andado | tivesse estado andando |
| Fut Subj | andar | estiver andando |
| Fut Perf Subj | tiver andado | tiver estado andando |

sentence, such as a verb, an adjective, or another adverb. The fact that the words we call adverbs are lumped into a single category, however, is a holdover from traditional grammars, and much work remains to be done to understand exactly how they work (Ilari 1996). Except for adverbs ending in *-mente* '-ly' (see below) there is no morphological feature that characterizes adverbs as such (Table 3.17).

As in English, so in Portuguese there are words that double as adjectives and adverbs. In 7a–7b *duro* and *rápido* add circumstantial information to the basic meaning of the verb. Likewise, in 7c–7d the adverb *cedo* and the phrase° *às três da manhã* bear the same structural relationship to the verb *levantei-me*.

(7)    a. *Ela trabalha duro.*
        'She works hard.'
    b. *A Fernanda subiu rápido.*
        'Fernanda climbed fast.'
    c. *Levantei-me cedo.*
        'I got up early.'
    d. *Levantei-me às três da manhã.*
        'I got up at three in the morning.'

Such examples show that the label "adverb" designates certain syntactic functions that can just as well be played by phrases that behave like adverbs. In fact some adverbs originate from lexicalized prepositional phrases, such as *depressa*

Table 3.16 *Verbs with double participles*

| Infinitive | Regular participle | Irregular participle | Infinitive | Regular participle | Irregular participle |
|---|---|---|---|---|---|
| *aceitar* 'accept' | aceitado | aceito,aceite | *acender* 'turn on' | acendido | aceso |
| *eleger* 'elect' | elegido | eleito | *inserir* 'insert' | inserido | inserto |
| *entregar* 'deliver' | entregado | entregue | *suspender* 'lift' | suspendido | suspenso |
| *gastar* 'spend' | gastado | gasto | *erigir* 'erect' | erigido | erecto |
| *limpar* 'clean' | limpado | limpo | *imprimir* 'print' | imprimido | impresso |
| *matar* 'kill' | matado | morto | *frigir* 'fry' | frigido | frito |
| *pegar* 'grab' | pegado | pego | *fritar* 'fry' | fritado | frito |
| *prender* 'arrest' | prendido | preso | *tingir* 'dye' | tingido | tinto |

| Infinitive | Participle | |
|---|---|---|
| *aceitar* | Reg. aceitado | CT: *Ele não tinha aceitado a conta.* 'He had not accepted the bill.' |
| | Irreg. aceito | Pas.: *A conta não foi aceita.* 'The bill was not accepted.' |
| | | Adj: *Os documentos estão aceitos.* (EP = *aceites*) |
| *acender* | Reg. acendido | CT: *Eu tinha acendido as lâmpadas.* 'I had turned on the lamps.' |
| | Irreg. aceso | Pas.: *As lâmpadas foram acendidas/acesas.* 'The lamps were turned on.' |
| | | Adj: *As lâmpadas estão acesas.* |
| *imprimir* | Reg. imprimido | CT: *Eles tinham imprimido/impresso os panfletos.* 'They had printed the pamphlets.' |
| | Irreg. impresso | Pass.: *Os panfletos foram imprimidos/impressos.* 'The pamphlets were printed.' |
| | | Adj: *Os documentos estão impressos.* 'The documents are printed [e.g. as opposed to handwritten].' |

CT: compound tense; Pas.: Passive; Adj.: Adjective.

'quickly' (*de* + *pressa* 'hurry'), *devagar* 'slowly' (*de* + *vagar* 'leisure'), *embaixo* 'underneath' (*em* + *baixo* 'low'), even though, oddly enough, *em cima* 'on top of, above' is written as two words.

Like nouns and adjectives, some adverbs may be modified by the diminutive suffix *-inho* (3.8.1). The resulting adverb has the same basic meaning and some added connotation:

> *logo* 'soon' > *loguinho* 'rather soon'
> *agora* 'now' > *agorinha* 'right now'
> *cedo* 'early' > *cedinho* 'rather early'
> *tarde* 'late' > *tardinho* 'rather late'

A useful distinction may be made between *deictic*° and *modal* adverbs. Deictic adverbs signal the location of something in relation to the speaker or some other point of reference. This is apparent in *locative* adverbs, some of which form triads such as *aqui* 'here, near the speaker,' *aí* 'there, near the hearer,' and *ali* and *lá* 'over there, near neither speaker nor hearer.' There is a clear

Table 3.17 *Adverbs*

| Deictic adverbs | | |
|---|---|---|
| | Locative | *aqui* 'here,' *aí* 'there,' *ali* 'over here' *cá* 'here,' *lá* 'there' |
| | Temporal | *ontem* 'yesterday,' *hoje* 'today,' *amanhã* 'tomorrow' |
| | | *antes* 'before,' *agora* 'now,' *depois* 'after' |
| Modal adverbs | | |
| | Manner | *bem, mal* |
| | Doubt | *talvez, quiçá* (obs.) |
| | Quantifiers or intensifiers | *muito, pouco, bastante, mais, menos* |
| | Affirmatives | *sim* |
| | Negatives | *não* |
| | Interrogatives | *quem? como? quando? onde?* |

parallel between these triads and the three-way distinction established by the demonstratives *este, esse, aquele* (3.3).

Time adverbs, as their name suggests, take a temporal frame of reference, as in *ontem* 'yesterday,' *hoje* 'today,' *amanhã* 'tomorrow.' A few adverbs, such as *antes* 'before,' *agora* 'now,' and *depois* 'after,' indicate a sequencing that is either spatial, or temporal, or both.

In contrast with deictic adverbs, modal adverbs characterize a set of circumstances, as in the case of manner adverbs, which include single words like *bem* 'well' and *mal* 'badly,' as in example 8 and adverbs ending in *-mente*.

(8)     *A gente comeu bem mas dormiu mal.*
        'We ate well but slept poorly.'

Although semantically equivalent to English '-ly,' *-mente* is not a suffix, but rather an independent word (Câmara 1972:105; Cintra 1983) that is attached to the feminine form of an adjective, if there is one (*atenta* 'attentive'+ *-mente* > *atentamente* 'attentively'), or directly to an adjective in *-e* (*alegre* 'happy' + *-mente* > *alegremente* 'happily'). There is some room for variation, though, as a few adjectives in *-or* or *-ês* escape this rule: *elas fazem isso superiormente* 'they do this in a superior fashion'; *as meninas trajavam portuguesmente* 'the girls were dressed in the Portuguese manner.' If two or more such adverbs are coordinated, *-mente* is usually attached to the last one only: *dançavam lenta e tristemente* 'they danced slowly and sadly.'

Other modal adverbs express doubt (9a), intensity (9b), or affirmation or negation (9c):

(9)     a. *Talvez chova.*
           'Maybe it'll rain.'
        b. *Quem pode mais, chora menos.*
           'He who is more powerful will cry less.'

    c. *Elas vêm? Sim ou não?*
       'Are they coming? Yes or no?'

Also traditionally listed as adverbs are the interrogative words that begin an information question, like *wh-* words in English: *quando*? 'when?,' *como*? 'how?' *onde*? 'where,' *quem*? 'who?,' BP *por que*? EP *porque?* 'why?' To these should be added BP *cadê?/quedê?* 'where is?' as in (10a–b), derived from the old expression *Que é feito de . . .?* 'what has become of . . .?'

(10)    a. *Cadê o teu irmão?*
        'Where is your brother?'
    b. *Quedê a pasta de dentes?*
        'Where is the toothpaste?'
    c. *E o cantil, quedê?*
        'And the canteen, where is (it)?'

## 3.7    Connectors: prepositions and conjunctions

Lexical words in utterances are linked by grammatical connectors that signal structural relationships. Prepositions can connect a variety of formants such as nouns (*rainha de copas* 'queen of hearts,' *café-com-leite* 'coffe with milk') or a noun and a verb (*pizza para levar* 'pizza to take out', *coisas por fazer* 'things to be done') or two sentences, as in 11:

(11)    *O pai trabalhava feito um burro para as filhas viverem feito rainhas.*
       'The father worked like a slave (lit. donkey) so the daughters could live like queens.'

A sentence formant such as a verb, a noun, or an adjective may require a specific preposition as a link to another formant that complements its meaning. Here are a few examples:

**Verb**

| | |
|---|---|
| *acabar (com)* 'to get rid of' | *Acabaram com os ratos naquele prédio.* 'They got rid of the rats in that building.' |
| *bater (em)* 'beat, spank' | *A polícia batia nos presos.* 'The police used to beat up the inmates.' |
| *depender (de)* | *O mundo depende do petróleo.* 'The world depends on oil.' |

**Noun**

| | |
|---|---|
| *doutor (em)* | *Joana é doutora em filosofia.* 'Joana is a doctor of philosophy.' |
| *obrigação (de)* | *Temos obrigação de pagar isso.* 'We have the obligation to pay that.' |
| *horror (a)* | *Tenho horror a gente burra.* 'I hate stupid people.' |

Table 3.18 *Prepositions*

| | |
|---|---|
| *a* | *fui a Lisboa* 'I went to Lisbon'; *escrito a mão* 'written by hand' |
| *ante* | *compareci ante o juiz* 'I appeared before the judge' |
| *até* | *fui até a esquina* 'I went as far as the street corner' |
| *com* | *saí com Marina* 'I went out with Marina' |
| *contra* | *somos contra esse governo* 'we are against this government' |
| *de* | *a bicicleta de Selma* 'Selma's bicycle' |
| *desde* | *estou a trabalhar desde as sete* 'I've been working since seven' |
| *em* | *Filomena vive em Viseu* 'Filomena lives in Viseu' |
| *entre* | *Cá entre nós: estamos entre amigos* 'between you and me: we are among friends' |
| *por* | *faço-o por ela* 'I do it for her' |
| *para* | *trouxeram flores para você* 'they've brought flowers for you' |
| *perante* | *estamos perante a autoridade* 'we are before the authority' |
| *sem* | *estou sem trabalho* 'I'm without a job' |
| *sob* | *fizemos isso sob ameaça de morte* 'we did that under threat of death' |
| *sobre* | *o dinheiro estava sobre a mesa* 'the money was on the table' |
| *como* | *ele vive como rei* 'he lives like a king' |
| *feito* (= *como*) | *ele trabalha feito escravo* 'he works like a slave' |
| *que nem* (= *como*) | *eles estavam rindo que nem loucos* 'they were laughing like crazy' |
| *conforme* | *vieram conforme as instruções* 'they came according to the instructions' |
| *durante* | *chegaram durante a noite* 'they arrived during the night' |
| *exceto* | *vieram todos exceto Norma* 'all arrived except Norma' |
| *mediante* | *o senador ficou rico mediante arranjos duvidosos* 'the senator got rich through shady deals' |

**Adjective**

| | |
|---|---|
| *forte (em)* | *Nunca fui forte em matemática.* 'I was never strong in math.' |
| *disposto (a)* | *O Juca está disposto a te ajudar.* 'Juca is willing to help you.' |
| *cheio (de)* | *Ele está cheio de dinheiro.* 'He's full of money.' |

Besides the basic prepositions shown in Table 3.18, other words may function as prepositions, such as *conforme* 'according to,' *durante* 'during,' *exceto* 'except.'

The class of conjunctions encompasses two types of connectors that perform rather different functions in structuring a sentence (Table 3.19).

*Coordinating* conjunctions join two or more like elements with like status. Such conjunctions may be *copulative*, like *e* 'and,' *ou* 'or,' and *nem* 'nor' in 12a–12c:

(12)    a. *Ele trabalha e ela estuda.*
        'He works and she studies.'

Table 3.19 *Conjunctions*

| | |
|---|---|
| Coordinating conjunctions: | |
| Copulative | *e, nem* (= *e não*) |
| Adversative | *mas* 'but,' *porém* 'however,' *senão* |
| Alternative | *ou* 'or' |
| Explicative | *logo, pois, por isso, portanto* |
| Subordinating conjunctions: | |
| Nominalizing | *que* |
| Time | *quando, sempre que, enquanto, antes que, depois que* |
| Cause | *porque, pois, porquanto, já que* |
| Condition | *se* 'if,' *contanto que* 'as long as,' *caso/desde que* 'as long as,' *a não ser que* 'unless' |
| Purpose | *para que, a fim de que* |
| Concessive | *embora, conquanto, ainda que, se bem que* |
| Consecutive | *de forma que, de maneira que* |
| Comparative | *como, como se* 'as if,' *assim como, que nem* |

b. *Vou e volto já.*
   'I'll go and come back soon.'
c. *O presidente não fala inglês nem francês.*
   'The president speaks neither English nor French.'

Other coordinating conjunctions have an *adversative* function and imply an excluded term, such as *mas* 'but,' *porém* 'however,' *senão* 'otherwise' in 13a–13b:

(13)     a. *Ele vai vir mas não vai falar.*
            'He's going to come but won't speak.'
         b. *Na América você tem que trabalhar feito uma mula senão não come.*
            'In America you have to work like a slave (lit. mule) or you won't eat.'

A third type, *alternative* conjunctions, like *ou*, signals a disjunctive, as in 14:

(14)     *Vocês querem beber vinho ou cerveja?*
         'Do you all want to drink wine or beer?'

*Explicative* conjunctions introduce an explanation or conclusion, as in 15:

(15)     *Eu estava sem dinheiro, logo não podia vir.*
         'I didn't have money, so I couldn't come.'

Finally, *comparative* conjunctions include *como* (16a) as well as words and constructions that have acquired this function, such as the participle *feito* (< *fazer*) and *que nem*, both meaning 'like,' as in 16a–16c:

(16)    a. *Ele vive como um rei.*
            'He lives like a king.'
        b. *Ele estuda feito louco.*
            'He studies like crazy.'
        c. *Ela ronca que nem um anjinho.*
            'She snores like a little angel.'

*Subordinating* conjunctions establish a syntactic relationship between two sentences by embedding° one in the other. Thus given two sentences, 17a and 17b, the subordinating conjunction *que* 'that' embeds 17b in 17a, yielding 17c. In such a construction, *que eu não minto* functions as a *subordinate* (or *dependent*) *clause*, and *você sabe* as the *main* (or *matrix*) *clause*.

(17)    a. *Você sabe* 'You know'
        b. *Eu não minto* 'I don't lie'
        c. *Você sabe que eu não minto* 'You know I don't lie.'

Specific subordinating conjunctions signal relationships, as in 18a–18:

(18)    a. Time: *Ele saiu **quando** a gente estava chegando.*
            'He went out when we were arriving.'
        b. Cause: *Não vou te pagar **porque** não tenho dinheiro.*
            'I'm not going to pay you because I don't have (any) money.'
        c. Condition: *Conto só **se** você fizer uma coisa.*
            'I'll tell it only if you do something.'
        d. Purpose: *Ele estava se matando **para que** o filho fosse alguém.*
            'He was killing himself so his son might be somebody.'

Whereas adverbs, prepositions, and conjunctions may be listed and, to a certain extent, analyzed in isolation, their full meaning only becomes clear in the context of complete constructions, as we will see in Chapter 4, which deals with the structure of sentences.

## 3.8    Word formation

Inflection modifies nouns and adjectives to signal variation in grammatical categories such as number (*fuzil/fuzis* 'rifle/s') or gender (*bonito/bonita* 'pretty'), and verbs to signal variation in tense, aspect, and person (*comi* 'I ate'/*comemos* 'we eat'). In such cases, the lexical meaning of the word remains the same. Furthermore, inflectional variation is limited to closed sets of desinences that generate entirely predictable forms. To put it in another way, inflection rearranges existing language stock within a self-contained system, but it does not create new words. Given enough time, some desinences, like the verb endings for *vós*, may cease to be used, but we cannot invent new desinences to signal a different kind of plural, or a new gender, or a new verb tense. In order to create new words other processes are used, such as *derivation, compounding, reduplication, clipping,* and *acronyms.*

### 3.8.1  *Derivation: prefixes and suffixes*

Unlike inflection, derivation is a creative process, using an existing word as a base for producing countless new words with related meanings. It would be impossible for a dictionary to list all possible derived words, since there are virtually infinite possible combinations of stems and two types of bound morphemes, namely prefixes° and suffixes° (collectively known as affixes°).

Prefixes come before a stem, as in *anti-* 'against' + *globalização* > *antiglobalização* 'antiglobalization.' Most Portuguese prefixes come from Greek or Latin (Table 3.20), where they already had this function, as in these simple examples:

> Gr *a-* or *an-* 'without:' *a-* + *theos* 'God' > *ateu* 'atheist'
> Lat *i-, in-* 'non:' *i-* + *legal* > *ilegal* 'illegal;' *in-* + *ativo* > *inativo* 'inactive'
> Lat *bis-* 'twice:' + *avô* 'grandfather' > *bisavô* 'great-grandfather'

In addition to these prefixes, a few Latin or Greek words have been adopted into Portuguese as prefixes:

> Lat *extra* 'outside, beyond:' *extra-oficial* 'unofficial,' *extrafino* 'very fine'
> Lat *multi* 'many:' *multicolor* 'many-colored,' *multilingüe* 'multilingual'
> Gr *macro* 'large:' *macrorregião* 'macroregion,' *macrodialect* 'macrodialect'
> Gr *micro* 'small:' *microcomputador* 'personal computer,' *micro-ondas* 'microwave'

*Derivative suffixes* are placed after a stem to form new words, as in *livro* + *-aria* > *livraria* 'bookstore.' They fall into two broad categories, namely modifying and transforming suffixes. Modifying suffixes (Table 3.21) include augmentatives and diminutives, the most productive of which are the augmentative *-ão/-ona* and the diminutive *-inho(a)/-zinho(a)* (*-ito(a)* is also current in EP, as in *livro* > *livrito*). Other diminutive suffixes exist in a fixed number of words (like *-ebre* in *casebre* 'hut,' a unique form) or very rarely combine with new

Table 3.20 *Some Portuguese prefixes*

**Of Latin origin**

| | | |
|---|---|---|
| a-, ad- | 'near, next to' | *acercar-se* 'to approach,' *adjunto* 'adjunct' |
| contra- | 'opposition' | *contra-revolucionário* 'counter-revolutionary,' *contraponto* 'counterpoint' |
| i-, im-, in- | 'negation' | *ilegal* 'illegal,' *impossível* 'impossible,' *infeliz* 'unhappy' |
| infra- | 'underneath' | *infraestrutura* 'infrastructure,' *infra-vermelho* 'infra-red' |
| mini- | 'small' | *minissaia* 'miniskirt,' *miniconto* 'very short story' |
| multi- | 'numerous' | *multimilionário* 'multimillionaire' *multicor, multicolor* 'many-colored' |
| pós- | 'after' | *pós-ditadura* 'post-dictatorship,' *pós-moderno* 'post-modern' |
| pró- | 'in favor of' | *pró-anistia* 'pro-amnesty,' *pró-arte* 'pro-art' |
| trans- | 'beyond' | *transportar* 'transport,' *transamazônico* 'beyond the Amazon' |
| sub- | 'under' | *subproduto* 'byproduct,' *subalugar* 'sublease' |
| sobre-, super- | 'above' | *sobrenatural* 'supernatural,' *superhomem* 'superman' |
| ultra- | 'beyond' | *ultramar* 'overseas,' *ultra-som* 'ultrasound' |

**Of Greek origin**

| | | |
|---|---|---|
| arqui-, arc- | 'superior' | *arcebispo* 'archbishop,' *arqui-inimigo* 'arch-enemy' |
| anti- | 'against' | *anti-capitalista* 'anticapitalist,' *anti-comunista* 'anticommunist' |
| aero- | 'air' | *aeródromo* 'aerodrome,' *aerograma* 'aerogram' |
| geo- | 'earth' | *geografia* 'geography,' *geotérmico* 'geothermic' |
| hemi- | 'half' | *hemiplegia* 'hemiplegia' |
| hiper- | 'very large' | *hipermercado* 'hypermarket,' *hipersensível* 'hypersensitive' |
| macro- | 'big' | *macroeconomia* 'macroeconomy,' *macróbio* 'long-lived' |
| micro- | 'small' | *microcirurgia* 'microsurgery,' *microônibus* 'microbus' |
| peri- | 'around' | *periférico* 'peripheral,' *perímetro* 'perimeter' |
| pseudo- | 'false, fake' | *pseudointelectual* 'pseudo intellectual' |

stems, like *-úsculo*, which appears in a few Latinate forms (*corpúsculo* 'corpuscle,' *arbúsculo* 'small shrub,' *opúsculo* 'opuscle') and every now and then yields a new one, like *grupúsculo* 'a small, unimportant group.'

Despite their name, the primary function of *augmentative* and *diminutive* *suffixes* is to convey positive or negative connotations such as appreciation, tenderness, irony, or scorn. Thus the same *jantar* 'dinner' may be referred to as a *jantarzinho* by a self-deprecating host or as a *jantarzão* by an appreciative guest. Likewise, the owner of a *fazenda* 'ranch' may call it his *fazendinha*, even though impressed visitors may think of it as a *fazendona*. Neither size nor intensity plays a role in an invitation like *Vamos tomar uma cervejinha/um uisquínho* 'let's have a (little) beer/whisky,' where the diminutive connotes a degree of informality or friendliness not present in the regular forms *cerveja* or *uísque*. Since context is crucial in interpreting the nuance intended, a statement like *eles compraram um carrinho/um carrão*, literally 'they bought a little car/a big car' may suggest admiration or disapproval that is only fully captured if we take into account the situation in which it is uttered.

Nouns formed with relatively unproductive suffixes often become lexicalized, that is "frozen" with a specific meaning that camouflages its derivational origin. Thus a *chaveta* (< *chave* 'key' + *-eta*) is a special kind of key (such as a slot key), and a *malote* (< *mala* 'suitcase' + *-ote*) is a specific bag used to transport correspondence or packages, and very different from a *maleta*, which is more like an attaché case.

Even derived forms with *-inho(a)/-zinho(a)* or *-ão* may lose some or all of their original size denotation and become lexicalized with a specific meaning, as in the following:

– *folhinha* (lit. 'small leaf'), meaning 'any calendar,' though originally one with daily removable pages
– *armarinho* (lit. 'small cabinet'): short for *loja de armarinhos* 'sewing notions store', 'haberdasher's', thus called because it used to be fitted with small cabinets for merchandise
– *casinha* (from *casa* 'house'): 'outhouse'
– *sombrinha* (from *sombra* 'shade'): a parasol
– *camisinha* (from *camisa* 'shirt'): 'condom'
– *mocinho* (from *moço* 'young man'): 'good guy (in westerns)'
– *cafezinho* (from *café* 'coffee'): 'a demitasse of coffee'

Other lexicalized diminutives originate from a comparison, as in *tatuzinho* 'sow bug, woodlouse' possibly due to some perceived similarity to a *tatu* 'armadillo,' or *abelhão* 'bumblebee,' likewise compared to an *abelha* 'bee.' Likewise, someone's *jeitão* (< *jeito* 'way') is simply their very personal aspect, and *solteirão* (< *solteiro* 'unmarried') means 'bachelor,' whereas *solteirona* has, for some speakers at least, the less charming connotation of 'spinster,' and BP *sapatão* (lit. 'big shoe') is a slang term for 'lesbian.'

Two *modifying suffixes*, *-íssimo/a* and *-érrimo/a*, function as adjective intensifiers in the creation of superlatives, e.g. *rico* 'rich' + *íssimo* > *riquíssimo* 'extremely rich' and *chato* 'boring' + *-érrimo* > *chatérrimo* 'extremely boring.' The morphology of superlatives is made slightly complex by the fact that *–íssimo/a* and *–érrimo/a*, which come from classical Latim *-issimus*, *-errimus* 'the most . . . of,' entered Portuguese already attached to a Latin or Latinized root, via Renaissance Italian. This process gave origin to a hybrid system in which some adjectives have a regular superlative while others preserve the original root and yet others have both, as shown in Table 3.21.

*Transforming suffixes* create new words that may belong to a different grammatical category from the original word. Some, like *-ada*, *-ida*, change verb stems into nouns denoting an action:

Table 3.21 *Some Portuguese modifying suffixes*

**Diminutive suffixes**

*-inho/a, -zinho/a:*
*livro > livrinho* 'little book'
*bicicleta > bicicletinha* 'small bicycle'
*lápiz > lapizinho* 'small pencil'
*cruz > cruzinha* 'small cross'

*-ito/a, -zito/a* (more common in EP)
*livro > livrito* 'little book'
*casa > casita* 'little house'

*-ete, -eta*
*pistola > pistolete* 'small pistol'
*mala > maleta* 'small suitcase'

*-ote(a)*
*menino/a > meninote/a* 'a child in his/her early teens'
*baixo/a > baixote* 'shortish'

*-usco, -ucho*
*velho > velhusco* 'oldish'
*negro > negrusco* 'blackish'
*gordo > gorducho* 'fatty'

*-eco, -ico*
*livro > livreco* 'a poor quality book'
*jornal > jornaleco* 'a trashy newspaper'
*namoro > namorico >* 'flirt'

**Augmentative suffixes**

*-ão(ona)*
*livro > livrão* 'big book'
*casa > casona* 'big house'
*grosseiro > grosseirão* 'very rude person'

*-(z)arrão, -eirão*
*cão > canzarrão* 'big dog'
*santo > santarrão* 'sanctimonious person'

*-aço, -aça*
*animal > animalaço* 'brute, ignoramus'
*barba > barbaça* 'big beard'

*-ázio*
*copo > copázio* 'large glass'

**Superlative suffixes**

| Base adjective form | Regular | With Latinate radical | |
|---|---|---|---|
| *elegante* 'elegant' | *elegantíssimo* | | 'extremely elegant' |
| *triste* 'sad' | *tristíssimo* | | 'extremely sad' |
| *fácil* 'easy' | *facilíssimo* | *facílimo* (< Lat *facilis*) | 'extremely easy' |
| *doce* 'sweet' | *docíssimo* | *dulcíssimo* (< Lat *dulcis*) | 'extremely sweet' |
| *humilde* 'humble' | *humildíssimo* | *humílimo* (< Lat *humilis*) | 'extremely humble' |
| *pobre* 'poor' | *pobríssimo* | *paupérrimo* (< Lat *pauper*) | 'extremely poor' |
| *negro* 'black' | *negríssimo* | *nigérrimo* (< Lat *niger*) | 'extremely black' |
| *cruel* 'cruel' | | *crudelíssimo* (< Lat *crudelis*) | 'extremely cruel' |
| *célebre* 'famous' | | *celebérrimo* (< Lat *celebris*) | 'extremely famous' |
| *íntegro* 'righteous' | | *integérrimo* (< Lat *integer*) | 'extremely righteous' |

*estudar* > *uma estudada* 'a quick study'
*subir* > *uma subida* 'a climb'
*andar* > *uma andada* 'a walk'

Others, such as *-dor(a)*, refer to an occupation or activity:

*fala(r)* > *falador(a)* 'talker'
*compra(r)* > *comprador/a* 'buyer'
*trepa(r)* > *trepadeira* 'a climbing vine'
*doma(r)* > *domador/a* 'tamer'

The suffixes *-ista*, *-ismo*, *-izar*, are used to form respectively adjectives, nouns, or verbs from adjectives: *social* + *-ista* > *socialista* 'socialist,' *social* + *-ismo* > *socialismo* 'socialism,' *social* + *-izar* > *socializar* 'to socialize.'

Since a derivative suffix becomes part of a word, it comes before any inflectional suffixes: *juiz* + *inho* + *-s* > *juizinhos* 'little judges,' *derrota* 'defeat' + *ista* + *-s* > *derrotistas* 'defeatists.' A derived word may in turn serve as a stem from which new words may be derived: *socializar* gives *socializ-*, which may be combined with other suffixes to form *socializável* 'socializable,' or *socialização* 'socialization.'

### 3.8.2    Compounding

Two or more words may combine to form a new lexical unit. They may do this by coalescing into a new word, as in *ponta* 'point' + *pé* 'foot' > *pontapé* 'a kick,' or *água* 'water' + *ardente* 'burning' > *aguardente* 'brandy' (lit. 'burning water'). They may also simply stand side by side, as in *carro esporte* 'sports car,' *apartamento kitchenete* 'studio apartment.' Finally, they may be linked by a hyphen (*diretor-gerente* 'managing director'), or by a preposition (*clube de campo* 'country club'), or by a conjunction (*cama e comida* 'room and board'). In principle, hyphens should signal a high degree of coalescence between the formants, but hyphenation rules are far from fixed and despite grammarians' efforts, tend to be used erratically. A distinction can be made between real compounds like *pé-de-meia* 'savings' (lit. 'a sock'; cf. American Eng *sock away* 'save money') and syntactic groups like *lança-foguetes* 'rocket launcher,' on the basis of the fact that the latter are "transparent" (Sandemann 1995:399). These distinctions, however, are not necessarily perceived alike by different speakers.

A compound is considered *coordinate* when its formants belong to the same word class and have the same status in the new word, like the nouns in *bar-restaurante* 'restaurant bar' or *país-membro* 'member country,' or the adjectives in (*assunto*) *político-religioso* 'political and religious (subject)' or (*acordo*) *brasileiro-uruguaio* 'Brazilian–Uruguayan (agreement).' A subset of

Table 3.22 *Some Portuguese transforming suffixes*

**Noun to noun**

| | |
|---|---|
| -ada | a verbal action: *estud(ar)* 'to study' *estudada* > 'a quick study,' *limp(ar)* 'to clean' > *limpada* 'a quick cleaning' |
| -ada | a collective: *criança* 'child' > *criançada* 'a group of children,' *cachorro* > *cachorrada* 'a band of dogs' |
| -ada | a typical action: *criança* 'child'> *criançada* 'a childish action,' *canalha* 'scoundrel'> *canalhada* 'a scoundrel's action' |
| -agem | an action: *pilh(ar)* > *pilhagem* 'pillage,' *clone* 'clone' > *clonagem* 'cloning' |
| -al | a plantation: *bambu* 'bamboo' > *bambual* 'bamboo grove,' *café* 'coffee'> *cafezal* 'coffee plantation' |
| -ança | *festa* > *festança* 'merrymaking' |
| -aria | abstract nouns: *carpinteiro* 'carpenter' > *carpintaria* 'carpentry,' *porco* 'pig'> *porcaria* 'filth' |
| | a collective: *lata* 'can' > *lataria* 'an amount of cans,' *fuzil* 'rifle' > *fuzilaria* 'a series of rifle shots' |
| | a business establishment: *papel* 'paper'> *papelaria* 'stationery store,' *livro* 'book'> *livraria* 'bookstore' |
| -(i)dade | *Brasil* > *brasilidade* 'brazilianness' |
| -eiro | agent, maker: *canoa* 'canoe' > *canoeiro* 'canoe maker,' *grafiti* 'graffiti' > *grafiteiro* 'grafiti writer,' *cozinha* 'kitchen' > *cozinheiro* 'cook' |
| -ez | quality: *líquido* 'liquid' > *liquidez* 'liquidity,' *macio* 'soft' > *maciez* 'softness' |
| -ida | verbal action: *benz(er)* 'to bless' > *benzida* 'a blessing,' *sa(ir)* 'to go out' > *saída* 'an outing' |
| -ismo | abstract nouns: Lula (name of Brazil's president) > *lulismo* 'Lula's political ideas,' *coronel* 'colonel, i.e. rural political boss' > *coronelismo* 'a political regime dominated by rural bosses' |
| -ista | follower of a person or an ideology: *comunista* 'communist,' *petista* 'follower of the *PT* [pe'te] i.e. *Partido dos Trabalhadores* 'Workers' Party' |
| -ite | illness or similar condition: *apêndice* 'appendix' > *apendicite* 'appendicitis,' *pulmão* 'lung' > *pulmonite* 'pulmonitis,' *paixão* 'passion,' > *paixonite* 'chronic passion,' *preguiça* 'laziness' > *preguicite* 'chronic laziness,' *pesquisa* 'research' > *pesquisite* 'obsession with research' |
| -ódromo | place: *aeródromo* 'aerodrome,' *cão* 'dog' > *canódromo* 'dog race track,' *samba* 'kind of dance' > *sambódromo* 'place for collective dancing' |
| -or | agent: *conduzir* 'drive' > *condutor* 'driver,' *acupuntura* 'acupuncture' > *acupuntor, reproduzir* 'to reproduce' > *reprodutor* 'reproducer' |

Adjective to noun:

| | |
|---|---|
| -(i)dade | quality: *oral* > *oralidade* 'orality,' *bom* 'good' > *bondade* 'goodness' |
| -eza | quality: *mole* 'soft' > *moleza* 'softness,' *baixo* 'low' > *baixeza* 'lowness' |
| -aria | quality: *baixo* 'low' > *baixaria* 'low action,' *velho* 'old' > *velharia* 'any old thing' |
| - ura | quality: *fresco* 'fresh'> *frescura* 'freshness,' *gostoso* 'pleasant' > *gostosura* 'intense pleasure' |
| -ância | a feature: *elegante* 'elegant' > *elegância*, arrogante 'arrogant' > arrogância 'arrogance' |

coordinate compounds are *additive*, because the meaning of a formant is added to the meaning of the preceding one, as in *dezesseis* (< *dez e seis*) 'sixteen.'

In *subordinate* (or *exocentric*) compounds a formant functions like a nucleus and is modified by another formant which usually follows it. The simplest type of subordinate compounding involves juxtaposing the formants, as in *navio-escola* 'training ship' or *escola-modelo* 'model school,' but in such cases the meaning of the resulting compound is more specific than either formant. As these examples suggest, nouns thus formed usually have the gender of the nucleus: *homem-rã* (m.) 'frogman,' *tartaruga macho* 'male turtle.' Other compounds follow the formula noun + adjective, as in *boina-verde* 'green beret (mil.)' or *bóia-fria* (lit. 'cold meal') 'a worker who eats a cold meal at his workplace.'

Subordination may be indicated by a preposition: *homem de negócios* 'businessman,' *filme para adultos* 'adult movie,' *cartão de crédito* 'credit card,' *água-com-açúcar* (lit. 'water-and-sugar') 'sappy, soppy,' as in *romance água-com-açúcar* 'a sappy novel, or 'very easy,' as in *esse problema é água-com-açúcar* 'that problem is like a breeze.'

*Endocentric* compounds, in contrast, lack a nucleus, and their meaning entails a reference to some understood word:

> *o limpa-trilhos* 'a device for cleaning rails'
> *o limpa-chaminés* 'chimney-sweep'
> *o tira-manchas* 'spot remover'
> *os sem-terra* 'landless persons'
> *o sem-modos* 'an ill-mannered person' (lit. 'without manners')

*3.8.2.1 Plural of compound nouns and adjectives*   There is a great deal of variation in the way compound nouns and adjectives form their plurals. If the two formants are connected by a preposition, only the first one varies:

> *fim-de-semana* > *fins-de-semana* 'weekend/s'
> *aspirante-a-oficial aspirantes-a-oficial* > 'officer candidate'

In coordinated compounds, both nouns vary: *bar-restaurante* > *bares-restaurantes* 'restaurant bar/s', and in exocentric compounds the general rule is that both elements vary whether they are nouns, or a noun and an adjective, or an adjective and a noun:

**Nouns**
*carro-bomba* > *carros-bombas* 'car bomb/s'
*salário-família* > *salários-famílias* 'family bonus/es'

**Noun + adjective**
*lugar-comum* > *lugares-comuns* 'cliché/s'
*prato-feito* > *pratos-feitos* 'one-dish meal/s'

### Table 3.23 *Types of compound nouns and adjectives*

**noun + noun**
*palavra-chave* 'key word'
*empresa-fantasma* 'ghost firm'
*carro-bomba* 'car bomb'
*diretor-chefe* 'head director'

**noun + adjective**
*homem público* 'public man'
*criado-mudo* 'night table'
*pão-duro* 'tightwad'
*dedo-duro* 'informer'

**noun + connector + noun**
*fim-de-semana* 'weekend'
*escova-de-dentes* 'toothbrush'
*água-com-açúcar*
   'easy, saccharine, soppy'
*cama-e-mesa* 'room and board'
*pau-para-toda-obra* 'factotum'

**adjective + adjective**
*azul-marinho* 'navy blue'
*verde-amarelo* 'green and yellow'
*auriverde* 'gold and green'
*rubro-negro* 'red and black'

**adjective + noun**
*pequeno almoço* (EP) 'breakfast'
*boa-pinta* 'good looking'
*terceiro-mundo* 'third world'
*mau-caráter* 'scoundrel'

**shortened adjective + adjective**
*ítalo-brasileiro* 'Italian-Brazilian'
*sino-brasileiro* 'Chinese-Brazilian'
*nipo-brasileiro* 'Japanese-Brazilian'
*franco-brasileiro* 'French-Brazilian'

**verb + noun**
*tira-manchas* 'spot remover'
*quebra-molas* 'road bump/ditch'
*guarda-costas* 'body guard'
*afia-lápis* 'pencil sharpener'

**verb + verb**
*vaivém* 'to-and-fro motion' (*vai e vem*)
*sobe-desce* 'up-and-down motion'
*espicha-encolhe* 'an indecisive situation
   or person'
*chove-não-molha* 'an indecisive situation or
   person'

**numeral + noun**
*quatro-olhos* 'four-eyes'
*terça-feira* 'Tuesday'
*quadrigêmeos* 'quadruplets' (*gêmeos*
   'twins')

**preposition + noun**
*de-comer* 'food'
*sem-terra* 'landless'
*sem-vergonha* 'shameless'
*à-toa* 'worthless'

**adverb + noun**
*mais-valia* 'surplus value'

**adverb + adjective**
*bem-amado* 'well liked'
*bem-falante* 'glib'
*mal-educado* 'rude'
*malvisto* 'suspect'

**adverb + verb**
*bem-estar* 'well being'
*bem-vindo* 'welcome'
*malversar* 'mismanage'
*malferir* 'to hurt badly'
*mal-estar* 'indisposition'

**synthetic compounds**
*leva-e-traz* 'busybody'
*pega-pega* 'free for all'
*sabe-tudo* 'know-it-all'
*bem-te-vi* 'a kind of bird'
*não-te-esqueças* 'forget-me-not'
*pega-pra-capar* 'free-for-all'

**Adjective + noun**
*gentil-homem > gentis-homens* 'nobleman.'

Exceptions are the shortened forms *grão* (m.), *grã* (f.) (*<grande*) and *bel* (< *belo*) which occur in a few low-frequency compounds such as

*grão-duque > grão duques* 'grand duke/s'
*grã-duquesa > grã-duquesas* 'grand duchess/es'
*bel-prazer > bel-prazeres* 'pleasure/s'

Although traditional grammars prescribe that only the first element should vary when its meaning is limited by the second, as in the exocentric compound *navio-escola > navios-escola* 'training ship/s,' actual usage shows considerable variation, as in *peixe-boi > peixes-bois* 'manatee/s,' *navio-oficina > navios-oficinas*, 'repair ship/s.' If the first formant is a verb or an invariable word, only the second varies:

*lança-rojão > lança-rojões* 'bazooka/s'
*beija-flor > beija-flores* 'humming bird/s'
*vice-presidente > vice-presidentes* 'vice president/s'

With words like *guarda*, however, there is variation, depending on whether the word is considered a noun ('guard') or a verb ('to guard, protect'). Thus we have *guarda-chuva > guarda-chuvas* 'umbrella/s,' *guarda-roupa > guarda-roupas* 'wardrobe/s,' but *guarda civil > guardas-civis* 'civil guard/s.' At least one such noun, *guarda-marinha* 'ensign (nav.),' has three possible attested forms: *guardas-marinha*, *guardas-marinhas*, and *guarda-marinhas*.

Compound adjectives also show considerable variation. *Surdo-mudo* 'deaf-mute' (n. or adj.) is always *surdos mudos*, but otherwise the generic norm for compound adjectives is that only the second formant agrees with the noun:

*suéter azul-claro > suéteres azul-claros* 'light blue sweater/s'
*camisa verde-clara > camisas verde-claras* 'light green shirt/s'

This rule also applies to compound adjectives with a short form in *–o* for the first formant, as in the following:

| | |
|---|---|
| *austríaco > austro* 'Austrian' | *austro-italiano* 'Austrian Italian' |
| *francês > franco* 'French' | *franco-prussiano* 'Franco-Prussian' |
| *africano > afro* 'Afro' | *afro-brasileiro* 'Afro-Brazilian' |

In compound adjectives made up of a color adjective followed by a qualifying noun, the tendency is for the first element to inflect (*painel verde-garrafa > painéis verdes-garrafa, painéis verdes-garrafas* 'bottle-green panel/s'). There are, however, examples of invariable compounds, as in *uniforme/s verde-oliva* 'olive green uniform/s,' *gravata/s amarelo-ouro* 'gold-yellow tie/s.' Variation is probably encouraged by the fact that the same compound may function as an adjective, in which case only the second formant varies (*terno azul-marinho > ternos azul-marinhos* 'navy-blue suit/s'), or as a noun, in which case both vary, as in *Comprei os azuis-marinhos* 'I bought the navy-blue ones.' The relatively low frequency of such compounds likely contributes to the fact that actual usage, even among the educated, can diverge considerably from normative grammar rules.

### 3.8.3    Other word-formation processes

A word may be created by clipping one or two syllables off an existing one, not only in common nouns but also in names, thus forming nicknames:

| | |
|---|---|
| *delegado > delega* 'police chief' | *José > Zé* |
| *pneumático > pneu* 'tire' | *Antônio > Tonio, Tonho* |
| *subtenente > sub* ['subi] | *Claudinê > Clau* |
|   'sublieutenant' | *Álvaro > Arvo* |
| *comunista > comuna* 'communist' | *Maria de Lurdes > Marilu* |
| *motocicleta >* BP *moto,* EP *mota* | *Mariângela > Mari* |
|   'motorcycle' | *Dorotéia > Doró* |
| *bicicleta > bici* 'bicycle' | *Maria Augusta > Magu* |

Clipping is productive in creating new prefixes, as in *motor > moto* (as in *moto-serra* 'an electric/gas chain saw'), *narcótico > narco* (as in *narcotráfico* 'drug traffic,' *narcodólar* 'narcodollar').

Sometimes an old prefix reincarnates with a new meaning. Gr *auto* 'self' is the basis for *automóvel,* originally 'self-moving' and later used as the name of a specific kind of self-propelled vehicle. *Automóvel,* in turn, has been clipped into the noun *auto* 'car,' used as a prefix meaning 'having to do with cars,' as in:

| | |
|---|---|
| *auto-estrada* 'highway' | *auto-peças* 'a store selling car parts' |
| *auto-escola* 'driving school' | *auto-estrada* 'expressway' |

Likewise *cinema* (originally from Gr *kínesis* 'movement,' hence *cinematograph* 'a machine that shows moving pictures') has yielded *cine-* 'related to cinema,' as in:

| | |
|---|---|
| *cine-revista* 'flick magazine' | *cineclube* 'film club' |
| *cine-drama* 'a dramatic movie' | *cinejornal* 'newsreel' |

The Gr prefix *tele* 'far' was used in new coinages like *telégrafo* or *telefone* (loan words from Fr *télégraphe, téléphone*) and *televisão* (from Eng *television*) to indicate devices for writing, speaking (Gr *graphein* 'writing,' *phono* 'sound'), or seeing (Lat *visio* 'vision') from a distance. In turn, *televisão* has been clipped to *tele*, which is used as a prefix meaning 'related to television' in a raft of coinages such as:

*telenotícias* 'telecast news'          *telenovela* a 'soap opera'
*telespectador* 'television viewer'     *telediário* 'news program'
*telecurso* 'television course'         *teleator* 'television actor'
*telever* 'to watch television'         *televizinho* 'someone who watches
                                         television at a neighbor's'

Reduplication is a rather active process, particularly in BP (Couto 1999). It consists in repeating a base form or a clipped version thereof, as in coll. *bunda* 'buttocks' > *bumbum* 'fanny.' This process is productive in nicknames involving repetition of either one of the syllable of a name (*Carlos* > *Cacá*, *José* > *Zezé*) or even a syllable bearing no resemblance to the name *Fafá* (*Maria Antonia*), > *Gigi* (*Wilma*), *Gugu* (*Adalgisa*). Some reduplicated kinship terms are virtually lexicalized:

*avô* 'grandfather'> *vovô*          *avó* 'grandmother' > *vovó*
   'grandpa'                            'grandma'
*pai* 'father'> *papai* 'daddy'      *mãe* 'mother' > *mamãe* 'mummy'
*tio* 'uncle' > *titio* 'nunky'      *tia* 'aunt' > *titia* 'auntie'

Reduplication of verb forms uses the third person singular, usually of the present indicative, as in:

*corre-corre* (< *correr* 'to run') 'a hurried situation'
*trepa-trepa* (< coll. *trepar* 'to screw') 'intense sexual activity'
*pinga-pinga* (< *pingar* 'to drop') 'a vehicle that makes many
   stops/landings to pick up/let off passengers'

Related verbs may be used, as in *pegue-pague* (< *pegar* 'to pick up,' *pagar* 'to pay'), a self-service market; *vai-vem* (< *ir* 'to go,' *vir* 'to come'), a situation where one is constantly on the move. Use of the preterit has a conditional connotation (if . . . then . . .) as in *pegou-comprou* (< *pegar* 'to pick up,' *comprar* 'to buy') 'if you touch it, you've bought it,'or *quebrou-pagou* (< *quebrar* 'to break,' *pagar* 'to pay') 'if you break it you'll pay for it.'

*Acronyms* are formed by two or more initials pronounced as a word:

*PT* [pe'te] < *Partido dos Trabalhadores* 'Workers' Party'
*PC* [pe'se] < *Partido Comunista* 'Communist Party'
*USP* ['uspi] < *Universidade de São Paulo* 'University of São Paulo'
*O.N.G., ONG, ong* ['õgi] < *organização não-governamental* 'NGO'

The referent need not be the thing or entity named by the acronym: *fenemê* is the name of a large truck bearing the maker's acronym, *FNM* (*Fábrica Nacional de Motores* 'National Motor Factory'). Once created, acronym-derived words may become stems for new derived words: *política petista* 'PT politics,' *normas uspianas* 'USP norms.' An acronym may be based on the Portuguese translation of a foreign term, as in *ONU* ['onu] 'UN' (*Organização das Nações Unidas*) or *sida* ['sidɐ] 'aids' (< *síndrome de deficiência imunológica adquirida*), but it may also be borrowed directly as in the case of *NASA* ['nazɐ] (*North American Space Agency*, *CIA* ['siɐ] (*Central Intelligence Agency*).

Synthetic formation creates a word out of a phrase with a sometimes distantly related meaning, as in *os afazeres* 'duties' (plural of *a fazer* 'to be done'), *o sabetudo* 'know-it-all,' *um chove-não-molha* (lit. 'rains-and-doesn't wet') 'an indecisive situation or person' or *um pega-pra-capar* (lit. '*grab for castrating*') 'a free for all.' Involving whole phrases, synthetic compounds are close to, and sometimes difficult to distinguish from, *idioms*, which are phrases functioning as lexical units with a meaning unrelated to the meaning of its formants. Thus *pé-de-moleque*, lit. 'street urchin's foot,' is a kind of peanut praline, and *bater as botas*, lit. 'to hit the boots,' and *esticar as pernas*, lit. 'to stretch one's legs,' are colloquial synonyms of 'to die,' not unlike the English idioms 'to kick the bucket' or 'to give up the ghost.' This is the area where morphology slides into the more complex area of phrase and sentence formation, which will be the topic of the next chapter.

# 4    Sentences

Whatever our native language, we intuitively know that the order of words is not haphazard but follows certain patterns, and that deviating from these patterns creates sequences that range from odd to meaningless. We know, for example, that in English *the rifle* and *my rifle* are acceptable sequences, whereas *the my rifle* is not. (The asterisk is conventionally used to mark a poorly formed construction that does not meet native speakers' criteria of acceptability.) This kind of judgment has nothing to do with the words themselves. Rather, it reflects our intuitive knowledge that whereas the orders *article + noun* and *possessive + noun* are all right, there is something wrong about the order *article + possessive + noun*. That there is nothing universal about these rules becomes apparent when we learn that Portuguese allows all three sequences:

| | |
|---|---|
| Art + N | *o fuzil* 'the rifle,' *os fuzis* 'the rifles' |
| Pos + N | *meu fuzil* 'my rifle,' *meus fuzis* 'my rifles' |
| Art + Pos + N | *o meu fuzil* 'my rifle,' *os meus fuzis* 'my rifles' |

These examples illustrate a phenomenon common to all languages, namely that word arrangements can be described by general rules. In this chapter we will analyze some rules governing the basic patterns of such arrangements in Portuguese, and we will pay closer attention to structures that usually require a bit more attention from learners. Part of the problem is that such constructions do not have a counterpart in English, or if they do (as in the case of articles and possessives), they are governed by different rules. Unless otherwise indicated, our presentation concentrates on standard usage acceptable to educated speakers. As in English, there is substantial variation between this educated standard and the non-standard usage found among the uneducated – what is often referred to as popular speech. A point to keep in mind, however, is that in spoken Brazilian Portuguese, colloquial usage among educated speakers shows many non-standard features typical of popular speech, which tends to depart significantly from that standard. Some of these labels – standard, non-standard, colloquial, and so on – are somewhat vague and denote ranges of language acceptability. We will return to these matters in Chapter 7.

## 4.1    Syntactic devices

Words are organized into *sentences*, which include a verb, as in 1a, and *phrases*°, which do not, as in 1b.

(1)    a. *Você quer sal?*          'Do you want salt?
          *Quem é?*                 'Who is it?'
          *Que horas são?*          'What time is it?'
          *Vamos entrar!*           'Let's go/come in.'

       b. *Saúde!*                  'Cheers!'
          *Feliz aniversário!*      'Happy birthday!'
          *Que horror!*             'How terrible!'
          *Branco ou tinto?*        'White or red?'
          *Este ou aquele?*         'This one or that one?'

Sentences and phrases are made up of both lexical words, which have an extralinguistic referent, and grammatical words, which signal structural relations between words (3.1). The meaning of a phrase or sentence depends partly on the meaning of its words and partly on its internal structure, that is the way the words relate to each other. *Syntax* (from Gr *syntassein* 'to ordain') is the analysis of such structures, which depend on devices that include (a) agreement, (b) word order, (c) grammatical words, (d) the syntactic information inherent in each word, and (e) coordination and subordination. We will take up each of these in turn.

### 4.1.1    Agreement

We saw in the section on inflection (3.2, 'Nouns and adjectives') that a noun's features of number or gender are replicated by the endings of accompanying words such as determinants or adjectives. The mechanism responsible for this process is called *agreement*.

*Nominal* agreement applies to nouns and adjectives. In *um chapéu e uma fita amarela* 'a hat and a yellow ribbon' the feminine adjective *amarela* agrees with *fita*, which is feminine, but not with *chapéu*, which is masculine. But *um chapéu e uma fita amarelos* the plural adjective *amarelos* agrees with both nouns, for when masculine and feminine nouns are qualified by the same adjective, the contrast in gender is neutralized and the adjective retains its masculine plural form.

Verbal agreement modifies a verb's person–number desinences (3.5) so as to match the subject's corresponding features, as in 2a–2c:

(2)     a. *Ela e eu já comemos.* 'She and I have already eaten.' (*ela e eu =
           nós* 'we')
        b. *Marta e Maria saíram.* 'Marta and Maria have left.'(*Marta e
           Maria = elas* 'they' (f.))
        c. *Tu e eu vamos ao clube.* 'You and I are going to the club.' (*tu e
           eu = nós* 'we')

### 4.1.2   Word order

The syntactic information encoded in word order lets us know that a headline like C*ACHORRO MORDE CARTEIRO* 'dog bites mailman' is news as usual, whereas C*ARTEIRO MORDE CACHORRO* 'mailman bites dog' is extraordinary news. If we compare the sentences in 3a–3b to those in 3c–3d, we realize how word order contributes to meaning:

(3)     a. *Romeu beijou Julieta.* 'Romeo kissed Juliet.'
        b. *Julieta esbofeteou Romeu.* 'Juliet slapped Romeo.'
        c. *Julieta foi beijada por Romeu.* 'Juliet was kissed by Romeo.'
        d. *Romeu foi esbofeteado por Julieta.* 'Romeo was slapped by Juliet.'

Most speakers understand that, insofar as meaning is concerned, sentences 3a and 3c tell us that Romeo did the kissing and Juliet got kissed, whereas sentences 3b and 3d state that Julieta did the slapping and Romeo got slapped. In syntactic terms, in 3a the noun *Romeu* is the subject° of the verb *beijou* and *Julieta* is its direct object°, whereas in 3b *Julieta* is the subject of the verb *esbofeteou* and *Romeu* is its direct object. A crucial syntactic feature is that the verb agrees with the subject in person and number.

### 4.1.3   Grammatical words

Grammatical words, the nuts and bolts that hold a sentence together, have structural meaning that concerns relationships between the formants of sentences or phrases. In examples 4a–4f, the relationship indicated by each preposition is shown in parentheses:

(4)     a. *A eleição foi adiada* pelo *governo.* (*por* = agent)
           'The election was postponed by the government.'
        b. *Marta passou* por *Paris.* (*por* = place)
           'Marta went through/by Paris.'
        c. *Dei-lhes a informação* por *cortesia.* (por = cause)
           'I gave them the information out of courtesy.'

    d. *Marta trabalha* de *intérprete.* (*de* = activity)
      'Marta works as an interpreter.'
    e. *Ela vinha* de *Pasadena.* (*de* = origin)
      'She came from Pasadena.'
    f. *Ele trouxe a bagagem* de *Daniel.* (de = possession)
      'He brought Daniel's luggage.'

### *4.1.4    Inherent syntactic information*

A word can be thought of as containing a bundle of inherent information related to the syntactic structures in which it can participate. Certain verbs, such as *sair, chegar,* ou *acordar*, may stand alone with their subject, as in *A Joana saiu?* 'Has Joan gone out?' Others, such as *comprar, vender* (and *esbofetear* and *beijar* in 3a–3d above), require a complement, as in 5a–5b. All the same, *O José comprou* can function as a full sentence, provided the complement is retrievable from the context, as in a reply to the question – *Quem comprou o bonde?* 'Who bought the street car?' (see 4.5.1).

(5)      a. *O José comprou um bonde no Rio e revendeu-o em São Paulo.*
         'José bought a street car in Rio and resold it in São Paulo.'
      b. *Os nativos vendiam flores.*
         'The natives sold flowers.'

### *4.1.5    Coordination and subordination*

Two processes for joining sentence formants are coordination and subordination. Coordination links words, phrases, or sentences sequentially, as in *Sílvio, Sérgio e Marco*; *de carro, de avião e de navio* 'by car, by plane, and by ship', or *Ondina cozinha, Danira ensina e Carolina estuda* 'Ondina cooks, Danira teaches, and Carolina studies.' Subordination in turn embeds a sentence into another by means of a function word such as the conjunction *que* 'that,' as in *Álvaro sabe que Mariano escreve* 'Álvaro knows that Mariano writes.' We will see more about coordinate and subordinate sentences in sections 4.10 and 4.11.

## 4.2    Syntactic functions vs. semantic roles

Besides the meaning of individual lexical words and the grammatical relationships expressed by syntactic devices, the meaning of a sentence depends on the *semantic roles* and the *syntactic functions* of its components. The distinction between these two categories may be grasped by examining sentences like those in example 6.

(6)     a. *Cardoso Gomes escreveu* Contracanto.
        'Cardoso Gomes wrote *Contracanto*.'
        b. Contracanto *foi escrito por Cardoso Gomes.*
        '*Contracanto* was written by Cardoso Gomes.'

In both sentences the noun *Cardoso Gomes* stands for the semantic actor°, that is the person who did the writing, whereas the book title *Contracanto* stands for the semantic patient°, that is what resulted from the action of writing. The semantic roles of *actor* and *patient* remain the same despite the fact that 6a and 6b have a different syntactic structures. In 6a *Cardoso Gomes* is the subject of the verb *escreveu* and *Contracanto* is its direct object. In 6b there is a passive construction (4.8.1) in which *Contracanto* is the subject of *foi escrito* while *Cardoso Gomes*, introduced by the preposition *por*, is the agent of the passive. Likewise, in 7a the nouns have the same semantic roles as in 7b:

(7)     a. *Lucrécia deu a maçã a Paulo.*
        'Lucretia gave the apple to Paul.'
        b. *A maçã foi dada a Paulo por Lucrécia.*
        'The apple was given to Paul by Lucretia.'

In either sentence *Lucrécia* is the semantic actor (the person who gives something), *maçã* is the semantic patient (the thing given) and *Paulo* is the semantic *benefactive°* (the person receiving something, irrespective of whether an actual benefit is involved). The syntactic functions of those words, however, vary in each case. In 7a *Lucrécia* is the subject of the verb *deu*, *Paulo* is its indirect object°, and *maçã* is its direct object; in 7b *maçã* is the subject of the passive construction *foi dada*, *Lucrécia* is the agent of the passive (characteristically introduced by the preposition *por*), and *Paulo* is the indirect object, introduced by the preposition *a*. English allows one more passive variation, in which the benefactive appears as the subject: *Paulo was given an apple by Lucretia*; this construction, however, does not work in Portuguese.

By substituting the verb *ganhar* 'to receive as a gift,' we create a new sentence, *Paulo ganhou a maçã de Lucrécia*, in which the benefactive (*Paulo*) appears as the subject and *Lucrécia*, the giver of the apple, as the semantic role *source*, introduced by the preposition *de*. Keeping semantic roles separate from syntactic functions (Table 4.1) helps us understand how the elements of a sentence interact with each other at the levels of semantic meaning and syntactic organization.

Table 4.1 *Correspondences between semantic roles and syntactic functions*

| Semantic roles | Syntactic functions |
| --- | --- |
| **Actor**: Whoever/whatever undergoes a process (*morrer* 'to die') or performs an action (*assaltar* 'to rob') | **Subject** (active sentence): ***Meu gato*** *morreu.* 'My cat died.' ***João*** *assaltou o banco.* 'John robbed the bank.' |
| **Patient**: The entity (person or thing) on whom the action is performed | **Direct object** (active sentence): *João assaltou* ***o banco****.* 'João robbed the bank.' **Subject** (passive sentence): *O **banco** foi assaltado.* 'The bank was robbed.' |
| **Benefactive**: Whoever receives a thing or favor (which is the semantic patient) | **Indirect object**: *Paulo deu um canivete **ao filho***. 'Paulo gave his son a pocket knife.' *Paulo entregou as flores **a Joana**.* 'Paulo handed the flowers to Joana.' |
| **Source**: Whoever or whatever originates a process (though not an action) | **Subject** (active sentence): *Joana recebeu uma herança de sua avó.* 'Joana received an inheritance from her grandmother.' |

## 4.3    Sentence types

Sentences may assert something, as in 8a–8b; ask a question, as in 8c–8d; or issue a comand, a request, an exhortation, or an invitation, as in 8e–8f. Any one of these three types may be either affirmative or negative.

(8)    a. *Eles moram em Lisboa.*
           'They live in Lisbon.'
      b. *Ela não vem hoje.*
           'She is not coming today.'
      c. *Você vem aqui sempre?*
           'Do you always come here?'
      d. *Vocês não querem vir com a gente?*
           'Won't you come along with us?'
      e. *Não comam essas maçãs.*
           'Don't eat those apples.'
      f. *Sente-se aqui ou ali, por favor.*
           'Please sit here or over there.'

A positive reply is made by repeating the verb of the question and placing the word *sim* 'yes' at the end (9a), whereas a negative reply is made by placing the word *não* before the verb; in BP a second *não* is placed after the verb as well (9b). Actually, in BP double or even triple negatives are perfectly correct and actually considered more polite in an answer (as in 9c) than using a single negative word.

(9)     a. – *Vocês falam inglês?* 'Do you speak English?'
            – *Falamos, sim.* 'Yes, we do.'
        b. – *Elas chegaram?* 'Have they arrived?'
            EP – *Não chegaram.* 'No, they haven't.'
            BP – *Não chegaram, não.* 'No, they haven't.'
        c. – *Já tomou o seu remédio?* 'Have you taken your medicine?'
            EP – *Não, ainda não tomei.* 'No, I haven't yet.'
            BP – *Não, ainda não tomei, não.* 'No, I haven't yet.'

## 4.4     Components of sentence structure

As mentioned above, a sentence (S) has a verb, which is the nucleus of its *verb phrase* (VP). The basic sentence format is S → NP + VP (that is, a sentence is generated as a noun phrase followed by a verb phrase) as in 10a. The verb phrase may include one or more noun phrases, as in 10b, or other phrase types, shown schematically in 11a–11c. Sentence structures are highlighted by bracketing in the examples.

(10)    a. [s [NP *Francisca*] [VP *chegou*]].
           'Francisca arrived.'
        b. [[s [NP *Francisca*] [VP [V *comprou*] [NP *carne*]]]].
           'Francisca bought meat.'

(11)    a. Adjectival phrase: [[s [NP *Selma* [[VP *está* [AdjP *alegre*]]]].
           'Selma is happy.'
        b. Adverbial phrase: [[s [NP *Nelson*] [[VP *fala* [AdvP *depressa*]]]].
           'Nelson talks fast.'
        c. Prepositional phrase: [[s [NP *Edwiges trabalha* [PrepP *por prazer*]]]].
           'Edwiges works for pleasure.'

Sentences 12a–12f include noun phrases made up of a pronoun (12a), a single noun (12b), coordinated nouns (12c), or a noun accompanied by a variety of modifiers, such as an article (12d), or a demonstrative and a possessive (12e), a demonstrative, a possessive and an adjective (12f).

(12)    a. [NP *Ela*] [VP *partiu*].
           'She left.'
        b. [NP *Francisca*] [VP *trabalha*].
           'Francisca works.'
        c. [NP *Selma e Margot*] [VP *estudam*].
           'Selma and Margot study.'
        d. [NP *O Fernando*] [VP *virá*].
           'Fernando will come.'

    e. [_NP_ *Aquele meu amigo*] [_VP_ *virá*].
      'That friend of mine will come.'
    f. [_NP_ *Aquela tua colega alemã*] [_VP_ *virá*].
      'That German colleague of yours will come.'

### 4.4.1     Verb phrases

In a structure like S → NP + VP the noun phrase constitutes the subject, and
the verb phrase, together with other sentence constituents, if any, make up the
predicate°. Adverbial phrases, shown in 13a–13c, provide additional information on how the action referred to by the verb is performed. Morphologically, an
adverbial phrase (AdvP) can include an adverb in -*mente* as in 13a, an adjective
functioning like an adverb as in 13b, or a prepositional phrase, as in 13c.

(13)    a. *Marina fala* [_AdvP_ [_Adv_ *rapidamente*]].
        'Marina talks fast.'
     b. *Greta anda* [_AdvP_ [_Adj_ *rápido*]].
        'Greta walks fast.'
     c. *Francisca lê* [_AdvP_ [_PrepP_ *com rapidez*]].
        'Francisca reads fast.'

### 4.4.2     Adverbial and prepositional phrases

A key difference between adverbial phrases and prepositional phrases is that
adverbial phrases can move around a sentence rather freely, as in 14, whereas
prepositional phrases remain attached to the sentence constituent they modify,
as in 15a, though not in the impossible 15b. (Constructions are possible in
certain poetic styles which need not concern us here.)

(14)    *Comprei a casa de manhã* ∼ *De manhã comprei a casa.*
     'I bought the house in the morning.'

(15)    a. *Comprei uma casa de tijolos.* 'I bought a brick house.'
     b. *\*De tijolos comprei uma casa.*

    Adverbs may be combined in sequences, as in 16a–16c. When two adverbs in
-*mente* are coordinated, it is possible to drop the suffix from all but the rightmost
one:

(16)    a. *Greta anda* [_AdvP_ [_Adv_ *muito*] [_Adv_ *rapidamente*]].
        'Greta walks very quickly.'
     b. *Jurema trabalhou* [_AdvP_ [_Adv_ *intensamente*] [_Adv_ *a noite toda*]]
       [_Adv_ *por prazer*]].
        'Jurema worked intensely all night for pleasure.'

c. *Ronalda estava cantando* [AdvP [Adv *rápida*], [Adv *intensa*]
*e* [Adv *alegremente*]].
'Ronalda was singing quickly, intensely, and happily.'

As well as functioning as adverbs, prepositional phrases signal a variety of relational meanings, as exemplified in 17a–17f:

(17)   a. Possession:   *Eu quero o carro* [PrepP *de Henrique*].
'I want Henrique's car.'
b. Company:   *Lucila saiu* [PrepP *com Marcelo*].
'Lucila went out with Marcelo.'
c. Place:   *Adagilsa está* [PrepP *in Coimbra*].
'Adagilsa is in Coimbra.'
d. Means:   *Elisa chegou* [PrepP *de táxi*].
'Elisa arrived by taxi.'
e. Manner:   *Selma acordou* [PrepP *em pânico*].
'Selma woke up in a panic.'
f. Motivation:   *Ela fez isso* [PrepP *por caridade*].
'She did that out of charity.'

In 18a–18b the prepositional phrase, introduced by *a* or *para* (the latter is far more common in BP but also occurs in popular EP) functions as an indirect object, which stands for the semantic benefactive.

(18)   a. *Entreguei o livro ao/para o Renato.*
'I handed the book to Renato.'
b. *Vou dar um presente a/para você.*
'I am going to give a gift to you.'

## 4.5      Subject and predicate

The subject, the element about which the sentence states something, is contained in the noun phrase with which the verb agrees. It may be simply a pronoun, as *eu* and *eles* in 19a or a noun (*as meninas chegaram* 'the girls arrived'). The subject may also be a verb in the infinitive, as in *compreender tudo isso é importante* 'understanding all that is important.' In such cases the verb is in the third person singular, e.g. *é* 'is' in 19b. All verbs, except impersonal ones (4.7), require a subject. The predicate, as its name suggests, contains information that is stated about the subject, e.g. *trabalho* and *ganham dinheiro* in 19a.

(19)   a. [S[Subj *Eu*] [Pred *trabalho*] *e* [Subj *eles*] [Pred *ganham dinheiro*]].
'I work and they make money.'
b. [S [Pred *É importante*] [Subj *compreender tudo isso*]].
'Understanding all that is important.'

### 4.5.1    Verb complements

Verbs like those in 20a–20b, which express a full meaning without the help of any complements, are called *intransitive°*.

(20)    a. *Meu cachorro morreu.*
           'My dog died.'
       b. *Chegou a primavera.*
           'Spring has arrived.'

Other verbs need a complement to complete the information they carry. Verbs like those in 21a–21b, which require a noun phrase that plays the syntactic function of direct object that corresponds to the semantic patient in active sentences (4.2), are called *transitive°*.

(21)    a. *Cláudia comprou os livros de Freud.*
           'Claudia bought Freud's books.'
       b. *Escreveste a carta?*
           'Have you written the letter?'

Like English, Portuguese allows transitive verbs without an overt direct object when used with a generic meaning (22a–22b). Unlike English, however, it also allows null direct objects that are understood from the context, as in the replies in 22c–22e:

(22)    a. *– O que ela faz? – Ela pinta e borda.*
           'What does she do?' 'She paints and embroiders.'
       b. *– O que é que você faz? – Eu importo e exporto.*
           'What is your line of work?' 'I import and export.'
       c. *– Vocês compraram os laptops? – Compramos, sim.*
           'Did you buy the laptops?' 'Yes, we bought [them].'
       d. *– Você quer um guarda-chuva? – Não, eu tenho.*
           'Do you want an umbrella?' 'No, I have [one].'
       e. *– Quando você vai escrever a carta? – Já escrevi.*
           'When are you going to write the letter?' 'I've already written [it].'

Other verbs, called *ditransitive°*, take both a direct object and an indirect object°. This component usually corresponds, in sentences like those in (23), to the semantic benefactive. Verbs that express the notion of giving something to someone (*dar* 'to give,' *oferecer* 'to offer,' *entregar* 'to hand over, to deliver,' *ofertar* 'to offer,' *emprestar* 'to loan'), or of requesting something from someone (*pedir* 'to ask,' *solicitar* 'to request,' *rogar* 'to beseech,' *implorar* 'to implore') fall into this category.

(23)     a. *Juca deu o dinheiro à Fernanda.*
            'Juca gave the money to Fernanda.'
         b. *Patrícia entregou as chaves do apartamento ao zelador.*
            'Patricia handed over the apartment keys to the custodian.'

There is also a category of verbs such as *agradar* 'to please,' *interessar* 'to interest,' and *pertencer* 'to belong,' called *indirect transitive*, that require an indirect object (but no direct object) expressed by an unstressed pronoun, as in example 24, or by a prepositional phrase, as in 25:

(24)     *Esse assunto não me agrada.*
         'That subject does not please me.'

(25)     *Eu acho que isso vai interessar a ele.*
         'I think this will interest him.'


### 4.5.2     Clitics

Clitics, or unstressed pronouns (3.4), have no stress of their own and function phonologically as an extra syllable attached to another word, usually a verb. They may come in *enclitic* position, that is, after the verb (26a) or in *proclitic* position, that is, before the verb (26b). A third possibility, namely *mesoclitic* position, with the clitic placed inside the verb, applies only to forms of the future or the conditional (26c–26d). Though used in European Portuguese, mesoclitic constructions only occur in BP as school-learned forms, usually in formal styles.

(26)     a. *Ele viu-me.*
            'He saw me.'
         b. *Ela me beijou.*
            'She kissed me.'
         c. EP *Entregar-lho-ei em Berkeley.*
            'I'll give it to you in Berkeley.'
         d. EP *Dar-te-iam os presentes.*
            'They would give you the gifts.'

Even for educated native speakers, clitic placement is one of the most vexing topics of Portuguese syntax, largely because it has been muddled by traditional grammars that neither reflect actual language use, nor take into account differences between speech and writing, or between BP and EP usage (Martins 1989:117). Our non-exhaustive presentation will deal first with the unstressed pronouns *me te se nos (vos) lhe lhes* (4.5.2.1), then with the unstressed third person pronouns *o a os as* (or their variants *lo la los las, no na nos nas*; see Table 3.5), which have a few pecularities of their own (4.5.2.2), then with *lhe/lhes* (4.5.2.3) and finally with the stressed pronouns used with prepositions (4.5.2.4).

*4.5.2.1 Position of me, te, se, nos (vos)*     In simple non-imperative verb forms in sentence-initial position, enclisis (27a–27b) is the general norm in EP and in formal BP. In unmonitored BP, however, proclisis is the general trend. Sentences like 27a–27c belong to a relatively careful level of speech in BP, where proclisis, even in utterance-initial position, is habitual in spontaneous speech, as in 27d.

(27)     a. *Parece-me que vai chover.*
             'It looks like rain to me.'
         b. *Pretende-se construir um hospital nesse lugar, mas eu duvido.*
             'They are planning to build a hospital in that place, but I doubt it.'
         c. *É, fala-se muito de processar os corruptos.*
             'Sure, they talk a lot about prosecuting the corrupt ones.'
         d. *Me parece que o coronel ainda não chegou.*
             'It seems to me that the colonel hasn't arrived yet.'

Whereas clitics in utterance-initial position are widespread in BP, literate speakers are often aware that this practice is frowned upon in formal usage and so may employ alternative constructions like 28:

(28)     a. *Estão pretendendo construir um hospital nesse terreno.*
             'They intend to build a hospital in that lot (on that site).'
         b. *Estão falando muito em processar os corruptos.*
             'They're talking a lot about prosecuting the corrupt ones.'
         c. *Tenho a impressão que ele ainda não chegou.*
             'I have the impression that he hasn't arrived yet.'

In imperative verb forms in utterance-initial positon, enclisis is the norm (29a–29b), although proclisis is widespread in BP (29c–29e). While 29a is possible in either EP or BP, 29b is normal in colloquial EP; given the general trend to avoid both clitic pronouns and direct commands, 29e would be a likely alternative in BP.

(29)     a. *Sente-se, por favor.*
             'Sit down, please.'
         b. EP *Chega-te cá, menina.*
             'Come closer, girl.'
         c. BP *Se enquadre!*
             'Stand at attention!'

    d. BP *Me desculpe, tá?*
       'Excuse me, ok?'
    e. BP *A senhora desculpe.*
       'I'm sorry, ma'am.'

If the verb is not in sentence-initial position, again EP tends to prefer enclisis (30), whereas BP prefers proclisis, as shown in 31.

(30)    a. EP *Isto irritou-me profundamente.*
        'That annoyed me deeply.'
    b. EP *A família juntou-se a ele mais tarde.*
        'The family joined him later.'
    c. EP *Eles perguntaram-me se queria vir.*
        'They asked me if I wanted to come along.'

(31)    a. BP *A Denise me pediu um favor.*
        'Denise asked a favor of me.'
    b. BP *Essas coisas me chateiam muito.*
        'Those things bother me a lot.'
    c. BP *Aí eles se juntaram.*
        'Then they shacked up together.'

Preference for proclisis in BP and for enclisis in EP extends to compound verb forms, where EP prefers to have the unstressed pronoun enclitic to the auxiliary, as in 32a–32b. BP, on the contrary, tends to have the pronoun proclitic to the main verb, with no hyphen, as in 32c–32d. The hyphenated variant used to be the norm in written BP but both forms coexist nowadays.

(32)    a. EP *Ele tinha-me falado desse assunto.*
        'He had talked to me about that subject.'
    b. EP *Elas estão-nos a observar.*
        'They are watching us.'
    c. BP *Eu tenho te visto na praia.*
        'I have seen you on the beach.'
    d. BP *Ela está te olhando.*
        'She's watching you.'

Likewise, if there is a modal verb° such as *dever, querer, poder* followed by either a simple or a compound tense, BP tends to prefer proclisis and EP tends to prefer enclisis to the modal, as in 33:

(33)    a. BP *Você devia me ver no trapézio.*
        'You should see me on the trapeze.'
    b. EP *Devias-me avisar.*
        'You should warn me.'

c. BP *Eles queriam me avisar desse problema.*
'They wanted to warn me about that problem.'

d. EP *Eu até que podia-te contar tudo, mas não vale a pena.*
'I could even tell you everything but it isn't worth it.'

Proclisis is generally conditioned by specific words, as in 34a–34l:

(34)    Negative words:
a. *Eu não te conto nada.*
'I'm not telling you anything.'

b. *Eu não me vejo fazendo isso.*
'I don't see myself doing that.'

Interrogative words:

c. *Quem me empresta o dinheiro do metrô?*
'Who will lend me the subway fare?'

d. *Quando te promoveram?*
'When did they promote you?'

Adverbs:

e. *Vocês sempre me dão problemas.*
'You always cause me problems.'

f. *Ontem me chamaram às três da madrugada.*
'Yesterday they called me at three in the morning.'

Relative pronouns:

g. *Acabou de passar aquele cara que te ligou hoje cedo.*
'That guy who called you up this morning has just come by.'

h. *Você precisa falar com quem tem autoridade para resolver isso.*
'You have to talk to who(ever) has authority to settle that.'

Subordinating conjunctions:

i. *Ele disse que me emprestava o dinheiro.*
'He told me he'd lend me the money.'

j. *Eu te chamo assim que me disserem alguma coisa.*
'I'll call you up as soon as they tell me something.'

A preposition that introduces a loose/independent infinitive:

k. *Ele trouxe um livro para te dar no Natal.*
'He brought a book to give you for Christmas.'

l. *Você tem um cigarro para me dar?*
'Have you got a cigarette to give me?'

*4.5.2.2 Position of o, a, os, as* Very much alive in EP, these unstressed pronouns have a low frequency in spoken BP. As mentioned in (3.4), these pronouns take the form *lo, la, los, las* after a verb form ending in *r*, *s*, or *z* (35a–35d) and the forms *no, na, nos, nas* after a nasal diphthong (35e).

(35)   a. EP *Queres vendê-los?* 'Do you want to sell them?'
       b. BP *Nós só queríamos cumprimentá-lo pelo seu aniversário.*
          'We just wanted to greet you on your birthday.'
       c. EP *Tomou o prato e pô-lo no microndas.*
          'P3sg took the dish and put it in the microwave.'
       d. EP *Faz bonecas de madeira, e fá-las muito bem.*
          'P3sg makes wooden dolls and makes them very well.'
       e. *Ponham-nas no armário.*
          'Put them in the closet.'

These pronouns also tend to be enclitic in EP except when proclisis is conditioned by the words mentioned in example 34, as exemplified in 36a–36b:

(36)   a. *Creio que não os tratamos muito mal.*
          'I think we don't treat them too poorly.'
       b. *É assim, se não me engano.*
          'That's it, if I'm not mistaken.'

While these clitics are used regularly in EP, there is a strong tendency in vernacular BP either to dispense with them altogether or to use *ele, ela, eles, elas* as a direct object (section 7.3.2.3), as shown in (37a)–(37c):

(37)   a. *É, não trataram eles muito bem, não.*
          'Yeah, they didn't treat them too well.'
       b. *Aquelas camisas, eu pus elas na cômoda.*
          'Those shirts, I put them in the dresser.'
       c. *Você sabe quando é que a gente vai poder ver ele?*
          'Do you know when we're going to be able to see him?'

The pronoun *o/lo/no* may refer to an aggregate of things or circumstances. In BP this practice is limited to monitored speech (38a), whereas in unmonitored speech the clitic may be left out altogether (38b):

(38)   *Já fez o que tinha que fazer?*
       'Have you done what you had to do?'
       a. *– Não, mas vou fazê-lo amanhã.*
          'No, but I'm going to do it tomorrow.'
       b. *– Não, mas vou fazer amanhã.*
          'No, but I'm going to do [it] tomorrow.'

*4.5.2.3 The pronouns lhe, lhes*    The clitic *lhe(s)* is essentially a third person indirect object pronoun which refers to the listener, as in 39a–39b, or to a third party, as in 39c. Although *lhe(s)* may occur with this function in monitored BP, it is rare in unmonitored speech. Besides, having either a second or third person referent makes *lhe, lhes* ambiguous, which may explain the marked preference for casting the indirect object as a prepositional phrase with *a/para* combined with *ele/s ela/s, você/s, o/s senhor/es, a/s senhora/s*, as in 40a–40b:

(39)    a. *Senhor Paulo, eu tenho um documento para lhe entregar.*
        'Mr Paulo, I have a document to give you.'
    b. *Senhores, amanhã eu vou lhes dar todas as intruções.*
        'Gentlemen, tomorrow I am going to give you all the instructions.
    c. *O gerente chamou o porteiro para lhe entregar o abono.*
        'The manager called the doorman to give him the bonus.'

(40)    a. BP *Aí eu entreguei o presente para ela.*
        'Then I gave her the gift.'
    b. BP *Quero dar isto aqui para o senhor.*
        'I want to give you this, sir.'
    c. BP *Ele queria oferecer um livro ao professor.*
        'He wanted to offer a book to the teacher.'

Perhaps to compensate for the low frequency of *o, a, os, as* as a direct object in unmonitored BP, many speakers – even educated ones – use *lhe* as direct object, creating sentences like those in 41a–41c, which traditional grammarians ineffectually frown upon. Such regular occurrence of constructions with direct object *lhe(s)* where normative grammar rules would call for *o/a(s)*, however, strongly suggests that a restructuring of the referential values of the pronoun system (Table 3.5) is taking place in BP.

(41)    a. BP *Seu Paulo, eu quero lhe ouvir sobre esse assunto.*
        'Mr. Paulo, I want to hear you about this subject.' (for *quero ouvi-lo*).
    b. BP *Se vocês mudarem para Santos, pode deixar que nós vamos lhes visitar.*
        'If you move to Santos, be sure we'll call on you.'
    c. BP *Então eu lhe espero à uma.*
        'Then I'll expect you at one (o'clock).'

*4.5.2.4 Prepositional pronouns*    As their name indicates, prepositional pronouns (Table 3.5) occur as complements in prepositional phrases, as in 42a–42b. As such, they often have the specific function of an indirect object introduced by either *a* or *para* (42c–42d). Another is that of agent of a passive construction, with *por* (42e–42f):

(42)  a. *Aparentemente você não acredita em mim.*
          'Apparently you don't believe in me.'
       b. *Não posso viver sem ti, meu amor.*
          'I can't live without you, my love.'
       c. EP *Ele entregou o jornal a ti, e não a mim.*
          'He handed the newspaper to you, not to me.'
       d. *Você trouxe aquele dinheiro para mim?*
          'Have you brought that money for me?'
       e. EP *Desculpa-me, mas esse documento deveria ser assinado por ti.*
          'Excuse me, but that document should be signed by you.'
       f. *Isso nunca foi aprovado por mim.*
          'That has never been approved by me.'

Another use is that of direct object, often with a slightly emphatic value, as in 43:

(43)  *Eles afirmaram que viram a mim no parque, eu, que nunca fui lá.*
       'They stated they saw me at the park, I, who have never been there.'

There are several areas in which educated usage contradicts normative rules. One example is the use in BP of the first person prepositional pronoun *mim* as the subject of a verb in the infinitive, as in 44a, where a prescriptive rule would call for *eu*, as in 44b:

(44)  a. *Esses arquivos são para mim guardar?*
          'Are these files for me to put away?'
       b. *Esses arquivos são para eu guardar?*
          'Are these files for me to put away?'

Another example, this time from EP, involves the stressed third person pronoun *si*. Originally a reflexive and regularly used as such (45a), *si* also occurs non-reflexively as a polite way of referring to one's interlocutor, thus precluding choice between intimate *tu*, or less formal *você*, or formal *o senhor/a senhora*, as in examples 45b–45d taken from an e-mail (7.3.2.3; 8.4).

(45)  a. *Ele só pensa em si.*
          'He only thinks about himself.'
       b. EP *Nessa revista encontrei, além de si, outros amigos que muito admiro.*
          'In that journal I found, besides you, other friends whom I admire a lot.'

    c. EP *Este livrinho é para si.*
      'This little book is for you.'
    d. EP *Isso foi feito por si?*
      'Was this done by you?'

## 4.6    Reflexive constructions

In a reflexive construction a clitic associated with the verb matches the subject in person an number, as in 46–48. In 46a–46c the verb conveys a truly reflexive action in which the actor and the patient have the same referent. In 47 there is an action but no actual patient to receive it, and *levantar-se* may be considered an intransitive verb like *acordar* 'to wake up' or *adormecer* 'to fall asleep' (as opposed, say, to *Eu levantei a mala* 'I lifted the suitcase,' where the verb is clearly transitive).

(46)    a. *E aí Judas se enforcou.*
       'And then Judas hanged himself.'
     b. EP *Banhas-te todos os dias?*
       'Do you bathe every day?'
     c. *Alice olhou-se no espelho.*
       'Alice looked at herself in the mirror.'

(47)    *Geralmente eu me levanto às sete horas e nunca me deito antes da meia-noite.*
     'Usually I get up at seven o'clock and never go to bed before midnight.'

   In 48a–48c the notion of semantic reflexivity is even more tenuous. In 48a the semantic experiencer *Selma* undergoes the (essentially involuntary) process of remembering something; similar verbs include *recordar-se* 'to remember,' *esquecer-se* 'to forget.' In 48b there is no action, reflexive or otherwise; the subject *minha cidade* 'our town' is inanimate, and the fact that *chamar-se* is morphologically reflexive is best interpreted as idiomatic. Finally, in 48c the verb *queixar-se* 'to complain' refers to an action without a patient/direct object and belongs to a subset of intransitive verbs requiring a semantically empty reflexive clitic. Other verbs in this group are *orgulhar-se (de)* 'to be proud (of),' *envergonhar-se (de)* 'to be ashamed (of).'

(48)    a. *Selma lembrou-se de que tinha um encontro.*
       'Selma remembered she had an appointment.'
     b. *A minha cidade se chamava Batatais.*
       'My town's name was Batatais / My town was called Batatais.'
     c. *O Daniel se queixa sem motivo.*
       'Daniel complains for no reason.'

As these examples suggest, the label "reflexivity" has two interpretations. One is the notion of an action whose actor and patient have the same referent, such as *cortar-se* 'to cut oneself,' *barbear-se* 'to shave oneself,' or *enforcar-se* 'to hang oneself.' Secondly, there is reflexivity as an idiosyncratic syntactic phenomenon, as in verbs like *queixar-se* 'to complain,' *esquecer-se* 'to forget,' *arrepender-se* 'to repent,' where the required clitic matches the subject in person and number, but lacks a semantic interpretation. It is not surprising that such reflexive clitics should be regularly dropped in unmonitored BP, as in 49a–49d, a topic to which we will return in 7.3.2.4.

(49)    a. *Eu deito e levanto muito tarde.*
           'I go to bed and get up rather late.'
        b. *Pára de queixar!*
           'Stop complaining!'
        c. *O banco abre às dez.*
           'The bank opens at ten.'
        d. *Eu arrependo muito de ter abandonado a faculdade.*
           'I very much regret having dropped out of college.'

### 4.6.1    Reciprocity

Reflexive constructions with a plural verb like those in 50a–50c are interpreted as involving a reciprocal action. In 50a each member of the subject noun phrase (*o patrão, eu*) is simultaneously an actor and a patient. Sentence 50b, in turn, ambiguously allows for two interpretations: one is reciprocal, along the lines of 50a, and in the other each actor performs a reflexive action. In this case the sentence may be seen as a compressed variant of two coordinate reflexive sentences, namely *o marido se matou e a mulher se matou* 'the husband killed himself and the wife killed herself.' Finally, 50c involves the singular noun phrase *a gente* as a substitute for the first person plural and is the equivalent of the slightly more formal *Nós nos falamos mas não nos beijamos.*

(50)    a. *O patrão e eu nos cumprimentamos na saída.*
           'The boss and I greeted each other on our way out.'
        b. *O marido e a mulher se mataram.*
           'The husband and the wife killed each other/themselves.'
        c. *A gente se fala, mas não se beija.*
           'We talk to each other but we aren't real buddies.' (lit. 'One talks to each other but one does not kiss each other.')

These sentences have the same syntactic structure, and the reason for the difference in interpretation lies in the semantics of verbs like *cumprimentar* 'to greet' (just like *chamar* 'to call,' *abraçar* 'to embrace,' *beijar* 'to kiss,' *espancar* 'to beat up,' *empurrar* 'to push'), which refer to actions in which the actor and the patient normally have different referents. On the other hand, verbs like *matar, cortar* 'to cut,' *barbear* 'to shave,' *pentear* 'to comb,' *coçar* 'to scratch' denote actions one can perform on oneself as well as on others. Thus, a sentence like 50a may be seen as containing two separate sentences, namely *O patrão me cumprimentou* and *Eu cumprimentei o patrão*. Such ambiguity may be avoided by adding phrases like *um ao outro* 'each other' as needed.

## 4.7     Null subjects

Portuguese allows omission of the subject, whether it is made explicit by the form of the verb, as in 51a, where *moramos* clearly refers to *nós*, or whether context permits identification of a third person subject, as in 51b:

(51)     a. *Moramos aqui.*
              'We live here.'
          b. *Ela descia o morro todo dia e dizia que adorava a praia.*
              'She walked down the hill every day and said [she] loved the beach.'

Certain verbs, however – such as those referring to weather phenomena (3.5.6), have no subject and occur only in the third person singular. Some linguists postulate for such sentences a structure NP + VP in which the noun phrase is semantically empty. Note that some such verbs can be used figuratively with a subject, 52b.

(52)     a. *– Nevou na serra?*
              *– Não, mas trovejou e choveu muito.*
              'Did it snow in the sierra?'
              'No, but it thundered and rained a lot.'
          b. *O senador trovejou insultos.*
              'The senator thundered insults.'

Other impersonal verbs are *fazer* 'to do' and *haver* 'to have' used to express time elapsed (53a–53b) as well as *haver* and *ter* (the latter being typical of BP) when used to indicate existence (53c–53d). This use of *haver/ter* is equivalent in meaning to English *there is/are*, but a crucial difference is that the accompanying noun phrase (*vários bancos livres, quatro soldados*) is the direct object of the verb:

(53)     a. *Faz tempo que não nos vemos.*
              'We haven't seen each other for a while.'
          b. *Fazia dez dias que não chovia.*
              'It had not rained for ten days.'

c. *Havia vários bancos livres na praça.*
'There were several free benches on the square.'
d. BP *Tinha quatro soldados esperando na saída.*
'There were four soldiers waiting at the exit.'

However, possibly because such subjectless constructions go against the general pattern of verbs, in unmonitored speech it is not unusual for the direct object to be interpreted as the subject, triggering the agreement rule in BP, yielding sentences like 54a–54c, which are rather common, despite being condemned by prescriptive grammar.

(54)    a. BP *Fazem oito meses que ele faleceu.*
'It's been eight months since he passed away.'
b. BP *Houveram muitos problemas.*
'There were many problems.'
c. BP *Tinham muitas pessoas na Noca ontem?*
'Were there many people at Noca's yesterday?'

## 4.8    Verb phrases with more than one verb

As we saw in 3.5.4, Portuguese uses compound tenses made up of one or two auxiliary verbs and a non-finite verb form:

| | | |
|---|---|---|
| *tenho falado* | *estou comendo* | *estou a comer* |
| 'I have spoken' | 'I am eating' | 'I am eating' |
| *tenho estado trabalhando* | *tenho estado a trabalhar* | *vou sair* |
| 'I have been working' | 'I have been working' | 'I'm going to leave' |

In such constructions the first auxiliary verb occurs in a conjugated form, but stripped of its original lexical meaning, and becomes a carrier of grammatical notions such as tense/aspect and person/number, while lexical meaning is conveyed by the main verb in a non-finite form (gerund, infinitive, participle). Although some grammarians insist on considering them periphrases rather than true tenses, from the language user's viewpoint these constructions have a unitary meaning and function just like the simple verb tenses. Other constructions with two or more verbs, however, present specific features that will be analyzed in the following sections.

### 4.8.1    *The passive construction and other* auxiliary + verb *constructions*

The label "passive," a holdover from Latin grammar (5.3.4), refers to a verb phrase in which a form *ser* combines with the participle of a transitive verb, as in

55a–55b. The subject noun phrase contains the semantic patient. The semantic actor, if there is one, appears in a prepositional phrase introduced by *por* (or, in archaizing styles, *de*). Unlike in compound verb tenses like *tenho amado* 'I have loved,' in passives the participle agrees with the subject in number and gender:

(55)     a. *O desfile da escola de samba foi patrocinado pela prefeitura.*
             'The samba club parade was sponsored by City Hall.'
         b. *Os bailes de carnaval são financiados pela máfia da droga.*
             'The Carnival balls are financed by the drug mafia.'

The examples in 56a–56f exemplify passive-like sentences in which a participle is combined with other auxiliaries, such as *estar* or *ficar*:

(56)     a. *A garota estava acompanhada por um médico.*
             'The girl was accompanied by a doctor.'
         b. *A casa esteve vigiada por dois guardas durante várias semanas.*
             'The house was watched by two guards for several weeks.'
         c. *A plantação está arruinada pela praga.*
             'The plantation is ruined by the pest.'
         d. *As passeatas estão proibidas pelo governo.*
             'The demonstrations are banned by the government.'
         e. *O trombadinha ficou enterrado no mato.*
             'The street kid got buried in the woods.'
         f. *Ficou confirmado que os dois carros estavam em mau estado de manutenção.*
             'It was confirmed that both cars were in a poorly maintained condition.'

Sentences 56a–56b are about states that result from actions and persist as long as the agents (expressed by the agent complement in *por + NP*) continue to perform those actions. In 56c the state expressed by the participle (*arruinada*) is irreversible, but in 56d it may be reversed, provided the prohibition is lifted. In 56e–56f *enterrado* and *confirmado* likewise convey a state created by an action, but the focus is the result rather than the action itself.

Analogous constructions with verbs such as *andar* 'to walk,' *viver* 'to live,' *achar-se* 'to find oneself,' *ver-se* 'to see oneself' express shades of meaning of *to be* and the participle functions here as a descriptive adjective. In 57a and 57b *anda* and *vive* suggest a continuing or repetitive situation, perhaps more intensely in the latter case. In 57d *acha-se* (or its synonym *encontra-se*) is a stylistically more sophisticated way of saying *está*.

(57)     a. *Adalgisa anda deprimida ultimamente.*
             'Adalgisa has been depressed lately.'

    b. *Ele vivia amargurado pela morte do filho.*
       'He was constantly embittered by his son's death.'
    c. *Teve um momento que quase eu me vi perdido, mas consegui
       superar.*
       'There was a moment when I was almost lost, but I managed to
       overcome it.'
    d. *Infelizmente o diretor acha-se completamente enganado.*
       'Unfortunately the director is completely mistaken.'

Like *estar*, which combines with a gerund to make up continuous verb tenses
(3.5.4), the verbs *andar* 'to walk,' *vir* 'to come,' and *ir* 'to go' also combine
with a gerund to form constructions that focus on the ongoingness of the event,
action, or process referred to by a verb:

(58)    a. *Ela anda bebendo muito.*
       'She has been drinking a lot.'
    b. *A gente vinha trabalhando sem ganhar nada mais de um mês.*
       'We had been working without earning anything for longer than a
       month.'
    c. *Aí eu disse para ele, "Espera aí na fila enquanto eu vou
       comprando as entradas."*
       'Then I told him, "Wait in line while I buy the tickets."'

## 4.8.2    Constructions with modals

Like auxiliaries, modals are verbs which combine with an infinitive or a gerund
to form two-verb constructions with the same subject. Unlike auxiliaries, modals
preserve their basic lexical meaning, as *dever* 'must, should, be probable' and
*poder* 'to be able to, may' in 59a–59b. Furthermore, *modal + verb* constructions
function like a unit that may be combined with an auxiliary to form a compound
tense, as in 59c–59d

(59)    a. *Eu acho que ela deve partir amanhã.*
       'I think she should leave tomorrow.'
    b. *Pode deixar isso em cima da mesa.*
       'You may leave that on the table.'
    c. *O avião dele devia estar saindo naquele instante mesmo.*
       'His plane must have been leaving that very minute.'
    d. *Ela disse que não vai poder trazer as taças de vinho.*
       'She said she would not be able to bring the wine glasses.'

Two modals may also be combined, as in 60, but while *dever* and *poder* are
combined directly with an infinitive, *acabar, começar,* and *continuar* combine
directly with a gerund, as in 61a–61c.

(60)    *O Daniel deveria poder ajudar você.*
        'Daniel should be able to help you.'

(61)    a. *Eu vou acabar votando no PT.*
           'I'll end up voting for the Workers' Party.'
        b. *O Daniel já começou falando mal do governo.*
           'Daniel has already started badmouthing the administration.'
        c. *E vocês duas continuam saindo juntas?*
           'And the two of you are still seeing each other?'

Other modals systematically combine with an infinitive by means of a specific connector, as in 62a–62e:

(62)    a. *Meu marido* acabou de *sair.*
           'My husband has just left.'
        b. *Os sequestradores* acabaram por *se entregar.*
           'The kidnapers ended by turning themselves in.'
        c. *Por que você não* deixa de *fumar?*
           'Why don't you give up smoking?'
        d. *Hoje eu não posso sair*, tenho que *cuidar das crianças.*
           'I can't go out today, I have to take care of the kids.'
        e. *A gente* tem de *acertar essa dívida o quanto antes.*
           'We must settle that debt as soon as possible.'

Finally, *haver de* combined with an infinitive, as in 63a–63b, suggests futurity combined with strong determination:

(63)    a. *Eu hei de me vingar daquele canalha.*
           'I'll get even with that scoundrel.'
        b. *Ela há de pagar o que me fez.*
           'She'll pay for what she did to me.'

Since modals may be combined with auxiliaries in passive constructions, strings of several verbs are possible (64a), although constructions of more than four verbs, like 64b, are not very frequent, probably because they involve redundancy that interferes with interpretation:

(64)    a. *Aquela casa* deve ter sido pintada *várias vezes.*
           'That house must have been painted several times.'
        b. *Esse assunto* deve ter estado sendo debatido *na imprensa com alguma freqüência.*
           'That subject must have been being debated in the press with some frequency.'

## 4.9 Actor indeterminacy

Certain syntactic constructions keep the semantic actor indeterminate, either because it is unknown, irrelevant, or obvious in the context, or simply because the speaker does not care to mention it. One way of doing this is by means of a passive without an agent phrase (65a–65c).

(65)  a. *Foram abertas vinte mil contas novas no mês passado.*
        'Twenty thousand new accounts were opened last month.'
      b. *Foram sequestrados dois industriais no fim de semana.*
        'Two industrialists have been kidnapped over the weekend.'
      c. *Os sequestradores foram presos na quinta-feira.*
        'The kidnapers were arrested on Thursday.'

Another device for signalling an indeterminate actor is the clitic *se* – often called "indeterminate *se*" – used with the approximate meaning of *one* or *you*, as in 66:

(66)  a. *Naquele tempo se estudava de verdade.*
        'In those days one studied really hard.'
      b. *Em Lisboa vive-se muito bem.*
        'One lives rather well in Lisbon.'
      c. *Comprava-se e vendia-se muito gado mas ninguém ficava rico.*
        'They bought and sold a lot of cattle but nobody got rich.'
      d. *Aluga-se quarto para rapaz solteiro.* (A sign.)
        'Room for rent for a young single man.'
      e. *Vendem-se apartamentos novos e usados.* (A sign.)
        'New and used apartments for sale.'
      f. *Conserta-se motos.* (A sign.)
        'Motorcycles fixed.'
      g. *Aqui se vende e se compra todas as coisas que você pode imaginar e mais algumas.*
        'Here they buy and sell everything you can imagine and then some.'

The indeterminate *se* is widely used in expositive style (Perini 2002a:268), e.g. in written recipes such as the one in example 67:

(67)  *Amassa-se bem meio limão e acrescenta-se a cachaça devagar. A seguir mexe-se bem, adicionando gelo moído. Adoça-se a gosto e então bebe-se em boa companhia.*
      'Crush half a lime and add the sugar cane brandy slowly. Then stir (it) well, adding crushed ice. Sweeten [it] to taste and then drink [it] in good company.'

Although historically derived from a reflexive form, the indeterminate *se* does not connote reflexivity but rather a semantically unspecified actor. This is particularly apparent when the verb is intransitive and thus cannot be related to a patient. Since reflexivity requires an actor and a patient with the same referent, intransitive verbs cannot participate in a reflexive action.

Another characteristic of the indeterminate *se* is that it is not normally used with verbs that describe a non-human action, such as *pastar* 'to graze.' Thus a sentence like *Pasta-se bem aqui* 'One grazes well here' receives a figurative interpretation, such as a comment on the quality of food or the manners of those eating.

A transitive verb such as *comprar, vender*, or *alugar* (66c–66d) appears in the third person singular form if the semantic patient is singular (*muito gado, quarto*). Prescriptive grammarians have traditionally adopted a formal interpretation for such constructions: the semantic patient is analyzed as the subject, and consequently its number will determine whether the verb should be singular as in 66d or plural as in 66e. Constructions without agreement, like 66f or 66g, however, occur regularly in the language and cannot be dismissed simply as resulting from poor grammar.

The indeterminate *se* construction is a unique combination of semantic and syntactic features (Azevedo 1976, 1980) and should not be analyzed as a variant of other sentence types, such as reflexives or passives. Sentences like 68a may have a reflexive reading, with *portas* as the apparent actor and patient, as when we interpret them to mean that opening and closing results from an automatic process. Likewise, in 68b *apartmentos* clearly is not the actor but rather the patient, and the apparent reflexivity is a metaphorical way of saying that selling them is so easy that it seems to happen of its own accord without a semantic actor's intervention. This is clearly different from a reflexive sentence with *vender* such as 68c.

(68)    a. *As portas se abrem às oito da manhã e se fecham às seis da tarde.*
            'The doors open at eight a.m. and close at six p.m.'
        b. *Esses apartamentos se vendem sozinhos.*
            'These apartments sell themvelves.'
        c. *Aquelas pobres mulheres tinham que se vender para comer.*
            'Those poor women had to sell themselves to eat.'

On the other hand, whilst in 69a there is no hint of human intervention (it might be a reference to doors that opened automatically), in 69b human intervention is assumed and there is no suggestion of any automatic process. Although the glosses in 69b suggest a semantic equivalence between the indeterminate *se* and agentless passives, it does not follow that they are structurally equivalent:

(69)    a. *As portas se abrem às oito.*
        'The doors open at eight.'
    b. *Aqui se abre as portas às oito.*
        'Here they open the doors/the doors are opened at eight.'

This analysis provides a basis to consider the indeterminate *se* as having the same function in all the sentences in 66. The subject–verb agreement in sentences like 68a is simply the result of the subject (*portas*) being interpreted as a plural and the structure being formally reflexive – without implying, however, semantic reflexivity (Perini 1998:270–272).

Other syntactic devices for leaving the semantic actor unidentified include verbs in third person plural, with or without the pronoun *eles*:

(70)    a. *Deixaram um pacote para você.*
        '[They]'ve left a package for you.'
    b. *Você não tem medo de eles acharem ruim?*
        'Aren't you afraid they may not like it?'
    c. *Ih, rapaz, eles estão dizendo que o governo vai soltar outro pacote econômico.*
        'Hey man, they're saying the government's going to bring out another economic package.'

Spoken BP goes one step further and favors a subjectless construction, as in 71, with the verb in the third person singular (7.3.2.5).

(71)    a. *Faz favor, como é que chega na Raposo Tavares?*
        'Please, how do you get to Raposo Tavares [highway]?'
    b. *Para desmontar a pistola, primeiro tira o carregador.*
        'To take the pistol apart, first [one] remove(s) the clip.'

## 4.10    Joining sentences: Coordination

Coordination (4.1.5) consecutively arranges two or more sentences which, while having the same status, may share a specific relationship, such as cause and effect (72a) or temporal sequencing (72b), either implicit or made explicit by specific coordinating conjunctions (3.7). The most frequent *additive* coordinating conjunctions are *e* 'and' and *nem* 'nor, neither.'

(72)    a. *Passei a luz vermelha, o meganha me multou, meu dia estragou.*
        'I went through the red light, the cop gave me a ticket, my day got ruined.'

b. *Vamos dar uma volta no quintal, chupar umas laranjas, e molhar os pés no ribeirão?*
'Shall we take a walk in the backyard, eat some oranges, and wet our feet in the creek?'

c. *Ele nem come nem deixa comer.*
'He neither eats nor lets (others) eat.'

*Adversative* conjunctions (*mas* 'but,' *porém* 'however') signal a contrast:

(73)    a. *Eles querem ficar ricos mas não trabalham.*
'They want to get rich but do not work.'

b. *O Antonio sabe ler inglês porém não fala.*
'Antonio can read English but does not speak it.'

*Disjunctive* conjunctions (*ou* 'or') indicate a contrast:

(74)    a. *Vens comigo ou vais com elas?*
'Will you come with us or will you go with them?'

b. *Ou é neste prédio ou é naquele.*
'It is either in this building or in that one.'

*Explicative* conjunctions (*pois* 'since,' *logo* 'therefore') signal an explanation:

(75)    a. *Não posso fazer nada, pois não tenho recursos.*
'I cannot do anything since I have no means.'

b. *Você não explica as coisas, logo eu não posso ajudar.*
'You don't explain things, therefore I cannot help.'

Coordination may also be brought about by a variety of locutions, such as the following (as shown in 76a–76c):

> *não só . . . mas também, não só . . . como também* 'not only . . . but also'
> *tanto . . . como* 'as much . . . as'
> *quanto mais/menos . . . (tanto) mais/menos* 'the more/less . . . the more/less'

(76)    a. *Isso* não *só é possível* como também *é indispensável.*
'This is not only possible but also indispensable.'

b. *Ele trabalha* tanto como *o outro rouba.*
'He works as much as the other steals.'

c. Quanto mais *a gente trabalha,* menos *dinheiro tem.*
'The more we work the less money we have.'

## 4.11    Joining sentences: Subordination

Subordination consists in embedding° one sentence (called the *subordinate* or *embedded* clause) in another (called the *matrix* or *main* clause). Once it becomes a constituent of the matrix, the subordinate clause functions like a noun (*nominal clause*), an adverb (*adverbial clause*), or an adjective (*adjective* or *relative clause*).

Subordination taxes listeners' memories by requiring them to recall what has been said in order to relate it syntactically to what is being said. This is probably why the incidence of subordination increases in direct proportion to the level of formality. Whereas an informal chat tends to rely more on coordination, a formal presentation (say, at a university lecture) is likely to rely more on subordination, particularly in technical and scientific fields (Marques 1995).

### 4.11.1   Subordinate nominal clauses

The syntactic function of a subordinate nominal clause (NomC) is determined by the type of the verb in the matrix. Thus the bracketed NP in 77a and the bracketed embedded sentence in 77b function as the direct object of the transitive verb *anunciaram*:

(77)    a. *Anunciaram* [NP *a chegada do avião*].
            'They've announced [NP the plane's arrival].'
        b. *Anunciaram* [NomC *que o avião chegou*].
            'They've announced [NomC that the plane has arrived].'

In such cases the verb is transitive, and the subordinate clause functions as its direct object, which may be introduced by connectors like *que* as in 77b or *se, quando, como,* as in 78a–78c. In such cases the subordinate clause may be replaced by an anaphoric demonstrative like *isso* or *aquilo* (that is, *sei/disse/perguntei isso/aquilo* 'I know/said/asked this/that').

(78)    a. *Eu não sei* [NomC *se eles vêm*].
            'I don't know [NomC if they are coming].'
        b. *Ele não disse* [NomC *quando vem*].
            'He didn't say [NomC when he's coming].'
        c. *Eu perguntei* [NomC *como eles vinham*].
            'I asked [NomC how they were coming].'

In 79, the bracketed nominal clause S functions as the subject of *é*. In this case a confirmation-seeking rejoinder might be *isso é verdade?* 'is that true?'

(79)    *É verdade* [NomC *que ele chegou à noite*].
        'It is true [NomC he arrived in the evening].'

A subordinate nominal clause may also function as the subject of an impersonal verb as in 80a–80b, or of an impersonal construction as in 80c–80d, or of a full matrix sentence as in 80e:

(80)   a. *Acontece* [NomC *que elas não querem vir*].
       'What happens is (As it happens) that [NomC they don't want to come].'
   b. *Parece* [NomC *que o trem está atrasado de novo*].
       'It seems [NomC the train is late again].'
   c. *Bom, o importante é* [NomC *que elas chegaram inteiras*].'
       'Well, what matters is [NomC that they arrived in one piece].'
   d. *O melhor da história foi* [Nom *que elas chegaram ensopadas*].
       'The best part of the story was [Nom that they arrived soaked].'
   e. *Me alegra muito* [NomC *que vocês entraram na faculdade*].
       'I'm very pleased [NomC that you got into college].'

Two or more subordinate nominal clauses may be joined by a connector as in 81a. If the same connector such as *que* is needed in both clauses, it may be omitted in the second clause in informal speech, as in 81b:

(81)   a. *Ela disse para a gente* [NomC [NomC *que ia viajar*] *e* [NomC *quando ia chegar*]].
       'She told us [NomC [NomC she was going to travel]] and [NomC when she was going to arrive].'
   b. *Eu sabia* [[Nom *que ele estava sem carro*] *e* [Nom *ia chegar atrasado*]].
       'I knew [[NomC he was without a car] and [NomC was going to be late]].'

### 4.11.2   Subordinate relative (or adjective) clauses

A subordinate adjective or relative clause (RelC) is embedded in the matrix clause by a relative pronoun such as *que* or one of the others shown in Table 4.2.

(82)   a. *Ontem eu fiquei conhecendo uma moça* [RelC *que fala espanhol muito bem*].
       'Yesterday I met a young woman [RelC who speaks Spanish very well].'
   b. *O rapaz* [RelC *que toca piano*] *é o meu irmão*.
       'The young man [RelC who plays the piano] is my brother.'

In 82a we understand that the subject of *fala* is *moça*, just as in 82b we recognize *o rapaz* as the subject of *estava tocando*. Also, the clause *que fala*

Table 4.2 *Relative pronouns*

| | Restrictive | Non-restrictive | After prep. | Free relative | Whole clause as antecedent |
|---|---|---|---|---|---|
| Invariable | | | | | |
| *que* 'that, who, which' | yes | yes | yes | – | – |
| *quem* 'who' | – | – | yes | yes | – |
| *o que* 'what' | – | – | yes | yes | yes |
| Variable | | | | | |
| *o qual* (m.sg.), *a qual* (f.sg.) 'which' | – | yes | yes | – | – |
| *os quais* (m.pl.), *as quais* (f.pl.) 'which' | – | yes | yes | – | – |
| *cujo* (m.sg.), *cuja* (f.sg.) 'whose' | yes | yes | yes | – | – |
| *cujos* (m.pl.), *cujas* (f.pl.) 'whose' | yes | yes | yes | – | – |
| Adverbial | | | | | |
| *onde* 'where' (place) | yes | yes | yes | yes | – |
| *como* 'how' (manner) | yes | – | – | – | – |

qualifies *moça* in the same way as the adjective *hispanoparlante* 'Spanish-speaking' in *Conheci uma moça hispanoparlante* 'I met a Spanish-speaking young woman.' Although *pianotocante* 'piano-playing' is not a recognized adjective in Portuguese, we can just as easily gloss *o rapaz que está tocando piano* as 'the piano-playing young man.'

*4.11.2.1 Restrictive vs. non-restrictive relative clauses*    A relative clause (RelC) may be *restrictive* or *non-restrictive*. A restrictive clause provides information essential to characterize the noun phrase functioning as its antecendent. Thus in 83a–83c the information contained in *me ajudou, é advogado, está em cima do piano* is restricted to the specific antecedent it characterizes (*o meu amigo, um primo meu, um martelo*); the assumption is that although there may exist other friends, cousins, or hammers, the speaker is only interested in the one that helped him/is a lawyer/is on the piano.

(83)    a. *O amigo* [RelC *que me ajudou*] *mora em Coimbra.*
            'The friend [RelC who helped me] lives in Coimbra.'
        b. *Eu posso perguntar isso para um primo meu* [RelC *que é advogado*].
            'I can ask that of a cousin of mine [RelC who is a lawyer].'
        c. *Faz favor, me traz um martelo* [RelC *que está em cima do piano*].
            'Please bring me the hammer [RelC that is on the piano].'

In contrast, non-restrictive clauses (also called *explicative*) simply provide additional but non-essential information about their antecedents, as in 84a and 84b. They are usually set off by commas that correspond to slight pauses in speech.

(84)    a. *A minha motoca,* [RelC *que é uma Yamaha 750*], *estava precisando de uma revisão.*
            'My motorcycle, [RelC which is a Yamaha 750], needed a tune-up.'
        b. *Aí ela apresentou o namorado,* [RelC *que estava meio sem jeito*].
            'Then she introduced her boyfriend, [RelC who was a bit embarassed].'

### 4.11.3    Subordinate adverbial clauses

A subordinate adverbial clause (AdvC) signals the same kind of relationship as indicated by an adverbial phrase, such as time, condition, cause, purpose, or manner. The adverbial clause is embedded in the matrix by a conjunction or a conjunction-like construction made up of *que* and one or two words:

| | |
|---|---|
| time: | *quando* 'when,' *enquanto* 'while,' *sempre que* 'whenever,' *assim que* 'as soon as' |
| condition: | *se* 'if,' *desde que* 'as long as' |
| cause: | *porque* 'because,' *porquanto* 'because,' *como* 'since' |
| purpose: | *para que* 'so that,' *a fim de que* 'in order to' |
| manner: | *como* 'as,' *conforme* 'as,' *segundo* 'as,' *de maneira que* 'so that' |
| concessive: | *embora* 'even though,' *conquanto* 'even though,' *apesar de que* 'even though' |

(85)  a. *A gente ia chegando* [$_{AdvC}$ *quando ele puxou o carro*].
        'We were arriving [$_{AdvC}$ when he drove away].' (time)

      b. *A gente vai passar o Carnaval em Ubatuba* [$_{AdvC}$ *se o Mário tiver folga*].
        'We'll spend Carnival in Ubatuba [$_{AdvC}$ if Mario is on leave].' (condition)

      c. *Nós acabamos o muro* [$_{AdvC}$ *como foi possível*.]
        'We finished soon the wall [$_{AdvC}$ as possible].' (manner)

      d. [$_{AdvC}$ *Como você não chegou na hora*], *a gente não esperou*.
        '[$_{AdvC}$ Since you did not arrive on time], we did not wait.' (cause)

      e. *Esse aí lava* [$_{AdvC}$ *se eu imploro*].
        'This (guy) will wash (the dishes) [$_{AdvC}$ if I beg (him to)].' (condition)

      f. *Papai trazia presentes* [$_{AdvC}$ *sempre que viajava*].
        'Dad brought gifts [$_{AdvC}$ whenever he traveled].' (time)

      g. *A gente vai na boate* [$_{AdvC}$ *quando sobra dinheiro*].
        'We go to a night club [$_{AdvC}$ when there is extra money].' (time)

Unlike nominal or relative clauses, adverbial clauses add information to the whole matrix clause, and not just to one of its elements. Consequently they may be moved around, so that 85g could just as well be *Quando sobra dinheiro, a gente vai na boate*, or *A gente, quando sobra dinheiro, vai na boate*. Since some connectors may be used in any one of the three types of embedded clauses 86a–86c, the classification of the subordinate clause depends on the function it performs in relation to the matrix clause.

(86)  a. (Nominal) *Eu sei* [$_{NomC}$ *quando você chega*].
        'I know [$_{NomC}$ when you arrive].'

      b. (Relative) *O dia* [$_{RelC}$ *quando ele chega*] *é amanhã*.
        'The day [$_{RelC}$ when he arrives] is tomorrow.'

      c. (Adverbial) *Eu saio* [$_{AdvC}$ *quando você chega*].
        'I leave [$_{AdvC}$ when you arrive].'

### 4.11.4    Relative pronouns

The most frequent relative pronoun is *que* (87), while *quem*, which applies to human antecedents only, is used after a preposition (88a–88b) and as a free relative, without an overt antecedent (88c):

(87)    *Você conhece o cara que ganhou na loteria?*
        'Do you know the guy who won (in) the lottery?'

(88)    a. *Aquele homem para quem a Joana estava olhando*
           *é meu vizinho.*
           'That man that Joana was looking at is my neighbor.'
        b. *Onde está o garoto de quem você estava cuidando?*
           'Where is the kid you were taking care of?'
        c. *Quem não trabalha não come.*
           'Whoever does not work does not eat.'

A bit clumsier because of its mandatory agreement in number and gender with its antecedent, *o/a qual / os/as quais* is largely restricted to formal speech and writing, where it serves to avoid ambiguity between two possible antecedents: in 89a *que* may refer to either *o instrutor* or *aquela garota*, but agreement of *o qual/a qual* makes the reference unmistakable in 89b, where *a qual* refers to *garota*, as well as in 89c, where *o qual* refers to *instrutor*:

(89)    a. *O instrutor daquela garota,* [$_{RelC}$ *que você quer conhecer*],
           *é do Rio.*
           'The instructor of that girl, [$_{RelC}$ who you want to meet], is
           from Rio.'
        b. *O instrutor daquela garota,* [$_{RelC}$ *a qual você quer conhecer*],
           *é do Rio.*
           'The instructor of that girl [$_{RelC}$ you want to meet] is
           from Rio.
        c. *O instrutor daquela garota,* [$_{RelC}$ *o qual você quer conhecer*],
           *é do Rio.*
           'That girl's instructor, [$_{RelC}$ who you want to meet], is
           from Rio.'

The relative *cujo* 'whose' signals a relation of possession regarding its antecedent but agrees in number and gender with the accompanying noun, as in 90a–90b. Although it hardly ever occurs outside formal speech and writing (7.3.2.7), some speakers use it in the approximate sense of *o qual*, to reiterate an already-mentioned element 90c:

(90)    a. *Este é o senhor* [RelC *cujo carro foi roubado*].
        'This is the gentleman [RelC whose car was stolen].'
    b. *O livro* [RelC *cujas páginas estavam rasgadas*] *foi substituído.*
        'The book [RelC whose pages were torn] was replaced.'
    c. *O governo quer fazer o congresso aprovar um pacote de leis muito drásticas,* [RelC *cujo pacote não vai melhorar em nada a situação*].
        'The government wants to make Congress pass a package, [RelC which package won't improve things at all].'

*Onde* 'where' (alone or combined with one of several prepositions, such as *de onde, donde* 'from where,' *para onde* 'where to') and *como* 'how' (when used with an antecedent referring to manner) function as relative pronouns. In 91a–91b *onde* and *como* are equivalent to the preposition + relative pronoun construction shown in parentheses:

(91)    a. *A casa* [RelC *onde* (= *na qual*) *a gente morou*] *foi vendida.*
        'The house [RelC where (= in which) we used to live] was sold.'
    b. *Não estou lembrando o nome da cidade* [RelC *para onde* (= *para a qual*) *a Cidinha se mudou*].
        'I can't remember the name of the town [RelC where Cidinha moved to].'
    c. *Meu pai acha que o jeito* [RelC *como* (= *do qual*) *eu me visto*] *é um escândalo.*
        'My father thinks the way [RelC I dress is a scandal].'

Finally, *o que* 'what' is used to refer to a whole aggregate of circumstances, expressed by one or several clauses (92a–92b), or with no antecedent at all (92c):

(92)    a. *Eles não trouxeram nada para o piquenique,* [RelC *o que pegou mal*].
        'They didn't bring anything for the picnic, [RelC which looked bad].'
    b. *Ela não tinha nenhum diploma, falava muito mal e além disso não tinha boa aparência,* [RelC *o que naquele tempo era inaceitável*].
        'She didn't have a degree, spoke very poorly and besides she was not presentable, [RelC which at that time was unacceptable].'
    c. *Eu faço* [RelC *o que o senhor me mandar*].
        'I'll do [RelC whatever you tell me].'

In BP there is a sharp contrast between the standard use of relative pronouns and their use in informal speech, where *que* functions as an all-purpose pronoun, replacing virtually all other forms, either combined with a subject pronoun preceded by a preposition (93a–93c) or simply alone (93d–93e):

(93)    a. *O cara* [$_{RelC}$ que *eu queria falar* com ele] *não veio.* (= st. *O cara*
        com quem/com o qual *eu queria falar não veio.*)
        'The fellow [$_{RelC}$ I wanted to talk to didn't show up].'
    b. *Aquela cidade* [$_{RelC}$ que *você queria ir* nela], *lembra?* (= st.
        *Aquela cidade* aonde/à qual *você queria ir, lembra?*)
        'That town [$_{RelC}$ where you wanted to go], remember?'
    c. *Ela tinha uma amiga* [$_{RelC}$ que *o pai* dela (= st. *cujo pai*)] *era*
        *brigadeiro.*
        'She had a friend [$_{RelC}$ whose father] was a general.'
    d. *Em Paris, todos os restaurantes* [$_{RelC}$ que (= st. aonde/aos quais) *a*
        *gente foi,*] *a comida era excelente.*
        'In Paris, (in) every restaurant [$_{RelC}$ where we went], the food was
        excellent.'
    e. *Aquele porteiro* [$_{RelC}$ que (= st. a quem/ao qual) *você perguntou o*
        *endereço*] *não sabia nada.*
        'That doorman [$_{RelC}$ whom you asked about the address] didn't
        know anything.'

## 4.12    The subjunctive

For a speaker of English, which does not have the subjunctive as a fully characterized tense, the mandatory choice between indicative and subjunctive in a
Romance language can be a real challenge. What is called the subjunctive in
English is not a verb tense with its own forms, but rather a syntactic construction
(McArthur 1992:997) that survives primarily in formal usage, with the infinitive (the citation form of the verb), as in *I require that the witness take* (rather
than *takes*) *the stand now*, which contrasts with, say, *I know that the witness*
*takes the stand whenever necessary.* Likewise, in the past, the infinitive would
also be used, as in *Her lawyers insisted that she take* (as opposed to *took*) *the*
*Fifth Amendment.* In if-clauses with the verb *to be*, the subjunctive construction
appears, again in formal style, as *were: If I were rich, she'd be my wife; but if*
*she were my wife, I'd be poor.* In colloquial usage the regular past form is used:
*If I was rich; if she was my wife.*

In contrast, Portuguese has six full subjunctive tenses contrasting with the
indicative's nine (Table 4.3). The subjunctive occurs primarily in subordinate
clauses, where it is governed by an element present in the matrix. Since the
nuances expressed by the subjunctive would require a whole volume, this section
will be limited to an overview of its main uses.

### 4.12.1    *The subjunctive in nominal clauses*

In sentences like those in 94a–94e, the subjunctive may be explained by the
presence in the matrix of a verb (94a), noun (94b), or adjective (94c) that signals

Table 4.3 *Indicative and subjunctive tenses contrasted*

| Indicative | | Subjunctive | |
| --- | --- | --- | --- |
| present | *falam* | present | *falem* |
| present perfect | *têm falado* | present perfect | *tenham falado* |
| future | *falarão* | future | *falarem* |
| future perfect | *terão falado* | future perfect | *tiverem falado* |
| imperfect | *falavam* | | |
| preterit | *falaram* | past | *falassem* |
| conditional | *falariam* | | |
| pluperfect | *falaram/tinham falado* | past perfect | *tivessem falado* |
| conditional perfect | *teriam falado* | | |

either some sort of command or request, or a subjective evaluation (94d–94e) regarding what is expressed by the verb in the subordinate clause.

(94)  a. *Quero [NomC que você venha amanhã].*
          'I want [NomC you to come tomorrow].'
       b. *Minha preferência é [NomC que ele trabalhe até as oito].*
          'My preference is [NomC that he should work till eight].'
       c. *É preferível [NomC que a reunião não comece tarde].*
          'It's preferable [NomC that the meeting should not begin late].'
       d. *Lamento [NomC que você não possa vir].*
          'I regret [NomC that you cannot come].'
       e. *É uma pena [NomC que esse acidente tenha acontecido].*
          'It's a shame [NomC that that accident has happened].'

By contrast, in 95a–95c the verb, noun, or adjective in the main clause simply conveys the assumption that what comes in the subordinate clause is factual, and so the indicative is used.

(95)  a. *Sei [NomC que você vem amanhã].*
          'I know [NomC you are coming tomorrow].'
       b. *A informação é [NomC que ele trabalha até as oito].*
          'The information is [NomC that he works till eight].'
       c. *É sabido [NomC que as reuniões não começam tarde].*
          'It is known [NomC that the meetings do not begin late].'

Exhortative sentences have a subjunctive form introduced by *que* as in 96a–96c, and may be considered subordinate to a deleted main sentence containing a volition verb, that is, one expressing a wish or desire:

(96)  a. *Os outros [NomC que se ocupem disso].*
          'Let the others [NomC take care of that].'

b. *Eles* [NomC *que se danem!*]
'Let them [NomC be damned!]'
c. *Eu não comi nada, quem comeu* [NomC *que pague*].
'I didn't eat anything, [NomC whoever ate, let them pay].'

After deletion of the matrix, the subject may be moved to a position before *que* or altogether deleted, as in 97:

(97)    *Eu quero que eles se danem* → *que eles se danem* →
*eles que se danem* → *que se danem.*

Such sentences commonly occur in exchanges like 98a–98b, where the volition verb present in the question is understood in the reply.

(98)    a. – *Quer alguma coisa de Miami?*
'Do you want (me to bring you) something from Miami?
b. – *Muito obrigado, só* [NomC *que faça boa viagem*].
'(No) thank you, only [NomC that you have a good trip].'

An element of doubt or denial, or a subjective attitude or evaluation expressed in the main clause, likewise determine the subjunctive in the subordinate clause. Doubt may be conveyed by a verb such as *duvidar* 'to doubt,' *negar* 'to deny,' or by a negative construction such as *não crer* 'not to believe,' *não acreditar* 'not to believe,' or by impersonal constructions with *ser* followed by a noun or adjective such as *possível, impossível, duvidoso*, and so on, as shown in 99:

(99)    a. *Duvidavam* [NomC *que o Lula ganhasse a eleição*].
'They doubted [NomC Lula would win the election].'
b. *É duvidoso* [NomC *que ela chegue na hora*].
'It is doubtful [NomC that she will arrive on time].'

In the sentence pairs in 100 and 101 the sentence with the subjunctive (b) reflects an element of doubt that is absent from the corresponding sentence with the indicative (a).

(100)    Q.: *A Gabriela vem trabalhar amanhã?*
'Is Gabriela coming to work tomorrow?'
A.: a. *Eu imagino* [NomC *que ela vem, sim*].
'I guess [NomC she is].'
b. *Eu imagino* [NomC *que ela venha, sim*].
'I guess [NomC she may].'

(101)    Q.: *A Gabriela vem trabalhar amanhã?*
'Is Gabriela coming to work tomorrow?'
a. *Acredito* [NomC *que ela vem, sim*].
'I believe [NomC she is].'

b. *Acredito* [NomC *que ela venha, sim*].
    'I believe [NomC she may].'

Subjective evaluations, in turn, may be expressed by a verb like *agradar* 'to please,' *gostar* 'to like,' *adorar* 'to be very fond of,' *lamentar* 'to regret,' or an impersonal construction made up of *ser* and an adjective or noun, as in (102):

(102)    a. *Não me agrada* [NomC *que ela chegue tão tarde*].
             'I am not pleased [NomC that she should arrive so late].'
         b. *Lamento* [NomC *que ele tenha falecido tão jovem*].
             'I regret [NomC that he passed away so young].'
         c. *É pena que* [NomC *ele não fale inglês*].
             'It's a shame [NomC he does not speak English].'

### 4.12.2   The subjunctive in relative clauses

The key factor in choice between the indicative and the subjunctive is the speaker's assumptions about the relative pronoun's antecedent in the matrix clause (Table 4.2). The indicative suggests an antecedent perceived as actual and specific, as in 103a. If that antecedent is viewed as a hypothetical entity, however, the verb will be in the subjunctive 103b:

(103)    a. *Eu quero comprar a moto* [RelC *que foi anunciada no jornal de ontem*].
             'I want to buy the motorcycle [RelC that was advertised in yesterday's paper].'
         b. *Eu quero comprar uma moto* [RelC *que tenha pouca quilometragem*].
             'I want to buy a motorcycle [RelC that has low mileage].'
         c. *Eu quero comprar uma moto* [RelC *que foi anunciada no jornal de ontem*].
             'I want to buy a motorcycle [RelC that was advertised in yesterday's paper].'
         d. *Eu quero comprar a moto perfeita,* [RelC *que gaste pouca gasolina e não exija manutenção*].
             'I want to buy the perfect motorcycle [RelC that would use little gas and require no maintenance].'

Since nouns referring to known entities are often introduced by the definite article, we may assume that use of the definite article *a* in sentence 103a implies a definite motorcycle. Not so in 103b, where the subjunctive *tenha* suggests that no specific motorcycle with low mileage is known to exist, even though there is nothing improbable about its existence. In 103c cooccurence of an indefinite article (*uma moto*) and an indicative form (*tem*) suggests the speaker is aware of a specific motorcycle, which may simply be out of sight at the moment of the utterance. In 103d, finally, the definite article suggests a specific entity, but its cooccurrence with the subjunctive suggests it is hypothetical – for example, an ideal motorcycle that the speaker knows has yet to be made. These possibilities may be described by means of two variables, *definite* and *hypothetical*, to which we assign positive or negative valences, yielding four combinations:

|  | + Hypothetical | – Hypothetical |
|---|---|---|
| + definite | *Ainda estou por conhecer a sogra que **trate** bem o genro.* | *Finalmente conheci a sogra que **trata** bem o genro.* |
| | 'I have yet to meet the mother-in-law who would treat her son-in-law nicely.' | 'Finally I have met the mother-in-law who treats her son-in-law nicely.' |
| – definite | *Quero conhecer uma sogra que **trate** bem o genro.* | *Quero te apresentar uma sogra que **trata** bem o genro.* |
| | 'I want to meet a mother-in-law who who treats her son-in-law nicely.' | 'I want you to meet a mother-in-law who treats her son-in-law nicely.' |

### 4.12.3    The subjunctive in adverbial clauses

Subordinate adverbial clauses are introduced by conjunctions that fall into three large classes (Table 4.4), depending on whether the verb of the adverbial clause is (a) in the indicative, (b) or in the subjunctive, or (c) either in the indicative or the subjunctive.

With conjunctions in group (1), which introduce clauses that carry an assumption of reality (104a–104c), there is no choice and therefore no contrast in mood.

(104)    a. *O chefe cortou as diárias* [$_{AdvC}$ *porque ninguém mais vai viajar*].
         'The boss has cut the perdiem [$_{AdvC}$ because nobody is going to travel anymore].'
      b. [$_{AdvC}$ *Visto que você não veio*], *nós cancelamos a reunião.*
         '[$_{AdvC}$ Since you didn't show up], we canceled the meeting.'
      c. [$_{AdvC}$ *Já que ia ter inspeção*] *a gente teve que limpar o alojamento.*
         '[$_{AdvC}$ Since there was going to be an inspection] we had to clean the lodging.'

Likewise, conjunctions in group (2) introduce adverbial clauses that convey something contrary to fact or hypothetical, or describe a future, yet to be

Table 4.4 *Conjunctions introducing subordinate adverbial clauses (After Perini 2002a)*

| (1) Conjunctions that introduce an adverbial case with the verb always in the indicative | (2) Conjunctions that introduce an adverbial case with the verb always in the subjunctive | (3) Conjunctions that introduce an adverbial case with the verb in either the indicative or the subjunctive |
|---|---|---|
| *assim como* 'just so as' | *a não ser que, a menos que* 'unless' | *quando* 'when' |
| *dado que* 'given that' | *ainda que* 'although' | *depois que* 'after' |
| *já que* 'since' | *antes que* 'before' | *enquanto* 'while' |
| *porque* 'because' | *caso, em caso de que* 'in case' | *logo que* 'as soon as' |
| *visto que* 'given that' | *contanto que* 'as long as, provided that' | *quanto mais . . . mais* 'the more . . . the more' |
| | *embora* 'although' | *sempre que* 'as long as,' 'whenever' |
| | *mesmo que* 'even if' | |
| | *nem que* 'not even if' | |
| | *para que* 'so that, in order to' | |
| | *sem que* 'unless' | |

fulfilled, event. There is no contrast, since the verb is always in the subjunctive, as in (105a)–(105c).

(105)   a. *Não faço isso* [_AdvC_ *nem que me paguem*].
          'I don't do that [_AdvC_ even if they pay me].'
        b. *Trabalhou cinco meses* [_AdvC_ *sem que lhe pagassem nada*].
          'He worked for five months [_AdvC_ without them paying him anything].'
        c. *Eu trabalho* [_AdvC_ *para que me paguem*].
          'I work [_AdvC_ so they'll pay me].'

Finally, adverbial clauses introduced by conjunctions of group (3) may have the verb either in the indicative or in the subjunctive. Mood choice here corresponds to whether the event in the adverbial clause is perceived by the speaker as fulfilled (indicative) or as yet to be fulfilled, either because it is non-factual or because it is still in the future (subjunctive).

The prototypical conjunction case is the temporal conjunction *quando* (106a–106h):

(106)   a. *Vamos jantar* [_AdvC_ *quando vocês chegarem*].
          We'll have dinner [_AdvC_ when you arrive].'
        b. *Vou fazer o café* [_AdvC_ *tão logo ela saia do banheiro*].
          'I'll make coffee [_AdvC_ as soon as she gets out of the bathroom].'

   c. *A gente põe o vídeo* [$_{AdvC}$ *assim que eles chegarem*].
     'We'll start on the video [$_{AdvC}$ as soon as they arrive].'

   d. *Eu vou fazer isso* [$_{Adv}$ *desde que vocês não me chateiem*].
     'I'll do that [$_{AdvC}$ as long as you don't bug me].'

   e. *Eu entrego o dinheiro* [$_{Adv}$ *desde que vocês me dêem um recibo*].
     'I'll hand in the money [$_{AdvC}$ as long as you give me a receipt].'

   f. *Eu entreguei o dinheiro,* [$_{Adv}$ *desde que eles me deram um recibo.*]
     'I handed in the money, [$_{AdvC}$ because they gave me a receipt].'

   g. *Eu entreguei um recibo* [$_{Adv}$ *depois que me deram o dinheiro*].
     'I handed in a receipt [$_{Adv}$ after they gave me the money].'

   h. *Eu só vou entregar o dinheiro* [$_{AdvC}$ *depois que me derem um recibo*].
     'I'm only going to hand in the money [$_{AdvC}$ after they give me a receipt].'

### 4.12.4    *The subjunctive with* se *in contrary-to-fact adverbial clauses*

Adverbial clauses introduced by the conjunction *se* imply a condition. A verb in the indicative signals the assumption that the condition has been fulfilled.

(107)   a. [$_{AdvC}$ *Se você tem carro*], *não vai ficar sozinho.*
     '[$_{AdvC}$ If you have a car], you won't lack for company.'

   b. [$_{AdvC}$ *Se ela conhece esse software*], *vai conseguir emprego fácil.*
     '[$_{AdvC}$ If she knows that software], she'll get a job easily.'

   c. *Meu filho,* [$_{AdvC}$ *se você tem fé*], *não vai ter problema.*
     'My son [$_{AdvC}$, if you have faith], there won't be any problem.'

In contrast, a verb in the subjunctive signals an unfulfilled condition. This may be a permanent situation, as in the case of a past event calling for the verb in the past subjunctive (108a–108b). In 108c–108d the verb in the future subjunctive signals a condition that may yet be fulfilled.

(108)   a. [$_{AdvC}$ *Se você tivesse trazido o passaporte*], *a gente podia ir a Tijuana.*
     '[$_{AdvC}$ If you had brought your passport] we'd be able to go to Tijuana.'

   b. *Ele ainda teria o emprego* [$_{AdvC}$ *se não falasse tanto*].
     'He'd still have the job [$_{AdvC}$ if he didn't talk so much].'

   c. [$_{AdvC}$ *Se a gente quiser ir à ópera*], *temos que comprar as entradas logo.*
     '[$_{AdvC}$ If we want to go to the opera] we have to buy the tickets soon.'

   d. *A gente pode cuidar disso* [$_{AdvC}$ *quando vocês chegarem*].
     'We can take care of that [$_{AdvC}$ when you arrive].'

## 4.12.5    *The subjunctive in independent clauses*

Subjunctive forms in independent (that is, non-subordinated) sentences (109a–109b) are limited to a handful of formulaic constructions in which the verb is preceded by specific words such as *talvez* 'maybe,' *tomara que* 'let's hope that' (a lexicalized° form of *tomar* 'to take'), *quiçá* 'maybe' (related to an old form of *quem sabe* 'who knows'), or *oxalá* 'let's hope that' (from Ar *wa xa illah* 'and may God wish'). *Talvez* has the particularity of taking the subjunctive when it comes before the verb as in 109a, and the indicative when it comes after the verb (*Ele chega hoje talvez* 'Maybe he'll arrive today'), without any noticeable change in meaning.

(109)  a. *Talvez ele chegue hoje.*      'Maybe he'll arrive today.'
       b. *Oxalá ela tenha êxito.*       'Let's hope she'll be successful.'
       c. *Quiçá ele seja de Minas.*     'Maybe he's from Minas.'
       c. *Tomara que chova!*            'Let's hope it rains!'

## 4.13    The inflected infinitive

Inflection of the infinitive for subject and number (3.5.2) is an idiosyncrasy of Portuguese, and its use is fraught with uncertainty (Cunha and Cintra 1985:473). In BP it is far more used in writing and in formal, monitored speech than in unmonitored speech, where its frequency is rather low. Perhaps because of that it has been suggested (Martin 1976) that speakers of BP who learn the inflected infinitive do so through formal instruction rather than natural aquisition.

The only forms that show inflection are those for *tu, vós, nós,* and *eles/vocês.* Since however in BP *vós* is no longer used, *tu* is used only regionally, and *nós* tends to be replaced by *a gente* in informal speech (Freitas 1995), most actual cases of the inflected infinitive naturally belong to *vocês/eles.* In EP, where *tu* and *nós* are regularly used, one would expect a higher incidence of inflected infinitive forms.

Even so, data from spontaneous speech are scarce, and consequently the phenomenon is far from being fully understood and linguists underscore the provisionality of their claims (Perini 1997:7, 1998:200). This brief presentation concentrates on the essentials and follows the main lines of the analysis given in Perini (1998, 2000a).

In 110a–110d the inflected infinitive occurs in a sentence that serves as a complement to another sentence, to which it is connected by a preposition. A key factor here is whether or not an overt subject is associated with the verb in the infinitive, which is inflected if its overt subject is different from the subject of the other sentence, as in 110a–110b. If there is no overt subject, inflection occurs if the subjects are different, as in 110c, and it is optional if the subject is the same, as in 110d.

(110)    a. [*A Dora deixou umas revistas*] [*para nós lermos*].
                '[Dora left some magazines] [for us to read].'
         b. [*Eu vou fazer umas pipocas*] [*para vocês comerem*].
                '[I'm going to make some popcorn] [for you to eat].'
         c. [*Comprei uma garrafa de vinho*] [*para bebermos hoje de noite*].
                '[I have bought a bottle of wine] [for us to drink tonight].'
         d. [*Vamos comprar uma garrafa de vinho*] [*para beber/bebermos
                hoje de noite.*]
                '[Let's buy a bottle of wine] [for us to drink tonight].'

If the infinitive in a construction like 110c is not inflected, the resulting
sentence is grammatical, but it may mean something else, as in 111:

(111)    *Comprei uma garrafa de vinho para beber hoje de noite.*
         'I bought a bottle of wine to drink tonight.'

To understand how the inflected subjunctive is bypassed, as it were, in spoken
BP, compare the sentences in 110 with their homologues in 112a–112d:

(112)    a. *A Dora deixou umas revistas para a gente ler.*
                'Dora left some magazines for us to read.'
         b. *Eu vou fazer umas pipocas para vocês comer.*
                'I'm going to make some popcorn for you to eat.'
         c. *Comprei uma garrafa de vinho para a gente beber hoje de noite.*
                'I have bought a bottle of wine for us to drink tonight.'
         d. *Vamos comprar uma garrafa de vinho para beber hoje de noite.*
                'Let's buy a bottle of wine for (us) to drink tonight.'

The inflected infinitive also occurs when the first sentence includes a verb of
perception or suasion:

| **Verbs of perception** | **Verbs of suasion** |
| --- | --- |
| *ver* 'to see' | *mandar* 'to command' |
| *ouvir* 'to hear, to listen' | *ordenar* 'to order' |
| *escutar* 'to hear, to listen' | *fazer* 'to make [someone do something]' |
| *observar* 'to watch' | *deixar* 'to let' |

(113)    a. *Ontem eu vi Madalena dançar.*
                'Yesterday I saw Madalena dance.'
         b. *Ontem eu a vi dançar.*
                'Yesterday I saw her dance.'
         c. *Ontem eu vi as Roquetes dançar.*
                'Yesterday I saw the Rockettes dance.'
         d. *Ontem eu vi as Roquetes dançarem.*
                'Yesterday I saw the Rockettes dance.'

In 113a *Madalena* is perceived as being both the actor/subject of *dançar* and the patient/direct object of *vi*, which is why *Madalena* may be replaced by a direct object clitic, as in 113b. If we replace *Madalena* with a plural noun phrase, then the infinitive may be inflected or not, as in 113c–113d. This means that in constructions involving a verb of perception followed by a noun phrase and an infinitive, the infinitive may or may not agree with the noun phrase.

The situation is made a little more complex because not every native speaker agrees that sentences like 114b can have an inflected infinitive if the clitic is in the plural:

(114)   Q.   – *Você já viu as Roquetes dançarem?*
                'Have you seen the Rockettes dance.'
        A. a. – *Eu já as vi cantar, mas não dançar.*
           b. – *Eu já as vi?*cantarem, mas não?*dançarem.*
                'I've seen them sing, but not dance.'

With verbs of suasion, the infinitive may likewise be inflected to agree with the subject noun phrase, as in 115b. In spoken BP, where *ele(s)* is regularly used as a direct object (7.3.2), either agreement or non-agreement is possible, as in 116a–116b:

(115)   a. *Eu mandei os meninos fazer umas compras.*
            'I sent the boys out to buy a few things.'
        b. *Eu mandei os meninos fazerem umas compras.*
            'I sent the boys out to buy a few things.'

(116)   a. *Eu sempre deixo eles brincar na rua.*
            'I always let them play on the street.'
        b. *Eu deixo elas irem a tudo quanto é baile.*
            'I let them go to all kinds of dances.'

## 4.14   Information distribution and word order

We have seen (4.1.2) that the order of words within a sentence constituent obeys certain constraints. In a noun phrase, articles come before possessives and nouns, not after (*a minha bicicleta*, not *minha a bicicleta*, nor *minha bicicleta a*). In a verb phrase the auxiliaries precede rather than follow the main verb (*tinha falado*, not *falado tinha*), and so on. On the other hand, where word order may vary, sentence constituents are distributed in information bundles so as to facilitate comprehension.

The generic or unmarked order of a Portuguese sentence is subject + verb + object (SVO). The subject is the head noun phrase (NP), and the verb (V), together with the object (NP) and other complements (such as prepositional phrases and adverbial phrases, if any) constitute the *predicate*. In the sequence $NP_1$ VP $NP_2$ the relative ordering of the noun phrases reflects the unmarked order SVO, and consequently *Paulo viu Maria* and *Maria viu Paulo* mean different things. Adding a prepositional phrase like *de manhã*, which has an adverbial function of time, makes possible other arrangements such as *Paulo viu Maria de manhã* or *De manhã Paulo viu Maria*.

Variation in word order modifies the distribution of information by focusing on one component or another. Although the decision regarding which element is informationally more important is the speaker's and cannot be predicted, we can analyze word order in terms of processes that distribute information in different sentence patterns.

A key notion is topic°, defined as the constituent that tells us what the sentence is all about. What lies outside the topic constitutes the *commentary*.° In the unmarked order SVO, the subject usually corresponds to the topic, while the predicate (again formed by the verb, objects, and complements) constitutes the commentary. Placed at the beginning of the sentence, the topic provides a background for the main information; the latter, being placed toward the end, is likely to remain more vividly in the listener's memory.

A productive process for varying word order consists in inverting the terms of the unmarked order. Example 117a is an ordinary sentence of the type SV, which if given as a reply to a question like *E a Selma?* 'What about Selma?' simply conveys information about the subject; the latter, having already been mentioned, carries old information. In 117b the verb *chegou* provides a background for the new information contained in *Selma*; this sentence might be uttered as a reply to *Quem chegou?* 'Who has arrived?' and the information focus is on *Selma*. This displacement of a component to topic position is known as topicalization.°

(117)    a. *A Selma chegou.* 'Selma has arrived.'
         b. *Chegou a Selma.* 'Selma has arrived.'

The passive construction allows topicalization° of the semantic patient by making it the subject and placing it at the beginning of the sentence. In sentence 118a, the information focus is on what City Hall did, namely to sponsor a parade by a samba club named *Morro Branco* ('White Hill'). In 118b passivization topicalizes the reference to the parade, placing the information focus on the new information regarding who did the sponsoring, which constitutes the commentary.

(118)    a. *A Prefeitura patrocinou o desfile da Morro Branco.*
            'City Hall sponsored the Morro Branco parade.'
         b. *O desfile da Morro Branco foi patrocinado pela Prefeitura.*
            'The Morro Branco parade was sponsored by City Hall.'

There are other processes for moving sentence constituents around. The unmarked SVO distribution of sentence 119a is an unexceptional statement, but the speaker can choose to create an emphatic sentence by using a syntactic device known as *left-dislocation*. This process shifts the element to be focused on to the leftmost position, yielding 119b, where the reference to *na minha casa* 'at my home' becomes a backdrop to the statement *eu mando* 'I give orders.' If subject–verb inversion is also applied, we have sentence 119c, with information focus on *eu*, highlighting who gives orders, against the background of where order-giving takes place.

(119)   a. *Eu mando na minha casa.* 'I give orders in my home.'
       b. *Na minha casa, eu mando.* 'In my home, I give orders.'
       c. *Na minha casa, mando eu.* 'In my home, *I* give orders.'

Likewise, given an unmarked word order such as in 120a, we may use left-dislocation to topicalize *amanhã*, placing it at the head of the sentence, as in 120b where the notion of car-buying appears as a commentary on what will happen tomorrow. Since the speaker is free to choose what will be topicalized, other arrangements are possible.

(120)   a. *Eu vou comprar aquele carro amanhã.*
          'I'm going to buy that car tomorrow.'
       b. *Amanhã eu vou comprar aquele carro.*
          'Tomorrow I'm going to buy that car.'

Yet another way topicalization operates is by cleft sentences (121), which are created by placing the topicalized element in the main clause as the subject of a form of the verb *ser*. The main clause then becomes the matrix of a subordinate clause introduced by a relative pronoun such as *que*. (As shown in 121c, *quem* is possible if the antecedent is human.) In 121d topicalization affects the adverbial *amanhã*, possibly to underscore the speaker's decision to stop putting off buying the car. As in the preceding sentences, a cleft sentence switches *amanhã* to topicalized position:

(121)   a. *Foi esse povinho que invadiu a fazenda.*
          'It was that riff-raff who invaded the farm.'
       b. *Fui eu que pus os convites no correio.*
          'It was I who mailed the invitations.'
       c. *Foi ela quem trouxe essas revistas.*
          'It was she who brought these magazines.'
       d. *É amanhã que eu vou comprar aquele carro.*
          'Tomorrow is when I'm going to buy that car.'

A similar construction, called *pseudo-cleft sentence* (122a–122c), uses a relative pronoun without an antecedent (such as *quem* or *o que*) to place the topicalized element at the end of the sentence, again as the subject of a form of the verb *ser*:

(122)    a. *Quem invadiu a fazenda foi aquele povinho.*
             '(The people) who invaded the farm were that riff-raff.'
         b. *Quem pôs os convites no correio fui eu.*
             '(The person) who mailed the invitations was I.'
         c. *O que eu vou comprar amanhã é aquele carro.*
             'What I'm going to buy tomorrow is that car.'

In the preceding sections we have simply touched upon the essentials of high-frequency syntactic constructions which learners are likely to encounter. Since developing a feel for sentence construction is one of a language learner's most important skills, it is recommended that learners use this chapter as a blueprint for identifying and analyzing sentences found in speech and writing, with a view to understanding different ways in which it can be modified.

# 5    Portuguese in time

In Chapter 1 we glanced at the external history of Portuguese, and in Chapters 2 through 4 we examined aspects of its sounds, word forms, and the structure of phrases and sentences. In doing this we followed a synchronic° perspective, looking at the language in its contemporary state, without taking into account historical factors, as though the language were fixed in time.

As time goes by, however, every language undergoes a variety of diachronic° processes that substantially affect all of its components and which constitute its internal history. Such modifications affect sounds (phonetic and phonological change), the shape of words (morphological change), the structure of phrases and sentences (syntactic change), the make-up of the lexicon (lexical change), and the meaning of words (semantic change). Given enough centuries, a language can be changed into a substantially different one. In this chapter we will consider some of the diachronic processes responsible for transforming popular spoken Latin into Portuguese.

## 5.1    The Latin source

Although it is difficult to observe diachronic processes directly, we have sufficient data about Latin and early forms of Romance, provided by ancient manuscripts, inscriptions, and grammarians' comments about the language. By comparing such information with data from today's Romance languages, we can make reasonable conjectures about what happened. A major obstacle, however, is that understanding those processes requires a knowledge of Latin, which most students nowadays lack. Consequently, we will only sketch a few of the major processes involved in the development of Portuguese, and complement our diachronic view with samples of earlier stages of the language, in order to give a panoramic notion of how it grew.

In the heyday of the Roman Empire, the speech of the cultivated patrician minority, on which literary, or classical, Latin was based, was a highly inflected language. Its nouns, adjectives, and determinants were distinguished by case° endings which varied to show syntactic function. Nouns were organized into five classes known as declensions°, each of which had six case endings for the singular and another six for the plural. Despite considerable overlapping, there were enough case endings to ensure that a noun's syntactic function was specified. Accompanying words such as adjectives and determinants, as well as pronouns, were likewise marked by case endings.

There was also enough social variation in Latin to differentiate the educated elite's *sermo urbanus,* or 'city speech' (from Lat *sermo* 'speech' and *urbs* 'town') from the rural dwellers' *sermo rusticus* or 'country speech' (from Lat *rus* 'country') and from the lower classes' *sermo vulgaris* or 'popular speech' (from Lat *vulgus* 'common people,' not "vulgar" in today's sense of 'in poor taste, obscene'). In this popular Latin, spoken by the majority of the population, the inflection system tended to be simplified. As case endings were merged or dropped, two compensatory devices became indicators of syntactic function. One involved more extensive use of prepositions; the other was a more fixed word order. As in Portuguese or English today, popular speech also used many words not found in literary works, although many have survived in graffiti (see below). Likewise, literature employed many terms that were not used in the spoken language. Today's Romance languages grew out of this popular variety, traditionally known as "Vulgar Latin," about which we have information from a variety of sources, to wit:

- Inscriptions on monuments, tombs, and ruins found all over the territory once occupied by the Roman Empire.
- Graffiti, like those found in the excavated towns of Pompeii and Herculaneum, buried by a volcanic eruption of Mount Vesuvius in the year 79 AD (Väänänen 1966, 1981).
- The pronunciation of some Latin words incorporated in other languages.
- The representation of the speech of rustic characters in popular works such as Plautus' comedies or Gaius Petronius' *Cena Trimalchionis* ('Trimalchio's Supper'), written ca. 61 AD.
- The language of personal letters and non-literary works of a practical nature, such as medical, cooking, agricultural, and architectural treatises.
- Popular works on religious themes like the *Peregrinatio ad loca sancta* ('Pilgrimage to the Holy Places'), attributed to Egeria, a nun from the north of the Iberian Peninsula in the early fifth century.
- Didactic comments by Latin grammarians criticizing features of popular speech, such as the *Appendix Probi*, or 'Probus' Appendix,' a list of 227 word pairs comparing forms considered correct with their supposedly incorrect popular counterparts. It deserves special mention.

Compiled anonymously, likely in the third century AD, the *Appendix* owes its name to having been found attached to a copy of a manuscript attributed to Marcus Valerius Probus, a Roman grammarian of the first century AD (*Probi* is the form of the genitive, or possessive, case, corresponding to Eng *Probus's*.) Long thought to have been written in the third century AD, its compilation is now dated after AD 568. In spirit as well as in form, the *Appendix* has much in common with the lists of the type "say it like this, not like that" found in newspaper and magazine columns purporting to teach readers to talk genteel. Ironically, the forms it criticizes include features of popular Latin that became the basis of the corresponding forms in the Romance languages, as can be seen in the following sample, where bracketed numbers are those provided by Väänänen (1981:200–203):

(a) replacement of *e* by *i* (probably a palatal glide /j/):
   [55] vinea non vinia 'vine'
   [80] solea non solia 'a kind of sandal'
   [72] lancea non lancia 'lance'
   [63] cavea non cavia 'cage'

(b) loss of an unstressed vowel:
   [11] oculus non oclus 'eye'
   [142] stabulum non stablum 'stable'
   [130] tabula non tabla 'board'
   [201] viridis non virdis 'green'

(c) loss of a consonant or a syllable:
   [155] auctoritas non autoritas 'authority'
   [154] auctor non autor 'writer'
   [221] vobiscum non voscum 'with you (pl.)'
   [220] nobiscum non noscum 'with us'
   [224] olim non oli 'formerly'
   [152] tensa non tesa 'wagon for transporting images of gods to public spectacles'

By the early ninth century, however, unmistakably Romance words were appearing in documents written in notarial Latin, bearing evidence of a new popular speech that differed widely from the school-learned Latin of the literate classes (copyists, writers, translators, notaries); and by the middle of the eleventh century an anonymous hand was making the first deliberate record in a Hispanic Romance language, in the form of glosses written into a Latin manuscript at the monastery of San Millán de la Cogolla in Rioja, Spain.

## 5.2    Sound change

The primary motor of language change is sound change. It involves complex processes largely arising from a widespread tendency to relax the articulation of some speech sounds, and to compensate for this by exaggerating the articulation of others. Sound change begins with minor variations in pronunciation like those that characterize regional accents°. Eventually, it affects the contrasts between phonemes, thus leading to changes in the phonological system.

Phonological change happens when one phoneme coalesces with another, or splits into two new ones, or simply is lost altogether. Such rearrangements often induce modifications in the morphology of words, affecting morphemes that signal syntactic relations. This is what happened to Latin case endings. Since sound changes take place over a period of time and then cease to operate, a detailed study of a language's development would require taking into account the relative chronology of intervening processes. Given its generic aim, however, our presentation will be limited to examining some of the processes that occurred in the formation of Portuguese, without regard to their absolute chronology.

### 5.2.1   Kinds of sound change

Changes induced by a neighboring sound are called *conditioned*. Such changes may involve simple modifications of a phonetic nature. For example, voiceless consonants may become voiced in intervocalic (between vowels) position, possibly due to their assimilation to the vowels, which are voiced. In the examples below, the Latin phonemes /p/, /t/, and /k/ (represented in spelling by the small capitals P, T, K) became voiced as /b/, /d/, /g/ in intervocalic position in Portuguese as in Spanish, though not in Italian. The forms are cited, unless otherwise indicated, in the accusative° singular, which ended in /m/; the case ending -M is placed in parentheses as a reminder that it was generally lost in popular Latin.

| Latin | Portuguese | Spanish | Italian | |
|---|---|---|---|---|
| LUPU(M) | lobo | lobo | lupo | 'wolf' |
| SAPONE(M) | sabão | jabón | sapone | 'soap' |
| PRATU(M) | prado | prado | prato | 'field' |
| PASSATU(M) | passado | pasado | passato | 'past' |
| AMICU(M) | amigo | amigo | amico | 'friend' |

Conditioned change was also involved in the nasalization of vowels by assimilation to a following nasal consonant, which was in turn lost after nasalization. Thus Portuguese ended up with a set of nasal vowels before syllable-final consonants and in word-final position. In the examples in the right-hand column, the original word-final vowel was fused with the preceding nasal vowel:

| Before syllable-final consonants | In word-final position |
|---|---|
| TANTU(M) > *tanto* ['tãtu] 'so much' | BONU(M) > *bõo* > *bom* [bõ] 'good' |
| CAMPU(M) > *campo* ['kãpu] 'field' | RANA(M) > *rãa* > *rã* [rã] 'frog' |
| CANTARE > *cantar* [kã'tar] 'to sing' | LANA(M) E *lãa* > *lã* [lã] 'wool' |

Table 5.1 *Latin stressed vowels and diphthongs and their result in Portuguese*

| Class. Lat | Pop. Lat | Pg | Class. Lat | Pop. Lat | Pg |
|---|---|---|---|---|---|
| /i:/ VITAM | vita | vida | /a/ LATUM | latu | lado |
| /i/ PILUM | pelo | pelo | /o/ PORTA | porta | porta |
| /e:/ TRES | tres | três | /o:/ FAMOSUM | famosu | famoso |
| /e/ PETRAM | petra | pedra | /u/ BUCCA | boca | boca |
| /a:/ PACEM | paz | paz | /u:/ ACUTU | acutu | agudo |
| /aj/ CAESAR | Cesar | César | /oj/ POENA | cena | cena |
| /aw/ AURUM | auru | o(u)ro | | | |

Changes that cannot be ascribed to specific factors in the phonetic environment are said to be *unconditioned*. A major unconditioned sound change in the popular Latin of the Iberian Peninsula was the loss of duration as a phonological contrast. Classical Latin distinguished between short (single) and long (double) consonants. Loss of this distinction caused double consonants to became short, that is, single in Portuguese. Since voiceless consonants derived from Latin double consonants remained voiceless, we can assume that voicing process was no longer operative by the time double consonants were shortened:

CUPPA > *copa* 'cup'      CAPPA > *capa* 'cloak'

LITTERA > *letra* 'letter'      GUTTA > *gota* 'drop'

BUCCA > *boca* 'mouth'      VACCA > *vaca* 'cow'

Loss of duration also affected the vowels. Classical Latin had five long vowels, Ā Ē Ī Ō Ū (phonetically [a: e: i: o: u:]) that contrasted with five short ones, represented as Ă Ĕ Ĭ Ŏ Ŭ ([a e i o u]). (The superscript signs ⁻ and ˘, used to show long and short vowels respectively, are a relatively modern invention.) As the long vs. short distinction gave way to a contrast involving vowel quality, some vowels merged with others while others simply changed quality. Vowel duration, no longer signaling a phonological contrast, became a function of word stress: all stressed vowels became long and unstressed vowels became short. The result of such changes in the speech of Galicia was a system of seven vowels in stressed position that has persisted in contemporary Galician and Portuguese (Table 5.1).

Classical Latin also had three diphthongs, Æ /aj/, Œ /oj/, and AU /aw/. The first two were reduced to simple vowels in popular Latin, as in Æ /aj/ > /ɛ/ CESAR > *César*, Œ /oj/ > /e/ POENA > *pena* 'punishment'; AU /aw/ yielded /ow/, as in AURU > *ouro* 'gold,' and in the sixteenth century this diphthong, too, was monophthongized° (/ow/ > /o/) in the south of Portugal, although the diphthongized pronunciation is preserved in northern regions.

A major result of sound change was that popular Latin lost meaning-bearing contrasts in case endings. Let us take an example from the first declension. A noun like POETA 'poet' assumed several forms, according to case:

nominative (subject) case: a short final /a/ POETĀ 'the poet'
genitive (possessive) case: a diphthong /aj/ POETÆ 'of the poet'
accusative (direct object) case: an /m/ POETAM 'the poet'
ablative (indirect object) case: a long /a:/ POETĀ 'to the poet'

With the loss of diphthongs and length as a distinctive factor, and the loss of the accusative ending /m/, these contrasting forms were reduced to a single ending in /a/, POETA. Since plural forms were also reduced to the accusative, which ended in /s/, the resulting contrast between *poeta* (sg.) and *poetas* (pl.) gave rise to -*s* as a plural marker. These changes may be summarized as follows:

| | Latin (accusative form) | | Portuguese | | |
|---|---|---|---|---|---|
| *Declension* | *Singular* | *Plural* | *Singular* | | *Plural* |
| 1st | POETAM | POETAS | poeta | poetas | 'poet/s' |
| 2nd | LIBRUM | LIBROS | livro | livros | 'book/s' |
| 4th | LACUM | LACUS | lago | lagos | 'lake/s' |
| 3rd | PRINCIPEM | PRINCIPES | príncipe | príncipes | 'prince/s' |
| 5th | SERIEM | SERIES | série | séries | 'series' |

Changes in the Latin system of eleven consonants gave rise to new consonants in Romance (Table 5.2).

### 5.2.2    Palatalization

Such remarkable sound changes, including the creation of new sounds, stemmed from palatalization that a moderately detailed study of this process gives an idea of sound change as a whole. Palatalization involves displacing the point of articulation to an area closer to the palate. While palatalization gave rise to no new vowels, it frequently altered their quality. The single most effective agent of palatalization was the palatal glide /j/. This sound, which already existed in Classical Latin, became much more common through the operation of various processes in popular speech. The front or palatal vowels /i/ and /e/, when unstressed and forming a hiatus (2.2.1) with a following vowel, became palatal glides. This is the process documented in examples like *lancea non lancia* found in the *Appendix Probi* (5.1). In other words, the presence of the palatal vowel /i/ or the palatal glide /j/ conditioned the consonant to acquire a palatalized articulation.

Table 5.2 *Comparison of Latin and Portuguese consonants*

| | Latin | | | | | | Portuguese | | | | | | |
|---|---|---|---|---|---|---|---|---|---|---|---|---|---|
| | bilabial | lab-dental | dental | alv pal | velar | glottal | bilabial | lab-dental | dental | alv | palatal | velar | glottal |
| stops | p b | | t d | | k g | | p b | | t d | | | k g | |
| fricatives | | f | | s | | h | | f v | | s z | ʃ ʒ | | |
| laterals | | | | l | | | | | | l | ʎ | | |
| vibrants | | | | r | | | | | | ɾ | | R | |
| nasals | m | | | n | | | m | | | n | ɲ | | |

Such glides palatalized all immediately preceding consonants, except labials /p/, /b/, and /r/. Thus the Latin alveolar lateral /l/, when followed by /j/ (written LI), yielded the palatal lateral /ʎ/: FILIU > *filho* 'son,' MULIERE > *mulher* 'woman.' A similar trend is noticeable today in Brazilian Portuguese in the casual pronunciation of nouns like *familia* 'family' (< FAMILIA) as [fa'miʎɐ] or *mobília* 'furniture' (< MOBILIA) as [mu'biʎɐ] instead of [fa'miliɐ], [mu'biliɐ]. The same goes for the name *Júlio* (< JULIU), pronounced as ['ʒuʎu] (= *julho* 'July') instead of ['ʒuliu].

A similar merger joined the alveolar nasal /n/ to an immediately following /j/ to form the palatal nasal /ɲ/ as in SENIORE > *senhor* 'sir,' VINEA/VINIA > *vinha* 'vine' (VINIA is listed in the *Appendix Probi*; see 5.1). Today this process appears in Brazilian Portuguese, in popular pronunciations such as *demonho* for st. *demônio* (< DEMONIUM) 'devil' or *Antonho* for *Antônio*. On the outcomes of dental /t/, /d/, and velar /k/, /g/ consonants plus /j/, see below.

Another important source of the palatal glide /j/ was syllable-final velar consonants. The velar became a palatal glide which in turn palatalized, and merged with, immediately following consonants. Thus /gn/ became /jn/, which, just like /nj/, yielded the palatal nasal /ɲ/, as in PUGNU > *punho* 'fist.' Likewise, palatalization modified the alveolar fricative /s/ followed by /j/ (written SSE or SSI), producing the palatal consonant /ʃ/, as in RUSSEU 'red' > *roxo* 'purple' or PASSIONE > *paixão* 'passion.'

Velar consonants that became syllable-final through syncope, that is loss of following vowels, also became palatal glides, as in OCULU > /oklo/ > /ojlo/ > *olho* 'eye,' where the sequence /jl/ gives precisely the same result as the sequence /lj/. Palatalized velar consonants regularly palatalized preceding vowels when the following consonant was not affected, as in FACTU > /fajto/ > *feito* 'deed,' where the open central vowel /a/ became the mid front (palatal) vowel /e/ in contact with the following /j/. Note that in this instance the palatal glide still exists in Portuguese. In fact, the palatal glide often palatalized both the immediately following consonant and the preceding vowel. An example of this is popular Lat *basiu*, where the glide first jumped to the preceding syllable, i.e. /bajso/, then palatalized both the alveolar sibilant /s/ and the open central vowel /a/, yielding *beijo* 'kiss.'

The consonant clusters /pl/, /kl/, and /fl/ (written PL, CL, FL) also palatalized, originating the palatal affricate /ʧ/, source of the fricative /ʃ/, as in the set below:

> PLORARE > *chorar* 'to cry'     CLAVE > *chave* 'key'
> FLAMMA > *chama* 'flame'     PLUVIA > *chuva* 'rain'

In another set of words, however, /pl/, /kl/ and /fl/ yielded respectively /pr/, /kr/, /fr/:

> PLACERE > *prazer* 'pleasure'     CLAVU > *cravo* 'nail'
> FLACCU > *fraco* 'weak'     PLAGA > *praga* 'plague'

Palatalization also affected the velar consonants /k/, /g/ in contact with following palatal (that is, front) vowels. This process created affricate and fricative consonants, some of which, however, did not end up being palatal themselves. The shift of the point of articulation of /k/ and /g/ from the velum toward the palate went on beyond the latter to the alveolar ridge. Thus in word-initial position /k/ before /i/ or /e/ became the voiceless dorsoalveolar affricate /ts/, as in CENTU ['kentu] > *cento* /tsentu/ 'hundred.' In intervocalic position, just like the voiceless stop consonants /p/, /t/, and /k/ (see section 5.2.1), the same affricate /ts/ became voiced /dz/, as in PLACERE > /pradzer/ > *prazer* 'pleasure.'

It seems likely that the alveolar articulation of /ts/ and /dz/ as products of /k/ before front vowels came about through the merger of the palatalized products of /tj/ and /kj/. In other words, both the dental /t/ and the velar /k/ before the palatal glide /j/ yielded the same dorsoalveaolar affricates, /ts/ and /dz/, that are the products of /k/ before front vowels, and in similar conditions. Thus FORTIA /fortja/ > *força* 'force,' LANCEA /lankja/ > *lança* 'lance,' with voiceless /ts/, and RATIONE /ratjone/ > *razão* 'reason,' with voiced /dz/.

Portuguese is exceptional among the Romance languages of the Iberian Peninsula in that the affricate /ts/ derived from /kj/ was not normally subject to lenition° : FACIE /fakje/ > *face* 'face.' Likewise, in intervocalic position palatalization of /t/ before /j/ (written TI or TE) also yielded either the voiceless affricate /ts/, as in ORATIONE > *oração*, PRETIU > *preço* /pretsu/, GRATIA > *graça* 'grace,' or the voiced affricate /dz/, as in RATIONE > *razão* 'reason,' PRETIARE > *prezar* 'to prize.' Another source of /ts/ was palatalization of intervocalic /k/ (written C) before /e/ or /i/, as in PLACERE > *prazer*, VICES > *vezes* 'times.'

Palatalization of the voiced velar occlusive /g/ yielded consistently palatal results. The velar occlusive /g/ became a voiced affricate /dʒ/ in word-initial position, or in syllable-initial position after a consonant, and this affricate /dʒ/

then lost its occlusive element, becoming the voiced fricative /ʒ/, as in GINGIVA > *gengiva* 'gum' or GENTE > *gente* 'people.' The Latin palatal glide /j/ also became a voiced affricate, phonetically identical to the palatalized outcome of the voiced velar /g/, not only in word-initial position but also intervocalically: IANUARIU > *janeiro* 'January,' CUIU > *cujo* 'whose.' In the latter environment, i.e. between vowels, the development of /g/ and the voiced dental occlusive /d/ before the palatal glide /j/ coincided with that of the original Latin glide, thus ADIUTARE > *ajudar* 'to help.' Unlike its voiceless counterpart /k/, before the front vowels /i/, /e/ the voiced velar /g/ disappeared: REGINA > *rainha* 'queen,' DIGITU > *dedo* 'finger.'

In medieval Portuguese, the dorsoalveolar affricates /ts/, /tz/, resulting from the palatalization of /k/, /kj/, and /tj/ mentioned above, contrasted with the apicoalveolar sibilant fricatives /s/, /z/, which descended from Latin /s/. The voiced sibilant /z/ is also a product of lenition, i.e. Latin /s/ was voiced in intervocalic position. The four phonemes were distinguished in spelling:

| **Palatal affricates** | | **Apicoalveolar fricatives** | |
|---|---|---|---|
| /ts/ | ç before a, o, u: PALATIU > *paaço* > *paço* | /s'/ | s initially: SIC > *sim* 'yes' |
| | c before e, i: ACCEPTARE > *aceitar* 'to accept' | | -ss- intervocally: PASSU > *passo* 'step' |
| /dz/ | z *COCERE > *cozer* 'to cook' | /z'/ | -s- intervocally: CASA > *casa* 'house' |

By the end of the Middle Ages, the affricates /ts/, /dz/ lost their occlusive articulation and became the dorsoalveolar sibilant fricatives /s/, /z/, which continued to contrast with the two apicoalveolar fricatives /s'/ and /z'/. This four-way contrast, based on the manner of articulation (dorsoalveolar vs. apicoalveolar) and on the voiced/voiceless feature, was described in 1536 by Fernão de Oliveira (2000:96–97):

| **Pre-dorsodental fricatives** | | **Apicoalveolar fricatives** | |
|---|---|---|---|
| /s/ | ç before a, o, u: PALATIU *paço* 'palace' | /s'/ | s initially: SIC > *sim* 'yes' |
| | c before e, i: ACCEPTARE > *aceitar* 'to accept' | | -ss- intervocally: PASSU > *passo* 'step' |
| /z/ | z: *COCERE > *cozer* 'to cook' | /z'/ | -s- intervocally: CASA > *casa* 'house' |

By the end of the sixteenth century this four-way contrast had been simplified in most of the country (with the exception of a small area in the northeast) into two distinct two-way contrasts. One of these, in the area south of the Douro,

Table 5.3 *Examples of palatalization of consonants*

| Class. Lat | Changes | Mod. Pg | Class. Lat | Changes | Mod. Pg |
|---|---|---|---|---|---|
| CENTUM | /k/ > /ts/ > /s/ | cento | PLORARE | /pl/ > /tʃ/ > /ʃ/ | chorar |
| MULIEREM | /lj/ > /ʎ/ | mulher | CLAMARE | /kl/ > /tʃ/ > /ʃ/ | chamar |
| OCULUM | /kl/ > /ʎ/ | olho | COGNATUM | /gn/ > /ɲ/ | cunhado |
| FLAMAM | /fl/ > /tʃ/ > /ʃ/ | chama | VINEAM | /nj/ > /ɲ/ | vinha |

involved the dorsopalatals /s/ : /z/. The other, north of that river, in the Beira region, involved the alveopalatals /s'/ : /z'/. In either case the contrast between -ç- and -ss- became a matter of a spelling convention devoid of any relevance to pronunciation, as the following scheme shows:

/s/    initially:        c- before e, i: *célebre*        s-: *sou* '(I) am,' *sim* 'yes'
                          'famous,' *cidade* 'town'

       intervocally:    -ç-: *paço* 'palace,' *maça*      -ss-: *passo* 'step,' *massa*
                          'mace'                            'mass'

/z/    intervocally:    -z-: *cozer* 'to cook'            -s-: *casa* 'house'

In the seventeenth and eighteenth centuries the affricate /tʃ/ lost its occlusive feature (Castro 1991a:258), originating the palatal fricative /ʃ/ in most of the country, although the pronunciation [tʃ] persists to this day in conservative northern dialects, as in *chorar* [tʃurarɨ] vs. st. [ʃurarɨ] 'to cry' (Mota 2001:33).

### 5.2.3    Phoneme addition

Besides modifying one or more features of a phoneme, sound change may involve either addition or loss of an entire phoneme. Evidence of this process in popular Latin is provided by graffiti found in Pompeii showing that an initial /i/, written I, tended to be added to words beginning with /s/ followed by a consonant, as in *Ismurna* for SMYRNA, the name of a town, or *ispose* for SPONSAE '(of a) wife.' This phonological process, known as *prothesis*, has continued in Portuguese: any word-initial sequence of /s/ + consonant must be preceded by /e/ (phonetically EP [ɐ] and BP [i]), as in STATUA > *estátua* 'statue,' SCUTU > *escudo* 'shield,' or SPHAERA > *esfera* 'sphere.' This process applies regularly to new loan words beginning in /s/ + consonant, such as *standard* > *estândar* or *stress* > *estresse*.

Addition of a phoneme within a word is called *epenthesis*. For instance, sequences of vowels in hiatus often became separated by a consonant, the nature of which was conditioned by the phonetic features of one of those vowels, usually the preceding one. Thus MEA > mĩa > *minha* 'mine,' where the consonant /ɲ/ retains both the palatal articulation and the feature of nasality of the vowel /ĩ/. In turn, the vowel then lost its nasal articulation. In UNA > ũa > *uma* the epenthetic consonant /m/ shows the features of nasality and labial articulation of the preceding /u/.

A sequence of glide + vowel could also undergo epenthesis, as in LAU-DARE > LOARE > LOAR > *louvar* [lo'var] ~ [low'var] 'to praise.' In this case the epenthetic /v/, a voiced labiodental fricative, shares the features of voice and labial articulation with the labiovelar glide /w/. Epenthesis could also undo a consonant group, as in the insertion of /a/ between the /b/ and /l/ in BLATTA > *barata* 'cockroach.' In Brazilian Portuguese an epenthetic /i/ is regularly inserted in consonant sequences such as *-dv-* or *pn-*, as in *advogado* [adʒivo'gadu] 'lawyer' or *pneu* [pi'new] 'tire' (7.3.1.2).

Addition of a phoneme in final position, known as *paragoge*, explains changes like ANTE > *antes* 'before,' possibly by analogy with *depois* 'after.' Addition of a paragogic *e* [ə] or [ɨ] at the end of infinitives is common in European Portuguese, as in *falar* > [fa'larə] ~ [fa'larɨ] 'to talk.'

### 5.2.4    Phoneme loss

Phonemes may be lost in word-initial, word-medial, or word-final position. Loss in initial position, or *apheresis*, occurred in words like HOMINATICUM > *homenagem* > *menagem* 'house arrest' (cf. *torre de menagem* 'castle keep'), IMAGINARE > *imaginar* > dial. *maginar* 'to imagine,' or HORRORE > horror > *ror* 'a large amount,' as in pop. *um ror de gente* 'a lot of people.'

The last three examples also show loss of a phoneme in final position, or *apocope*, as in SALE > *sal* 'salt,' MALE > *mal* 'evil', and MENSE > MESE > *mês* 'month.' The loss of word-final /m/ in the accusative of nouns and adjectives (5.3.2) and verb forms like AMABAM > *amava* 'P1sg loved' (5.3.4) are also cases of apocope.

The loss of vowels in word-medial position is called *syncope*, and was especially frequent in unstressed syllables, whether posttonic or not. This was the case with SPECULUM > pop. SPECLU > *espelho* 'mirror' and OCULUM > pop. OCLU > *olho* 'eye' (as found in the *Appendix Probi*, 5.1) where -CL- /kl/ palatalized and yielded /ʎ/, as mentioned earlier. Syncope of pretonic F e/ (written E) and subsequent voicing of the occlusive consonant in the resulting intervocalic cluster produces e.g. OPERARE > *obrar* 'to work' or SUPERARE > *sobrar* 'to be left over.' This process also took place in word-medial position, as in the case of intervocalic /l/ (written L), creating a hiatus, which remained as such, as in SALIRE > *sair* 'to go out,' or resulted in the fusion of the two identical vowels as in COLORE > *coor* > *cor* 'color,' VOLUNTATE > *voontade* > *vontade* 'will.'

Table 5.4 *Examples of addition and loss of phonemes*

| Addition | Loss |
|---|---|
| Word-initial position (prothesis) | Word-initial position (apheresis) |
| STATUA > *estátua* 'statue' | HOMINATICUM > *homenagem* > *menagem* |
| STELLA > *estrela* 'star' | 'house arrest' |
| SPHAERA > *esfera* 'sphere' | APOTHEKA > *bodega* 'tavern' |
| Word-medial position (epenthesis) | Word-medial position (syncope) |
| LAUDARE > LOARE > LOAR > *louvar* | NUDU > *nuu* > *nu* 'nude' |
| 'praise' | NIDU > *ninho* 'nest' |
| STELLA > *estrela* 'star' | SPECULUM > pop. SPECLU > *espelho* 'mirror' |
| REGESTU > *registro* 'register' | |
| Word-final position (paragoge) | Word-final position (apocope) |
| ANTE > *antes* 'before' | SALE > *sal* 'salt' |
| | SUNT > *são* 'are' |

## 5.3    Morphological change

Morphological change, caused in part by sound changes and in part by a simplifying tendency already noticeable in popular Latin, yielded a radically different system of determinants, nouns, adjectives, and pronouns, and profoundly modified verb conjugation.

### 5.3.1    Determinants

As we have seen, the class of determinants (3.3) includes articles, demonstratives, and possessives. Although Classical Latin did not have a definite article, it had a set of six fully declined demonstratives. One of the most common of these, ILLE–ILLA–ILLUD, developed into a definite article in popular Latin. Thus a phrase like ILLA MULIER, which meant 'that woman' in the literary language, came to mean 'the woman' in popular speech.

The Portuguese definite article developed from the accusative forms ILLU(M), ILLA(M), with loss of the first syllable IL- in most cases. Thus in pre-literary Portuguese, there were four forms of the definite article, inflected for gender and number: *lo, la, los, las.* These forms were reduced to *o, a, os, as* in syntactic contexts where the initial *l-* stood between vowels, as in *de + lo + noun, a + las + noun.* (This was the same regular deletion of /l/ that occurred within words, as in PALATIU > *paaço* > *paço* 'palace.') Eventually, *o, a, os, as* became generalized as the only forms for the definite article.

The cardinal number UNUS, UNA 'one' was used in Latin to suggest indefiniteness, as in UNUS CASSIUS 'a certain Cassius,' and eventually became the

Table 5.5 *Origin of Portuguese determinants*

| Articles | Demonstratives | Possessives | |
|---|---|---|---|
| **Definite** | | | |
| ILLU > OP lo > o | *ACCU[1] + ISTE > OP aqueste > este | MEU > meu | MEA > OP mia > minha |
| ILLA > OP la > a | *ACCU + ISSE[2] > OP aquesse > esse | TUU > OP tou[3] > teu[4] | TUA > tua |
| | *ACCU + ILLE > aquele | SUU > sou[3] > seu[4] | SUA > sua |
| **Indefinite** | | NOSTRU > nosso | NOSTRA > nossa |
| UNU > ūu > um | | VOSTRU > vosso | VOSTRA > vossa |
| UNA > ūa > uma | | | |

[1] Hypothetical form, from ECCE, used in combination with demonstratives.

[2] IPSE > pop. Lat ISSE.

[3] Dial. in N. Portugal.

[4] By analogy to *meu*.

indefinite article UNUM > uu > *um*, and UNAM > *ua* > uma, which developed plural forms with the meaning of 'indefinite small number of': *uns, umas*.

The Latin demonstratives ISTE and IPSE 'same, self' respectively yielded *este, esse*. ILLE was also preserved as a demonstrative, but with the addition of the expletive adverb *ACCU (itself a hypothetical form supposedly derived from AD ECCU), so that ACCU ILLE evolved into *aquele*. In medieval and early modern Portuguese, the other two demonstratives often appeared with initial *aqu-* (*aqueste, aquesse*), by analogy with *aquele*.

The derivation of Portuguese possessives from Latin ones was quite straight-forward, with some important adjustments: *teu, seu* were modeled after *meu* < MEU(M), and the etymological *nostro* < NOSTRU(M) was replaced by *nosso*, which likely resulted from a hypothetical NOSSUM. The second person plural form VESTRUM of Classical Latin left no trace, since the Romance languages presuppose the analogical form VOSTRU(M) > *vostro*, which in Portuguese yielded to *vosso*. As mentioned in section (5.3), the feminine possessive MEA produced *minha* through nasalization of the stressed vowel and subsequent development of the nasal palatal /ɲ/.

## 5.3.2 *Nouns and adjectives*

The paradigms of nouns and adjectives were radically simplified in popular Latin by three developments. First, several processes of amalgamation reduced the declensions of nouns and adjectives from five to three. Secondly, the neuter gender disappeared as a formal category, leaving only vestiges, such as the so-called neuter determinants *isto, isso, aquilo* (3.3). Finally, nouns and adjectives lost the case inflections that indicated their syntactic functions. In consequence, variation in gender was reduced to masculine and feminine only. In Portuguese and other Ibero-Romance languages, noun and adjective forms descend regularly from the accusative form of Latin nouns and adjectives. As mentioned earlier, since the accusative plural in all declensions ended in /s/, this phoneme ended up as a plural marker, as in PORTA(M) 'door' – PORTAS 'doors.'

Popular Latin retained three declensions, classified according to their theme vowel, -A, -U, or -E. Nouns in -A were mostly feminine: ROSA 'rose,' STELLA 'star,' FILIA 'daughter,' but POETA 'poet' (m.). Nouns in -U were mostly masculine, e.g. SERVU 'slave,' FILIU 'son,' CARRU 'cart,' but MANU 'hand' (which originally belonged to the fourth declension) was feminine. Finally, nouns in -E were either masculine (PRINCIPE 'chief,' CONSULE 'consul') or feminine (VIRGINE 'maiden,' TURRE 'tower'). Since in Portuguese most nouns in -u were masculine and those in -a were feminine, the endings -o and -a ended up being associated, respectively, with the masculine and feminine.

Neuter singulars in -u were reinterpreted as masculine, e.g. CORNU 'horn,' CORPU[S] 'body' as in Portuguese *corno*, *corpo* (the -s removed by analogy, since it had become the plural marker). Feminine singulars in -u (usually, but not always, from the fourth declension) either became masculine, as in PINU > Pg *pinho* 'pine tree,' or, in order to mark feminine gender explicitly, had their endings shifted to the first declension. For instance the Classical Latin forms SOCRU 'mother-in-law' and NURU 'daughter-in-law' appear in the *Appendix Probi* (5.1) in their popular forms SOCRA, NURA, which produced Pg *sogra*, *nora*. Plural neuter nouns ending in -a, such as OPERA 'works' or LIGNA 'firewood,' were reinterpreted as being singular feminine; consequently, their Portuguese descendants, *a obra* 'work' and *a lenha* 'firewood,' are feminine, sometimes with a collective or generic meaning traceable to the original plurality. (Compare Pg *lenho* 'log, tree trunk' < LIGNU(M) 'stick of wood' with *lenha*.)

### 5.3.3     Pronouns

First person and second person subject pronouns have changed relatively little: EGO > *eo* > *eu*, TU > *tu*, NOS > *nós*, VOS > *vós*. Direct and indirect object pronouns descend from the Latin accusative forms, ME > *me*, TE > *te*, NOS > *nos*, VOS > *vos,* but they lost their stress and became clitics (4.5.2). The pronominal objects of prepositions, which are stressed, go back to the Latin datives MIHI and TIBI, thus MIHI > OP *mi* > *mim* (with nasalization of /i/ by assimilation to initial /m/), TIBI > ti. The plural forms, as objects of prepositions, are identical to the subject pronouns.

Combinations of pronouns with the preposition CUM 'with' had a separate development. In Latin CUM followed, rather than preceded, its pronominal object, which stood in the ablative case, thus MECUM 'with me,' NOBISCUM 'with us,' TECUM 'with you (sg),' and VOBISCUM 'with you' (pl). This usage can be seen in the traditional greeting *Dominus tecum/vobiscum* '(may) the Lord (be) with you,' and MECUM survives in the noun *vade-mecum* (literally 'go with me'), meaning something, e.g. a book, constantly carried for use. Regular phonetic loss of final -M and voicing of intervocalic -C- reduced the singular form MECU > *mego* and TECU > *tego*, and then, by analogy with the prepositional objects OP *mi/ti*, to *migo/tigo*. The plural forms *nosco, vosco* were formed from a combination of the preposition with the pronouns *nós/vós* in place of the original datives/ablatives NOBIS/VOBIS. As time went by, however, speakers ceased to identify the terminal segments *-go/co* with their primitive meaning 'with,' and consequently they started combining those forms with *com*, creating *comigo, contigo, consigo, conosco* (EP *connosco*), *convosco*.

Instead of a specific pronoun for the third person, Latin used the demonstrative IS–EA–ID to refer to someone other than the speaker or the hearer, or to something not associated with either. In popular Latin IS was replaced by the demonstrative ILLE–ILLA–ILLUD, whose paradigms furnished most of the forms of the third person subject and object pronouns in Romance. Exceptionally, the third person subject pronouns preserved a Latin nominative, i.e. the masculine singular ILLE, which yielded *ele*. The feminine form could come from either the nominative or the accusative, ILLA or ILLA(M) > *ela*. The plural forms *eles, elas* were formed by adding *-s* to the singular. These four forms also function as objects of prepositions and, in popular Brazilian Portuguese, as direct objects (7.3.2.3).

The direct object pronouns became clitics, like *me/te*, discussed above, with apheresis of the first syllable: (IL)LU(M) > *lo*, (IL)LA(M) > *la*, (IL)LOS > *los*, (IL)LAS > *las*. Loss of the resulting initial *l-* when it followed a vowel then yielded *o, a, os, as*. However, the *l* was preserved after a consonant, leading to preservation of allomorphs of the direct object pronouns with initial *l-*, as in *fazê-lo* 'to do it (m.),' *comê-la* 'to eat it (f.).'

The third person object pronouns, unlike those of the first and second persons, maintained a formal distinction between direct and indirect objects. The latter descend from the Latin datives (IL)LI and (IL)LIS, where apheresis of the first syllable yielded OP *li, lis*. Apheresis also modified the pronominal sequence dative + accusative (IL)LI ILLU(M) 'to him + it.' Subsequent palatalization of the initial consonant in the resulting LI ILLU yielded *ljelo* > *lhelo* > *lheo* > *lho*. The latter form served as a basis for the indirect object pronoun *lhe*, which replaced *li*, and *lhes* was formed analogically.

To express reflexivity (4.6), the first and second person object forms *me, te, nos, vos* function as reflexives with no formal distinction. In Latin, the single form SE, which embraced all genders and numbers of the third person reflexive, yielded Pg *se*, which became a clitic like *me/te*. The dative form SIBI, like TIBI, became the object of prepositions, *si*. The ablative form SE combined with the

Table 5.6 *Origin of Portuguese pronouns*

| | | | |
|---|---|---|---|
| EGO > *eo* > *eu* | ME > | *me* | MIHI > OP *mi* > *mim* |
| NOS > *nós* | | *nos* | |
| TU > *tu* | TE > | *te* | TIBI > *ti* |
| VOS > *vós* | | *vos* | |
| ILLE > *ele* | | | SIBI > *si* |
| ILLA > *ela* | | *la* > *a* | |
| ILLU > | | *lo* > *o* | |
| (IL)LI ILLU(M) > *ljelo* > *lhelo* > *lheo* > *lho* > *lhe* | | | |

preposition CUM in the same way as did ME and TE, with similar outcomes: SECUM > *sego*, *sigo* (by analogy with *si*), *consigo*.

### 5.3.4    Verbs

Like the other Romance languages, Portuguese inherited the basic structure of the Latin verb system, with major modifications in the general design and many morphological changes. What follows is a very streamlined overview.

The core of the Latin verb system included four formal categories called conjugations. In addition to the denotative, that is lexical, meaning of the verb, a Latin verb could display up to four categories of grammatical information, namely, (1) tense (present, past, or future); (2) mood (indicative, subjunctive, or imperative); (3) person and number; and (4) voice (active or passive). Thus in a form such as *amabamus* 'we loved' (whence the Portuguese imperfect *amávamos*), the verbal root *am-* carries the lexical, meaning; the stem vowel *-a-* shows the verb belongs to the conjugation in -ARE (AMARE > Pg *amar* 'to love'). Next the morpheme *-ba-* signals both the tense (imperfect) and the mood (indicative); the person ending *-mus* shows this form corresponds to the first person plural (Lat *nos* 'we'). The category of voice is revealed by the contrast between *amabamus* 'we loved' and *amabamur* 'we were loved,' which belonged to a parallel passive conjugation, vanished in Romance, about which more will be said below.

Portuguese has kept only three of the Latin conjugations, those with verbs stressed on the stem vowel in the infinitive forms (AMARE 'to love,' DEBERE 'to have to,' AUDIRE 'to hear'). The third-conjugation verbs (LEGĚRE 'to read'), with unstressed endings in the infinitive forms, were absorbed into the other conjugations. Some phonological anomalies caused the third conjugation verb PONĚRE 'to put' to lose intervocalic *-n-* and subsequently the resulting hiatus was reduced to a single vowel: PONĚRE > */ponére/ > /pōer/ > /por/ *pôr* 'to put.' Consequently, Portuguese ended up with three conjugations, namely –*ar* (*amar*), -*er* (*dever*), and -*ir* (*dormir*), and a kind of extra conjugation made up of *pôr* and its compounds, as in the following scheme, where only the singular forms are shown for the sake of brevity:

|         | 1st | 2nd | 3rd | (3rd) | 4th |
|---------|-----|-----|-----|-------|-----|
| Latin   | **AMARE** | **DEBERE** | **LEGĔRE** | **PONĔRE** | **DORMIRE** |
|         | AMO | DEBEO | LEGO | PONEO | DORMIO |
|         | AMAS | DEBES | LEGIS | PONIS | DORMIS |
|         | AMAT | DEBET | LEGIT | PONIT | DORMIT |

|            | 1st | 2nd |     |      | 3rd |
|------------|-----|-----|-----|------|-----|
| Portuguese | **amar** | **dever** | **ler** | **pôr** | **dormir** |
|            | amo | devo | leio | ponho | durmo |
|            | amas | deves | lês | pões | dormes |
|            | ama | deve | lê | põe | dorme |

The Latin tense system included a contrast between two aspects°, which conveyed the speaker's perception of how a verbal action was carried out. One aspect was the *infectum*, or *imperfective*, meaning an action not completed. The other was the *perfectum* (from Lat PER- 'completely' + -FECTUM 'done'), or *perfective*, meaning an action fully carried out. The relationships between imperfective and perfective forms can be seen in the scheme below (based on Penny 1991:141):

|          | *Indicative* | | *Subjunctive* | |
|----------|--------------|-----------|----------------|------------|
|          | Imperfective | Perfective | Imperfective | Perfective |
| Present  | **AMO** | **AMAVI** | **AMEM** | AMAVERIM |
| Past     | **AMABAM** | | AMAREM | AMAVERIM |
| Future   | AMABO | AMAVERO | | |
| Anterior | | **AMAVERAM** | | **AMAVISSEM** |

Of these tenses, only those in boldface have survived. The imperfective present and past, respectively AMO > *amo* 'I love' and AMABAM > *amava* 'I loved/used to love' passed to Romance more or less intact. The future tense (AMABO 'I will love'), however, was replaced by a periphrasis° made up of an infinitive followed by a form of HABERE 'to have,' e.g. AMARE HABEO 'I will love.' The forms of HABERE (P1sg *habeo*, P1pl *habemus*, etc.) functioned at first as an auxiliary verb°, but eventually they coalesced with the infinitive, forming a single word, thus AMARE HABEO > *amar hei* > *amarei* 'I will love,' AMARE HABEMUS > *amar emus* > *amaremos* 'we will love,' and so on.

The basic meaning of the tenses of the *perfectum* shifted from 'completed, punctual' to 'anterior' or 'past' and underwent radical changes, e.g. AMAVI > *amei*, a preterit, and AMAVERAM > *amara*, a past perfect (that is, 'anterior') or pluperfect. Further, AMAVI was restricted to the past punctual meaning where it contrasted with AMABAM. As a result, it is only in the past tense that a formally marked aspectual contrast now exists, that is, between the preterit ("punctual past") *amei* < AMAVI and the imperfect ("durative past") *amava* < AMABAM.

New tenses were created, usually by means of periphrases combining HABERE (and later TENERE) as an auxiliary verb placed before the participle, as in HABEO AMATUM, which yielded *hei amado*. This later became *tenho amado* 'I have loved,' when *ter* (from Lat TENĚRE 'to have') became the preferred auxiliary verb of the perfect tenses (instead of *haver*).

By analogy, the periphrasis HABEO AMATUM (VS. AMAVI) spawned other parallel constructions, such as HABEBAM AMATUM > *havia/tinha amado* 'I had loved.' This periphrasis initially contrasted with AMAVERAM > *amara* 'I had loved,' but no aspectual difference in fact existed, and eventually the new compound tense displaced the latter non-periphrastic past anterior in the common language, although *amara* is preserved in formal styles (as is *havia amado*, considered more formal than *tinha amado*). A periphrastic future perfect was also formed, namely HABERE HABEO AMATUM (VS. AMAVERO), which yielded *haverei amado,* or more commonly *terei amado* 'I shall have loved.'

Of the Latin subjunctive the only survivors were the present AMEM > (present) *ame* and the pluperfect AMAVISSEM > (past) *amasse*. A brand-new future subjunctive developed to indicate a hypothetical future situation in constructions like *quando nós amarmos* 'when we may love.' According to a generally accepted explanation, it came about from the fusion of the future anterior (perfect) indicative AMAVERO with the present anterior (perfect) subjunctive AMAVERIM. Since in regular verbs, the forms of the inflected infinitive (see below) coincide with those of the future subjunctive, the morphological peculiarity of the latter tense is more apparent in verbs with changes in the radical, such as FECERIMUS > [*quando nós*] *fizermos* '[when we] may do'.

Following the general model of periphrastic constructions with HABERE, a present perfect was created as HABEAM AMATUM > *haja / tenha amado*, as was a past perfect (or pluperfect) as HABUISSEM AMATUM > *houvesse/tivesse amado*.

Another Romance novelty was the creation of a new mood, the conditional, which signals an eventuality less certain in the speakers' minds than that associated with the future (*amarei* 'I will love'), which is regarded as more certain to happen. The conditional was morphologically like the future but with the past tense of the auxiliary verb: AMARE HABEBAM > *amaria* 'I would love.' Following the model of the future, a compound conditional also came about as *teria amado* 'I would have loved.'

Like other Romance languages, Portuguese retained only two forms of the Latin imperative, yielding P2sg AMA > *ama (tu)* and P2pl AMATE > *amai (vós)*. For the other persons, as well as for the negative forms of these two imperatives, forms of the present subjunctive are used.

Three non-finite or uninflected Latin verb forms had special significance in the development of Portuguese verbs. One was the infinitive per se, the *infectum* form AMARE, a verbal noun. Another was the past passive participle, AMA-TUM/A/OS/AS, a verbal adjective (and as such inflected for gender and number like other adjectives); the third was the gerund, AMANDO, fundamentally a verbal adverb.

Portuguese is the only Romance language with an infinitive with person/number inflections. Thus the full Portuguese reflection of the Latin infinitive AMARE is *amar, amares, amar, amarmos, amardes, amarem*, as in *Ela pediu para nós falarmos* 'she asked (for) us to sing.' Both the uninflected and the inflected infinitives participate in perfect and passive constructions: *termos/havermos amados* 'to have [we] loved,' *haver amado* 'to have loved,' *termos/havermos sido amados* 'to have [we] been loved,' *haver sido amado* 'to have been loved.'

As hinted above, Latin had two parallel conjugation sets, distinguished by their desinences and referred to as "voices." In the active voice, which was the source of the verb system in Romance, the subject corresponded to the semantic actor (4.2). In the passive voice, the subject corresponded to the semantic patient. In the past tenses, the passive used a periphrastic construction made up of a past participle followed by a conjugated form of the verb ESSE 'to be':

| Active voice | Passive voice |
|---|---|
| **Present** | |
| AMO 'I love' | AMOR 'I am loved' |
| AMAS 'you love' | AMARIS 'you are loved' |
| AMAT 'he/she loves' | AMATUR 'he/she is loved.' |
| **Preterit** | |
| AMAVI 'I loved | AMATUS SUM 'I was loved' |
| AMAVISTI 'you loved' | AMATUS ES 'you were loved' |
| AMAVIT 'he/she loved' | AMATUS EST 'he/she was loved' |

In popular Latin the inflected passive was lost, and the passive preterit construction, made up of a participle + *sum/es/est* was retained with a present meaning, originating the Portuguese periphrastic construction *ser* + participle (*sou/és/é amado* 'I am/you are/he/she is loved'), which grammarians have continued to call the "passive voice" for the sake of tradition. The new construction accepted an explicit agent of the passive (4.2), introduced by a preposition which in early stages of Portuguese was *de*. Eventually, *por* became the regular marker of the agent, as in *Violeta foi abandonada por seus amantes* 'Violet was abandoned by her lovers.' Nonetheless, *de* survives in this function in set phrases such as *estimado dos amigos* 'liked by friends.'

In the new periphrastic perfect tenses, the participle was originally passive in meaning, and agreed in gender and number with the direct object of the verb, as in *tenho escritas cartas* 'I have written letters' vs. *tenho escritos livros* 'I have written books.' This concordance was lost in perfect constructions in Portuguese (*tenho escrito cartas/livros* 'I have written letters/books'). In passive constructions, however, the participle retains its adjectival character, and thus agrees with the subject of the verb in gender and number.

Finally, the gerund grew out of a Latin verbal form which, while functioning as a noun, strongly connoted the idea of a continuing action, as in AMANDO 'by loving.' In Portuguese this gerund formed periphrases, especially with the verb *estar* (from Lat STARE), that expressed actions in progress (hence the label "progressive" or "continuous" for tenses like *estou falando* 'I am speaking'). In turn, the original present active participle AMANS 'loving' acquired the status of either a noun or an adjective, as for instance AMANTE(M) > *amante* 'lover.'

### 5.3.5    Adverbs

Classical Latin formed manner adverbs with specific endings, e.g. *-ter*, as in *fortiter* 'bravely,' or *-e*, as in *romanice* 'in the Roman manner,' from which the noun *romance* was derived (3.6). This adverb-forming process fell in disuse in popular Latin, which used instead constructions such as AD SIC 'thusly' which gave OP *assi* > *assim* 'thus.' Another process used word combinations like the following:

| | |
|---|---|
| demonstrative + noun | HAC HORA 'this hour' > *agora* 'now' |
| preposition + adjective + noun | IN BONA HORA 'in good hour'> *embora* 'although' |
| preposition + adverb | DE MAGIS > 'of more' > *demais* 'too much' |

The most productive adverb-forming process, in Portuguese (3.6) and other Romance languages, involves adding *mente*, derived from the noun MENTE 'mind,' to a feminine adjective, as in PLACIDA MENTE 'with a quiet mind,' that is 'quietly' or TRISTE MENTE 'with a sad mind,' or 'sadly.' Table 5.8 shows the origin of some adverbs.

### 5.3.6    Connectors: Prepositions and conjunctions

Use of prepositions as a syntactic device, common in popular Latin, increased in Romance, allowing many Latin prepositions to survive in Portuguese. In addition, one way to create new prepositions consisted in combining two or more existing ones (DE IN ANTE > *denante* > *diante* 'in front of'). Another was to use as prepositions words from other categories, such as the present participle *durante* 'during,' from *durar* 'to last, to endure.' Portuguese conjunctions, on

## Table 5.7 *Origin of Portuguese verb tenses*

| Latin | | Portuguese — From Latin | | Romance creations |
|---|---|---|---|---|
| **Indicative** | | | | |
| Present | AMO | Present | *amo* | Present perfect > *hei*/*tenho amado* |
| Imperfect | AMABAM | Imperfect | *amava* | |
| Preterit | AMAVI | Preterit | *amei* | |
| Pluperfect | AMAVERAM | Pluperfect | *amara* | Past perfect *tinha amado* |
| Future | AMABO | — | | Future *amar hei* > *amaréi* |
| Future perfect* | AMAVERO | | | Future perfect *terei amado* |
| | | | | Condicional *amar ia* > *amaria* |
| | | | | Conditional perfect *teria amado* |
| **Subjunctive** | | | | |
| Present | AMEM | Present | *ame* | Present perfect *tenha amado* |
| Imperfect | AMAREM | — | | |
| Perfect | AMAVERIM | — | | Future* *amar, amares, amar* . . . |
| | | | | Future perfect *tiver amado* |
| Pluperfect | AMAVISSEM | Imperfect | *amasse* | Past perfect *tivesse amado* |
| Future perfect | AMAVERIMUS | — | | |
| **Imperative** | | | | |
| Present | AMA, AMATE | Imperative | *ama* (tu), *amai* (vós) | |
| Future | AMATO, AMATOTE | — | | |
| **Infinitive** | | | | |
| Present | AMARE | Infinitive | *amar* | Inflected infinitive: *amares, amarmos, amardes* . . . |
| Perfect | AMAVISSE/AMASSE | — | | |
| Future | AMATURUS ESSE | — | | |
| **Participles** | AMATUS | Participle | *amado* | |
| Present | AMANS, -ANTIS | | *amante* (adj.) | |
| Future | AMATURUS, -A, -UM | — | | |
| **Gerund** | | Gerund | | |
| Genitive | AMANDI | | | |
| Dative | AMANDO | | | |
| Accusative | AMANDUM | | *amando* | |
| Ablative | AMANDO | | | |
| Supine: | AMATUM | — | | |

\* Except for the first person, the forms of the future perfect indicative and the perfect subjunctive (AMAVERO/AMAVERIM) were identical.

Table 5.8 *Origin of Portuguese adverbs*

| Latin | Pg | Latin | Pg | Latin | Pg |
|---|---|---|---|---|---|
| **Time** | | | | | |
| HAC HORA > | agora | AD POST > | após | DE EX POST > | depois |
| AD *MANIANA > | amanhã | HODIE > | hoje | NUNQUAM > | nunca |
| CITO > | cedo | JAM > | já | SEMPER > | sempre |
| **Place** | | | | | |
| AD ILLIC > | ali | DE INTRO > | dentro | AD TRANS > | atrás |
| *ACCU HIC > | aqui | AB ANTE > | ante | DE TRANS > | de trás |
| AD IBI / HIC > | aí | LONGE > | longe | AD CIMA > | acima |
| **Manner** | | | | | |
| DE MAGIS > | demais | AD SIC > | assim | BENE > | bem |
| QUOMODO > | como | TALI VICE > | talvez | MALE > | mal |

the other hand, include only a few inherited from Latin and many more created in the language (Table 5.9).

## 5.4    Syntactic change

To make up for the loss of word-final contrasts that once expressed syntactic functions in Latin, two devices were widely used in Romance, namely a more fixed word order and an increase in the use of function, or structural, words.

### 5.4.1    Word order

By relying on case endings to signal the syntactic function of determinants, nouns, adjectives, and pronouns, Latin allowed considerable variation in word order. This meant that a sentence like *Puellam mula momordit* 'the mule bit the girl' always had the same meaning even though word order might vary, as in these arrangements:

*mula puellam momordit    momordit puellam mula    momordit mula puellam*
*puellam momordit mula    mula momordit puellam    puellam mula momordit*

In all such orderings the nominative desinence -*a* and the accusative desinence -*m* make it clear that *mula* is the subject and *puellam* is the direct object. Swapping those endings creates a different sentence: *Puella mulam momordit* 'the girl bit the mule,' again irrespective of word order.

As contrasting case endings were lost, prepositions and word order were increasingly relied upon to signal syntactic function. A more rigid order then tended to favor the sequence subject – verb – object (SVO) as a kind of default,

Table 5.9 *Origin of Portuguese connectors*

**Prepositions**

| Latin | Pg | Latin | Pg | Latin | Pg |
|---|---|---|---|---|---|
| A > | a | DE > | de | SINE > | sem |
| ANTE > | ante | IN > | em | SUB > | so (arch.)[1] |
| CUM > | com | INTER > | entre | SUPER > | sobre |
| CONTRA > | contra | PER/PRO > | por | TRANS > | trás |

**Compound prepositions**

| Latin | Pg | Latin | Pg | Latin | Pg |
|---|---|---|---|---|---|
| DE IN ANTE > | diante | AD POST > | apos | PER AD > | pera (arch.) |
|  |  |  |  |  | > para |
| DE TRANS > | detrás | DE EX DE > | desde | PER ANTE > | perante |

**Conjunctions**

| Latin | Pg | Latin | Pg | Latim | Pg |
|---|---|---|---|---|---|
| ET > | e | MAGIS > | mas | AUT > | ou |
| NEC > | nem | PRO INDE > | porém | QUID > | que |
| QUOMODO > | como | QUANDO > | quando | SI > | se |
| QUE > | que |  |  |  |  |

[1] MP *sob* is a learned form.

or unmarked°, order, as in *puella momordit mula*. This is reflected in today's preference: in *a menina mordeu a mula* the noun phrase *a menina* is invariably interpreted as the semantic subject. Other orderings, though possible, tend to be marked°. The order *verb – object – subject,* for example, is used when we want to focus the subject, as in 1a–1b:

(1)   a. *Patrulhará a cidade o Exército.*
        'The Army will patrol the town.'
      b. *Chegarão amanhã os astronautas.*
        'The astronauts will arrive tomorrow.'

The use of prepositions increased in Romance as a device for signaling syntactic function. A Latin construction like 2a, where the *ae* marks *Tulliae* as the indirect object (dative case), was rephrased in popular Latin as 2b, with the preposition *a* marking the indirect object. (Cf. *to* in *Julia gave a great gift to Tullia.*)

(2)   a. *Julia Tulliae donum magnum dedit.*
        'Julia gave Tullia a great gift.'
      b. *Julia dedit donu magnu a Tullia.*
        'Julia gave a great gift to Tullia.'

A combination of fixed word order and preposition was used in developing the noun-forming pattern *noun + preposition + noun,* in which the first noun is modified by the construction *preposition + noun*: *carro de combate* 'combat car,' *casa de campo* 'country house,' *filho de algo* > *fidalgo*, originally 'man of means' (*algo* 'something') and later 'nobleman.' The pattern *noun + noun*, in which the second noun qualifies the first without being connected to it by any explicit syntactic link, is another productive noun-forming device, as in *caminhão-tanque* 'tanker truck,' *moda praia* 'beach fashion,' *oferta Natal* 'Christmas special,' and so on.

### 5.4.2    Indeterminate constructions

As seen in 4.8.1, the passive construction makes possible sentences like *Os bondes foram comprados* 'The street cars were bought,' which describe an action without mentioning any actor. Latin had other devices for omitting information about the actor. One of these consisted in using the noun *homo* 'man' generically, as a kind of indeterminate actor (HOMO DICIT 'one says'), which survived in old Portuguese as *homem: Quanto homem vive, vê mais* 'the more man [=one] lives, the more one sees' (Bueno 1955:208). Another device was a construction with the third person reflexive pronoun SE, as in SE DICIT 'one says' (Elcock 1940:104) or LITTERA SE SCRIBIT 'the letter is written' (Coutinho 1962:326), which was the source of the indeterminate *se* (4.9).

### 5.4.3    Other constructions

Inevitably, Old Portuguese had features that have disappeared from the modern language. One such feature was the adverb *hi* or *i* (comparable to Fr *y*), which preceded the verb *haver* with an existential meaning, as in *(h)averá i tristeza* 'there will be unhappiness' (Bueno 1955:205). Another was the use of the relative pronoun *cujo* 'whose' as an interrogative without an antecedent, as in *Cujo filho és?* 'whose son are you?' (Bueno 1955:219).

A feature may cease to be active in the common language and yet be retained in fossilized expressions. For example, the use of the past perfect indicative in *-ra*, *-ras*, *-ra* in hypothetical clauses, as in *como se foram* 'as if they were' (Silva Neto 1970:509), was replaced, with the same meaning, by the imperfect subjunctive, *como se fossem*. Nevertheless, the old form occurs in set expressions such as *se eu fora* 'if I were,' as in *Se eu fora rica você teria de tudo* 'if I were rich you would have everything.'

Uneven patterns of language change account for the fact that constructions no longer used in EP persist in BP. According to Bueno (1955:211–214) this is the case with subject pronouns used as direct objects (7.3.2.3), or the preposition *em* used with verbs of movement (7.3.2.8). Both uses occur in the following Old Portuguese examples:

(3)      a. *Perdi ela que foi a rem milhor.*
            'I lost her who was the best thing.'
         b. *Se a alma vai en paraíso . . . a alma está benta.*
            'If the soul goes to Paradise, the soul is blessed.'


## 5.5      Lexical change

Over the centuries the meaning of words can undergo several kinds of mod-
ification. Processes of semantic change include *generalization,* which turns a
word with a specific meaning into a generic term, as in the case of popular Lat
*caballu* 'nag' > *cavalo* 'horse,' or popular Lat *casa* 'shack' > *casa* 'house.'
Conversely, a generic term may become specific, as in Lat *venatu* 'any game
animal' > *veado* 'deer.'

Words acquired lowly or even negative connotations through a process known
as *pejoration,* as in the case of *alarife* 'master builder,' which has come to
mean 'scoundrel,' or popular Lat *villanu* > *vilão*, once 'village dweller' and
nowadays 'villain,' or, as we have seen, *vulgaris* 'pertaining to the *vulgus*
(common people),' which yielded *vulgar* 'vulgar, lowly.' The opposite change,
known as *melioration,* caused some words of humble connotations to acquire a
favorable meaning, e.g. Lat *servire* 'to serve as a slave' > *servir* 'to serve' (as
in *servir a Pátria* 'to serve one's country'); Lat *minister* 'servant' > *ministro*
'minister'; *brasileiro* 'collector of brazilwood' (a trade once engaged in by
former convicts) > *brasileiro* 'Brazilian'; *mineiro* 'miner' > *mineiro* 'from the
State of Minas Gerais.'

Besides changes in the meaning of existing lexical items, there has been a
continuing process of words becoming archaic and dropping from active use. A
common reason for this is the obsolescence of their referent. Thus, as gunpowder
rendered medieval weaponry and tactics obsolete, dozens of words related to
armor went out of use. Likewise, as motor vehicles became widespread in the
early twentieth century, the lexicon of traction vehicles, horses, harness, and
related equipment quickly began to fade from collective memory. Conversely,
in the course of technological and social change new words have come into
circulation.

The modern Portuguese lexicon is a hybrid, the heir to a variety of sources and
influences, not all of them transparent. From the languages of the inhabitants
of pre-Roman Hispania, a handful of lexical items are still used, even if the
exact source language is not always clear, e.g. *bezerro* 'calf,' *esquerdo* 'left,'
*páramo* 'prairie.' The bulk of the lexicon, however, is made up of patrimonial
words, that is those derived from popular Latin through Romance, to which
items created through derivation and composition (3.8) have been added on a
regular basis.

Over the centuries, thousands of new words have continuously been borrowed from the many languages with which Portuguese has come into contact. A primary source of such loan words was Greek, which pervaded ancient Roman culture in philosophy, the arts, literature, and science, enriching Latin, and subsequently Portuguese, with words such as CORONA > *coroa* 'crown,' GUBERNARE > *governar* 'to govern,' and MACHINA > *máquina* 'machine.' Words pertaining to intellectual activities, in which the Greeks excelled, included BIBLIOTHECA > *biblioteca* 'library,' PHILOSOPHIA > *filosofia* 'philosophy,' SCHOLA > *escola* 'school,' and THEATRUM > *teatro* 'theatre' (Väänänen 1981:11). Early Christianity, legalized in 312 and made the Roman Empire's religion in 380, used Greek as a scriptural language in preference to Latin, which was considered the language of paganism. Consequently a number of early religious terms were Greek in origin, such as *eucaristia* 'eucharist,' *igreja* 'church' (via Lat ECCLESIA), *apóstolo* 'apostol,' *bispo* 'bishop,' and *presbiter* 'presbyter.'

Germanic languages left a modest mark. Both the Visigoths and the other Germanic tribes that moved into the Iberian Peninsula had lived in imperial lands beyond the Pyrenees, where they had become partly romanized by learning some Latin along with Roman ways. A few of the words of Germanic origin that entered Iberian Romance in that period are related to everyday life, such as *espeto* 'skewer,' *roupa* 'clothing,' *sopa* 'soup.' Most, however, were related to the military arts in which their users excelled, and are still in the language:

| | | |
|---|---|---|
| *dardo* 'dart' | *elmo* 'helm' | *estribo* 'stirrup' |
| *espora* 'spur' | *guerra* 'war' | *trégua* 'truce' |
| *brandir* 'to brandish' | *marchar* 'to march' | *trepar* 'to climb' |
| *acha* 'axe' | *guarda* 'guard' | *guiar* 'to guide' |

Another source of new words was Arabic, which in the eighth century served as the vehicle of a civilization that in some technical aspects was ahead of Europe. In Portugal, where Arab-dominated territories were finally conquered in 1249, arabisms, while fewer than in Spanish, covered a range of fields, such as the following examples, given with their present-day glosses:

| **Botany** | **Agriculture** | **Military** |
|---|---|---|
| *açucena* 'lily' | *algodão* 'cotton' | *aljava* 'quiver' |
| *alecrim* 'rosemary' | *arroz* 'rice' | *alfanje* 'curved sword' |
| *alcachofra* 'artichoke' | *limão* 'lemon' | *alferes* 'second lieutenant' |
| *alfavaca* 'basil' | *laranja* 'orange' | *almirante* 'admiral' |
| | | |
| **Food** | **Technology** | **Business** |
| *almôndega* 'meat ball' | *acéquia* 'irrigation ditch' | *alfândega* 'customs house' |
| *álcool* 'alcohol' | *albarda* 'pack saddle' | *açougue* 'butcher's' |

| | | |
|---|---|---|
| *xarope* 'syrup' | *alfinete* 'pin' | *leilão* 'auction' |
| *marzipã* 'marzipan' | *alicerce* 'house foundation' | *quilate* 'carat' |

| **Activities** | **Construction** | **Science** |
|---|---|---|
| *alcagüete* 'pimp, informer' | *adobe* 'sun-dried brick' | *algarismo* 'digit' |
| *alfaiate* 'tailor' | *alcova* 'windowless bedroom' | *cifra* 'zero' |
| *algoz* 'executioner' | *andaime* 'scaffolding' | *zênite* 'zenith' |
| *almoxarife* 'store keeper' | *azulejo* 'ceramic tile' | *nadir* 'nadir' |

Through Arabic came a few Greek terms, such as *acelga* 'chard,' *alambique* 'still (n.),' *alcaparra* 'caper,' *guitarra* 'guitar'; a handful of them came through the Mediterranean trade, such as *botica* 'pharmacy,' *farol* 'lighthouse.' The other Semitic language of the Peninsula, Hebrew, left several religious terms that entered Portuguese through Latin:

| | | | |
|---|---|---|---|
| *aleluia* 'hallellujah' | *amén* 'amen' | *Belzebu* 'Belzebuth' | *éden* 'Eden' |
| *cabala* 'kabala' | *rabino* 'rabbi' | *sábado* 'sabbath Saturday' | |

As Portugal and other Christian peninsular kingdoms fought against Islam, they developed strong ties with the Christian kingdoms on the other side of the Pyrenees. Provençal influence, active in the context of troubadour poetry (5.6.1), appears in words like *viagem* 'journey' (< Pr *viatge* < Lat VIATICU(M), 'travel provisions'), *jogral* 'buffoon' (< Pr *joglar* 'singer,' related to Lat *jocularis* 'amusing'), *rouxinol* 'nightingale' (< Pr *roussinhol*), *trovar* 'to compose a song' (< Pr *trobar* 'to make verses').

French likewise provided a number of items that entered the language early: *dama* (< Fr *dame* 'high class married woman'), *chapéu* (< Fr *chapel* 'kind of hairdo'), *chefe* (< Fr *chef* 'head man'), *assembléia* 'assembly' (Fr *assemblée* 'meeting'), *jaula* 'cage' (< Fr *jaole* 'prison'), *manjar* 'dainty food' (Fr *manger* 'to eat; any food'). Many more would come in later centuries as French became an international language and its literature increased in importance.

Receptivity to Renaissance ideas entailed massive importing of Italian artifacts together with their names, e.g. in the military, *alarme* 'alarm' (< It *allarme* 'to arms'), *mosquete* 'musket' (< It *moschetto*), *coronel* 'colonel'(< It *colonello* 'commander of a column of soldiers'); or in the arts, *Arlequim* 'Harlequin' (< It Arlechino), *Colombina* 'Columbine'(< It *Colombina*), *palhaço* 'clown' (< *pagliaccio* 'circus buffoon'), *artesão* 'artisan' (< *artigiano* 'someone who works with his hands').

In addition to such regular loans, the intellectual trend from the Renaissance through the eighteenth century encouraged borrowing words directly from

Latin. A practical reason for such massive borrowing was that Portuguese prose, forged in the historiography of the late fourteenth and fifteenth centuries, while possessing a vocabulary apt for describing events and actions, was not fully equipped to handle abstractions in more philosophical and aesthetic genres. Borrowing thus contributed to creating a supplementary lexicon of learned terms, such as were employed by Camões his epic poem *Os Lusíadas* (1572), some of which are still used nowadays, if only in elevated styles. Since such borrowing came directly from Latin, instead of from the popular Latin accusative like patrimonial words, the items in the following sample are given in the nominative singular:

PUDICITIA > *pudicícia* 'modesty'      INSANUS > *insano* 'mad'
INCAUTUS > *íncauto* 'careless'      SORDIDUS > *sórdido* 'filthy'
PLUMBEUS > *plúmbeo* 'of lead'      ARGENTEUS > *argênteo* 'of silver'
PERTINAX > *pertinaz* 'tenacious'      ARMIGER > *armígero*
SAGITTIFER > *sagitífero*          'arms-bearing'
    'arrow-bearing'          NAUTICUS > *náutico* 'nautic'

Such was the prestige of Latin that some authors actually went a step beyond borrowing to meet expressive needs and endeavored to ennoble the lexicon by substituting Latin or latinized forms for patrimonial words that had been considered rustic, as in the following sample:

| Latin source | Patrimonial word | New loan word | |
|---|---|---|---|
| ASPECTU(M) | *aspeito* | *aspecto* | 'aspect' |
| DIGNU(M) | *dino* | *digno* | 'worthy' |
| LUCTA(M) | *luita* | *lucta* | 'struggle' |
| MALIGNU(M) | *malino* | *maligno* | 'evil' |
| ARBITRIU(M) | *alvedrio* | *arbitrio* | 'will' |

Another procedure consisted in dropping patrimonial words considered old-fashioned and substituting a morphologically unrelated Latin synonym spelled in the Portuguese manner (nouns are given below in the nominative singular):

| Latin source | Learned loan word | Patrimonial word | |
|---|---|---|---|
| VINCULUM | *vínculo* | *atamento* | 'bond, tie' |
| IMPEDIMENTUM | *impedimento* | *empacho* | 'encumbrance' |
| SANARE | *sanar* | *guarir* | 'to heal' |
| OBTINERE | *obter* | *gançar* | 'to obtain' |
| ADORNARE | *adornar* | *guarnir* | 'to decorate' |

An unforeseen result of such massive borrowing is that, since many new loan words had a counterpart that had evolved in the language, the Portuguese lexicon ended up with patrimonial/learned doublets the meaning of which can be just a shade apart or even substantially different:

| Popular Latin | Patrimonial form | Learned form |
|---|---|---|
| ARTICULU(M) | *artelho* 'toe' | *artigo* 'article' |
| DECRETU(M) | *degredo* 'banishment' | *decreto* 'decree' |
| INFLATU(M) | *inchado* 'bloated' | *inflado* 'filled (with air)' |
| LACUNA(M) | *lagoa* 'pond' | *lacuna* 'gap' |
| AURICULA(M) | *orelha* 'ear' | *aurícula* 'atrium (anat.)' |
| CATHEDRA(M) | *cadeira* 'chair' | *cátedra* 'bishop's throne' |
| STRICTU(M) | *estreito* 'narrow' | *estrito* 'strict' |
| DELICATU(M) | *delgado* 'slender' | *delicado* 'delicate' |
| LIMPIDU(M) | *limpo* 'clean' | *límpido* 'limpid, clear' |
| PLENU(M) | *cheio* 'full' | *pleno* 'full' |
| PULSARE | *puxar* 'to pull' | *pulsar* 'to throb' |
| APREHENDERE | *aprender* 'to learn' | *apreender* 'to aprehend' |
| PALPARE | *poupar* 'to save' | *palpar* 'to touch' |
| CAPTARE | *catar* OP 'to look' MP 'to pick' | *captar* 'to capture' |
| FABULARE | *falar* 'to talk' | *fabular* 'to invent, to lie' |
| LITIGARE | *lidar* 'to deal with' | *litigar* 'to litigate' |

From the fifteenth century on, maritime expansion took the Portuguese to Africa, Asia, and the Americas. Trade and colonization promoted contact with speakers of a variety of languages from which hundreds of items flowed to the lexicon of European languages. Either directly or through an intermediary language, Portuguese received many such words, of which a small sample is given below:

| Mandarin | Malay | Japanese |
|---|---|---|
| *chá* 'tea' | *cacatua* 'cockatoo' | *catana* 'sword' |
| *caolim* 'kaolin' | *orangotango* 'orangutan' | *quimono* 'kimono' |
| *ganga* 'kind of cloth' | *bule* 'coffee pot' | *biombo* 'divider' |

In proportions varying from one historical period to another, major European languages, particularly French and Italian, have remained a vital source of loan words that promoted lexical growth and renewal. In the second half of the eighteenthth century, the so-called neoclassical period, it became fashionable to borrow from literary Latin. In the following century, under the influence of Romanticism, foreign borrowings, particularly from French, again came into fashion. Since the second half of the nineteenth century, scientific advances have fostered an increase in technical terms, at first through French and then, particularly since the Second World War, through English, whose hegemony as an international language has made it a primary source of borrowings.

## 5.6    From the twelfth century on

By the twelfth century, language change had consolidated the long process of transforming the popular Latin of Galicia into the Romance speech which linguists have traditionally called Galician-Portuguese. Since language change tends to be gradual, over the decades each generation adjusted to it effortlessly as speakers passed on to their offspring a speech that diverged in minor ways from that which they had received from their own elders.

It took a long time for this new speech to appear in writing, and when it did it was sporadically at first, as occasional words and expressions slipped into texts written in a medieval Latin increasingly divergent from its classical ancestor. As elsewhere in the Romance area, so in Galicia language change widened the gap between Latin and everyday speech. By this time Latin was no longer anybody's native tongue and was preserved at monastic schools by a literate minority made up mostly of monks and lay brothers. The extent of the gap between Latin and the spoken language is evidenced by the Roman Catholic Church's decision at the Third Council of Tours (813) that preaching should no longer be in Latin but rather "in rusticam romanam linguam" – the "rustic" Romance vernacular – so it could be understood by the faithful.

### 5.6.1    Galician-Portuguese: from the early thirteenth century to about 1325

The development of poetry in Galician-Portuguese followed the troubadour tradition imported from Provence. The earliest extant poem, by Paio Soares de Taveirós, has been dated to about 1189. The following stanza is from a poem by Joan Garcia de Guilhade, from the middle of the thirteenth century, clearly of a satirical bent, listed under number 1486 in the collection entitled *Cancioneiro da Biblioteca Nacional*:

| | |
|---|---|
| *Ai dona fea! Fostes-vos queixar* | Oh ugly lady! You've complained |
| *Porque vos nunca louv' en meu trobar* | That I never praise you in my verses |
| *Mais ora quero fazer un cantar* | So now I want to make a song |
| *En que vos loarei toda via;* | In which I will praise you all the way; |
| *E vedes como vos quero loar:* | And see how I want to praise you: |
| *Dona fea, velha e sandia!* | Ugly lady, old and silly! |

As this style is rather sophisticated, we can safely assume this poem was preceded by many others, unfortunately lost or buried in some archive. Prose, on the other hand, took longer to grow, and its beginnings were practical rather than artistic. Already in the twelfth century, Galician-Portuguese words began to appear amidst the medieval Latin of notarial papers, and the two earliest extant texts that may be considered Portuguese are legal documents.

The first text is the unimposing draft of a *notícia de torto*, that is a notarial report (*noticia*) containing a complaint for wrongful acts (*torto* 'tort') filed by a landed squire against some neighbors. It comes from the region of Braga, in northern Portugal, and while the manuscript bears no date, internal evidence has made it possible to place it around 1214 and 1218 (Cintra 1986/1987:42; Castro 1991a:228). It begins thus:

*De noticia de torto que fecerũ a Laurrēcius Fernãdiz por plazo que fece Gõncauo Ramiriz antre suos filios e Lourēzo Ferrnãdiz quale podedes saber: e oue auer, de erdade e dauer, tãto quome uno de suos filios, daquãto podesē auer de bona de seuo pater.* (Castro 1991a:231)

[Report of a tort that was done to Lourenço Fernandes regarding an agreement made by Gonçalo Ramirez between his sons and Lourenço Fernandez, to wit: he should have received, in inheritance and property, as much as one of his sons, of all they might have from the goods/property from their father.]

Although the language is mostly Galician-Portuguese, notarial Latin pervades the document: *fecerũ, fece* are close to Lat *fecerunt, fecit* 'they made /he made;' the odd possessive *seuo* has been analyzed as a cross between the Romance form *seu* and Lat *suo* (Castro 1991a:235); *auer* (from Lat *habere*, MPg *haver*) preserves the full meaning of 'to have' which lasted until at least the late sixteenth century. Spelling is still far from regular, and although the tilde (originally a miniature *n* placed over a vowel) is used to signal a nasal vowel in *Laurrēcius, Lourēzo, Ferrnãdiz, podesē*, nasalization is marked with a full *n* in *antre* (MPg *entre*) and with both a tilde and a nasal consonant in *daquãnto*.

The next oldest known text in prose is the will of King Afonso II (reigned 1211–1223), written in Coimbra and dated June 4th of the year 1252 of the Julian calendar then in use, corresponding to 1214 in today's Gregorian calendar:

*En'o nome de Deus. Eu rei don Afonso pela gracia de Deus rei de Portugal, seendo sano e saluo, temēte o dia de mia morte, a saude de mia alma e a proe de mia molier raina dona Orraca e de me(us) filios e de me(us) uassalos e de todo meu reino fiz mia mãda p(er) q(ue) depos mia morte mia molier e me(us) filios e meu reino e me(us) uassalos e todas aq(ue)las cousas qu(ue) De(us) mi deu en poder sten en paz e en folgãcia. P(ri)meiram(en)te mãdo q(ue) meu filio infante don Sancho q(ue) ei da raina dona Orraca agia meu reino enteg(ra)m(en)te e en paz. E ssi este for morto sen semmel, o maior filio q(ue) ouuer da raina dona Orraca agia o reino entegram(en)te e en paz. E ssi filio barõ nõ ouuuermos, a maior filia q(ue) ouuermos agia'o. E ssi no tēpo de mia morte meu filio ou mia filia q(ue) deuier a reinar nõ ouuer reuora, segia en poder da*

*raina sa madre e meu reino segia en poder da raina e de me(us) uassalos ata q(uan)do
agia reuora.* (Castro 1991a: 197)

[In God's name. I, King Afonso, by the grace of God king of Portugal, being a sane
mind fearing the day of my death, the salvation of my soul and the interests of my wife
Queen Urraca, and of my children and of my vassals and of my whole kingdom, have
made my will so that after my death my wife and my children and my kingdom and
my vassals and all those things that God gave me in stewardship may be in peace and
tranquility. First, I command that my son the *infante* ('prince') dom Sancho, whom I
have from the queen dona Urraca, will have my kingdom, whole and in peace. And if
he should die without issue, the eldest son that I may have from the queen dona Urraca
will have the kingdon whole and in peace. And if we should not have a son, the eldest
daughter that we may have shall have it. And if by the time of my death my son or my
daughter who comes to reign should not be of age, let him/her remain in the power of
the queen his/her mother and let my kingdom be in the power of the queen of and of my
vassals until such time as they be of age.]

This text is actually far closer to today's Portuguese than its spelling might
suggest. Old Portuguese spelling was far from uniform, and manuscripts contain
many idiosyncratic creations by scribes who needed to invent ways to represent
Romance sounds that did not exist in Latin, the only language in which they were
literate. As Castro (1991a:215) points out, the *ci* in *gracia* (< Lat GRATIA) and
*folgã[n]cia* suggests the affricate pronunciation [ts] (that is, *gratsa, folgãntsa*)
that eventually yielded today's *graça, folgança*. Double vowels (*seendo*) signal
stress, and nasalization is marked by a tilde in *temēte, mãda, folgãça*, though
with an *n* in *infante*. Likewise, the palatal affricate /ʤ/ is represented as *gi*
where we would use *j* (*segia, agia* cf. mod. *seja, aja*), the lateral palatal /ʎ/
appears as *li* (*molier, filio, filia*), and the nasal palatal /ɲ/ hides behind a regular
*n* in *raina* (*raina*, mod. *rainha*). The *u* in *uasallos, reuora* and the double *uu* in
*ouuer, ouuermos* reminds us that Latin spelling did not differentiate between *u*
and *v*, which remained interchangeable well into the Modern Age.

In morphology we notice that the unstressed short form of the possessive (*sa
madre*) alternates with the full form (*meu filio*). *Sten* is the first person plural of
the present subjunctive of STARE, replaced in the sixteenth century by *estejam*,
formed by analogy to *seja*.

The vocabulary shows archaic items such as *madre* for *mãe, semmel* (< Lat
SEMINEM 'semen, seed' that is, 'descendants'), *proe* 'profit' (< Lat PRODIRE
'to advance'), and the verb *haver* (spelled without an *h*) used in the transitive
sense of Lat HABERE 'to have' (*meu filio . . . que ei da raina; o maior filio que
ouuermos; agia meu reino*). As one might expect in a legal document, there
are formulaic expressions such as *seendo sano e saluo* 'being of sane mind'
(nowadays, *em plena posse de minhas faculdades mentais* 'in full possession
of my mental capacities'), *mando que* 'I order,' and juridical terms like *mãda*
or *manda* 'a will' (from *mandar* 'to order, to dispose') and *reuora*, mod. *revora*
or *robora* 'legal age.'

Once these details have been mastered, comparison to a slightly modernized version shows that in fact the text is not really that far removed from what we are used to:

*No nome de Deus. Eu, Rei Dom Afonso, pela graça de Deus rei de Portugal, sendo são e salvo, temente o dia de minha morte, a saúde [= salvação] de minha alma e os interesses de minha mulher a rainha dona Urraca e de meus filhos e de meus vassalos e de todo meu reino, fiz minha manda [= meu testamento] para que depois de minha morte minha mulher e meus filhos e meu reino e meus vassalos e todas aquelas coisas que Deus me deu em poder estejam em paz e em tranquilidade. Primeiramente mando que meu filho infante dom Sancho, que tenho da rainha dona Urraca, tenha meu reino, integramente e em paz. E se este vier a morrer sem descendência, o filho mais velho que [eu] tiver da rainha dona Urraca haja o reino integralmente e em paz. E se filho varão não houvermos, a filha mais velha que houvermos haja-o. E se no tempo de minha morte meu filho ou minha filha que devier a reinar não houver maioridade, seja em poder da rainha sua mãe e meu reino seja em poder da rainha e de meus vassalos até quando haja maioridade.*

## 5.6.2    Old Portuguese: from about 1325 to 1536

The troubador-inspired fashion of writing courtly poetry in Galician-Portuguese persisted until the middle of the fourteenth century, after the death of King Dinis (1279–1325), the sixth monarch of the Burgundian dinasty and a prolific poet. By his time, however, the language had changed considerably and such poetry was already an archaizing literary exercise restricted to a cultivated minority.

An important reason for this was that Portugal's independence, recognized by Alfonso VII of Castile in 1143 and by Pope Alexander III in 1179, fostered cultural and linguistic differentiation. Victory against Castile at the battle of Ajubarrota in 1385 not only consolidated independence but reinforced the power of the new king, João I, first of the dynasty of Avis, directly supported by the Lisbon merchants who would underwrite the seaward expansion of the fifteenth and sixteenth centuries.

As the new language took shape, it occupied areas hitherto reserved for Latin, such as public administration and the law. Scholars date the beginning of Portuguese prose at 1255, when, during Afonso III's reign (1248–1279), the language started replacing Latin regularly in the royal chancery, a practice made mandatory by King Dinis in 1279. In what we would consider a more literary vein, Portuguese appears with increasing regularity in translations of saints' lives from Latin, and, with Fernão Lopes (1380–1464), in chronicles which are considered the beginning of historiography in Portuguese.

A certain amount of Portuguese–Spanish bilingualism was also fostered by intense political and cultural interaction between Portugal and Spain from the middle of the fifteenth century through the middle of the seventeenth century. As Teyssier (1959:293) points out, Spanish was a second language among educated Portuguese, and most sixteenth-century writers, such as Gil Vicente, Sá de Miranda, and Camões, also wrote in Spanish. Gil Vicente wrote nineteen bilingual plays (*autos*) in which each character speaks his or her own language, which suggest his audiences had no difficulty in understanding Spanish.

### 5.6.3    Classical Portuguese: from the mid-sixteenth century to the mid-eighteenth century

The period from about 1536 to the first half of the eighteenth century saw the development of Portuguese as a full-fledged language of culture and civilization. Such growth entailed changes that distanced it even more from the original Galician source. Among such changes were the replacement of the four-way contrast among the sibilants /s/, /z/, /s'/, /z'/ by the two-way contrast between /s/ and /z/, the change of the affricate pronunciation of *ch* for its fricative articulation (5.2.2), and the establishment of the contrast /v/ : /b/, all of which became the norm in the Lisbon-Coimbra region.

A major task begun in 1536 was the standardization of the language. Until then written Portuguese reflected the speech prevalent in each writer's region, even though the Royal Chancery exerted a certain uniformizing influence. In 1536, however, Fernão de Oliveira published his *Grammatica da Lingoagem Portuguesa*, the first of its kind, soon followed by João de Barros' *Grammatica da lingoa portuguesa* in 1539. Once spelling is slightly modernized, as in a recent edition (Oliveira 2000), Oliveira's diction appears remarkably familiar:

E o rei ou senhor, ainda que fosse estrangeiro e viesse de fora senhorear em alghũa terra, havia de apartar sua lingua e não na deixar corromper com alghũa outra, assi par'elle viver em paz, como também porque seu reino fique e persevere em seus filhos. Quanto de minha parte segundo eu entendo, eu juraria que quem folga d'ouvir lingua estrangeira na sua terra não he amigo da sua gente nem conforme à musica natural della. (Oliveira 2000:124–125)

[And the king or master, although he were a foreigner and came from abroad to rule in some land, should set aside his language and not allow it to be corrupted by any other, so as to live in peace, and also so that his kingdom will remain and prosper with his offspring. So far as I am concerned, I would swear that whoever is pleased to hear a foreign language in his land is not a friend of his people, nor attuned to its natural music.]

Such works, partly inspired by Nebrija's *Gramática de la lengua castellana* (1492), were followed during the next two hundred years by grammars, vocabularies, orthographic treatises, and pronunciation primers. Works in praise of the Portuguese language constituted a particularly rich genre, avidly cultivated between 1580 and 1640, when Portugal, for dynastic reasons, was under Spanish domination. This uninterrupted grammatical and lexicographic work was instrumental in shaping a written language that consciously avoided features from the northern regions of the country, which were regarded as old-fashioned or rustic. Gradually, a written code evolved, modeled regionally on the speech of southern Portugal – the Coimbra-Lisbon area – and socially on the usage prevalent among the upper classes, thus contributing to a rift between the educated standard and popular speech which would never cease to widen. Though the language had changed greatly in over ten centuries, its *urbanus* variety still kept its distance from its *rusticus* and *vulgaris* relatives.

### 5.6.4   Modern Portuguese

It is customary to give the label of "modern Portuguese" to the language from the mid-eighteenth century onward. Just as Renaissance ideas had been a major influence on the language in the sixteenth and seventeenth centuries, it was the Enlightenment of the eighteenth century, and the subsequent intellectual trends linked to scientific and technological advances, which contributed to a constant upgrading of the lexicon.

While such changes were taking place in Europe, the Portuguese language was being taken far afield by the people involved in the maritime enterprises which, from the fifteenth to the middle of the seventeenth century, made Portugal a major seafaring nation. As the language traveled far and wide, it was adopted in the newly established settlements by people who used it as their first or second language. In so doing they modified it to meet their communicative needs and to reflect the new natural, cultural, and linguistic environment in which they lived. In the next two chapters we will examine some aspects of this process.

# 6    The expansion of European Portuguese

The expansion of Portuguese in the world illustrates what can happen when a segment of a speech community moves out of its original territory to settle down thousands of miles away. There is an approximate parallel with the spread of Latin in the territories conquered by the Roman Empire, or, more recently, with the spread of English in the British Empire. In each situation the language has changed, sometimes drastically, borrowing words from other languages, developing some of its latent possibilities, and eventually acquiring a new countenance, close enough to the original model and yet unmistakably unique.

From the middle of the fifteenth century to the middle of the twentieth, thousands of Portuguese emigrated to other European countries, to Africa, to Asia, to the Americas and, more recently, to Australia. Throughout most of that period, once anchors had been cast off, oral communication was limited to one's immediate community on board or in the new settlements. As this happened, the language, unbeknownst to its speakers, started on a course of its own. In this chapter we will examine some of the ways in which the spread of Portuguese in continental Portugal and elsewhere in the world has fostered innovation.

## 6.1    Aspects of language variation

Reified expressions like "Portuguese language" or "Portuguese" convey an impression of uniformity which, while convenient for the theoretical analysis of language structure, camouflages the fact that any real language is riddled with variation. In fact, what we call "a language" is the sum total of its regional and social variants. Within each new community set up abroad, a variety of factors contribute to modify its speech. One such factor is *drift*, characterized by Sapir (1921) as a natural tendency for languages to change as time passes. Another is a leveling process: interaction among speakers from various regions in the original country tends to iron out salient differences, inducing in the speech of subsequent generations, born and raised in the new community, a degree of homogeneity in pronunciation, morphology, syntax, and the lexicon that will make their language contrast with that of the original community.

The first aspect of regional variation we tend to notice is *accent°*, the impression caused on the ear by pronunciation features – such as consonant articulation, vowel quality, the presence or absence of certain diphthongs, intonation, and so on – which characterize a given group of speakers. Everyone has an accent of some kind (Esling 1998), for even standard pronunciation can be characterized in terms of those features. Accents can be either regional (as in Brazilian vs. Portuguese, or American vs. British), or social, as in the case of British Received Pronunciation (also known as "BBC English") vs. popular varieties of British English such as Cockney. Some classifications cut both ways: whereas a rural accent may be related to a specific geographic location, the contrast "rural vs. urban" has social implications as well. If non-phonological features, such as morphology, syntax, or the lexicon, are involved, we no longer talk of an accent but rather of a language variety or dialect.

As used in linguistics, the term *dialect°* is merely a neutral way to designate the speech of a region or social group. The reason this term has connotations of folksy speech is that dialectal studies began, in the late nineteenth century, with a focus on rural varieties, contrasting these with the formal educated varieties associated with the written language. Nowadays, however, we realize that "urban vs. rural" or "educated vs. uneducated" are only some of the many possible dimensions of language variation. Urban varieties, prestigious or not, are also dialects, as is the written norm embodied in prescriptive grammars. It should be clear, then, that in linguistics the terms "dialect" and "language variety," or just "variety," are simply ways of referring to a specific manifestation of a language, be it regional or social. Social dialects or varieties are also called *sociolects°*, and some linguists prefer *lect°* as a generic term. The term "macrodialect°", in turn, refers to a set of dialects or varieties.

In Chapter 5 we saw some of the processes whereby popular Latin changed into Galician-Portuguese, which in turn split into Galician and Portuguese as two differentiated, if closely related, languages. From the twelfth century on, large groups of speakers migrated southward from the lands of the original Portucalense County to the Coimbra and Lisbon regions. The presence of the Court and the university (which was moved a couple of times between those two cities) ensured that the south would remain the prestige center of European Portuguese. As Portuguese society expanded and became more stratified, the language underwent changes in three dimensions, namely time, geographical space, and social context. Although we can focus on any one of these dimensions for purposes of analysis, all three need to be taken into account.

There is a relationship between a language's rate of change and its geographic spread. Icelandic, for instance, developed in Iceland from the speech of Norwegian settlers in the late ninth and early tenth centuries. About 37 per cent of a population of 277,906 live in the capital, Reykjavik, and except for immigrant communities (in e.g. the US and Canada), Icelandic has remained in its original territory of 39,768 square miles (103,000 square kilometers), with limited direct contact with other languages. Unsurprisingly, it has remained relatively homogeneous, and is defined linguistically in terms of usage in its home territory.

Portuguese, on the contrary, has spread world-wide, putting down roots in areas far vaster and more populated than its original territory. It has come into close contact with many other languages, from which it has borrowed new words, and the communities where it is spoken show a great deal of social variation. It is only natural that it should have changed considerably, to the point of providing a foundation for new languages, the Portuguese-based creoles (6.5.1); and it is thus a diversified language, with no single standard defined by a single speech community.

While diachronic change may look rather homogeneous when considered in abstraction, its effects on the language's territory are far more varied. For example, although loss of the occlusive element [t] in the original Galician-Portuguese phoneme /ʧ/ eliminated the contrast /ʧ/ : /ʃ/ in southern Portugal, that contrast still exists in the north of the country. From a dialectological perspective this diachronic change has not been complete, and decades may go by before [ʧ] completely disappears, if it ever does. Thus answers to questions like "does the sound [ʧ] exist in Portuguese?" or "do the sounds [ʧ] and [ʃ] contrast in Portuguese?" will depend on whether we take "Portuguese" in the broad sense of an ensemble of dialects, some of which have [ʧ], or in the narrower sense of the standard variety of the language, which does not have [ʧ].

Social stratification may be encoded, often in subtle ways, by some correlation between language features and social factors such as sex, age, ethnicity, education level, and socioeconomic standing. Pinto (1981:175–178, 192) points out that although grammarians began to label the sound [ʧ] as rustic at the end of the seventeenth century, as late as the early nineteenth century a respected grammarian such as Jerónimo Soares Barbosa insisted that [ʧ] and [ʃ] should be kept apart in educated pronunciation. In contrast, other contemporary grammarians believed that pronouncing *ch* as [ʃ] rather than [ʧ] was the correct choice. These opposing views were apparently influenced by scholars' place of birth or residence: those born or living in areas north of the Mondego River, where [ʧ] and [ʃ] contrasted, insisted on distinguishing between *ch* and *x*, whereas their colleagues from southern areas where that contrast had been lost accepted [ʃ] as the correct rendering for *ch*. Such variety of opinion suggests that although the norm had not yet been fixed at the time, there was already a tendency to consider *ch* = [ʃ] standard and to mark [ʧ] as geographically "dialectal" or as socially "rustic."

## 6.2    Continental Portugal

Taken as a whole, continental Portugal is quite homogeneous linguistically. Regional differences are relatively small in comparison to other European countries, such as neighboring Spain, which has three major Romance languages (Spanish, Catalan, and Galician), a few minor ones (Aranese [in Catalonia], Aragonese, and Asturian), and a totally unrelated language (Basque). Portuguese regional dialects in Portugal – usually labeled after the region's name, such as *Minhoto* in Minho or *Trasmontano* in Trás-os-Montes – are basically mutually intelligible, and other languages are restricted to rather small border regions (6.3). Cintra (1971:28) proposed for the whole area of Galician and Portuguese a phonology-based division into three primary dialectal zones, namely (a) Galician dialects, (b) Northern Portuguese dialects, and (c) Center–Southern Portuguese dialects.

Galician contrasts with Portuguese by the absence of nasal vowels, and the presence of a single voiceless alveolar fricative /s/, as opposed to Portuguese voiceless /s/ and voiced /z/ (*face:fase*). Likewise, Galician has only the voiceless palatal fricative /ʃ/, while Portuguese contrasts voiceless /ʃ/ with voiced /ʒ/ (*acho:ajo*). Finally, unstressed vowels tend to retain their quality in Galician, whereas in European Portuguese they tend to be reduced to [ə] or dropped altogether.

Differences between Northern and Center–Southern Portuguese dialects are likewise defined by a few phonological features. Regarding consonants, whereas Center–Southern speech contrasts bilabial /b/ and labiodental /v/, Northern has only the phoneme /b/, manifested by the allophones [b] and [β]. Consequently, while word pairs like *bala* 'bullet'/*vala* 'ditch' or *cabo* 'handle'/*cavo* 'I dig,' contrast in Center–Southern pronunciation, they are homophonous in the north. This difference forms the basis for the purely impressionistic popular notion that Northern speech mixes *b*s and *v*s, when in fact it has no *v*s to speak of.

Northern dialects also articulate /s/ and /z/ with enough palatalization to make them sound a bit like [ʃ] and [ʒ], as in *Viseu* [bi'ʒew], *esse* ['eʃə], as opposed to [vi'zew], ['esə] in Center–Southern pronunciation. Furthermore, as mentioned earlier, Northern speech follows Galician in preserving the contrast /ʃ/ : /ʧ/, while Southern speech has only /ʃ/ (orthographically *ch* or *x*).

As regards the vocalic system, two features involve reduction of diphthongs to simple vowels. In Center–Southern speech the original diphthong /ou/ has long been reduced to a simple vowel [o], as in *ouro* ['oru] 'gold,' *Douro* ['doru]. Although this pronunciation has been incorporated in the standard language, Northern speech preserves the /ou/ diphthong, phonetically either [ow] or [ɐw], according to the region. The other diphthong affected is /ej/, pronounced [e] in the south, as in *feira* ['ferə]. This feature, unlike the preceding ones, is not considered standard. Furthermore, the Lisbon variety of Portuguese renders the diphthong /ej/ as [ɐj], as in *feira* ['fɐjrɐ] 'fair,' thus preserving the contrast /ej/ : /e/, albeit with a different timbre.

Other features contribute to further characterize regional pronunciation. We have seen (5.2.2.) that medieval Portuguese had two contrasting pairs of sibilants, apicoalveolar /s'/ and /z'/ and dorsoalveolar /s/ and /z/. Changes in sound articulation have led to three different situations. One is the preservation of the old four-way contrast in a conservative area (roughly including Trás-os-Montes, Alto Minho, and part of Beira-Alta), as in the following scheme:

> /s/ *cego* 'blind,' *caça* 'hunting'      : /z/ *fazer* 'make'
> /s'/ *saber* 'knowledge,' *passo* 'step' : /z'/ *casa* 'house'

In another area (part of Minho, Douro, part of Beira Alta and Beira Baixa) there is only one contrast, involving the apicoalveolar sibilants, /s'/ : /z'/. Finally, in the central-southern region (including Lisbon) there is also only one contrast, but involving instead the two dorso-dental sibilants, /s/ : /z/, which are identified as being standard pronunciation (Cintra 1995:28, Riĩho 1999:62).

The dialect area extending from Beira Baixa to Algarve deserves mentioning (Cintra 1995:155) on account of articulatory changes in the vowel system that took place before the sixteenth century, and which linguists have called the "Portuguese Vowel Shift" (Rogers 1979, Silva 1988:337). The most salient contrast with the standard vowel system is the pronunciation of the stressed vowel /u/ with the tongue forward, resulting in a front rounded vowel [ü], as in *maduro* [ma'düru] instead of [ma'duru]. This feature occurs in the Castelo Branco–Portalegre dialect, thus named after the two towns that signal respectively its northern limit, Castelo Branco in Beira Baixa, and its southern limit, Portalegre in Alto Alentejo.

More extreme changes are found in the speech of Barlavento (Windward) do Algarve, on the southwestern tip of the peninsula. This dialect has two extra vowels in stressed position, namely /ü/ and /æ/, giving a total of eight stressed vowels, / i e ɛ ae a ɔ o ü/. The following examples (collected from Azevedo Maia 1975:10–23), show some phonetic realizations:

> /ɛ/ > [æ] *terra* ['tæRɐ]     for st. ['tɛRɐ] 'land'
>           *pedra* ['pædrɐ]     for st. ['pɛdrɐ] 'stone'
>           *pesca* ['pæʃkɐ]     for st. ['pɛʃkɐ] 'fishing'
> /ɔ/ > [o] *porca* ['porkə]     for st. ['pɔrkə] 'sow'
>           *cova* ['kovɐ]     for st. ['kɔvɐ 'pit'
>           *cobra* ['kobrɐ]     for st. ['kɔbrɐ] 'snake'
> /u/ > [ü] *tudo* [tüdᵊ]     for st. ['tudu] 'all'
>           *uma* ['ümɐ]     for st. ['ümɐ] 'one (f.)'
>           *azul* [a'zül ]     for st. [a'zul ] 'blue'

Survival of this regional vowel subsystem may have been due at least in part to the fact that the regions of Alentejo and Algarve were largely isolated from the rest of the country until relatively recent times. Azevedo Maia (1975:23) pointed out that while some of these variations seemed to be on the wane elsewhere in the country, in Algarve they were found in the pronunciation of people of all age groups. These features also appear in some of the island dialects (6.4).

## 6.3 Border talk

In Europe and elsewhere, most borders are artificial constructs established for political reasons rather than to mark linguistic or cultural differences. Nevertheless, over the centuries European borders have proved rather permeable as people from both sides crossed them to carry on their daily business. In such situations of language contact, which provide an ideal breeding ground for mixed speeches, inhabitants have been known to have varying degrees of proficiency in two or more languages. Despite Portugal's general linguistic homogeneity, a few pockets of diversity exist, usually in areas under Spanish jurisdiction that were settled by Portuguese speakers, or conversely, in areas settled by speakers of Galician, Leonese, or Spanish which are part of Portuguese territory.

In the process of settling border disputes with Spain, Portugal has kept several northern villages of Galician or Leonese speech (Santos 1964–1965:91). On several points along the border between Minho and the Galician region of Ourense there are towns (such as Soutelinho da Raia, Cambedo, and Lama de Arcos) where Portuguese coexists, in varying proportions, with Galician and/or Spanish. In the northern district of Bragança (Trás-os-Montes) there are border villages (Riodonor, Guadramil) where traces of Leonese dialects once spoken are still present in popular speech (Cruz *et al.* 1994).

When dialectal studies started in Portugal at the end of the nineteenth century (Vasconcellos 1970), such situations of language contact promoted conditions of bilingualism, trilingualism, or language mixture which were supported by the relative isolation of those rural regions and an extremely low literacy rate. Although it was remarked in the 1960s that some of those dialects were on the wane (Santos 1964–1965:138), factors such as the current revival of Galician, an open border, access to television and radio in Portuguese, Spanish, and Galician, and frequent travel may foster varying degrees of active or passive bilingualism among the inhabitants of those regions.

A resilient instance of non-Portuguese speech is found further west, in the district (*Concelho*) of Miranda do Douro in the Trás-os-Montes region, where Mirandese (*Mirandês*), a variety of Leonese, is spoken by a few thousand people. It has been suggested that Mirandese once covered a wider area along the border (Ferreira 2002:140) and that a situation of active bilingualism was prevalent until the sixteenth century, with Portuguese and Mirandese used for complementary communicative purposes in a diglossic° situation (Martins 1995). Its continuity, and perhaps survival, is assisted by a law passed in 1999, which recognizes

the right to cultivate and promote the Mirandese language, as a cultural asset and instrument of communication, and support of the identity of the region of Miranda . . . . [and] a child's right to learn Mirandese. [The law also authorizes] public agencies . . . in the *concelho* of Miranda do Douro . . . to issue their documents together with a version in the Mirandese language. (Law # 7/99, *Diário da República* # 24 /99)

While this law is clearly favorable to Mirandese, its wording implies that the original documents will continue to be issued in Portuguese, with a Mirandese version being optional.

Three subdialects of Mirandese have been identified, namely *Raiano, Central*, and *Sendinês*, although the relative independence of Sendinese from Mirandese has been maintainted by Ferreira (1994). A feature shared by all three is the preservation of intervocalic Latin /l/ and /n/, which have been lost in Portuguese, as in PLENU > Pg *cheio*, Mir. *cheno*, SOLU > Pg *só*, Mir *solo* 'alone.' Raiano and Central also have initial /ʎ/ corresponding to Ptg /l/, as in *llobo/lobo* 'wolf,' *lliebre/lebre* 'hare,' as well as a rising diphthong, /wo/ or /je/, where Portuguese has /o/ or /e/, as in *fuonte/fonte* 'fountain,' *cuorpo/corpo* 'body,' *mulhier/mulher* 'woman,' *bielho/velho* 'old.' In Sendinês, on the contrary, there is no initial /ʎ/ and instead of those diphthongs we find high vowels: *libre/lebre, tirra/terra, curpo/corpo*.

There is an old tradition of oral literature in Mirandese (Barros 2002:141–142) and efforts are currently under way to record and transcribe representative texts. The following passage was recorded in 1998 in the village of Picuôte:

*Era ua beç dues comadres, l tiu era pastor. I el fui-se a deitar cun la comadre, cun outra, cun la mulhier daquel pastor e apuis, pul meio de la nuite, staba l cura deitado na cama cun la tie i el batiu, i el metiu-se debaixo de la cama. Pula manhana, quando se lhebantou, bestiu las calças de l cura, l pastor. Quando andaba cun las canhonas: – Ai diabo que you trago las calças dun cura!* (Alves 1999:29)

[Portuguese:] *Era uma vez duas comadres, o marido era pastor. E ele foi-se deitar com a comadre, com outra com a mulher daquele pastor, e depois, pelo meio da noite, estava o padre deitado na cama com a mulher e ele bateu, e ele meteu-se debaixo da cama. Pela manhã, quando se levantou, vestiu as calças do padre, o pastor. Quando andava com as ovelhas: – Ai, diabo, que eu levo as calças dum padre!*

[Once upon a time there were two women, the husband was a shepherd. And he went to sleep with a woman, with another, with the wife of that shepherd, and later, in the middle of the night, the priest was lying in bed with the wife and he knocked, and he crawled under the bed. In the morning, as he got up, he put on the priest's pants. When he was walking with the sheep [he said]: "What the devil, I'm wearing a priest's pants!"]

A case of linguistic hybridism is found in the village of Barrancos, located on the Portuguese border between Beja in Baixo Alentejo and the Spanish provinces of Huelva and Badajoz (Extremadura). The Spanish presence in Barrancos goes back to 1253, when a land grant was made to a Spanish princess who married King Afonso III. Since the border in this area was not finally considered settled until 1926, it is not surprising that the inhabitants (under 3,000) speak a mixture of Portuguese and southern Spanish. A salient phonological feature, normal in southern Spanish though not in Portuguese, is the aspiration or loss of syllable-final /s/: *dois filhos* > *doi*[h] *filho*[h], *doi filho*, *detrás* > *detrá*[h], *detrá*. Another feature is the loss of final /r/ as in *correr* > *corrê*, *buscar* > *bu*[h]*cá* (Stefanova-Gueorguiev 2000).

On the Spanish side of the border there are a few Portuguese enclaves such as the town of Olivenza (Pg Olivença), but the general tendency is for the younger generations, particularly in urban environments, to be Spanish-speaking, or at any rate Spanish-dominant bilinguals. Nevertheless, efforts are being made (as in the case of Mirandese on the Portuguese side) to preserve at least some of that linguistic heritage. A decree passed in 2000 by the Culture Department (*Consejería de Cultura*) of the Autonomous Region of Extremadura recognized as a cultural asset the variety of Galician-Portuguese, with Leonese features, traditionally known as "A Fala," spoken in the towns of San Martín de Trevejo, Eljas, and Valverde del Fresno, in the Jálama Valley (Vázquez-Cuesta 1971: 76, Viudas Camarasa 2001).

While such legal measures provide conditions favorable to minority dialects, the extent of their effectiveness remains an open question. The pressure of the standard official language, public education, the media, and increased opportunities for travel and work in other countries of the European Community may work against their preservation. As one might expect, such varieties have tended to fare better in fast-shrinking rural areas than in towns. Whatever their outcome, such efforts evince a positive change of attitude toward regional varieties which, until relatively recently, were left to their own devices, when not persecuted outright.

## 6.4 The Atlantic islands: Madeira and the Azores

The Madeira archipelago (pop. ca. 271,000) comprises two inhabited islands, Madeira and Porto Santo, situated about 640 km (398 miles) off the Moroccan coast. The archipelago of the Azores (pop. ca. 237,000) includes nine islands divided into three groups: Eastern Azores (São Miguel and Santa Maria), Central Azores (Graciosa, Terceira, São Jorge, Pico, and Faial), and Western Azores (Corvo and Flores), located in the middle of the Atlantic, at about the same latitude as Beja in Portugal or Washington, DC. Settlement of these two hitherto uninhabited island groups began in the middle of the fifteenth century. Madeira and Porto Santo were settled quite successfully due largely to their mild climate and fertile soil, while the Azores were settled more slowly on account of low demographic resources and other factors (Mendorica 2000:21).

Rogers (1946, 1948, 1949) provides an ensemble view of the speech of both Madeira and the Azores. By and large the Azores are unevenly studied, with the speech of some islands, such as São Miguel, having received far more attention than that of others. The main phonological consonantal features in the speech of both island groups coincide with those of Central–Southern dialects, e.g. the /b/ : /v/ contrast and the occurrence of fricative [ʃ] rather than affricate [ʧ] in words written with *ch*.

In Madeira, however, there is palatalization of /l/ after [i] or [j], as in *vila* [vi'ʎɐ] 'village,' *telefone* [teʎi'fon]. Some features from northern Portugal occur in the vowel system, such as the pronunciation of /ei/ as [ej] instead of [e] and /ou/ as [ow] instead of [o]. Furthermore, [ow] alternates with [oj], as in *coisa/cousa* ['kowzɐ] / ['kojzɐ] 'thing.' Vocalic features found in Algarve which reappear in Madeira include the fronted vowel [ü] as in *escudo* ['ʃküdu] and the articulation of stressed /a/ as a back low–mid [ɔ] as in *casa* ['kɔzə]. There is also a tendency to diphthongize stressed high vowels, e.g. /i/ (*filho* ['fɐjʎu] for st. ['fiʎu]) or /u/ (*lua* ['lɐwɐ] for st. ['luɐ]).

Linguists (Silva 1988, Rogers 1948) have pointed out that *Miquelense*, the dialect of São Miguel, is the variety that departs most strikingly from standard European Portuguese. This is due primarily to the effects of the aforementioned Portuguese Vowel Shift, brought to the island in the sixteenth century by settlers from Algarve. The following examples (from Silva 1988:337) give an idea of the range of such divergence:

| | |
|---|---|
| /i/ > [i] *fita* ['fitɐ] for st. ['fitɐ] 'ribbon' | /a/ > [ɐ] *cabra* ['kɐbrɐ] for st. ['kabrɐ] 'goat' |
| /e/ > [ɛ] *pretu* ['prɛtu] for st. ['pretu] 'black' | /ɔ/ > [o] porca ['porkɐ] for st. ['pɐrkɔ] 'sow' |
| /ej/ > [e] *peixe* ['peʃ] for st. ['pejʃ] 'fish' | /o/ > [u] *porto* ['purtu] for st. ['portu] 'port' |
| /ɛ/ > [æ] *terra* ['tæʀɐ] for st. ['tɛʀɐ] 'earth' | /u/ > [ü] *uvas* ['üvɐʃ] fos st. ['uvɐʃ] 'grapes' |

Phonetic variation of vowels has been interpreted as socially significant by Silva (1988), who determined that pronunciation of /a/ as either central [a] or back [ɑ] or [ɔ], in the same person's speech, is not random. The variant [a], which coincides with the standard pronunciation, is the prestige form, while the variant [ɔ], traditionally considered typical of São Miguel pronunciation, is considered less prestigious by outsiders. The back variant [ɑ], in turn, seems to be a compromise solution: unlike [ɔ] and like [a], it is unrounded, but unlike [a] and like [ɔ], it is backed. In other words, it is sufficiently similar to [a] to share some of its prestige value and also close enough to [ɔ] to partake its value as an index of regional or ethnic identity.

A more recent analysis by Cruz and Saramago (1999), based partly on Cintra (forthcoming), suggests that Madeira and the Azores should be considered a dialect area in their own right because they share a number of features, some of which are either regional or non-existent in mainland Portugal. The authors support this view with data from their own acoustic analysis of vowel harmony (more intense in Azores) and final /s/ (more intense in Madeira). They also find that stressed vowel quality is unstable and affected by the quality of preceding unstressed vowels and by the quality of the final unstressed vowel. This phonological process, reportedly found on most Azorean islands but particularly evident on Terceira, involves changing the stressed vowel into a rising diphthong by inserting a semivowel whose articulation has the same tongue position as a preceding unstressed vowel or semivowel:

insertion of [j]:
> *e ferve* [iˈfjɛrvi]               st. [iˈfɛrvi] 'and (it) boils'
> *ceifar* [sejˈfjar]               st. [sejˈfar] 'to reap'

insertion of [w]:
> *buscar* [buʃˈkwar]          st. [buʃˈkar] 'fetch'
> *ao gato* [awˈɣwatu]         st. [awˈɣatu] 'to the cat'

The stressed vowel may in turn assimilate to the semivowel in area of articulation, becoming palatalized if the semivowel is [j], or velarized if the semivowel is [w]. Vowel instability is apparent in the fact that several forms may occur not only in the same dialect but in the speech of the same speaker:

> *cidade* [siˈðaði] ∼   [siˈðjäði] ∼   [siˈðɛði] for st. [siðaði]
> *fumar* [fuˈmwar] ∼ [fuˈmwɑr] ∼ [fuˈmɑr] for st. [fuˈmar]

This diphthongization process has been identified in continental Portugal (Beira Baixa, Alto Alentejo, Beira Alta). In Madeira, diphthongization of stressed vowels preceded by a syllable with a high vowel or a semivowel is likewise found, as in the examples below, although there is no further palatalization of a vowel preceded by a palatal semivowel.

> *inverno* [ĩˈvjɛrnu] for st. [ĩˈvɛrnu] 'winter'
> *comer* [kuˈmwer] for st. [kuˈmer] 'to eat'

In Madeira, when the stressed vowel is high, there is a tendency for unstressed high final vowels to be articulated as a relatively weak [i]:

> *limpo* [ˈlĩpi] for st. [ˈlĩpu] 'clean'
> *bico* [ˈbiki] for st. [ˈbiku] 'bird's beak'

Words ending in unstressed [u] may have their stressed vowel velarized, particularly if it is /a/, which may be pronounced as [ɑ] or even [ɔ], as in *carro* ['kɑʀu], ['kɔʀ] 'car' (with loss of the final vowel), contrasting with st. ['kaʀu]. This phenomenon apparently occurs, with varying frequency, in the speech of all Azorean islands.

As regards final /s/, on Madeira it may either be articulated as [ʃ] or [z] as in the mainland, or eliminated, or articulated as [j] when preceding a vowel beginning with a voiced consonant or a voiceless fricative, thus originating a falling diphthong, as in *os donos* [uj'donuʃ], st. [uʃ'donuʃ] 'the owners' or *os machos* [uj'maʃuʃ], st. [uz'maʃuʃ] 'the males,' or *as veias* [aj'vejɐʃ], st. [az'vejɐʃ] 'the veins.' On the Azores, and particularly on Flores, this process reportedly takes place regularly, occurring also before voiceless stops, as in *as pegadas* [ɐjpɛ'ʁaðɐʃ], st. [ɐʃ pɛ'ʁaðɐʃ] 'the footprints.'

With the exception of transformation of final /s/ into [j], these features of island speech also occur, albeit unsystematically, in continental Portugal. Cruz and Saramago hypothesize that their regular occurrence on the islands may result from a settlement pattern lacking "noticeable predominance of settlers from any given region" (1999:732). Furthermore, while the pressure of standard language has limited the occurrence of those features on the continent, lack of such pressure on the islands has made it possible for those features to be present in the speech of all social groups, thus contributing to the characterization of the islands as a whole as a dialect region.

## 6.5    Africa

The presence of the Portuguese language in Africa is the outcome of a colonial situation that began with the conquest of Ceuta by Portugal in 1415 and lasted until the middle of the 1970s. The five African countries where Portuguese has official status – Angola, Mozambique, Cape Verde, Guinea-Bissau, and São Tomé and Príncipe (see Table 1.1 for demographic data) – are collectively known by the acronym PALOP (*Países Africanos de Língua Oficial Portuguesa*).

Portuguese was adopted as a lingua franca° by the various ethnic groups involved in the struggle for independence from the early 1960s. This was an act of language planning as well as a conscious political decision to use Portuguese "as a bridge in the face of inter-regional barriers to communication" (Katupha 1994:91). Its retention as an official language after independence in the 1970s can also be seen as a pragmatic move. In multilingual countries such as Angola, Mozambique, and Guinea-Bissau, adoption of Portuguese has obviated the potentially divisive choice of an African language spoken by some ethnic groups but not others. In this context, Lopes (1997b:493) states:

the Portuguese language is and will most likely be, in our lifetime, the national lingua franca . . . [for] Mozambicans who speak different mother tongues.

When universal proficiency has been achieved, it will be no doubt advantageous for all citizens to share a language which, having been used for over eight centuries for all kinds of literary and non-literary purposes, can be a vehicle for the development of a national culture (Ferreira 1988), as well as for communication among those five countries and between them and Portugal and Brazil. There is, however no way of guessing how long it may take for a significant majority of the population to acquire that proficiency. At present, Portuguese is an exogenous language, spoken by less than 40 per cent of the population. Furthermore, it is the native or dominant language of a rather small percentage of the population. This situation, sharply different from that of Portugal or Brazil, where most people speak Portuguese natively, has specific implications for the future of the language in Africa. Furthermore, since in Cape Verde, Guinea-Bissau, and São Tomé and Príncipe several Portuguese-based creoles are also spoken, a brief overview of these languages should help put things in perspective.

### 6.5.1  Pidgins and creoles: An excursus

As mentioned in 1.3, a remarkable by-product of the contact of Portuguese with African languages in the fifteenth and sixteenth centuries was the development of hybrid languages called pidgins° and creoles°. A pidgin, often called a trade language on account of its customary association with business, is a much simplified, essentially oral language formed by combining elements taken from the languages of people trying to communicate without knowing each other's language. Its structure usually involves the vocabulary of the socially dominant language (called the *lexifier* or *superstrate* language), with a trimmed-down version of the grammar of the socially subordinate (or *substrate*) language. Although a pidgin is nobody's native language, when the offspring of pidgin speakers acquire it as their first language, it becomes a creole.

A well-known instance of a pidgin is *Sabir* (< *saber* 'to know'), which was spoken by merchants, sailors, and warriors round the Mediterranean in the Middle Ages. It had an Italian and Occitan lexical basis and was still in use, in various forms, in places on the North African coast in the early nineteenth century. Its other name, *Lingua Franca* – that is, "language of the Franks," as Europeans were called by non-Europeans – survives as a designation of a language which, like English, is used for a variety of communicative purposes by speakers of other languages.

Since the early fifteenth century, contact with African languages, and the familiarity the Portuguese had with techniques for simplifying their own language to communicate with foreigners, promoted the rise of pidgins. Although the precise circumstances surrounding their genesis continues to be a topic of debate (see, for example, Whinnom 1965; Naro 1978, 1981; Clements

1992, 2000, Holm 2004), Portuguese-based pidgins were formed and used not only between Europeans of various nationalities and Africans, but also among Africans who did not share a common language. This process contributed to rise to the creoles currently spoken, with regional variations, in Guinea-Bissau, on Cape Verde, and on São Tomé and Príncipe. A creole is also spoken on the island of Annobón, which was originally settled by the Portuguese and was a Spanish colony from 1778 to 1968, when it became part of the territory of the Republic of Equatorial Africa (formerly known as Spanish Guinea).

Like pidgins, creoles are structurally simplified, but whereas a pidgin may hold, at least in its initial stages, a kind of dialectal relationship with its lexifier, a creole is an autonomous entity. Consequently, in dealing with language-planning issues such as the establishment of a standard grammar or the compilation of a dictionary that can be used by speakers of partially divergent varieties, it is necessary to find solutions that take into account the creole's own structure rather than the structure of the original lexifier language. There are substantial differences among the different Portuguese-based creole varieties found in Africa, for even though a large portion of their lexicon is Portuguese, each has a number of loan words from different African languages. It has been argued that such differences do not necessarily alter the shared structure of Portuguese creoles (Ploae-Hanganu 1998), but nonetheless each creole – like any language – follows its own process of diachronic change, and differences tend to accumulate over the years.

If the lexifier coexists with a creole – as Portuguese does in Cape Verde, São Tomé and Príncipe, and Guinea-Bissau – its very presence may turn out to be an obstacle – though not necessarily an insurmountable one – to the use of the creole in socially prestigious activities such as education, the media, and the administration. Rather than accept the creole as it is, the educated segments of society, whose social prestige benefits from their command of the lexifier, may consider that the value of the creole depends on its ability to approximate to the lexifier in spelling or vocabulary. Since creoles are essentially oral, however, there may be a great deal of regional variation, and consequently the task of developing a viable writing system requires choosing a specific variety as a point of reference.

The decision processes involved in such language planning are fraught with technical and social problems. First, creoles are not necessarily discrete entities but form a continuum where it is not always clear where one variety ends and another begins. Secondly, decisions on how to represent sounds and sound combinations in spelling require an informed view on whether, and to what extent, the written creole should or should not look like the lexifier language. Further, deciding which syntactic structures should be taken as a basis for the standard may prove a vexing issue, encroaching upon the prestige of speakers of competing varieties. Given such a diversified situation, it is no surprise that the task of developing a relatively standardized norm for Portuguese-based creoles is still in its early stages.

The extent to which a creole both resembles and differs from its lexifier language can be appreciated by comparing a text in Guinea-Bissau creole with its translation into Portuguese:

*I ten ba un bias un omi ku tene kandonga, ma i ka tene kusa riba. I tene un kacon tras. I mbarca son un amparante ku sukundi na kacon. I bai i bai tok i ciga na Safin. Jintis e bin pidi buleia. I inci jintis karu. Suma cuba na cobi i mbarka kil jintis tras. E bai tok e ciga na Jugudul. Cuba para, cuba para son. Amparante manera ku i miti dentru di kacon i iabri son kacon. Ku velosidadi ku karu na bin ba ki jintis oja son manera ku kacon iabri. Omi lanta. Kada kin na kai na si ladu. Kada kin na kai. Te pa e ciga Gan-Mamudu, tudu ku sta ba na karu e muri. Amparante boka mara. Ma i bin fala elis kuma i cuba ku pul ba i miti dentru di kacon. Ami i ka kuma di difuntu. I ka algin ku muri ku tenedu na kacon. Bu obi.* (Couto 1994: 131)

*Havia um homem que tinha uma candonga que não tinha teto. Na carroceria havia um caixão. Em seguida o cobrador embarcou e se escondeu dentro do caixão. Assim foram até chegar a Safim. Algumas pessoas pediram carona. O homem encheu o carro de gente. Estava chovendo muito, mas embarcaram todos atrás [na carroceria]. Continuaram a viagem até chegar a Jugudul. A chuva parou. O cobrador saiu de dentro do caixão. Na velocidade em que o veículo corria todos viram o caixão se abrir. O homem se levantou. Cada uma das pessoas caiu para um lado. Todos caíram. Todos que estavam na candonga caíram, até chegar a Gã Mamudu todos morreram. O cobrador ficou sem fala (boquiaberto). Apesar de ele lhes ter dito que não era defunto, que se metera dentro do caixão por causa da chuva.* (Couto 1994:131)

[There was a man who had a candonga (bush taxi) that did not have a roof. In the back there was a coffin. Then the conductor got on and hid inside the coffin. They went on like that until they got to Safim. Some people asked for a ride. The man filled the car with people. It was raining a lot, but they all climbed in the back. The trip went on until they got to Jugudul. The rain stopped. The conductor got out of the coffin. At the speed at which the vehicle was running everyone saw the coffin open. The conductor got up. Every person fell out by the wayside. Everyone fell out. The conductor was speechless (open-mouthed). Every one who was on the candonga fell off, by the time they got to Gã Mamudu everyone died. Even though he told them he was not a corpse, that he had got into the coffin because of the rain.]

## 6.5.2    The continental countries: Angola, Mozambique, and Guinea-Bissau

As pointed out by Lopes (2002b:22), Angola, Guinea-Bissau and Mozambique have considerable linguistic diversity, in the sense that no single language is spoken by over 50 per cent of the population. Furthermore, the close links between linguistic diversity and ethnic variety impinge upon efforts to bring about language unification. The three countries originated from colonial entities created by fiat following the Berlin Congress in 1884, at which European powers agreed to partition Africa without regard for existing ethnic groups. Consequently, the task of establishing a post-colonial nationhood was one for which their previous experience had not prepared them (Cahen 1994). Portuguese remains primarily an urban language, and major cities, such as Luanda and Benguela in Angola, and Maputo and Beira in Mozambique, are predominantly Portuguese-speaking (Barbeitos 1985:422; Castro *et al.* 2001:234–236). In Angola, for example, about 46.4% of the residents of urban areas speak Portuguese, as opposed to about 11.9% in the countryside (MICS 1997:29). In rural or semi-rural areas, however, teaching Portuguese as a second language is likely to remain a priority task for some time to come.

Consensus is lacking regarding figures pertaining to languages, not only because of a lack of reliable statistics but also because some linguists consider as separate languages what others would classify as dialects of the same language. Available information, however, shows that in Angola and Mozambique bilingualism or even multilingualism is the rule for the majority of the population. Although pidgin varieties may have existed (Holm 1989:271), there are at present no Portuguese-based creoles.

In Mozambique about 3% of the population speak Portuguese as a native language (Lopes 2002c:51), and about 43% speak it as a second language. Of the native languages, Emakhuwa is spoken by about 25% of the population (Lopes 2002b:23), three fourths of whom speak at least one of some twenty Bantu languages, distributed with considerable geographic overlapping and none with a clear majority. Non-Bantu languages such as Swazi or Zulu are also spoken in border areas. Surrounded by countries where English has official status, interacting directly with South Africa, and having joined the British Commonwealth in 1995, Mozambique has witnessed a growth of interest in learning English, which seems destined to play the role of every educated person's "third language," that is after a native African language and native or school-learned Portuguese (Matusse 1997:551). As regards geographic distribution, 79% of the speakers of Portuguese live in urban areas, whereas 74% of the speakers of African languages live in rural areas (Castro *et al.* 2001:234–238).

In Angola there are about 40 languages, belonging primarily to the Bantu family. Some 29.8% of the population speak Umbundu (the only language spoken only in Angola), followed by 26.3% who speak Portuguese, with Kimbundu in third place with 15.4% (MICS 1997:29). Kimbundu seems to be in a process of replacement by Angolan Popular Portuguese. Kikongo is spoken by some 1.5 million people (Barros 2002:37–38). Fluency in Portuguese is limited, and most speakers speak a variety of European Portuguese influenced by native languages (Mingas 2000, 2002:47).

Even more than in Angola and Mozambique, in Guinea-Bissau, where over fifteen African languages are spoken, Portuguese was spoken at the end of the twentieth century by only 0.03% of the population (Couto 1991:116). Balanta is spoken by some 27% (Lopes 2002b:23), and there are three creole varieties, namely that of Bissau and Bolema on the coast, that of the town of Bafatá in the hinterland, and that of Cacheu in the north of the country. Depending on the source chosen, between 50% and 90% of the population speak a Portuguese-based creole that is widely used in urban areas.

The complex relationship between creole and Portuguese involves a continuum linking standard Portuguese to creolized Portuguese, to Lusitanized creole, to traditional creole, to creole influenced by African languages, and to the African languages themselves. The transition from one link to the next is relatively smooth, and "only the ends of that continuum are completely alien to each other" (Couto 1994:53). Varieties can also compete with each other. For example, a Lusitanized variety known as *kriol lebi* (*crioulo leve* or 'light creole'), spoken primarily in the Bissau and Bolema area, competes in the media with the traditional *kriol fundu* (*crioulo fundo* or 'deep creole') associated primarily with the Cacheu area. At the time of writing (2004), a trend was reported in favor of using a variety of *kriol fundu* in certain sectors of the media, so as to take advantage of "its inherent richness and mechanisms for expanding itself to report on themes that have typically been reserved for *kriol lebi* or Portuguese" (Brian King, personal communication).

If a creole variety were to become the language of national communication, it would offer the considerable advantage of not belonging to any ethnic group in particular and so it could be shared by everyone without impinging on ethnic pride. During the anticolonial struggle in the 1960s and 1970s, creole was taken to the hinterland by revolutionaries, who used it as a language of intra-ethnic communication. After independence, efforts have been made to increase media use of light creole, officially or officiously called Kriol (Henriques 1985), which has been adopted by government agencies such as the National Assembly and the Supreme Court "to ensure the clarity of the proceedings" (King 2001:35–41).

### 6.5.3  *The island countries: Cape Verde and São Tomé and Príncipe*

The two island countries, Cape Verde (ten islands) and São Tomé and Príncipe (two islands), were uninhabited when the Portuguese arrived in the second half of the fifteenth century. Their population comprises mostly Africans from the mainland and descendants of Portuguese settlers, many of whom were exiles or deported convicts. Intermarriage of Europeans and Africans accounts for an Afro-Portuguese socioeconomic elite.

In colonial times islands of both archipelagos served as trading posts for the traffic of slaves, who went to São Tomé from the kingdom of Benin (in today's Nigeria) and later from the regions of Congo and Angola. Slaves from several ethnic groups went to Cape Verde from the region that is now Guinea-Bissau.

Cape Verde comprises two groups of islands, Sotavento (Leeward) and Barlavento (Windward). Virtually everyone speaks a creole as a first language and an educated minority is fluent in Portuguese. The creole variety of the island of São Vicente (located in Barlavento) is known for its "light" features, which bring it closer to Portuguese than to other creoles, such as the one spoken on the island of Santiago (Holm 1989, 2000; D. Pereira 2000; Espírito Santo 1985). The creole of Barlavento has a reputation of being particularly different from those of Sotavento, although recent work has shown that São Vicente creole seems to be "more permissive, among other reasons, because of the importance of the European presence in the settlement of the island," whereas Santiago creole "is more resistant" to outside influences (D. Pereira 2000:44).

On São Tomé there are two creole varieties, known as *Sãotomense* or *Forro* (spoken by some 85,000 speakers, clearly the majority of the population) and *Angolar* (about 9000 speakers). The latter is spoken by an ethnic community of descendants of slaves who escaped from the plantations. The creole known as *Principense* or *Lunguyè*, spoken on Príncipe, has about 4000 speakers. Both Angolar and Principense are said to have few young speakers and to be used primarily by older persons, "and even so only in very private situations," and may thus be on the wane, whereas Forro may be undergoing a decreolization process (Mata 1998:33–34).

The island societies are thus essentially bilingual and creoles constitute their main native languages. Command of Portuguese ranges from the European standard, spoken by a minority, to vernacular Portuguese and on to the creole-influenced, rudimentary Portuguese spoken by the less educated (Ramos 1985). The lack of a regional norm of Portuguese has been pointed out as an obstacle to the teaching of the language (Pontífice 2002:57–58).

### 6.5.4    Whither Portuguese?

Due to the fast pace of national and international events, assessments of social situations must be considered provisional, and linguistic matters are no exception. While negative feelings about the former status of Portuguese as a colonial language seem to have been largely overcome, the absence of local roots may limit some of its effectiveness as a language of national solidarity in multilingual societies (Lorenzino 2000:446). Portuguese may, nevertheless, turn out to be a viable "supra-national" alternative to the national African languages. Given the many obstacles, such as lack of funds for education and a shortage of teachers, for most of whom Portuguese is a school-learned rather than native language, new learners' proficiency is likely to continue ranging from rudimentary fluency to a vernacular Portuguese influenced by local languages, to standard European Portuguese spoken by an educated urban minority.

Diglossia°, which will be discussed in some detail in section 8.2, is a situation characterized by a relationship of social subordination between two varieties of the same language or between two different languages. The subordinate variety is usually a vernacular used at home, in community life, and sometimes in some popular literature. The superordinate variety is reserved for formal venues, such as formal education, law courts, and serious literature. Learning it usually requires years of formal training that is not necessarily available to a majority of the population.

In the African case, Portuguese functions as the superordinate variety, while creoles and African languages play a subordinate role and are generally limited to informal contexts, although this situation may be changing somewhat in Guinea-Bissau, as mentioned in 6.5.2. Two factors are particularly important. One is the role of Portuguese since the beginning of the struggle for independence, as a symbol of national unity (Larsen 2003); another is its prestige and power, for as underscored by Lopes is a comment applicable to all PALOP countries, "Portuguese has provided Mozambican speakers with unprecedented power for mobility and advancement in society" (1997a:21). Since much more widespread proficiency than is currently the case would be necessary for Portuguese to serve effectively as a common language for all citizens, a situation with diglossic features may endure for some time.

In the early days of colonization native languages were used in education by the Jesuits, but this practice was forbidden in 1759 by the Portuguese government, which expelled the Jesuits from the colonies. Portuguese was introduced as an instructional medium and was maintained through a succession of educational reforms aiming primarily at integrating Africans into the labor market. African languages were kept out of the education process and students were punished if caught using them at school (Martinho 1991:167).

Use of standard European Portuguese as the exclusive medium of education, even when students do not understand it, tends to work against efforts to increase literacy in Portuguese. Some scholars believe that speakers of African languages or creoles would stand a better chance of becoming fluent and literate in Portuguese if they could learn it as a second language after having become literate in their own native language (Couto 1994:62–65). This approach, however, is hampered by the circumstance that native languages and creoles are essentially oral and lack a written system as well as a tradition of use in formal education. Whatever solutions are ultimately envisaged, it is clear that any serious language policy must take indigenous languages into account (Firmino 1995a, 1995b).

Efforts to develop writing systems for African languages in Angola and Mozambique have yielded only modest results, on account of the large number of languages involved and also of the intrinsic difficulty of choosing a variety acceptable to a majority of speakers. The technical aspects of developing a workable writing system, already mentioned in relation to creoles, are another obstacle.

Although school instruction is conducted in Portuguese, creole is used on radio and television, as well as in some of the press, and thus a struggling, though apparently viable, body of publications in creole is under way. This includes not only comic books and fiction works but also publications of a more practical content such as election materials, health education, technical information, and so on. Publishing in creole is hampered by dialectal variation, and although proposals have been made for a unified written norm, that goal is far from having been reached (Augel 1998:35–37). The essentially oral nature of creoles, bound by no single grammatical standard and tolerating a great deal of variation in pronunciation, syntax, and the lexicon, contributes to the preservation of creole continua. Since developing a writing system requires choosing a specific variety and therefore excluding others, the process of establishing a norm raises issues akin to those involved in developing a writing system for African languages.

According to King (2001:41), in Guinea-Bissau in the 1980s "at least two standardized Kriol alphabets were elaborated, yet no single standard was adopted or promoted by the state." Eventually, the Bissau variety of "crioulo aportuguesado" or Lusitanized creole "completely superseded the other two principal dialects" (King 2001:35) in most written materials. Ironically, increased use of this variety of creole may lead to a "decreolization process [that] accelerates every passing day" (Couto 1994:66). The fact that differences between creoles are sometimes deep enough to interfere with mutual intelligibility – as in the case of Guinea-Bissau's *fundu* and *lebi* varieties, or in that of the Capeverdian variety spoken on the island of São Vicente (D. Pereira 2000) – further complicates standardization efforts.

It has been suggested that learners' linguistic background also interferes with their formal learning of Portuguese, particularly among children from families of low socioeconomic standing, who speak non-standard Portuguese, alone or in combination with a native language and/or a creole (Pontífice 1991). African languages also borrow words from Portuguese, usually with phonological adaptations. Examples of this process include oral diphthongs reduced to vowels (*caixa* > *kaxà* 'box') or split by a glide (*queijo* > *kexjù* 'cheese'); nasal diphthongs are made oral and reduced to simple vowels (*pão* > *pawu* 'bread'); consonant groups are split by a vowel (*grade* > *gàradà* 'grille,' *cerveja* > *sàràvhexjà* 'beer'). At the morphological level we find verb infinitives marked by two Bantu elements, such as the prefix *ku-* and the infinitive-marking suffix *-a* (*passear* > *kùpàsìyàrà* 'to stroll,' *arrumar* > *kùrùmàrà* 'to fix') (Sitoe 1991:109–110).

Linguists have pointed out that there is something artificial in a situation in which European Portuguese remains the standard for language teaching and use, even though most speakers and learners have little or no contact with that variety (Lopes 1997a:41; Silva 1991:102). Because Portuguese is learned as a second language by persons who get little or no feedback from native speakers of standard European Portuguese, their language tends to undergo a process of nativization, whereby it acquires specific features from African languages. This happens not only at the lexical level, where borrowing from the national languages is to be expected, but also at the phonological and morphosyntactic levels (Mingas 2000).

Some scholars (such as Gonçalves (1985, 1996), Firmino (1995a, 1995b), Lopes (1997a), and Marque (1985)) have debated the issues involved in defining an African variety (or varieties) of Portuguese, with specific features for each country. Endruschat (1995) analyzed differences in the placement of clitic pronouns between EP and Angolan and Mozambican varieties, and research carried out in Mozambique (Stroud and Gonçalves 1997–1998) has yielded a corpus of oral production for systematic analysis. Loan words from African languages are found not only in the colloquial language but also in the literary variety, as in the following items from Quimbundu: *kixima* > *cacimba* 'rain water well,' *kubata* > *cubata* 'house,' *muamba* 'chicken stew,' *maka* 'fight, confusion,' *quinda* 'basket,' *soba* 'chief, chieftain,' *gimbo* 'money,' *guimbo* 'machete,' *milongo* 'medicine,' *quituxe* 'crime' (Santos 1991; Oliveira 1991).

A sign of integration of loan words into the lexicon is their use in the formation of new words by derivation (3.8.1). In Mozambique, for example, a borrowed noun such as *lobolo* 'a fee paid to a bride's father by her betrothed' has yielded the derived verb *lobolar* (< *lobolo* + *-ar*) 'to pay the tribute owed to one's bride's father.' Another regular process is the extension of the meaning of a Portuguese word, such as *alarmar* 'to startle,' as in *alarmar um carro* 'to install an alarm system in a car.' Semantic extension may involve syntactic change, as in the use of *nascer* 'to be born' in the transitive sense of 'to give birth to,' e.g. *eu nasci três vezes: duas meninas e um rapaz* 'I gave birth three times: two girls and a boy' (Lopes 2002a). Making a verb transitive is easily achieved by omitting the preposition required in standard EP, as in the following examples from Gonçalves (1996:74):

(1)  a. MoP *Não queriam* **obedecer ordens** *dos professores.*
      'They did not want to obey the teachers' orders' (cf. EP *obedecer às ordens*).
     b. MoP *O inspector* **acertou** *aqueles indivíduos.*
      'The inspector hit (with a shot) those individuals' (cf. EP *acertou naqueles indivíduos*).

Generalized transitivity makes possible passive sentences in which a semantic benefactive (4.2) occurs in the syntactic function of the subject, a construction not considered grammatical in EP, as in these examples from Gonçalves (1996:75):

(2)    a. MoP *O irmão foi concedido uma bolsa de estudos.*
'The brother was awarded a scholarship.'
b. EP *Uma bolsa de estudos foi concedida ao irmão.*
'A scholarship was awarded to the brother.'

(3)    a. MoP *Segundo nós fomos explicados isso deve-se a questões de ordem prática.*
'As we were explained (= was explained to us), that is due to practical reasons.'
b. EP *Segundo foi-nos explicado, isso deve-se a questões de ordem prática.*
'As was explained to us, that is due to practical reasons.'

Possibly because it is a school-learned language, spoken and written Portuguese tends to include words and expressions that would be considered literary, or at any rate typical of formal written styles, in European Portuguese. This usage creates blends of formal and informal styles in the same sentence as in example 4, where formal items such as *fundos, alocar, execução, empreitada* cooccur with the nearly-slang expression *comer o dinheiro* 'to embezzle,' literally 'to eat the money.'

(4)    *Os fundos alocados para a execução da empreitada não chegaram, porque comeram o dinheiro.* (Lopes 2002a)
'The funds allotted to the project did not suffice because [they] ate the money.'

Such a situation underscores the need pointed out by Lopes (1997b:499, n. 16) for linguistic analysis to take into account "considerations of syntax, idiom, style and usage related to social and cultural features of the Mozambican way of life," a line of research further developed by Lopes *et al.* (2002). Much work remains to be done, for as scholars have argued (Brito 1999), the evidence available is fragmentary and based largely on data that have yet to be submitted to statistical analysis, and consequently it would be premature to evaluate claims about the formation of country-specific varieties of Portuguese. Clearly, issues related to language acquisition and the definition of regional standards are likely to remain topics of lively debate in the foreseeable future.

## 6.6    Asian twilight

As mentioned in Chapter 1, Portugal's seafaring and trade activities in Africa and Asia in the fifteenth and sixteenth centuries made Portuguese an international language. It was used in oral and written communication, not only between Portuguese seafarers and administrators and local rulers, but also by

Dutch and English explorers and explorers of other nationalities in their African and Asian contacts (Cintra 1999a:293). Portuguese also provided a foundation for pidgins and creoles, and it has been suggested (Clements 2000) that a generic Portuguese-based pidgin participated in the formation of creoles in Asian communities formed by Portuguese settlers, their native spouses or companions, and eventually by their descendants, for whom that pidgin became a creole. Recent research (Tomás 1992) suggests the presence of African elements in Asian Portuguese creoles.

The development of creoles in Asia was aided by the circumstance that the number of native speakers of Portuguese in the colonies was relatively small, and shrank further as Portugal's maritime empire was gradually lost to the British and the Dutch in the seventeenth century. Goa, Daman (Pg *Damão*), and Diu remained Portuguese until 1961, when they were taken over by India and reorganized as a single Union Territory. Even during the colonial period, however, the Portuguese language was spoken only by an educated minority, while the general population spoke Indo-Portuguese creole, Konkani, or other Indian languages. After 1961 the new Indian administration continued operating in Portuguese for a few years as it converted to English, and schools likewise changed to English on a gradual basis. Although still spoken as a family language by some people and taught at the university as a foreign language, Portuguese is clearly on the wane in India (Rodrigues 2000; Cahen *et al.* 2000).

This situation was aptly summed up by Teyssier (1985:47), who underscored the residual nature of Portuguese or Indo-Portuguese creoles in a few remaining Asian communities. The Portuguese-based creole of Sri-Lanka, for example, was still spoken by about 1,000 people or less in the early 1970s (Theban 1985:276), although "prospects for its survival can only be described as bleak" (Smith 1978:32). In Macau (pop. 453,700, area 25.4 square kilometers, 9.8 square miles), by the end of twentieth century Chinese had become the language of young people (Batalha 1985). When sovereignty was returned to China in December 1999, the region became the Macao Special Administrative Region, and Putonghua was recognized as the official language, with Portuguese remaining official but in a secondary role (Mann and Wong 1999:32). There is no reason to expect it to regain any significant ground.

A similar situation obtains in Hong Kong, where a once viable Portuguese-based creole was reported as having disappeared a decade ago (Charpentier 1992; Baxter 1990). In Malaysia, Papia Kristang ('Christian talk') or simply Kristang, spoken in Malacca by some 1,000 people, is "the last surviving variety of Creole Portuguese in South East Asia which still functions as a mother tongue and home language of a speech community" (Baxter 1988:vii). It remains to be seen whether the adoption of Portuguese in 2002 as a cooficial language (with Tetum) in East Timor will signal the beginning a new life cycle for Portuguese in Asia. Even if it does, teaching it as a second language to a population with low literacy levels in their own native languages (Costa 1995) may prove a formidable task, if for no other reason then because Portuguese has to compete with English, widely used throughout Asia as a second language with a much wider international reach.

## 6.7    Emigration and contact with other languages

Emigration from continental Portugal and the islands increased considerably in the twentieth century, so that between 1964 and 1974, according to Bloemraad (1999:103), "about 100,000 Portuguese were leaving the country every year." Motivated primarily by the need to find work opportunities, emigration led to the establishment of Portuguese-descent immigrant communities in several countries around the world.

The presence of Portuguese immigrants in Western European countries became statistically significant after the 1960s, and although most countries received at least some immigrants, the most numerous communities are found in France and Germany. In France there were about 765,000 Portuguese in the late 1980s, about half of them in the Paris region. In Germany there were slightly fewer than 110,000 in 1981 and as they started going back to Portugal that figure decreased to about 77,000 by 1986 (Dias 1989:18). With the establishment of the European Union and increasing ease of travel thanks to affluence and better roads in Spain and Portugal, frequent visits to the homeland have become commonplace.

Prolonged contact with the host country's language(s) and increasing bilingualism within the community have contributed to the development of distinctive, though not necessarily stable, varieties of mixed speech referred to as *emigrês* 'Emigrese' (Dias 1989). The development of an Emigrese variety does not seem to have taken place in Germany, where influence of German on the speech of Portuguese immigrants and their descendants is limited to the kind of interference that is expected when languages come into contact (Dias 1989; Sousa-Möckel 1995). French, on the other hand, seems to have left a deeper mark, linguistically as well as socially, on the immigrants and their descendants, as noted in studies on French-dominant adolescents attending school in Portugal (Mesquita 1986; Afonso 1998; Bendiha 1998; Matos 1991).

An analysis of immigrants living in Paris by a Portuguese psychiatrist (Barros Ferreira 1988) revealed regular patterns of French influence. As one might expect, there were many loan words that represented unknown or unfamiliar terms, such as Fr *veau* > *vô* for Pg *vitela* 'veal,' Fr *poubelle* > *pubela* for Pg *caixote do lixo* 'dustbin,' Fr *vacances* > *vacanças* for Pg *férias* 'vacation.' Other loan words, however, either replaced ordinary Portuguese terms (Fr *seau* > *sô* for Pg *balde* 'pail,' Fr *balai* > *bàlé* for Pg *vassoura* 'broom,' Fr *serpillière* >

*sarapilheira* for Pg *esfregão* 'cleaning rag'). Others were simply adapted for ease of pronunciation, as Fr *lessive* > *lessivia* for Pg *lexívia* 'bleach.'

Morphological loans included regular change of the French adjective-forming suffix *-eux* into *-oso*, as in *affreux* > *afrôso, malheureux* > *malerôso, dangereux* > *dangeroso* for Pg. *terrível* 'terrible,' *infeliz* 'unhappy,' *perigoso* 'dangerous,' respectively.

Borrowing sometimes yielded unexpected results, as in the case of Fr *retraite* 'retirement' > *retrete* (cf. Pg *retrete* 'outhouse'). French verbs in *-er* and *-ir* were systematically changed into Portuguese verbs in *-ar* and *-ir*, respectively, as in *Meu marido trompava-me* for *Meu marido enganava-me* 'my husband was betraying me,' from Fr *tromper* 'betray' > *trompar*.

Contact with English has been particularly significant in Australia, South Africa, and above all North America. Portuguese emigration to Australia involved no more than 1,000 individuals until the middle of the twentieth century, and increased through the 1980s mostly due to an exodus from the former African colonies and from East Timor. By the end of that century there was an estimated community of 65,000 people of Portuguese origin (though only under 18,000 Portugal-born), with over 50% of them living in New South Wales (Rocha-Trindade 2000a:23).

In South Africa Portuguese immigration also grew in the second half of the twentieth century, mainly from Madeira, and by the last decade of the century the Portuguese-descent community had increased by some 100,000, including people coming from Angola and Mozambique after decolonization, to reach about 600,000–800,000 (Dias 1989:16; Rocha-Trindade 2000a:23).

In Canada, where Portuguese immigration started in 1953, there are "approximately 292,185 individuals . . . who claim a Portuguese ethnic origin" (Nunes 1998:i). About 92% of the Portuguese-Canadians live in the provinces of Ontario, Quebec, and British Columbia. Major concentrations live in the metropolitan regions of Toronto (48%) and Montreal (13%) (Nunes 1998:i). Now in its third generation and increasingly integrated in Canadian society, this community seems to be undergoing a process of language attrition as young people either fail to learn Portuguese or stop using it. Researchers suggest that in the Toronto area the retention of Portuguese fell from 83% in 1971 all the way to 60.5% in 1991 (Helms-Park 2000:128). Interference from other languages seems particularly intense in Quebec, where Portuguese-Canadians tend to learn and use both English and French (Dias-Tatilon 2000).

The largest communities of Portuguese ancestry in North America are in the United States, and their establishment can be traced to the second half of the nineteenth century, when whalers from the Azores, and later from Cape Verde, started arriving in New England, California, and Hawaii.

Despite restrictive immigration laws in the 1920s, the influx of Portuguese immigrants increased again after the 1950s, thanks to legislation favoring victims of the volcanic eruption on the Azorean island of Fayal in 1957–1958, but then slackened off in the 1980s. Portuguese-American communities exist today on the East Coast, in and around New Bedford, Fall River, Lowell, and Boston, and there are other significant communities in Newark, Providence, Philadelphia, New York, and Hartford. The other significant community – again mostly of Azorean origin, with Madeirans running a distant second – is located in California, where immigrants started arriving in the second half of the nineteenth century, again attracted to the fishing industry, and ended up primarily in the San Francisco Bay area, all the way south to San José and inland in the San Joaquín Valley. In Hawaii, a Portuguese-American community, likewise descended primarily from Azoreans and Madeirans, was established around 1878.

Reliable data about actual use of the Portuguese language in the USA and Canada are scarce, and systematic large-scale sociolinguistic research has yet to be carried out. A favorable sign is the existence, in the United States and Canada, of a small but viable literature (Almeida 2001, Vaz 2001). A less favorable one is that the press in Portuguese in California, once thriving, seemed limited to two bimonthly bilingual papers in 2003. A few websites in Portuguese have appeared in both Canada and the United States but it is difficult to estimate their readership. Radio programs in the language are reportedly dwindling, as are television programs, although cable television may play a relevant, if small, role.

According to data from the USA Census Bureau (www.census.gov), in 1990 429,860 respondents declared Portuguese as their home language; in 2000 that figure had jumped to 564,630, a difference of 134,770 that seems to require careful scrutiny. Home use of the language is likely to be primarily by the older generations, and the younger segment of the Portuguese-descent population appears to be not only bilingual but increasingly English-dominant. A survey of 100 Portuguese-American high school students (Borges 2001) found that fewer than 50% of their parents used Portuguese at home. About 15% of the respondents used the language because their immigrant parents did not speak English, whereas another 15% reported talking to their parents in English, even though the latter used Portuguese to address their own parents. The same author reports that in 1998 secondary schools in the San Joaquín Valley cities of San Jose, Turlock, Hilmar, Los Banos, and Tulare had about 550 students in Portuguese language classes, while in all of California there were only seven community-supported night schools offering language courses to fewer than 500 students. On the East Coast, Bento (1998) reports that at a language school in Newark the number of enrollments dropped from 550 in 1983–1984 to 400 in 1988–1989 and to 250 in 1997–1998.

Works such as Pap 1949 and Dias 1989 give an idea of the processes involved in forming this Emigrese variety. Intense borrowing, primarily at the lexical level, includes not only single words but compounds and full idiomatic phrases. Loan words are systematically adapted to Portuguese phonology, with the resulting loss of certain contrasts that are functional in English. Thus the English high front vowels (Table 2.4) /i/ (*beet*) and /ɪ/ (*bit*) are both interpreted as Pg /i/, as in *milker > milca, freeway > friuei*. Eng /ɪ/ (bit), however, may also be interpreted as /ej/, as in *television > televeija, air conditioning > arcandeixa*. Eng /t/, articulated as [ɾ] in intervocalic position (*waiter, water*), tends to be interpreted phonetically as [ɾ], as in *automatic > arameque; starter > estara, radiator > radieira*. Diphthongs are usually preserved, as in /ej/ *bacon > beica, brake > breique*; /aj/ *dryer > draia, size > saize*.

While phonological adaptations are more or less predictable from a comparison of the two phonological systems, it is more difficult to predict which specific words will be borrowed, since this will depend on the specific needs of the community. On the basis of compiled lists, however, one can detect a tendency to borrow the names of technological items that did not exist in the immigrants' original environment. Once brought into the lexicon of the community, items may stay on indefinitely, even if the next generations, who are usually bilingual, more educated, and likely to be English-dominant, are familiar with the English word.

It should be kept in mind that strange as the spelling of some items may appear, it merely reflects an attempt to represent in writing what is essentially a strictly oral adaptation to Portuguese phonology. The phonological processes involved parallel those responsible for the anglicization of Spanish words like *burrito, tortilla, Los Angeles* or *San Jose* to [ˈbəɾɪtə], [təɾˈtɪlə], [ləsˈændʒələs], [ˈsənəzej], making them unrecognizable to Spanish speakers from other countries. Below are some items that illustrate the borrowing and phonological adaptation process:

**Technology**
*television > televeijo*
*market > marqueta*
*carpet > carpeta*
*store > estôa*
*manager > maneja*
*bookkeeper > boquipa*
*grocery (store) > grosseria*

**Culture-specific**
*sheriff > charêfe*
*tenement > tanamento*
*vacation > vaqueixa*
*undertaker > anatêca*
*radiator > radiera*
*son of a gun > sanabagana*
*go to hell! > gorele!*

**New activities**
*to trim the bushes > trimar os buxos*
*to drop a course > dropar un curso*
*to drive > draivar*

**Clothing**
*overalls > alverozes/*
*  alveroles*
*overshoes > alvachús*
*overcoat > alvacote*

Another regular borrowing process is loan translation, in which an English word or expression is literally translated into Portuguese: *high school > escola alta* (Pg *escola secundária*), *black coffee > café preto* (Pg *café simples*), *boarding house* > *casa de bordo* (Pg *pensão*), *to watch television* > *vigiar televeijo* (*ver televisão*).

Activities are often encoded by combining an action verb and a noun, usually involving direct translation:

> *fazer o parque* 'to park' (Pg *estacionar*)
> *fazer a estoa* 'to go to the store' (Pg *fazer compras*)
> *fazer o fainaute* 'to find out' (Pg *descobrir*)
> *fazer uma direita/esquerda* 'to make a right/left' (Pg *virar à direita/esquerda*)
> *dar para trás* 'to give back' (Pg *restituir, devolver*)
> *dizer para trás* 'to talk back' (Pg *replicar*)
> *mandar para trás* 'to send back' (Pg *devolver*)

Semantic extension, in turn, involves adding to an existing Portuguese word the meaning of a like-sounding English word, as in the following items (with spelling adjusted to approximate the pronunciation, since this is an oral variety without regular written expresion):

| Portuguese word | Meaning | Immigrese (English-influenced meaning) |
| --- | --- | --- |
| *cela* | cell (e.g. prison) | cellar |
| *mecha* | wick | match |
| *especial* | special (adj.) | special (item on sale) |
| *bordar* | to embroider | to board |
| *grau* | degree (e.g. temperature) | school grade |
| *aplicar* | to apply (e.g. a compress) | apply for something |

Code-switching is also an active communicative device, as seen in these examples cited by Dias (1989:103–104):

(5)    a. *Pintei a minha casa de* blue. *Ficou* nice.
             'I painted my house blue. It turned out nice.'
        b. *A senhora não dá* juice *para o meu* kid?
             'Won't you give my kid some juice?'
        c. *Não sei* why *tu foste com ela.*
             'I don't know why you went with her.'

On returning to their place of origin, either on a visit or permanently, immigrants take back some of these items, which may end up adopted by their less mobile compatriots. Borges (1960) points out that most such items collected by her on the island of São Miguel, in the Azores, were listed in Pap (1949) as occurring in Portuguese-American speech.

Similar though apparently less extended interference phenomena from English and French are noticeable in the Portuguese of Quebec, where Dias-Tatilon has registered a variety of calques such as the following (2000:153, adapted):

| Luso-Québécois | Québécois French or English | Standard Portuguese |
|---|---|---|
| *inecessário* | unnecessary | *desnecessário* |
| *permitir algumas semanas* | allow some weeks | *esperar algumas semanas* |
| *levar vantagem* | to take advantage | *aproveitar-se* |
| *dopar-se* | se doper | *drogar-se* |
| *apontamento* | appointment | *hora marcada* |
| *mesmo se é duro* | même si c'est dur | *mesmo se é difícil* |
| *o secondário* | le secondaire | *o liceu* |

The varieties of Portuguese spoken and written in the regions covered in this chapter are, linguistically and culturally, an extension of European Portuguese. The Azores and Madeira are of course a part of the Portuguese Republic, and despite regional features, their language remains unmistakably Portuguese. The PALOP countries have kept cultural links with Portugal, and while the Portuguese spoken in those countries shows some specific features, not enough time has elapsed for the development of autonomous varieties, although this may come to pass. It is worth recalling that Portuguese-based creoles, as said earlier, are autonomous languages and should not be thought of as dialects of Portuguese.

As for immigrant communities around the world, if developments in North America may serve as a point of reference, interference from contact languages is likely to go on, coupled with increasing dominance of the national language(s) among the young and decreasing numbers of native speakers as the immigrant generations pass away. It is unclear to what extent Portuguese is likely to be kept, beyond emblematic use, by the new heritage speakers, despite a sense of ethnic identity which appears to endure, independently of language maintenance (Stephens 1989; Noivo 2000: 163; Rocha-Trindade 2000:29).

As of late, Brazilians have been making their presence felt in growing numbers in the world immigration scene, especially in the United States, where since the 1980's their number has grown, particularly in California, Florida, New York, and the Boston and New Jersey regions, where they share some space with Portuguese-origin communities. Although reliable statistics are virtually non-existent, partly because many such immigrants are undocumented, off-the-record estimates by consular officials range between 500,000 and 1,000,000 for the whole country. This would make the 2000 census figure of 181,076 Brazilians sound rather low, in view of the 200,000 reported in the Miami area alone (*The Brasilians* 2003 (May), 16-P) and some 40,000 in the Atlanta (Georgia) area alone, where schools in Cobb County supposedly have some 5,000 Brazilian pupils.

Although no large-scale systematic studies of the speech of Brazilians living in the United States have been carried out, casual observation reveals similar patterns of adaptation of English words to everyday, as in the sample below:

| Adapted term | Source/meaning | Standard Portuguese |
|---|---|---|
| *enforçar* | to enforce (a law) | *fazer cumprir (uma lei)* |
| *afordar* | to afford | *poder pagar* |
| *tiquetar* | to ticket | *pôr uma multa* |
| *rentar* | to rent | *alugar* |

(6)    a. *Tem uma lei contra, mas eles não **enforçam** ela.*
       'There is a law against (it) but they don't enforce it.'
    b. *A gente queria **rentar** um **penthouse**, mas não dá para a gente*
       ***afordar**, é muito caro.*
       'We wanted to rent a penthouse but we can't afford [it], it's too expensive.'

Another topic to be researched in the next decade is the outcome from contact between the two varieties of Portuguese, either in the already mentioned regions in the United States or in Portugal itself, where immigration from Brazil has grown steadily in the last twenty years and an estimated 100,000 Brazilians, both legal and undocumented, currently live (Beatriz Padilla, personal communication; see also Rocha-Trindade 2000). Brazilian television programs, and particularly soap operas, are extremely popular and contribute to foster familiarity with Brazilian Portuguese. This is important, because the situation of the language in Brazil is very different from that in the other regions commented on in this Chapter. Having grown primarily out of the speech of the original sixteenth- and seventeenth-century settlers, it has taken deep roots and become the native language of vast majority of the population, who may understand European Portuguese, but do not identify with it. Though significantly diversified and endowed with an educated standard of its own, Brazilian Portuguese has an unmistakable profile, about which we will talk in the next chapter.

# 7    Brazilian Portuguese

Like any language spread over a large territory occupied by a stratified society, Portuguese as spoken in Brazil encompasses a raft of partially overlapping regional and social varieties that show a significant amount of contrast in pronunciation and syntax. The present chapter will review some of the specific features of Brazilian Portuguese.

## 7.1    Variation in Brazilian Portuguese

A great deal of such variation is directly related to speakers' educational level, which in turn is linked to their socioeconomic situation. In fact, some of the most salient contrasts within Brazilian Portuguese are not regional but social. There is considerable divergence between the vernacular° speech of the majority of the population, the speech of the educated minority, and the normative° language codified in prescriptive° grammars. Traditionally, such grammars have been based primarily, if not exclusively, on the formal written usage found in Portuguese (and, as of the 1920s, also Brazilian) literary works spanning over four centuries. In principle, there is nothing wrong with this, for it is necessary to have reliable descriptions of the language used in literature. The error, however, has consisted in taking the literary variety as being the only valid one, and in condemning varieties diverging from it – such as the vernacular – as the result of decay caused by speakers' poor language habits. In addition, it has been determined that poor theoretical principles and unsystematic selection of examples have led normative grammars to contradict each other (Castilho 1989a:57). Linguistic research carried out in the second half of the twentieth century has invalidated this view, and work on Brazilian linguistics over the last four decades shows that features of vernacular speech are an integral part of the language.

Contradiction between grammar manuals and actual language use has long been a major stumbling block not only for foreign learners but also for Brazilian students, particularly those from the lower social strata who are not exposed to educated varieties of speech. For many of those students, formal varieties of Portuguese constitute, if not a "foreign" language, certainly a dialect

211

very distant from the linguistic reality to which they are accustomed. Such a situation, puzzling to outsiders, has not gone unnoticed by perceptive writers. Early in the twentieth century the modernist author Mário de Andrade (1893–1945) described a picaresque character named Macunaíma studying "the two languages of the country, namely spoken Brazilian and written Portuguese" (Andrade 1978:111). More recently, a Brazilian linguist wrote:

O português (que aparece nos textos escritos) *não* é a nossa língua materna. A língua que aprendemos com nossos pais, irmãos e avós é a mesma que falamos, mas não é a que escrevemos. As diferenças são bastante profundas, a ponto de, em certos casos, impedir a comunicação . . . há duas línguas no Brasil: uma que se escreve (e que recebe o nome de "português"); e outra que se fala (e que é tão desprezada que nem tem nome). E é esta última que é a língua materna dos brasileiros; a outra (o "português") tem de ser aprendida na escola, e a maior parte da população nunca chega a dominá-la adequadamente. (Mario Perini, *Sofrendo a gramática*, 35–36. Italics in the original.)

[Portuguese (as it appears in written texts) is *not* our mother tongue. The language we learn from our parents, siblings, and grandparents is the same as we speak, but it is not the one we write. Differences are very deep, enough, in certain cases, to prevent communication. . . . there are two languages in Brazil: a written one (which receives the name of 'Portuguese') and a spoken one (which is so despised that it does not even have a name). The latter is the mother tongue of Brazilians; the other ('Portuguese') has to be learned at school and the majority of the population never manage to master it properly.]

To understand this situation, it is helpful to visualize it as a triangle. One of its vertices represents Vernacular Brazilian Portuguese (VBP), the essentially oral variety spoken natively by the majority of the population. Another vertex represents what we will call Prescriptive Portuguese, is the norm embodied in traditional grammar manuals based primarily on literary sources. Although Prescriptive Portuguese is essentially a school-learned variety, persons who grow up in highly educated environments, where its use is a mark of prestige, can speak and write it fluently. While it is no exaggeration to say that for educated Brazilians, Prescriptive Portuguese remains, at least in theory, an ideal of language correction and elegance, in the informal situations that make up the bulk of everyday communication, we encounter the variety that constitutes the third vertex of our triangle. This variety, still imperfectly analyzed, may be referred to as Standard Brazilian Portuguese. It may be characterized, somewhat loosely, as the variety used by educated speakers in casual speech and less formal kinds of writing – such as correspondence with intimates, which in recent years includes e-mailing – which do not call for Prescriptive Portuguese. This is, of course, a simplification, for the complex relationships among these three facets of the language constitute a thorny linguistic issue which has long occupied a growing number of linguists.

The coexistence of a vernacular and a standard in the same language community need not constitute a problematic issue if the two varieties can be kept reasonably apart. In the case of Brazil, however, vernacular features pervade the unmonitored speech of the educated with a (to many, disquieting) regularity that suggests that, rather than discrete entities, VBP and SBP are an integral part of Brazilian Portuguese as a whole. As Holm puts it, even the most extreme modalities of the vernacular and the standard belong to "a continuum of lects° that relate more to social class and education than to race" (2004:58).

Since vernacular forms are either frowned upon or downright condemned by prescriptive grammars, educated speakers find themselves in an ambivalent position. On the one hand, they are aware that vernacular features in their speech contribute to defining the colloquial styles that are essential for effective communication in settings where standard or prescriptive forms would create distance between the interlocutors. This is not only the case with casual conversation with social equals but also crucial in communicating with VBP speakers at work, on the street, or in a variety of daily interactions with service people. On the other hand, being aware that language correctness is held as a mark of educational excellence and social status, educated speakers feel pressured to follow norms of prescriptive grammar in formal and semi-formal situations. Some individuals feel comfortable codeswitching along the gamut of possibilities between vernacular and standard. For others – particularly the semi-educated trying to climb the social ladder – the ease with which vernacular features occur in their speech as soon as self-monitoring is relaxed can be a source of embarrassment and loss of face. It is not surprising that stock phrases like *para usar a linguagem popular* 'to use popular language' or *como se diz na gíria* 'as they say in slang' are widely used as an excuse for vernacular forms that pop up in conversation, like country cousins showing up uninvited at an smart party.

To complicate things, while prescriptive grammars are based, as already mentioned, on literary usage, a reasonably complete descriptive grammar of non-literary educated usage has yet to be produced. The language of the press, for example, shows a great deal of variation. In the same newspaper or news magazine, the language of editorials tends to adhere to prescriptive usage, while feature articles often use constructions, idioms, and vocabulary close to vernacular usage, or at any rate to what one could describe, somewhat loosely, as rather colloquial BP. Furthermore, some forms accepted by the style manuals of some publications are eschewed by those of others, just as forms used in speech or writing by some educated persons are frowned upon by others with as much claim to being educated. Together, these factors foster a situation of linguistic insecurity that is exploited by media mavens ready to foist advice – often contradictory and without a solid linguistic basis – upon a disoriented public.

For foreign learners of BP, initiated through textbook dialogs and edited reading selections, such variation can be, to put it mildly, confusing. If they persevere, however, they will likely understand that it is a reflection of a multifaceted social situation that must be grasped on its own terms. This presentation will contrast educated usage with vernacular forms and, when appropriate, indicate those which are, for purely social reasons, considered inappropriate for educated discourse.

### 7.1.1    Research on Brazilian Portuguese

As an academic subject and a research area, linguistics is a relatively recent activity in Brazil, and as recently as the early 1970s, there was only a handful of scholars with a doctoral degree in linguistics. Thus it is only in the last few decades that a suffecent critical mass of scholars have begun to study BP systematically. (For an overview, see Naro 1976 or Altman 1998.)

Nevertheless, objective analysis of the characteristics of Brazilian Portuguese began much earlier, with individual efforts focusing on specific instances of linguistic variation. One of these was Amadeu Amaral's *O Dialecto Caipira* (1920), a description of the main features of rural speech in the backlands of the State of São Paulo. Another was Antenor Nascentes's *O Linguajar Carioca* (1922), which analyzed popular speech in the city of Rio de Janeiro. Yet another was Mário Marroquim's *A Língua do Nordeste (Alagoas e Pernambuco)* (1934), a study of the speech of the northeastern region. Nascentes (1953) characterized two large dialectal areas according to the vowel quality (2.4.3.2), namely Northern (with open pre-tonic vowels) and Southern (with closed pre-tonic vowels). He also tentatively proposed a division of Brazil into six dialectal regions: *Amazon, Northeast, Bahia, Fluminense* (state of Rio de Janeiro), *Mineiro* (part of the state of Minas Gerais), and *Southern*. Work on linguistic atlases following the European tradition of focusing rural speech on a number of pre-selected points over a geographical area began with Nelson Rossi's *Atlas Prévio dos Falares Baianos* (Rossi *et al.* 1963), followed up more recently by regional linguistic atlases such as Ribeiro *et al.* 1977, Aragão and Menezes 1984, Ferreira *et al.* 1987, Aguilera 1994, and others reportedly in progress. A dialectological description on a national level is reportedly under way. For an overview of current dialectology work in Brazil see Cardoso 1999, 2001; Ferreira 1995; and Head 1996, and for sociolinguistics, Paiva and Scherre 1999.

The diachronic study of Brazilian Portuguese, essential to a comprehension of the process of regional differentiation, is likely to benefit greatly from the project *Para a História do Português Brasileiro*, based on corpora drawn from archival sources such as private letters, documents, and newspapers (Castilho 1998; Silva 2001; Duarte and Callou 2002; Alkmin 2002, among others).

Regarding the description of actual spech, one major project, started in 1969, is the *Projeto NURC (NURC = Norma Urbana Culta* or 'Educated Urban Norm'), based on recorded interviews with educated informants (defined as individuals with full college-level instruction) from the five state capitals of Porto Alegre, Recife, Rio de Janeiro, Salvador, and São Paulo (Cunha 1985). Partial studies published so far not only confirm clear differences between the prescriptive norm and actual educated speech (Lucchesi 2002:65), but also reveal the systematic occurrence of vernacular features (Castilho 1989a, 1990a, 1990b, 1990c; Castilho and Preti 1987; Castilho and Basilio 1996; Abaurre and Rodrigues 2002; Neves 1999; for an updated account of other equally relevant projects, see Castilho 2002).

It should be pointed out that the very notion of an "educated speaker" is open to debate. When the *NURC* project was launched, there were relatively few universities, admission to which was controlled, particularly at the public institutions, by strict entrance exams. Universitites and colleges have since mushroomed – between 1993 and 2003 alone, their number jumped from 1,100 to 2,000, while enrollments rose from 1.5 million to 3.5 million. Significantly, on national exams designed to evaluate the performance of graduating seniors, the lowest averages (2.0 out of a possible 10.0) were earned by students in Colleges of Letters (*faculdades*), which train language teachers (Weinberg 2003:74). One can only wonder to what extent low salaries and heavy class loads drive away from the teaching profession those employable elsewhere, and what impact this situation has on the quality of instruction, particularly when one considers that "the great majority of teachers, particularly those in charge of the first school levels, share the language varieties of the majority of their students, and have no means to acquire, and thus to teach, the standard idealized for the school" (Silva 1996:398).

## 7.2     The development of Brazilian Portuguese

BP began during the colonial period, as settlers – mostly men – from different regions in Portugal moved to Brazil. According to Pessoa (1998:244), the development of BP can be divided into three periods, namely an initial period during which regional varieties began to take shape (1534–1750), a second period during which a common BP came into existence (1750–1922), and a third period, from 1922 on, during which a Brazilian literary standard became established.

One way in which Brazilian speech moved away from EP was through a process of linguistic leveling° that ironed out major differences among the early settlers' dialects. Furthermore, in the eighteenth century EP went through a process of reduction and elimination of unstressed vowels, which led to its present consonantal quality and syncopated rhythm. In particular, weakening and elimination of final unstressed vowels has caused EP to have consonants in final position which do not occur in Brazilian speech, as in:

come 'P3sg eats'       EP [kɔm] vs. BP ['kɔmi]
cabe 'P3sg fits'       EP [kab] vs. BP ['kabi]
pega 'P3sg grabs'      EP [pɛg] vs. BP ['pɛgi]

In Brazil, however, vowels have continued to be pronounced fully, even though some regional accents, such as Mineiro, tend to slur and drawl them. Another change that took place in the Lisbon variety but not in Brazil concerns the articulation of the vowel /e/ as a low central [ɐ] before a palatal consonant, creating contrasts such as the following:

beijo 'kiss'       EP ['bɐjʒ"] vs. BP ['bejʒu] ~ ['beʒu]
feixe 'bundle'     EP ['fɐjʃ] vs. BP ['fejʃi] ~ ['feʃi]

Differentiation was also influenced by the fact that certain syntactic features which became regional or archaic in Portugal remained in general use in Brazil. One instance of this process involves the construction *estar + gerund* (Table 3.15), which was replaced in the nineteenth century in standard EP by *estar a + infinitive* (i.e. *estou falando* vs. *estou a falar*). The earlier construction, however, has been preserved not only in Brazil but also in regions such as Algarve (Azevedo Maia 1975:97) and Alentejo. There is nothing unusual about this: peripheral areas (as Brazil used to be during the colonial period) often tend to preserve features that have become archaic in the variety spoken in metropolitan areas.

Not surprisingly, the lexicons of Portuguese in Brazil and in Portugal have diverged noticeably. Certain words current in one variety are not used in the other, or are used only regionally, or have partially or completely different meanings. Despite the importance of the lexicon in communication, such differences do not affect the structure of the language, even though they are the first thing that catches one's attention. The sample in Table 7.1 should suffice for illustrative purposes and interested readers will find abundant information in Villar (1989) and Prata (1994).

### 7.2.1    Colonial times (1500–1808/1822)

A certain amount of language variation was likely fostered not only by contact with other languages but also by the lack of public education, in keeping with the Crown's decision to exploit the colony exclusively for its (the Crown's) own enrichment. Whilst in Spain's American colonies universities were created early in the colonial period (Santo Domingo, 1538; Lima and Mexico, 1551; Bogotá, 1652; Caracas, 1721; La Habana, 1728), only elementary instruction existed in colonial Brazil, offered at a few Church-sponsored schools or by more or less improvised teachers. The offspring of the elite, if interested in studying at all, attended university in Portugal or perhaps elsewhere in Europe. Until

Table 7.1 *Some lexical differences between Brazilian Portuguese and European Portuguese*

| EP | BP | |
| --- | --- | --- |
| o autoclismo | a descarga | flush system (on a toilet) |
| a camioneta | o ônibus | bus |
| a camisola | a camisa esporte | sports shirt |
| a camiseta | a camisa polo | polo shirt, T shirt |
| a casa de banhos | o banheiro | bathroom |
| o comboio | o trem | train |
| o durex | a camisinha | condom |
| o eléctrico | o bonde | street car, tramway |
| a esquadra | a delegacia | police station |
| o estendal | o varal | clothes line |
| o estore | a persiana | blind |
| a factura | a nota fiscal | sales receipt |
| o fato | o terno | suit of clothes |
| o fiambre | o presunto cozido | cooked ham |
| o gasóleo | o diesel | diesel |
| o gelado | o sorvete | ice-cream |
| a hospedeira | a aeromoça | stewardess |
| o leitor de cassetes | o toca-fitas | casette player |
| as pastilhas elásticas | a goma de mascar | chewing gum |
| a quinta | o sítio | rural property |
| a sanita | a privada | toilet |
| o sumo | o suco | (fruit) juice |
| o talho | o açougue | butcher's shop |
| as tapas | os canapés | hors d'oeuvres |
| o utente | o usuário | user |
| a velharia | a antiguidade | antique |

1808 neither institutions of higher learning nor printing presses were allowed in Brazil, and all publications – censored if legal, and liable to prosecution if not – came from Portugal. Not surprisingly, the levels of illiteracy, high in the mother country, were also high in the colony.

Except for specific areas in the backlands, settlement developed primarily along the coast, where most of the population was concentrated until the middle of the twentieth century (Prado Junior 1945: 33). It is not clear whether any one region in Portugal contributed a preponderance of settlers to Brazil, although the north, being more densely populated than the south, would likely have provided a proportionately larger share. There were also settlers from the Azores, who from the early seventeenth century until the eighteenth century arrived in the northern regions of today's states of Pará and Maranhão, as well as in the today's southern states of Santa Catarina and Rio Grande do Sul (Silva Neto 1976:43–45).

Between 1500 and 1760 about 70,000 mostly male Portuguese settlers moved to Brazil (IBGE 2000; www.imigrantes.no.sapo.pt). Since most of them came from the rural lower classes and tended to be illiterate, their language accordingly reflected conservative usage (Silva Neto 1970:587). As the colony's population grew, fostered by intermarriage among settlers, Indians, and Africans brought in as slaves, the proportion of native speakers of EP decreased in relation to those born in Brazil. Limited EP input also meant that language changes occurring in Portugal failed to influence Brazilian speech. As dialect leveling° eliminated the more obvious differences among the settlers' dialects, the speech of their descendants was progressively pushed away from the original models.

### 7.2.2    Indian and African influence

When the early settlers arrived in Brazil there were an estimated one thousand indigenous languages with some three million speakers. The languages of a major family, Tupi-Guarani, were spoken along the coastal area stretching between today's states of Bahia and Rio de Janeiro.

Although that original Tupi population disappeared as a result of wars, enslavement, and intermarriage, their speech survived as the *Língua Geral* ("General Language"), a once widespread koine° which served as a lingua franca and was spoken in colonial times by natives and settlers alike. According to Rodrigues (2001), the tendency was for *Língua Geral* to be spoken by families where "only the husband and, after a certain age, the male children were bilingual in Portuguese." *Língua Geral* was progressively taken to the backlands by expeditions aiming at prospecting and enslaving Indians, and managed to survive into the early twentieth century. A similar linguistic situation developed in the northern area ocupied by today's states of Pará and Maranhão, where another koine developed in colonial times, *Nheengatu*, is still spoken in the Amazon region.

Besides serving the population at large, *Língua Geral* was also used by Jesuits as a medium for teaching and indoctrination. Whatever its consequences for spiritual matters, this practice fostered bilingualism in *Língua Geral* and Portuguese, which was widespread well into the seventeenth century, at which point two new factors contributed to reinforce the hegemony of Portuguese. One was a renewed influx of settlers from Portugal, headed for the newly discovered gold and diamond mines in the region of today's state of Minas Gerais. The other was the Crown's decision in 1758 to expel the Jesuits from the colony, ban *Língua Geral* as a medium of instruction, and enforce the use of Portuguese in government and education. Ultimately, the influence of Indian languages on BP became limited to the lexicon, since it was natural for colonial speakers, bilingual or not, to use Indian words related to the environment, food, and other everyday matters. Thus, except for a handful of words in general use, most

Table 7.2 *Brazilian Portuguese words from indigenous languages*

**Plants**

*abacaxi* 'pineapple,' *buriti* 'a kind of palm tree,' *caju* 'cashew,' *capim* 'grass,' *cipó* 'vine,'
   *cupim* 'anthill,' *jacarandá* 'jacaranda,' *mandioca* 'manioc,' *maracujá* 'passion fruit'

**Fauna**

*piranha* 'piranha,' *pirarucu* 'pirarucu,' *quati* 'coati,' *sucuri* 'anaconda,' *tatu* 'armadillo,'
   *capivara* 'capivara' (large rodent), *arara* 'macaw,' *jibóia* 'boa,' *tamanduá* 'ant eater,'
   *caitetu* 'wild pig,' *jacarutu* 'kind of snake,' *içá* 'female winged ant'

**Toponomy**

Towns: Aracaju, Avaí, Ubatuba, Caraguatatuba, Parati, Piracicaba, Guaratinguetá, Itu, Niterói
Town districts: Paquetá, Guanabara, Jabaquara, Jacarepaguá, Tijuca, Jaraguá, Morumbi

**Geography**

*caatinga* 'arid region in the NE of Brazil, with drought-resistant vegetation' (< Tupi *ka'a*
   'wood,'+ *tinga* 'white')
*capoeira* 'new-growth area' (Tupi *ko* 'plantation,' + *pwera* 'which was')
*capão* 'small thicket or grove' (< Tupi *ka'a* 'wood' + *puã* 'round')
*pororoca* 'wave caused by the shock of the water of the Amazon River with the ocean'
   (< Tupi *poro'roka* 'loud noise')

**Personal names**

Araci, Jaci, Iracema (f.), Ubiratã, Ubirajara, Moacir (m.), Juraci, Jair (m./f.)

**Supernatural beings**

Tupã 'thunder god, supreme being' (< Tupi *tu'pã*)
Saci 'a one-legged, pipe-smoking black boy who frightens cattle and travelers'
   (< Tupi *sa'sïe*)
Caipora 'forest-dwelling humanoid who lives in the woods and brings bad luck or death to
   those who see him' (Tupi *kaa'pora*)
Curupira 'forest-dwelling humanoid with feet turned backwards' (< Tupi *kuru'pira*)

lexical items of Indian origin are regionalisms (Houaiss 1985:65) having to do
with plants, animals, the landscape, and things related to indigenous cultures
(Table 7.2).

Another source of lexical items were the languages spoken by the approximately four million African slaves imported between 1530 and 1850
(*Almanaque Abril* 2002a:376). During the sixteenth and seventeenth centuries
slaves were primarily of Bantu origin and spoke languages such as Kikongu or
Kimbundu. Destined initially for the labor-intensive sugar cane industry and
later for mining and for coffee plantations, a number of slaves who worked in
homes acquired varying degrees of fluency in Portuguese through interaction
with members of the household. Today African influence is noticeable at the
lexical level, where several hundred words are incorporated – often, as in the
case of words of Indian origin, regionally – in everyday vocabulary, involving
various aspects of social life. Some of the more widespread terms include the
following, of Kimbundu origin:

| | |
|---|---|
| *senzala* 'slave quarters' | *caçula* 'youngest offspring' |
| (< K. *sanzala*) | (< K. *kasula*) |
| *moleque* 'young boy, street urchin' | *molambo* 'rag' (< K. *mu'lambu*) |
| (< K. *mu'leke*) | *macambúzio* 'gloomy' |
| *mucama* 'female household slave' | (< K. *kubanza*) |
| (< K. *mu'kama*) | *munguzá* 'cooked corn meal |
| *fubá* 'corn flour' (K. *fuba*) | dish' (< K. *mu'kunza*). |
| *quilombo* 'escaped slaves's | *tanga* 'loin cloth' (< K. *ntanga*) |
| settlement' (< K. *kilombu*) | |
| *berimbau* 'a one-string instrument' | *molambo* 'rag' (< K. *mulambo*) |
| (< K. *mbirim'bau*) | |

Slaves from West Africa (today's Nigeria, Benin, and Togo) arrived in the eighteenth and nineteenth centuries. They spoke Sudanese languages such as Yoruba or Ewe. Words of Yoruba origin related to African-Brazilian religions include priests' titles such as *babalaô, babalorixá*, names of specific rituals like *umbanda, macumba, mandinga*, and names of African deities or *orixás*, such as *Exu, Iemanjá, Ogum, Oxum, Xangô*. In regions such as the state of Bahia, where the population contains a high percentage of African-Brazilians, religious practices include liturgical vocabularies and prayers from African languages.

The extent to which African languages influenced other aspects of Portuguese in Brazil, such as phonology or morphosyntax, remains open to debate (Megenney 2001, 2002; Castro 1980, 1983, 1997), as does the topic of the supposed creole origins of Vernacular Brazilian Portuguese, which will be taken up in 7.2.4.

### 7.2.3    Independence and beyond

The arrival of the Portuguese Royal Court in Rio in 1808 (1.6) had a powerful impact on Brazilian culture. Between 1808 and 1820 the Crown created schools which included a Naval Academy (1808), a Military Academy (1812), schools of Medicine and Engineering, a Royal School of Science, Art, and Trades which later became the Academy of the Arts, and a variety of trade schools for utilitarian purposes. A fledgling press began, also in 1808, with the *Correio Braziliense*, printed in London, soon followed by the *Gazeta do Rio de Janeiro*, the first paper printed in Brazil, well over two centuries after printing had been introduced in Peru.

The sudden arrival of some ten thousand native speakers of European Portuguese also provided a powerful linguistic input that supposedly lies at the origin of the articulation of post-vocalic /s/ as a palatal fricative [ʃ], typical of Carioca° pronunciation, but also found in areas in the northeastern region, such as the states of Alagoas and Pernambuco (Leite and Callou 2002:32). The presence of those new speakers, however, was not enough to reinstate EP as the model for Brazilian speech, which at that point had probably drifted irreversibly away from its European source.

The earliest reference to specific features of Brazilian Portuguese appears in a text written in French in 1824–1825, and thus soon after independence in 1822, by Domingos Borges de Barros, Viscount of Pedra Branca. It lists words with different meanings in Brazil and Portugal, and words used in Brazil and unknown in Portugal (Pinto 1978:9–11). Throughout the nineteenth century an awareness of differences between European and Brazilian usage grew among intellectuals, fiction writers, and journalists. Their views, documented by Pinto (1978), show concern with lexical matters, particularly regarding neologisms originating from popular creation or coined by writers of fiction. Another theme of debate was gallicisms, that is French loan words and loan constructions that entered the language on both sides of the Atlantic, condemned by purists and defended by those who considered them a legitimate means of linguistic and cultural renovation (Silva Neto 1976:212–218). Even authors who strongly defended what they saw as typically Brazilian modes of expression, however, tended to stop short of accepting the vernacular syntax. Then as today, popular speech not only diverged substantially from educated usage but also provided a number of shibboleths that have traditionally served to separate the two varieties and identify who should or should not be considered educated.

Although nationalistic fervor theoretically encouraged avoidance of EP norms that contradicted Brazilian usage, most literate speakers were not prepared to relinquish the Portuguese tradition in the written language. Throughout the nineteenth century, the grammar manuals used in Brazil came from Portugal and naturally took Portuguese literary works as reference. Significantly, this practice was followed by Brazilian grammarians: it was only a century after independence that a manual (Silveira 1923) included examples drawn from Brazilian literary works. Even so, in the second half of the twentieth century, Brazilian grammars (such as Brandão 1963 or Almeida 1967) remained strongly conservative, and even a few more progressive manuals (such as Cunha and Cintra 1985 or Bechara 1999) have retained a cautiously prescriptive stance based on literary models. Only very recently have a few usage-based grammars and dictionaries (such as Neves 1999, 2003; Borba 2002; Perini 1998, 2002a; Houaiss 2001) offered more accurate guidance to users of BP.

Some scholars have interpreted adherence to Portuguese linguistic tradition as resulting from the nineteenth-century Brazilian "elite's wish to live in a White and European country," which "made it react systematically against anything that distinguished [Brazilians] from a certain Lusitanian linguistic standard" (Faraco 2002:43). There were, however, powerful social reasons for this: then as today, the vernacular was the language of the poor and the disenfranchised, and speaking correctly, however defined, was, and continues to be, a mark of social distinction. It is difficult to imagine how things could have been otherwise, given the unrivalled prestige of European cultural models and the stratification of Brazilian society at the time. Nevertheless, despite adherence to Portuguese models, the interest shown by nineteenth-century romantic authors in popular language and traditions helped pave the way for two important trends. One was the work of the regionalist authors of the late nineteenth and early twentieth centuries, who collected and used a variety of forms typical of rural language. The other was the work of modernist authors beginning in the 1920s, whose representation of both rural dialects and urban sociolects° helped rekindle the question of what was distinctive about Brazilian Portuguese (Lessa 1976; Barbadinho Neto 1972, 1977).

## 7.3    Main features of Brazilian Portuguese

As already mentioned, although VBP is primarily the language of the uneducated, vernacular features occur, in varying proportions, in the unmonitored speech of educated speakers. Linguistically speaking, there is nothing wrong with those features per se, though there may be something awry about a social situation in which people are discriminated against because of the way they talk. Nonetheless, learners should be aware that using vernacular features in formal contexts that call for standard forms may affect their success in communicating. In informal contacts, failure to use vernacular features may put an undesirable distance between them and their interlocutors. Learning to pick the right form, vernacular or standard, constitutes the process of learning to "talk Brazilian," which unfortunately cannot be learned from a book. All we can do is present the main features of the vernacular and attempt to compare them with their standard counterparts.

### 7.3.1    Phonology

Brazilian Portuguese pronunciation was commented on in Chapter 2. This section will focus on those features considered typical of unmonitored speech, focusing on those that may be considered non-standard.

7.3.1.1 *Vowels*    General features include phonological processes that involve turning a vowel into a diphthong or, conversely, reducing a diphthong to a simple vowel.

Diphthongization° of a vowel by inserting the glide [j] before syllable-final /s/ is widespread. It may be light or strong, depending on whether the glide is articulated softly or in full, and it is particularly common in monosyllables such as *mas* [majs] 'but' (which thus sounds exactly like *mais* 'plus'), *luz* [lujs] 'light,' *pôs* [pojs] 'P3sg puts,' *três* [trejs] 'three.' The latter item accounts for the use of *meia* (*dúzia*) 'half (a dozen)' to clearly distinguish between *três* [trejs] and *seis* [sejs] 'six' as when reading out figures, so that a number like 666, for example, would be spoken as *seis-seis-seis* in Portugal and *meia-meia-meia* in Brazil. Monitored pronunciation, however, particularly in formal contexts, tends to avoid this diphthongization, particularly in nouns or adjectives such as *inglês* 'English,' *francês* 'French,' *português* 'Portuguese,' *arroz* 'rice,' and so on.

In unmonitored speech the orthographic diphthong *ei* tends to lose the glide and be pronounced [e] before /r/, /ʒ/ or /ʃ/, although in monitored speech the full diphthong [ej] may be restored:

| | | | |
|---|---|---|---|
| *primeiro* | [pri'meru] | ~ | [pri'mejru] 'first' |
| *dinheiro* | [di'ɲeru] | ~ | [di'ɲejru] 'money' |
| *feixe* | ['feʃi] | ~ | ['fejʃi] 'bundle' |
| *seixo* | ['seʃu] | ~ | ['sejʃu] 'pebble' |
| *queijo* | ['keʒu] | ~ | ['kejʒu] 'cheese' |
| *beijo* | ['beʒu] | ~ | ['bejʒu] 'kiss' |

Likewise, in unmonitored speech the orthographic diphthong *ou* tends to lose the glide and be pronounced [o], although as in the preceding case the full diphthong [ow] may be restored in formal pronunciation:

| | | | |
|---|---|---|---|
| *couro* | ['koru] (rhyming with *coro* 'choir') | ~ | ['kowru] 'leather ' |
| *ouro* | ['oru] (rhyming with *soro* 'serum') | ~ | ['owru] 'gold' |
| *outro* | ['otru] | ~ | ['owtru] 'other' |
| *loura* | ['lorɐ] | ~ | ['lowrɐ] 'blonde' |

*7.3.1.2 Consonants    Occlusives.* Voiced /b d g/ are always occlusive [b d g] in every position, never fricative [β ð ɣ] intervocalically as in some varieties of EP. Articulation of /t/ and /d/ before [i] (spelled *i* or *e*) varies from a stop [t], [d], which is the traditional pronunciation, to moderate affrication [tˢ dᶻ] or full affrication [tʃ dʒ], as in *tio* ['tiu] ~ ['tˢiu] ~ ['tʃiu] ~ [tʃiw] 'uncle,' *dia* ['diɐ] ~ ['dᶻiɐ] ~ ['dʒiɐ] 'day.' Devoicing° and loss of unstressed [i] in final position results in words with a final affricate, as in *este* [estʃi] > [estʃ] 'this' or *leite* ['lejtsi] > [lejts] 'milk.'

Lenition and loss of /d/ in gerunds is habitual in vernacular VBP (Lipski 1975:64) but occurs also in unmonitored educated speech (*falando* [fa'lɐnu], *comendo* [ku'menu], *pedindo* [pi'dʒinu]), although /d/ tends to be restored in monitored pronunciation ([fa'lẽdu]).

*Fricatives.* Articulation of syllable-final /s/ varies between an alveolar [s] and a palatal [ʃ], which are respectively voiced as [z] or [ʒ] before a voiced sound: *os dois, as amigas.* Post-vocalic /s/ (*este, dois*) occurs as either [s] or [ʃ] in all five capitals analyzed in the NURC project (7.1.1), but whereas in

Salvador the proportion is about 50% for each variety, [s] clearly predominates in São Paulo and Porto Alegre, whereas in Recife and Rio de Janeiro the rates for [ʃ] are about 70% and 90% respectively (Leite and Callou 2002: 45–46).

*Liquids.* Articulation of syllable-final /l/ as velar [ɫ] can be heard in recordings of popular songs from the 1930s and 1940s (Alves, n/d). It used to be the norm and is still common in some regions, such as Porto Alegre in the state of Rio Grande do Sul (Leite and Callou 2002:48). Elsewhere it is recessive (as in the city of São Paulo, where it occurs in the pronunciation of older speakers). Despite some grammarians' insistence on the desirability of preserving [ɫ] (Bechara 1999:78), in most of the country [ɫ] has largely been replaced by [w], as in *alto* ['awtu] 'tall' or *mal* [maw] 'evil,' respectively pronounced like *auto* 'car,' *mau* 'bad.' The glide [w] is kept even when a vowel follows, as in *sal e limão* 'salt and lemon' [sawili'mẽw], but in compounds in which /l/ comes before a vowel the pronunciation may be either [w] or [l], sometimes in the same individual's speech: *mal-educado* [mawidu'kadu] ∼ [malidu'kadu] 'boorish,' *mal-humorado* [mawumo'ɾadu] ∼ [malumo'ɾadu] 'ill-tempered.'

The contrast between the vibrants /ʀ/ and /ɾ/ is only functional intervocalically (*carro* 'car' – *caro* 'car'); initially or after /n/ or /s/, only /ʀ/ occurs (*rato* 'rat,' *honra* 'honor,' Israel). In other positions, that contrast is neutralized and the phonetic rendering varies from the alveolar tap [ɾ] or trill [r] to a velar fricative [x], a uvular vibrant [ʀ], a velar aspiration [h] or a retroflexed [ɹ] (see below). The phoneme /r/ in post-vocalic position (*arma, porta*) appears as a simple vibrant apical [ɾ] primarily in São Paulo and Porto Alegre, whereas in Rio de Janeiro, Salvador, and Recife it occurs mostly as the velar fricative [h] (Leite and Callou 2002:43–44).

Except in closely monitored deliberate speech, loss of final /r/ is universal in infinitives (*falar* [fa'la] 'to talk,' *comer* [ku'me] 'to eat,' *sair* [sa'i] 'to leave'). Loss of final /r/ in words of other classes is considered socially less acceptable (*senhor* [si'ɲo] 'mister,' *cantor* [kẽ'to] 'singer,' *ator* [a'to] 'actor.' If a vowel follows, [ɾ] may be articulated or not (*falar alto* [fa'la'ɾawtu] ∼ [fa'la'awtu]).

Retroflex [ɹ], known as *r Paulista*° 'São Paulo r' or *r Caipira*° 'rural r' (approximate glosses), is heard in the interior of the state of São Paulo and part of the state of Minas Gerais (Head 1973; Rodrigues 1974). The urbanization process of the second half of the twentieth century has brought to the city thousands of people who regularly use this [ɹ], and their growing presence at university and in the professions may have contributed to its increased acceptance. In regions where it is native – such as the environs of the city of Piracicaba in the state of São Paulo – it occurs in the speech of most people, regardless of their level of formal education. The actual distribution of [ɹ], however, varies somewhat regionally. For example, according to Ferreira Netto (2001:99–100), in western São Paulo one hears [ɹ] after vowels (*porta* ['pɔɹtɐ] 'door') and in consonant clusters (*prato* ['pɹatu] 'dish'), whereas in other areas, such as northeastern São Paulo, [ɹ] occurs after vowels (*porta* ['pɔɹtɐ] 'door') but not in consonant clusters (*prato* ['pɾatu] 'dish').

Far less accepted socially, however, are certain phonological processes that yield vernacular pronunciations traditionally associated with low educational levels. One is rhotacism, that is the replacement of /l/ by /r/, phonetically [ɹ]. It may happen in syllable-final position, as in *calma* ['kaɹmɐ] 'calm,' *alma* ['aɹmɐ] 'soul,' *soldado* [soɹ'dadu] 'soldier,' *alguma* [aɹ'gumɐ] 'some,' *calça* ['kaɹsɐ] 'pants,' *papel* [pa'pɛɹ] 'paper,' *mal* [maɹ] 'evil.' Rhotacism is also responsible for the replacement of /l/ by the vibrant /r/, phonetically [r] or even [ɹ] in clusters:

| | | | | |
|---|---|---|---|---|
| *planta* | ['prẽtɐ] | ~ | ['pɹẽtɐ] 'plant' |
| *Cláudia* | ['krawʤɐ] | ~ | ['kɹawʤja] |
| *Clóvis* | ['krɔvis] | ~ | ['kɹɔvis] |
| *reclame* | [he'krɐmi] | ~ | [re'kɹɐmi] 'ad' |

Also frowned upon is the loss of /l/ in word-final position, as in *avental* [av ẽ 'ta] 'apron,' *papel* [pa'pɛ] 'paper,' or in clusters, as in *caboclo* [ka'boku] 'country dweller,' *arreglo* [a'hegu] 'arrangement.'

Likewise regarded as an indicator of lack of education is the substitution of the glide /j/ for the lateral palatal /ʎ/ as in *malha* ['maja] 'sweater,' *olho* ['oju] 'eye,' *galho* ['gaju] 'branch.'

A common phonotactic° process involving consonant sequences other than clusters of stop + liquid or /f/ + liquid consists in separating those two consonants by inserting /i/, as in *psiquiatra* [pisikiatrɐ]. Some words have alternative pronunciations with [i] or [e], such as *advogado* [adevo'gadu] ~ [adʒivo'gadu] 'lawyer' or *pneu* [pi'new] ~ [pe'new] 'tire' (Câmara 1972:48). Though widespread, this extra /i/ may lead to pronunciations that at least some educated speakers would frown upon. Thus *opção* 'option' may be [op'sɐ̃ω] in monitored pronunciation and [opi'sɐ̃w̃] in casual speech. In certain formal contexts, one's communicative effectiveness or social acceptability would be jeopardized by pronouncing the first person singular of the verb *optar* 'to opt,' *opto* 'I opt,' as [o'pitu] (rhyming with *apito* 'I blow a whistle,' from *apitar*) instead of ['ɔptu].

## 7.3.2    Morphology and syntax

Morphological and syntactic aspects of vernacular BP contrast not only with European Portuguese but also with Brazilian standard usage. However, half a century ago, Bueno (1955) showed that a number of features condemned by prescriptive grammarians as popular Brazilianisms already existed in sixteenth-century European Portuguese, and he suggested that those features may simply have been preserved in Brazil, where they were excluded from formal usage and relegated to the vernacular. It should be kept in mind that morphological and syntactic vernacular features tend to be relatively rare in public writing, since newspapers and magazines have their own style manuals, editors, and correctors, and consequently reflect educated usage more closely. Even so, a substantial difference can be noticed between the language of editorials, usually more conservative, and that of feature articles, some of whose writers favor a style closer to the spoken language.

*7.3.2.1 Non-agreement in the noun phrase*    Standard nominal agreement (4.1.1) requires pluralization of adjectives and determiners accompanying a plural noun. In the vernacular, however, pluralization is more erratic; in the extreme case, the plural marker is moved to the leftmost determiner and the noun and other accompanying formants remain in the singular, as in 1a–1d.

(1)    a. *As mulher* (st. *as mulheres*).
          'The women.'
       b. *As primeira chuva* (st. *as primeiras chuvas*).
          'The first rains.'
       c. *Aquelas coisa* (st. *aquelas coisas*).
          'Those things.'
       d. *Esses quatro caixote* (st. *esses quatro caixotes*).
          'Those four crates.'

Although lack of agreement is strongly condemned by prescriptive grammars, examples from educated speakers (2a–2c) show that application of the pluralization rule tends to vary according to the level of formality (Campos and Rodrigues 1999:129), as seen in these examples from an informal conversation:

(2)    a. *Logo mais a gente vai comer umas pizza e tomar umas cerveja*
          *por aí.* (st. *umas pizzas, umas cervejas*)
          'Later on we'll go and eat some pizzas and drink some beers
          somewhere.'
       b. *Prova uns docinho . . .* (st. *uns docinhos*)
          'Try a few sweets . . .'
       c. *Aquelas revista que eu te emprestei, você já leu?* (st. *aquelas*
          *revistas*)
          'Those magazines I lent you, have you read them?'

*7.3.2.2 Non-agreement in the verb phrase*    Standard verbal agreement (4.1.1) requires a conjugated verb to match its subject in person and number. Non-agreement in VBP is related to the reduction of verb paradigms to three, two, or even a single form, as shown in Table 7.3. This process is responsible for constructions like 3a–3c:

(3)     a. VBP *Vocês vai lá e fala com ele* (st. *vocês vão lá/falam*).
           'You go there and talk to him.'
        b. VBP *As casa (es)tava suja demais da conta* (st. *As casas estavam sujas*).
           'The houses were way too dirty.'
        c. VBP *Quando é que eles chegou?* (st. *Quando é que eles chegaram?*)
           'When did they arrive?'

Some vernacular varieties extend the first person plural ending *-emo(s)* of *-er/-ir* verbs to verbs in *-ar*, as in 4a–4b:

(4)     a. VBP *Nós falemo ontem* (st. *nós falamos*).
           'We talked [to them] yesterday.'
        b. VBP *Nós cheguemo aqui tudo dia de madrugada* (st. *nós chegamos*).
           'We arrive here every day at dawn.'

Although cooccurrence of verbal non-agreement and nominal non-agreement is strongly condemned by prescriptive grammars, it occurs in the colloquial speech of educated informants, as in 5a–5c:

(5)     a. VBP *Eles era grosso, não tinha condições* (st. *Eles eram grossos, não tinham condições*).
           'They were rude, they were unprepared' [an engineering student].
        b. VBP *Nessas hora – te deixava os amigo – te deixava os conhecido – te deixava até os parente* (st. *Nessas horas te deixavam os amigos, te deixavam os conhecidos, te deixavam até os parentes*).
           'At those times you got dumped by friends, by acquaintances, even by relatives.'
        c. VBP *Quando é que chega as visitas?* (st. *chegam*)
           'When will the guests arrive?'

In such constructions, variability in verbal agreement in casual speech seems to be encouraged by the low phonological contrast between forms such as P3sg *fala* vs. P3pl *falam*. Postponement of the subject also seems to play a role, even if the phonological contrast is more salient, as in 6a–6b:

(6)    a. VBP *Ontem só veio o Paulo e a Délia* (st. *só vieram*).
       'Only Paulo and Délia came yesterday.'
       b. VBP *Os organizadores vai ser o Professor X e eu* (st. *vamos ser*).
       'The organizers will be Professor X and I.'

Another point of variation in subject–verb agreement involves subjects represented by a singular collective noun, e.g. *pessoal* 'people,' *turma* 'gang (of friends, or workers),' or partitive expressions such as *uma porção de* 'a number of,' *uma parte de* 'a part of.' In a sentence like 7a, prescriptive grammars insist on agreement with the singular noun *uma porção* 'a number of,' which is the nucleus of the subject noun phrase. Such constructions, however, often occur in educated speech with the verb in the plural, in agreement with the collective notion expressed here by *alunas* 'students (f.)' (Bueno 1955:216):

(7)    a. *[Ele] disse que uma porção de alunas estavam te procurando*
          *porque queriam falar com você.*
          '[He] said that a number of students were looking for you because
          [they] wanted to talk to you.'
       b. *Olha, tem um pessoal aí que disseram que isso não pode ser.*
          'Look, there are some people here who said this can't be done.'
       c. *A turma quer começar mais tarde, falaram que dez horas é muito*
          *cedo.*
          'The guys want to start later, [they] said ten o'clock is too early.'

*7.3.2.3 Pronouns*    Table 3.5 shows all pronoun forms that function as subject or object. It includes the lexicalized forms of direct address *você*, *o/a senhor/a* and *a gente*, which take a third person verb form (*falava, falavam*). We will first consider the personal pronoun system in BP, then the patterns of occurrence or non-occurrence of subject and object pronouns, and finally the placement of object pronouns in relation to the verb. Since possessives also refer to the persons of speech, they are included in the following discussion.

Noticing that the frequency of overt subjects in BP has increased since the second half of the nineteenth century, linguists have linked this phenomenon to an increase in the occurrence of null object clitics° (Tarallo 1983; Galves 1993; Morais 2003). The dialog in (8a) illustrates the contrast between the BP tendency to use null objects and the EP preference for null (or covert) subjects whose referent is understood from the verb morphology or the communicative context. (Raposo 1986). Use of a subject pronoun in BP is more than a matter of clarity; in direct address, a question like 8b, without the subject pronoun, may be perceived as more intimate than 8c, which is more deferential. Consequently, omission of *o senhor* in such cases might sound disrespectful.

(8)   a. *– Você me chamou?* (cf. EP *Chamou-me?*)
      *– Eu chamei porque eu precisava falar com você.*
      (cf. EP *Chamei-o porque precisava falar consigo.*)
      'Did you call me?'
      'I called because I needed to talk to you.'
      b. *Como vai?*
      'How are you?'
      c. *Como vai o senhor?*
      'How are you, sir?'

There seems to be a link between use of overt subjects in BP and the morphological reduction of verb paradigms to forms whose ending does not readily identify the subject. Whereas in a sentence like 9a the subject is clearly *tu*, in 9b the subject of *falou* can be either the listener (*você/o senhor/a senhora*) or a third party (*ele/ela*). BP precludes such ambiguity by using overt subjects as in 9c.

(9)   a. *Falaste com o chefe?*
      'Did you talk to the boss?'
      b. *Eu quero saber se falou com o chefe.*
      'I want to know if you/he/she talked to the boss.'
      c. *Eu quero saber se você falou com o chefe.*
      'I want to know if you talked to the boss.'

Overt subjects are favored in BP even when the verb form redundantly indicates the subject, as in the dialogue fragment in 10, where in six out of seven cases a subject pronoun (*eu*) is used:

(10)  *Eu fiquei pensando assim em ganhar dinheiro . . . então eu achei que
      Letras . . . eu podia lecionar . . . quer dizer – eu podia sair . . . então
      eu falei – ah – então eu vou escolher Letras mesmo. E escolhi por
      causa disso.* (Recorded interview)

      'I thought about making money . . . then I thought about (the course
      of) Letters . . . I could teach . . . that is – I could go out . . . then I – said
      ah – then I'm going to choose Letters. And that's why I chose [it].'

The pronouns *eu* and *nós* occur in vernacular usage in direct object function (11a–11b). In addition, *eu* occurs as the object of a preposition (12a) and *nós* as the object of the preposition *com* 'with' (12b), the standard forms with *com* being *comigo* 'with me' and *conosco* (EP *connosco*) 'with us.' As 13a–13b show, *eu* also occurs as the object of other prepositions in the vernacular (Galves and Abaurre 1996:288).

(11)    a. *O tenente falou que viu eu fumando maconha* (st. *me viu*).
'The lieutenant said he saw me smoking pot.'
b. *Será que ele não viu nós?* (st. *Será que ele não nos viu?*)
'Maybe he did not see us?'

(12)    a. *Ela não quer brincar com eu* (st. *comigo*).
'She does not want to play with me.'
b. *Ela não fala mais com nós* (st. *conosco*).
'She doesn't talk to us anymore.'

(13)    a. *Isso aí é pra ele ou pra eu?* (st. *para ele ou para mim*).
'Is that for me or for him?'
b. *. . . (es) tava contra eu* (st. *contra mim*).
'[he] was against me.'

Use of *a gente* for *nós* or *eu* is can be a device of self-effacement (for modesty, self-protection, and the like). The general trend, however, is simply for *a gente* to function as replacement for *nós* (Ilari *et al.* 1996:97) in referring to the speaker, either alone (14a) or with someone else (14b), or as a vague reference to an indeterminate actor (14c). *A gente* appears with this function in sixteenth-century documents, although the process was not completed until the nineteenth century according to Lopes (2002:44). Data from Rio de Janeiro speech show an incidence of 59% for *a gente* against 47% for *nós*. More conservative usage is reflected in data from Porto Alegre, in the state of Rio Grande do Sul, with 72% for *nós* and 28% for *a gente* (Leite and Callou 2002:54). If *a gente* has a plural referent it may appear in the vernacular with a plural verb as in 15. This construction, which also occurs in popular EP, can be found in sixteenth-century writings (Bueno 1955:214), but is considered non-standard nowadays.

(14)    a. *Se o senhor mandar, a gente faz.*
'If you give the order I'll do it.'
b. *A Martinha e eu queríamos convidar você para vir jantar com a gente amanhã.*
'Martinha and I would like to invite you to have dinner with us tomorrow.'
c. *Agora, se a gente tenta aprender da noite para o dia, não dá.*
'Now if one tries to learn [it] overnight, it isn't possible.'

(15)    a. *Amanhã a gente não podemo vim* (st. *a gente não pode*).
'Tomorrow we cannot come.'
b. *A que hora a gente chegamos?* (st. *a gente chega*).
'At what time will we arrive?'
c. *Se o sior* (st. *senhor*) *quer, a gente trazemo ele* (st. *a gente traz*).
'If you want we'll bring it.'

Use of *você, o senhor/a senhora, a gente* in object function, as in (16), is universal:

(16)    a. *Eu vi você no teatro ontem.*
        'I saw you [sg.] at the theater yesterday.'
    b. *Pode deixar que eu acordo o senhor às oito.*
        'Don't worry, I'll wake you up at eight.'
    c. *Deixa a gente ir lá trás?*
        '[You'll] let us ride in the back?'

Although the second person pronoun *você* has largely replaced *tu* in BP, the corresponding third person pronouns (*o/a, lhe*) and possessives (*seu/sua*) have not fully replaced *te, teu*. Instead, *você* cooccurs with *te, teu* in colloquial usage, generating constructions like 17a, condemned by traditional grammars as "mixture of pronouns." Available evidence, however, suggests that a re-arrangement of the pronoun system has created a new norm in BP (Galves and Abaurre 1996:288).

(17)    a. *Você não quer me emprestar o teu guarda-chuva? Amanhã eu*
        *te devolvo.*
        'Won't you lend me your umbrella? I'll return [it] to you
        tomorrow.'
    b. *Você tem um minutinho? Eu precisava te dizer uma coisa.*
        'Have you got a moment? I needed to tell you something.'

The prepositional pronoun *ti* (as in *para ti* 'for you,' *de ti* 'from you'), used in regions where *tu* occurs, has been replaced elsewhere by *você*, as in 18a. (Note that use of *preposition + si* (where *si* = 'you'), habitual in EP as in 18b, is unusual in BP.) Although the lexicalized form *contigo* 'with you' can be heard (18c), it is infrequent. Furthermore, *consigo* is widely used in EP with the meaning 'with you' as in 18d, where it functions as a neutral option between less formal *com você* and formal *com o senhor* (18d). Though less common than in EP, this usage occurs, with a connotation of courtesy, in BP (18e); if reflexivity is intended, however, it tends to be signaled by *mesmo/mesma* 'self' as in 18f:

(18)    a. BP *Esse sanduiche é para você.*
        'This sandwich is for you.'
    b. EP *Desculpe, creio que isto é para si.*
        'Excuse me, I think this is for you.'
    c. BP *Então, até depois. Olha aí, contamos contigo, hem!*
        'So long then. Look, we are counting on you, eh!'
    d. EP *Estava preocupada consigo.*
        'I was worried about you.'

e. BP *Ah, então eu quero ir consigo!*
   'Oh, then I want to come along with you!'
f. BP *Ele andava falando consigo mesmo.*
   'He used to talk to himself.'

As mentioned in 5.3.3, the third person subject pronouns *ele/ela* originated from anaphoric demonstratives whose referent was neither the speaker nor the addressee. According to Bueno (1955:210–212), use of *ele/ela* as a direct object has been in the language for centuries. Though condemned by prescriptive grammars, this conspicuous vernacular feature is frequent in unmonitored educated speech, as in 19a–19b.

(19)    a. VBP *Você já chamou eles?* (st. *já os chamou*).
           'Have you already called them?'
        b. VBP *Passa ela para cá* (st. *passe-a*).
           'Hand it over.'

Further, *ele/ela*, as well as *eu* and *nós*, tend to occur in structures like 20a–20b where the pronoun functions both as the direct object of a preceding verb and as the subject of an infinitive.

(20)    a. VBP *O professor deixou ele sair mais cedo.* (st. *deixou-o sair*).
           'The professor let him leave early.'
        b. VBP *Por que você não deixa eu cuidar disso?* (st. *não me deixa cuidar*).
           'Why don't you let me take care of that?'
        c. VBP *O Seu João quer fazer nós trabalhar no domingo mas nós não quer não* (st. *quer fazer-nos trabalhar*; st. *nós não queremos*).
           'Mr. João wants to make us work on Sunday but we don't want to.'

Bagno (2000) has linked this use of stressed pronouns as objects with the tendency of Brazilian Portuguese to use overt subjects. He analyzed a corpus of speech transcriptions culled from newspaper texts and determined that in 85.7% of the occurrences of command forms *deixa* or *deixe* ('let'), the following object pronoun was one of the pronouns *eu/ele/ela(s)*, whereas in written texts the proportions were reversed, that is, the non-standard object *eu/ele/ela(s)* were 2.3 times less frequent than the standard forms (Bagno 2000:212–218).

As we saw in Chapter 4, there is a strong preference in BP for placing clitics to occur in proclitic° position, that is before the verb, as in 21a. This placement contrasts with EP, where the default position is enclitic°, or after the verb, as in 21b, which would be considered more formal in BP.

(21)   a. BP *O Paulo me viu.*
       'Paulo saw me.'
       b. EP *O Paulo viu-me.*
       'Paulo saw me.'

Probably because prescriptive grammars insist that unstressed pronouns should not occur in sentence-initial position, enclisis is slightly more common in that position in monitored speech (Schei 2003:58). Even so, unmonitored BP favors proclitic placement even in sentence-initial position, in statements (22a) or requests (22b). Actually, this construction is found with some frequency even in the popular press (22c).

(22)   a. BP *Me parece que ele não vai chegar* (cf. EP/ formal BP
       *Parece-me que ele não vai chegar*).
       'It seems to me he will not arrive.'
       b. BP *Me dá um café e um copo dágua aí, chefe?*
       'Give me a cup of coffee and a glass of water, buddy?'
       c. BP *Se dá mal ao tentar fugir.*
       '[Inmate] was unlucky in trying to escape.' (Newspaper
       headline – *A Gazeta* – Acre, October 26, 2002)

As in EP, proclitic placement is usual in BP when the verb is preceded by a relative pronoun (23a) or negative or limiting words like *não* 'no,' *nunca* 'never,' *ninguém* 'nobody's,' *só* 'only,' and others (23 b–23 d) (Perini 2002a:389; Raposo 1995:459).

(23)   a. ... *a garota que me chamou.*
       '... the girl that called me.'
       b. *Ninguém me entregou chave nenhuma.*
       'Nobody gave me any key.'
       c. *Eu nunca te disse?*
       'Didn't I ever tell you?'
       d. *Só me dói assim.*
       'It only hurts me in this way.'

With two-verb constructions like perfect tenses (*ter* + *participle*) or continuous tenses (*estar* + *gerund*), BP favors a proclitic pronoun phonetically linked to the second verb like an initial unstressed syllable, as in 24. Thus in the following four-line stanza, each line scans in four beats, as shown by dashes:

| | |
|---|---|
| *Vo-cê-ti-nha* | 'you had |
| *me-cha-ma-do* | called me |
| *de-ban-di-do,* | a criminal, |
| *de-ta-ra-do.* | a pervert.' |

This placement contrasts with EP, where the clitic *me* would become a final unstressed syllable attached to the auxiliary (hyphenated in spelling): *tinha-me chamado* 'P3sg had called me.' Proclisis to the auxiliary (25) is also a possibility in BP, albeit a less usual one.

(24)    a. BP *Ele tinha me chamado* (cf. EP *Ele tinha-me chamado*).
        'He had called me.'
        b. BP *Ele estava me chamando* (cf. EP *Ele estava-me a chamar*).
        'He was calling me.'

(25)    a. BP *Ele me tinha chamado*.
        'He had called me.'
        b. BP *Ele me estava chamando*.
        'He was calling me.'

Likewise in combinations made up of a modal and an infinitive (*queria visitar* 'wanted to visit'), the default solution in BP is a pronoun proclitic to the infinitive (26a). Proclisis to the modal (26b) is also possible, although a little less usual, whereas enclisis to the infinitive (26c) or to the modal (26d) are formal variants.

(26)    a. *Ele queria me visitar.*
        'He wanted to visit me.'
        b. *Ele me queria visitar.*
        'He wanted to visit me.'
        c. *Ele queria visitar-me.*
        'He wanted to visit me.'
        d. *Ele queria-me visitar.*
        'He wanted to visit me.'

Given the tendency in BP to use subject pronouns as direct objects, the range of occurrence of clitics in unmonitored speech is more limited than in formal speech or in writing. The clitics *o/a(s)* do occur in educated speech, nonetheless, particularly if linked to an infinitive in subordinated clauses, as in *não seria conveniente mudá-lo* 'it wouldn't be practical to change it' (Galves and Abaurre 1996:289).

Use of clitics is further limited by a tendency to omit anaphoric° object pronouns whose referent is either explicit in the discourse or can be understood from the context (Raposo 1986; Schwenter and Silva 2002). Clitic omission is exemplified in 27a–27e, where the subscript $_i$ stands for an omitted anaphoric clitic in a reply to a question where its referent is explicit:

(27)    a. – *Você encontra muito contraste entre os alunos?*
        – *Bom, toda classe tem $_i$, não é? Toda classe tem$_i$ muito.*

'Do you find many contrasts among the students?'
'Well, every class has [them], doesn't it?'
b. – *Você sabe se já trouxeram as caixas?*
– *Entregaram $_i$ hoje de manhã e o zelador pôs$_i$ no apartamento.*
'Do you know if they've brought the boxes?'
'They delivered [them] this morning and the janitor put [them] in the apartment.'
c. – *Você não trouxe passaporte?*
– *Aí é que está, eu trouxe$_i$ mas como não precisei mostrar$_i$ deixei$_i$ no hotel.*
'Haven't you brought [your] passport?'
'That's the point, I did, but since I didn't have to show [it], I left [it] at the hotel.'
d. – *Você não me viu na platéia?*
– *Vi$_i$, mas como você estava acompanhado, não quis incomodar$_i$ i.*
'You didn't see me in the audience?'
'I did, but since you had company, I didn't wish to disturb you.'
e. – *Aí eu falei para ela, se você quiser, compra$_i$ e dá$_i$ de presente para ele.*
'Then I said to her, if you wish, buy [it] and give [it] to him as a gift.'

Such verbs are understood as having a covert or null object which is retrieved by the listener. In 28a–28b, however, the omitted clitic$_i$ has no overt antecedent and is interpreted contextually as referring to something that has either been mentioned in an earlier utterance or is evident from the context (e.g. *compre-a* 'buy it,' *faça-o / faça isso* 'do it/do that').

(28)    a. *Se você acha que vale a pena ir lá, faça$_i$.*
        'If you think going there is worth your while, do [it].'
        b. *Olha, você quer saber duma coisa? Eu vou comprar$_i$, e o cartão que se dane.*
        'You know what? I'm going to buy [it], and damn the credit card.'

An indirect object may be signaled either by a clitic as in 29a or, more commonly, introduced by the preposition *para* (or *a*) followed by a prepositional pronoun (29b). This feature creates contrast with the preference shown by EP for clitic indirect objects, as in BP *Vou perguntar para ela* vs. EP *Vou-lhe perguntar* 'I'm going to ask her.' Only the strong pronouns *mim* and *ti* are exclusively prepositional; as mentioned earlier, *ti* is usually limited to regions where *tu* is used. The clitics *lhe* and *nos* are uncommon in indirect object function in casual speech (Galves and Abaurre 1996:288), which favors the preposition *para* followed by a stressed pronoun, as in 29c–29e.

(29)    a. *Ele não te ofereceu um lugar?*
        'He didn't offer you a seat?'
        b. *A Rose entregou o cedê para mim.*
        'Rose gave me the CD.'
        c. *Depois papai dá procê* (< *para você*).
        'Daddy will give it to you later.'
        d. *Quando o Dr. Gláucio chegar você entrega esse envelope para ele.*
        'When Dr. Gláucio arrives you'll give him this envelope.'
        e. *Você não quer comprar isso para a gente?*
        'Won't you buy this for us?'

One consequence of preference for the indirect object expressed as *para* + *NP* is that the third person pronoun *lhe* is relatively rare in casual speech. When it does occur (as in 30a), it refers invariably to the hearer, not to a third party. Although this is condemned by prescriptive grammars, *lhe* also occurs as a direct object, as in 30b–30d, even in the speech (and sometimes in the writings) of educated speakers (Thomas 1969:100).

(30)    a. *Eu tenho um presente para lhe dar.*
        'I have a gift to give you.'
        b. *Depois eu quero lhe ouvir* (st. *eu quero ouvi-lo / ouvir você*).
        'I want to hear you later.'
        c. *A gente queria lhe convidar para a festa, doutor* (st. *queria convidá-lo/convidar o senhor*).
        'We wanted to invite you to the party, doctor.'
        d. *Eu lhe contatei para falar de um assunto muito importante* (st. *Eu o contatei/contatei você*).
        'I contacted you to talk about a very important subject.'

Indirect object clitics may be also be omitted, though less commonly than direct object clitics (Cyrino 1999:615), as in 31, where a subscript $i$ stands for a direct object clitic and $e$ for an indirect object clitic. Omission of such anaphoric indirect object pronoun is particularly common when it may be recovered from the communicative context:

(31)    – *Você quer entregar as entradas$_i$ para os alunos$_e$ agora?*
        'Do you want to hand out the tickets to the students now?'
        – *Eu entrego [$_i$, $_e$] quando a gente chegar lá, senão eles perdem$_i$ $_e$ vai dar problema.*
        'I will hand [them$_i$] out [to them$_e$] when we get there, otherwise they will lose [them] and there will be trouble.'

Although some speakers (like the present writer) acquire the clitic *o* (and its variants shown in Table 3.5) naturally, from growing up in a home environment where standard forms are insisted upon, it is a fact that such pronouns are rather rare in unmonitored BP and virtually non-occurring in the vernacular. Consequently, it makes sense to regard their occurrence in BP as a whole as resulting primarily from formal learning rather than native language acquisition. In fact, it has been suggested (Galves and Abaurre 1996) that the demise of clitics reflects a qualitative change in BP in relation to EP. Be that as it may, learners would do well to master the rules of clitic usage, since they occur in all varieties of EP and in the more formal varieties of BP. Familiarity with contractions like *mo, to, lho* (Table 3.6) is likewise useful, since they occur in EP as well as in Brazilian literary texts up to until the first two or three decades of the twentieth century.

*7.3.2.4  The vanishing reflexive*    As we saw in Chapter 4, some verbs are conjugated with a reflexive clitic that does not denote a truly reflexive action that has the subject as both actor and patient), e.g. *levantar-se* 'to get up,' *sentar-se* 'to sit down,' *lembrar-se (de)* 'to remember,' *esquecer-se (de)* 'to forget,' *queixar-se* 'to complain' (4.6). In BP such verbs occur without a clitic, as in 32a–32c. Omission of the clitic may be compensated for by a different construction, as in 32d, where the verb *ficar* combined with the participle stands for *preocupar-se* 'to worry.'

(32)  a. *Não quer entrar e sentar?* (st. *se sentar*).
      'Don't you want to come in and sit down?'
    b. *Eu esqueci de trazer a pastinha* (st. *me esqueci*).
      'I forgot to bring the folder.'
    c. *Eu não agüento, ela queixa demais* (st. *se queixa*).
      'I can't stand it, she complains too much.'
    d. *Não precisa ficar preocupado com isso* (st. *se preocupar*).
      'Don't worry about that.'

Research has shown not only that reflexive clitics are rare in the vernacular, but also that speakers of this variety do not find it easy to understand clitics when they hear them (Veado 1982:45; Bortoni-Ricardo 1985:227). Loss of awareness of the function of the clitic accounts for the vernacular tendency to amalgamate the pronoun *se* with the infinitive, as in 33a. This feature, however, occurs more than just sporadically in colloquial educated speech, as in 33b. This vernacular feature also occurs in popular EP (Mota 2001:32).

(33)  a. *Eu não consigo se esquecer do que ele fez para a minha mãe*
      (st. *me esquecer*).
      'I can't forget what he did to my mother.' [Rural informant]
    b. *Agora nós temos que ir se trocar* (st. *nos trocar*).
      'Now we need to go and change.'

*7.3.2.5 Actor indeterminacy, the pronoun* se, *and* se-*deletion*    As we have seen (4.9), Portuguese has several ways to indicate an indeterminate semantic actor. One of these, the indeterminate *se*, is relatively infrequent in spoken BP in general and even more so in the vernacular, except perhaps in set phrases like *isso não se diz/faz* 'one doesn't say/do that.' A less formal version of the recipe quoted in section 4.9 would simply use infinitives, as in 34a, and if given orally, would likely use *você* (usually shortened to *cê*), as in 34b:

(34)    a. *Amassar bem meio limão, acrescentar cachaça, adicionar gelo moído, adoçar a gosto e então disfrutar em boa companhia.*
        'Crush half a lime, add in sugar cane brandy, add crushed ice, sweeten [it] to taste and then enjoy [it] in good company.'
        b. BP (*Vo*) *cêamassa . . . acrescenta. . adoça . . . adiciona . . . disfruta . . .*

BP makes extensive use of (*vo*)*cê* as an indeterminate actor (very much like unstressed *you* 'someone in general'), as in the following dialogue segment about the requirements for winning an election, an activity in which neither interlocutor was involved:

(35)    *. . . Eles têm que fazer assim – você não vai ganhar uma eleição sem dinheiro, então você têm que conseguir o dinheiro, e aí você faz de tudo para conseguir.*

        'They have to act like that, you aren't going to win an election without money, and so you've got to get the money – and then you'll do anything to get [it].'

A more drastic reduction omits any reference to an indeterminate semantic actor, resulting in constructions with a third person singular verb without a subject, as in 36:

(36)    a. *Como é que sai da estação?* (st. *Como é que se sai . . .*).
        'How does [one] get out of the station?'
        b. *Onde é que toma o ônibus de Valinhos?* (st. *que se toma . . .*).
        'Where does [one] take the bus for Valinhos?'

*7.3.2.6 Verbs*    Two striking features of verbs in BP are the streamlining of the conjugation paradigm through reduction of forms, and the low frequency of certain verb tenses.

The tenses shown in the conjugation paradigms seen in Chapter 3 represent the theoretical possibilities of the language, but in actual speech some restructuring takes place. The forms corresponding to *vós* have long ceased to be used except in formal oratorical styles. Furthermore, the forms corresponding to *tu* are limited to certain regions in the south (Rio Grande do Sul, Santa Catarina), north, and northeast, and tend to alternate with third person forms (e.g. *Tu vai?/Tu vais*).

Table 7.3 *Standard and vernacular verb paradigms in Brazilian Portuguese*

|            |         | -AR          | -ER          | -IR            | PÔR                  |
|------------|---------|--------------|--------------|----------------|----------------------|
| **Present** |        |              |              |                |                      |
| Standard   | P1sg    | falo         | bebo         | parto          | ponho                |
|            | P2/P3sg | fala         | bebe         | parte          | põe                  |
|            | P1pl    | falamos      | bebemos      | partimos       | pomos                |
|            | P2/P3pl | falam        | bebem        | partem         | põem                 |
| Vernacular | P1sg    | falo         | bebo         | parto          | ponho                |
|            | P2/P3sg | fala         | bebe         | parte          | põe                  |
|            | P1pl    | falemo/fala  | bebemo/bebe  | partimo/parte  | ponhemo/põe          |
|            | P2/P3pl | fala         | bebe         | parte          | põe                  |
| **Preterit** |       |              |              |                |                      |
| Standard   | P1sg    | falei        | bebi         | parti          | pus                  |
|            | P2/P3sg | falou        | bebeu        | partiu         | pôs                  |
|            | P1pl    | falamos      | bebemos      | partimos       | pusemos              |
|            | P2/P3pl | falaram      | beberam      | partiram       | puseram              |
| Vernacular | P1sg    | falei        | bebi         | parti          | pus [pujs]           |
|            | P2/P3sg | falô         | bebeu        | partiu         | pôs [pojs]           |
|            | P1pl    | falemo/falô  | bebemo/bebeu | partimo/partiu | ponhemo/pôs [pojs]   |
|            | P2/P3pl | falaro/falô  | bebero/bebeu | partiro/partiu | ponharo/pôs [pojs]   |
| **Imperfect** |      |              |              |                |                      |
| Standard   | P1sg    | falava       | bebia        | partia         | punha                |
|            | P2/P3sg | falava       | bebia        | partia         | punha                |
|            | P1pl    | falávamos    | bebíamos     | partíamos      | púnhamos             |
|            | P2/P3pl | falavam      | bebiam       | partiam        | punham               |
| Vernacular | P1sg    | falava       | bebia        | partia         | punha/ponhava        |
|            | P2/P3sg | falava       | bebia        | partia         | punha/ponhava        |
|            | P1pl    | falava       | bebia        | partia         | punha/ponhava        |
|            | P2/P3pl | falava       | bebia        | partia         | punha/ponhava        |

A comparison of standard and vernacular verb paradigms (Table 7.3) shows that in VBP tenses with four forms are reduced to three, two, or even a single form for all persons. The contrast between P2sg and P3sg, on the one hand, and that between P2pl/P3pl on the other, are lost in the present indicative, and the resulting system shows a three-way distinction. In other tenses, a two-way contrast remains. There is also sharp reduction of contrasts in the preterit, from four forms to three or two. The forms of the imperfect are reduced from three to a single one. The verb *pôr* appears in the vernacular with an allomorph in *ponh-* derived from the first person singular (*ponho*).

In unmonitored educated speech, contrasts of the type *fala/falam* are more likely to be neutralized than salient contrasts involving different morphemes such as *é/são* (Guy 1981:260). Even so, salient contrasts may be partially lost. The occurrence of vernacular forms in unmonitored educated speech shows such speakers have at their disposal the grammar of both the standard and the vernacular varieties of the language. The rules of verbal agreeement, which are mandatory in the standard, become variable in unmonitored educated speech, and thus closer to the vernacular. Since passive exposure to the standard norm may favor the acquisition of salient contrasts, one would expect to find fewer P3sg vs. P3pl contrasts in the vernacular spoken in more isolated communities than in that of urban environments where normalizing factors are at work, such as formal schooling, the media, and direct contact with speakers of standard BP.

Statistical analyses (Pontes 1973; Hutchins 1975) show certain tenses occur very infrequently in speech. Using a corpus of spontaneous conversations recorded on amateur radio frequencies, Hutchins determined that, out of 81,091 verb forms, the most frequent inflected tenses were the present indicative (39.54%) and the preterit indicative (15.18%). The future indicative accounted for only 1.96% of tokens, contrasting with the future construction *ir + infinitive*, with 4.14%.

These findings dovetail with Pontes's comment (1973:93) that the future indicative is "extremely rare in speech" and that besides the "stereotyped expression *será que*" "I wonder if" all examples in (her) corpus do not convey futurity as such but rather an element of doubt or unreality. Thus a question like *A Maria virá amanhã?* 'Will Maria come tomorrow?' would likely be interpreted as suggesting doubt about Maria's arrival, whereas *A Maria vem amanhã?* is a straight request for information.

The conditional occurs in eight out of 1500 tokens in Pontes's corpus and in 0.92 of Hutchin's tabulation. These findings confirm the trend to replace it by the imperfect indicative, as in 37:

(37)    a. *Tendo tempo, a gente podia chegar até lá* (st. *poderia chegar*).
          'If there is time we could go there.'
        b. *Com um pouco mais eu comprava um Tercel* (st. *compraria*).
          'With a little more I would buy a Tercel.'

In Hutchins's study all subjunctive forms accounted for less than 5% of the total. Most cases of the future subjunctive (1.92%) occurred with verbs that have an irregular stem in that tense (*querer/quiser, poder/puder, ter/tiver, ser/for, estar/estiver, ir/for, vir/vier, haver/houver*). This datum suggests that the persistence of these future subjunctive forms may be due to the fact that irregular forms are more resistant to loss than regular ones. For regular verbs, however, there are only three forms (P1/P2/P3sg *chegar*, P1pl *chegarmos*, P3pl *chegarem*), which are reduced to just P1sg and P3pl when *a gente* is substituted for *nós*. Vernacular examples show that the contrast P1sg/P2sg in regular verbs is easily neutralized by loss of the *-em* (phonetically [ẽj]) desinence, as in 38a–38b. In vernacular speech, the present indicative may occur in the subordinate clause instead of the subjunctive, as in 38c:

(38)   a. *Se eles precisar* (st. *precisarem*) *da gente, aí a gente vai lá.*
       'If they need us, then we'll go there.'
       b. *Quando* (*v*)*ocês chegar* (st. *chegarem*) *em Miami, dá um toque pra*
       *gente.*
       'When you (pl.) arrive in Miami, give us a call.'
       c. *Se a senhora paga* (st. *pagar*) *um pouco mais nós limpa*
       (st. *limpamos*) *a varanda também.*
       'If you pay a little more we clean the porch too.'

In fact, although the contrast between indicative and subjunctive (4.12) holds well in monitored educated speech and in written styles, it may easily be neutralized in casual educated speech and in the vernacular (Martins and Medeiros 1998). This suggests there is a tendency to use the indicative even in constructions where the matrix clause has a verb expressing volition, a belief, or a presupposition, as in 39:

(39)   a. *A gente quer que vocês vêm jantar lá em casa amanhã*
       (st. *venham*).
       'We want you (pl.) to come and have dinner at our place
       tomorrow.'
       b. *Eu estou muito contente que você passou no concurso* (st. *tenha*
       *passado*).
       'I'm very happy that you passed the contest.'

There are also alternate constructions that make it possible to avoid the subjunctive, like the use of constructions with *para* + $NP_{subject}$ + *infinitive* (40a) or with the infinitive (40b):

(40)   a. *O gerente disse para a gente ficar aqui* (st. *O gerente disse que a*
       *gente ficasse aqui*).
       'The manager said for us to stay here.'
       b. *Ela me mandou trazer o pacote* (st. *mandou que eu trouxesse*).
       'She told me to bring the package.'

Another strategy, common in contrary-to fact-sentences, involves switching the narrative to the present even though the events focused on are in the past, as in 31.

(31)   *Que pena, se o senhor fala com a gente antes a gente trazia a serra*
       *elétrica sem problema* (st. *se o senhor tivesse falado . . . a gente teria*
       *trazido*).
       'What a shame, if you had talked to us earlier we'd have brought the
       electric saw, no problem.'

Although prescriptive grammars require a subjunctive form for commands related to *você*, the third person singular of the present indicative "is half again as common . . . as the standard third person command" (Hutchins 1975:63), as in 32:

(32)    a. *Entrega esse envelope para a secretária e depois vem aqui de novo que eu preciso falar com você* (st. *entregue . . . venha*).
'Give this envelope to the secretary and then come back here for I need to talk to you.'
    b. *Põe esse dinheiro no bolso que aqui você não paga nada* (st. *ponha*).
'Put that money back in your pocket because here you don't pay for anything.'

**7.3.2.6.1 Double negation.**    In all varieties of Portuguese, the default way of negating a verb consists in placing *não* 'no' before it (33a). As pointed out in section 4.3, double (or even triple) negatives are normal in BP. In replying to a question, a single negative (33b), while correct, may be perceived as less courteous than a double one (33c). This *não . . . não* construction also occurs in EP. Negation by a single *não* postposed to the verb (33d), however, is widespread in VBP. Furthermore, the postposed *não* may be replaced by *nada* 'nothing'(33e) or reinforced by it (33f).

(33)    a. *Desculpe, eu não falo inglês.*
'I'm sorry, I don't speak English.'
    b. – *Você quer mais sobremesa?*
       – *Não quero, obrigado.*
'Do you want more desert?'
'No, I don't (want it), thank you.'
    c. – *Você quer mais sobremesa?*
       – *Não quero não, obrigado.*
'Do you want more desert?'
'No, I don't (want it), thank you.'
    d. – *Tem correspondência para mim, seu Pedro?*
       – *Tem não, doutor.*
'Is there mail for me, Mr. Pedro?'
'No, doctor, there isn't.'
    e. *Ele não sabe andar a cavalo nada!*
'He can't ride a horse at all!'
    f. *Eu não acredito que ela dormiu com ele nada não, ela estava é com conversa.*
'I don't believe she slept with with him at all, she was just babbling.'

Double negatives are an old feature of the language and can be found in old Portuguese texts, as pointed out by Bueno (1955:225), who listed several examples, as in 34a. Amaral (1920:65) lists the double negative *ninguém não* (pronounced *num* [nũ]) as common in rural VBP:

(34)    a. *A ninguém não me descubro.*
        'I do not doff my hat to anyone.'
    b. *Ninguém num viu.*
       'Everybody saw.'

**7.3.2.6.2 The gerund.** A more recent use of the gerund in BP involves constructions like 35a–35b, which apparently became widespread in business circles at the end of the twentieth century. This practice, dubbed *gerundismo*, has generated an adverse reaction among grammarians far out of proportion to its importance. In the absence of detailed studies, however, there is no basis to determine whether it is, as some have suggested, a calque from English, or simply a spontaneous creation which may or may not be retained.

It is interesting to note that marginal gerund constructions have played a role as indicators of specific nuances, as in the reply in 35c, where *não estou tendo* conveys a connotation of a temporary state that would be absent if the simple present were used.

(35)    a. *Eu vou estar transferindo a sua ligação* (for *vou transferir*).
        'I'll be transfering your call.'
    b. *Nós vamos estar mandando uma circular para todos os clientes*
       (for *vamos mandar*).
       'We'll be sending a circular to all clients.'
    c. – *Cê num tem cerveja preta?*
       – *Cê sabe que eu não estou tendo?*
       'Have you got dark beer?'
       'You know I don't have it (right now)?'

**7.3.2.6.3 *Haver* and *ter*.** A great deal of variation is found in the agreement of the verbs *haver* and *ter*. Although both verbs should be invariable when used impersonally in the sense of 'to exist,' in VBP they often occur in the plural, possibly because speakers reinterpret the direct object noun phrase as a subject, as in 36a–36b

(36)    a. *Houveram muitas causas para esse problema* (st. *houve*).
        'There were many causes for that problem.'
    b. *Tinham vários jeitos de resolver a questão* (st. *tinha*).
       'There were several ways to solve that question.'

Grammars and usage manuals have systematically insisted on prescriptive use of *haver* and condemnation of *ter*, although for no good reason. Use of impersonal *ter* to indicate existence has been documented in old Portuguese (Bueno 1955). Callou and Avelar (2002) found a proportion of 22% instances of *ter* against 78% instances of *haver* in their analysis of ninetenth-century newspaper adverts, which in their view suggests a much higher incidence of *ter* in the spoken language.

*7.3.2.7 Resumptive and clipped relative clauses*     The use of relative constructions shows sharp differences between unmonitored and monitored speech. Spoken BP has long used *que* as an all-purpose relative pronoun (Amaral 1920:63; Bechara 1999:200) and limits the other relative pronouns to semi-formal and formal styles. This is particularly noticeable in cases where in standard usage a relative pronoun would be preceded by a preposition (*com, de, para*), as in 37a, 38a, 39a. Such constructions, perfectly possible in formal conversation, are far less common than the alternative construction, called a *resumptive° relative* (37b, 38b, 39b). In this construction the antecedent of *que* is represented by a resumptive third person pronoun whose referent is the antecedent of *que*.

Another alternative, called the *clipped relative* (37c, 38c, 39c), involves elimination of the resumptive pronoun (Kato 1993:224). In the absence of any explicit reference to the antecedent of *que*, this latter kind of sentence requires a contextual interpretation.

(37)     a. *O funcionário **com quem** eu conversei não tinha nenhuma informação.*
         b. *O funcionário **que** eu falei **com ele** não tinha nenhuma informação.*
         c. *O funcionário **que** eu falei não tinha nenhuma informação.*
         'The official with whom I talked didn't have any information.'

(38)     a. *A casa **de que** eu te falei já foi vendida.*
         b. *A casa **que** eu te falei **dela** já foi vendida.*
         c. *A casa **que** eu te falei já foi vendida.*
         'The house I told you about has already been sold.'

(39)     a. *A cachaça **de que** eu mais gosto é a de alambique velho.*
         b. *A cachaça **que** eu mais gosto **dela** é a de alambique velho.*
         c. *A cachaça **que** eu mais gosto é a de alambique velho.*
         'The sugar cane brandy that I like best is that from an old-style still.'

Combinations of preposition and the locative relative *onde* 'where' are likewise replaced by *que*, combined with the place adverb *lá* 'there' as in 40 and 41:

(40)    a. *O departamento **para onde** eu tinha que escrever mudou.*
        b. *O departamento **que** eu tinha que escrever **para lá** mudou.*
        c. *O departamento **que** eu tinha que escrever mudou.*
           'The department (which) I had to write to has moved.'

(41)    a. *A cidade **de onde** eles vieram não tinha nada.*
        b. *A cidade **que** eles vieram **de lá** [= **dela**] não tinha nada.*
        c. *A cidade **que** eles vieram não tinha nada.*
           'The town they had come from had nothing.'

The disappearance of the relative *cujo* 'whose' (4.11.4) from unmonitored speech seems to entail restructuring of relative clauses, as shown in 42b–42c and 43b–43c:

(42)    a. *Eu conheci uma brasileira **cujo** filho é bolsista.*
        b. *Eu conheci uma brasileira **que** o filho **dela** é bolsista.*
        c. *Eu conheci uma brasileira **que** o filho é bolsista.*
           'I met a Brazilian woman whose son is a scholarship-holder.'

(43)    a. *Vou consertar aquele livro **cuja** capa está rasgada.*
        b. *Vou consertar aquele livro **que** a capa **dele** está rasgada.*
        c. *Vou consertar aquele livro **que** a capa está rasgada.*
           'I'm going to fix that book whose cover is torn.'

Besides agreeing in gender and number with the noun it modifies (*filho*), *cujo* in 42a associates a possessive function with its antecedent (*uma brasileira*). When *que* replaces *cujo*, the possessive function is expressed, if at all, by the preposition *de* combined with a pronoun (*ela*), endowed with an anaphoric function and the same features of person, gender, and number as the antecedent, as in 42b. Thus in 42b if the antecedent were changed to *um brasileiro*, the relative clause would be *que o filho dele*. The relative construction exemplified by 42c, in turn, leaves unmarked the relationship of possession between *filho* and *brasileira*, which has to be retrieved from the context: the listener assumes the woman in question is the mother of the person referred to as *filho*. Likewise the link between *capa* and *livro* is expressed by *cuja* in 43a, by *dele* in 43b and solely by the contex in 43c. In 44b a similar relationship is expressed between *escritor* 'writer' and *livro* 'book,' but in 45a–45b there is no necessary relationship between *cara* 'guy' and *livro*, and consequently such sentences appear less likely to occur unless, as in this example, they are clarified by the context.

(44)    a. *Tem muito escritor **que** os livros **dele** não vendem.*
        b. *Tem muito escritor **que** os livros não vendem.*
        'There are many writers whose books don't sell.'

(45)    a. *Tem muito cara **que** os livros dele não vendem.*
        b. *Tem muito cara **que** os livros não vendem.*
        'There are many guys that the (= whose) books don't sell.'

In BP the clipped relative is more common than the resumptive relative among educated speakers (Tarallo 1983:120 ff.; Bagno 2000:195). Despite their high frequency in BP, however, neither construction is a Brazilianism. The resumptive relative goes back to popular Latin (Ilari 1992:113), and resumptive and clipped relatives also occur in EP (Peres and Móia 1995:276–277, 288).

*7.3.2.8 Regency*    Verbs expressing movement such as *ir, vir, chegar* are systematically construed with *em* instead of with *a* as required by prescriptive grammars. This use of *em* seems to go back to Latin and its occurrence in BP, shown in 46, may be a survival from sixteenth-century language (Bueno 1955:214).

(46)    a. *Que hora que a gente chega em Campinas?*
        'What time do we arrive in Campinas?'
        b. *Você não quer ir na casa dele escutar uns discos?*
        'Don't you want to go to his place to listen to some records?'
        c. *Vamos lá na fazenda domingo?*
        'Shall we go to the farm on Sunday?'

A series of verbs that require a preposition in prescriptive usage is systematically construed without that preposition not only in the vernacular but also in unmonitored educated usage. A sample of such verbs follows:

| | |
|---|---|
| Agradar (a) | *A fala do presidente desagradou os gramáticos* (for *desagradou aos*). |
| | 'The president's speech displeased the grammarians.' |
| Aspirar (a) | *Eu ainda aspiro chegar a chefe* (for *aspiro a chegar*). |
| | 'I still hope to get to be the boss.' |
| Assistir (a) | *Nós fomos assistir uma apresentação* (for *assistir a uma*). |
| | 'We went to attend a presentation.' |
| Comparecer (a) | *Aquela reunião que você não compareceu* (for *à qual você*). |
| | 'That meeting you didn't show up for.' |
| Gostar (de) | *Ela faz o que ela gosta* (for *faz o de que ela gosta*). |
| | 'She does what she likes.' |

| | |
|---|---|
| Obedecer (a) | *Ela não obedece ninguém* (for *obedece a*). |
| | 'She does not obey anyone.' |
| Perdoar (a) | *O presidente perdoou os prisioneiros* (for *perdoou aos prisioneiros*). |
| | 'The president pardoned the prisoners.' |
| Responder (a) | *Você não vai responder o que ele perguntou?* (for *responder ao que*). |
| | 'Aren't you going to answer what he asked?' |
| Suceder (a) | *Vamos ver quem vai suceder o presidente* (for *suceder ao*). |
| | 'Let's see who will succeed this president.' |
| Visar (a) | *Essas medidas visam o barateamento dos alimentos* (for *visam ao*). |
| | 'These measures aim at lowering the price of food.' |

Other verbs, on the contrary, are used with prepositions not required in the prescriptive language:

| | |
|---|---|
| Preferir | *Eu prefiro mais dançar do que caminhar* (for *prefiro dançar a caminhar*). |
| | 'I prefer dancing to walking.' |
| Chamar | *Chamou o presidente de ladrão* (for *chamou o presidente ladrão*). |
| | 'He called the president a thief.' |
| Namorar | *O meu filho estava namorando com a filha da vizinha* (for *estava namorando a filha*). |
| | 'My son was going out with the neighbor's daughter.' |

*7.3.2.9 Word order and topicalization* As discussed in section 4.15, an utterance provides a frame for organizing bundles of information in the format of a full sentence (which has a verb), or a phrase or a sentence fragment (which have no verb). In a sentence like *Eu estou cansado desse projeto* 'I am tired of this project', that information is organized by means of syntactic functions such as a subject (*eu*) and a predicate (*estou cansado desse projeto*).

Word order reflects the relative informativeness of the sentence elements. The general principle is that background information tends to be presented first so as to pave the way for relatively more important information. As shown by Pontes (1987), the default or unmarked word order in declarative sentences in BP is subject + verb + direct object (SVO), found in neutral statements, that is, those that are neither contrastive nor emphatic. The order verb + subject (VS) is marked, and used when the subject is felt to be more informative than the verb, to provide information that is either contrastive, or emphatic, or simply new.

Thus in the context of a question such as *Quem chegou?*, in the reply *Chegou o meu pai* the verb *chegou* simply echoes the question, while the actual information is contained in *o meu pai*, which might, in fact, constitute a full reply. As an answer to an open-ended question such as *O que aconteceu?*, however, either ordering would do, depending on whether the information focus was on the arrival (*O meu pai chegou*) or on the person who arrived (*Chegou o meu pai*).

Distribution of information in an utterance may be analyzed in terms of a topic° followed by a commentary°. The topic contains information on what the utterance is about (Matthews 1997:380) and consequently it tends to come at the beginning, announcing what is going to be said. In a sentence like 47a, topicalization is brought about by the passive construction. Here the commentary coincides with the predicate (*foi morto pela polícia*), while the topic coincides with the subject (*o chefe da gangue*).

Passives, however, are relatively uncommon in unmonitored BP, and there is no reason why their topic need be the subject: in 47b–47c the subject is *a polícia* and the topic is *o chefe da gangue*. The difference is that unlike in 47a, in 47b *ele* is an anaphoric direct object that refers to the topic *o chefe da gangue*. As for 47d, though it is theoretically possible, the low frequency of the clitic *o/a* makes it unlikely except in formal styles.

(47)    a. *O chefe da gangue foi morto pela polícia de madrugada.*
        'The gang leader was killed by the police at dawn.'
    b. *O chefe da gangue, a polícia matou ele de madrugada.*
        'The gang leader, the police killed him at dawn.'
    c. *O chefe da gangue, a polícia matou de madrugada.*
        'The gang leader, the police killed at dawn.'
    d. *O chefe da gangue, a polícia matou-o de madrugada.*
        'The gang leader, the police killed him at dawn.'

The topicalized element may have a variety of syntactic functions, such as the direct object (48a), or the complement of a preposition (48b), or a predicative complement (48c), or an adverbial complement (48d). In all of these cases, as in 47b–47d, the topic is said to be left-dislocated, meaning that its natural place would have been somewhere to the right (in the place indicated by a wedge ▲):

(48)    a. *Essa moto eu comprei ▲ em Santos.*
        'This motorcycle I bought (it) in Santos.'
    b. *Com ela, eu dançava ▲ a noite toda.*
        'With her, I'd dance all night.'

    c. *Zangada ela ficou* ▲, *mas que é que eu vou fazer.*
      'Mad she got, but what can I do.'
    d. *Aqui, ele não põe mais os pés* ▲.
      'Here, he won't set foot again.'

Placing an element at the head of the sentence is one way of topicalizing it. Another is to split the sentence by inserting in it a frame made up of the verb *ser + que*, thus creating a cleft sentence° as in (49):

(49)    a. *É ele **que** quer falar com o senhor.*
        'He is the one who wants to talk to you.'
    b. *É com o senhor **que** ele quer falar.*
        'It's with you that he wants to talk.'
    c. *É falar com o senhor **que** ele quer.*
        'To talk to you is what he wants.'

Topicalization is not unique to BP; rather, it may be seen as a further development of processes that occur regularly in EP, as studied by Duarte (1996). In discursive topicalization (Perini 2002a:542), the topicalized element does not have a clear syntactic relationship with the rest of the sentence. In some cases it operates as an antecedent to an anaphoric pronoun that may function either as subject (50a), direct object (50b), or indirect object (50c).

(50)    a. *A Susana, eu acho que ela não gosta muito disso não.*
        'Susan, I think she doesn't like that very much.'
    b. *Essa moto, eu comprei em Santos.*
        'This motorcycle I bought (it) in Santos.'
    c. *A minha mãe, eu dou um presente para ela todo Natal.*
        'My mother, I give her a gift every Christmas.'

In other cases, there is no such resumptive pronoun to link the sentence to the topic, which simply provides a background for the information in the sentence, and the relationship between the two must be interpreted from the context, as in 51a–51b.

(51)    a. *O Lula presidente, você acha que as coisas estão melhorando?*
        'Lula [being] president, do you think things are getting better?'
    b. *Horário de verão, eu nunca lembro de acertar até alguém me dizer.*
        'Daylight saving time, I never remember to set (my watch) until someone tells me.'

## 7.4     The creole hypothesis

Having identified some of the main features of Brazilian Portuguese, including its vernacular variety, we are now in a position to briefly review the question of its possible origins.

African slaves started arriving in Portugal in 1441 (Teyssier 1957:228) and communication between Portuguese navigators and Africans was facilitated by a Portuguese-based pidgin which, according to Naro (1978:341), had originated "with the officially instituted training of translators" established by the Portuguese. That pidgin was "later extensively used throughout West Africa" as a reconnaissance language and African characters speaking it "began to appear in the popular literature." In fact, the literary representation of pidgin- or creole-speaking Africans first appeared in Garcia de Resende's *Cancioneiro Geral*, published in 1516 (1.2). Gil Vicente's plays depict it in a stylized manner, as shown by the following brief sample:

| | |
|---|---|
| *Que inda que negro soo* | Although I am black, |
| *bosso oyo he tam trabessa,* | your eye is so mischievous, |
| *tam preta, que me matoo.* | so dark, that it has killed me. |
| *Senhora, quem te frutasse* | Lady if one could enjoy you |
| *por o quatro dia no maas* | for four days, no more |
| *e logo morte me matesse,* | and then death might kill me |
| *que mas o dia nam durasse* | that more the day would not last |
| *pollo vida que boso me das.* | for the life you give me. |

(Gil Vicente, *Frágua de Amor*, p. 146)

Though stereotyped, such representation gives an idea of salient phonological features of that speech. Use of *b* for *v* (*bosso* for *vosso* 'yours,' *bos* for *vós* 'you') suggests underdifferentiation of the phonemes /b/ and /v/, a feature found in Northern EP (6.2). Other features are shared by creoles and VBP (7.3.1.2), such as [j] instead of [ʎ], as indicated by **lh** replaced by **i** (*olho > oyo*).

Metathesis°, that is an alteration in the normal position of sounds, as in the case of *r* and *u* in *furtasse > frutasse*, is common in VBP (e.g. *caderneta >* VBP *cardeneta* 'notebook,' 'problem,' *estupro >* VBP *estrupo* 'rape'). The same goes for monophthongization° of *ou* [ow] *> o* [o] (7.3.1.1), represented by *oo* as in *sou > soo, matou > matoo*. Morphological features include lack of nominal agreement (7.3.2.1), as in *o quatro dia* for *os quatro dias; oyo . . . trabessa* for *oyo travesso, pollo vida* for *polla vida*.

The occurrence of similar features in both VBP and African Portuguese-based creoles has given rise to the idea – apparently first suggested by the Portuguese scholar Adolpho Coelho (1880–1886) – that VBP might have roots in one or more creoles spoken by African slaves in colonial times. This hypothesis has since been revisited by several linguists, including Machado (1940), Silva Neto (1976), Câmara (1975), Jeroslow (1974), Melo (1971), Holm (1987, 1989,

1992, 2004), Guy (1981, 1989), Baxter and Lucchesi (1997), and Baxter (1998). Melo (1971:75) stated that there may have existed in colonial times a Yoruba-type creole and a Bantu-type creole, both of which disappeared as successive generations acquired Portuguese. Guy (1981) has suggested that a creole might have been widespread among the colonial lower classes and that VBP would be the result of a decreolization process that took place under the influence of the standard variety spoken by both native speakers of EP and the educated Brazilian-born minority.

Other scholars (Naro 1978; Naro and Lemle 1976; Naro and Scherre 1993; Scherre and Naro 1993, 2000), however, have rejected the creole-origin hypothesis, suggesting that VBP can be explained as resulting from diachronic change undergone by the language spoken by sixteenth-century settlers. One factor influencing the later development of a specifically Brazilian variety of Portuguese would be the presence of the metropolitan standard, related to increased immigration from Portugal in the eighteenth century. Another factor would be the arrival of the Portuguese court in 1808, with a following of some ten thousand speakers of EP whose presence constituted a powerful model of prestigious speech.

The view of the non-creole origin of VBP finds support in McWhorter's (2000) Afrogenesis hypothesis, according to which New World creoles grew out of pidgins which originated in West African trade settlements and were brought over by slaves who had learned them in Africa. The fact that VBP is not a creole, but "at best lightly 'semicreolized,'" suggests that the slaves who came to Brazil originally were not speakers of a Portuguese-based pidgin. Once in Brazil, they could have learned "a relatively full [that is, non-creolized] variety of Portuguese despite massive disproportion of black to white" (McWhorter 2000:204–205).

Scherre and Naro (2000) further point out that the notion of creolization in Brazil cannot be linked to any specific ethnic group. In their view, the recently reported speech of small commmunities of African descent living in hamlets like Helvécia in the state of Bahia (Megenney 2002), or Cafundó in the state of São Paulo (Vogt and Fry 1996, 2000), should be analyzed as varieties of rural VBP, relexified° to a certain extent with words of African origin. Scherre and Naro "reject the position that BP has a creole history, is a semi-creole, or has a light underlying creolization," suggesting instead that the features and structures of present-day vernacular BP were already "present from the beginning. The basic change was in the general tendency of the frequency of the forms" (2000:8).

This is not to say that creoles did not exist in colonial Brazil, but that their range was likely geographically limited. A widespread creole variety could hardly have been so thoroughly decreolized without leaving behind a post-creole continuum of the kind found in areas such as Jamaica (Le Page and De Camp 1960). In that case we would expect to find a stratified situation with an *acrolect* (standard Portuguese) at the top, a *basilect* (that is, one or more creole varieties) at the bottom, and a series of *mesolects*, or intermediate varieties, connecting those two extremes. This situation, however, does not obtain in Brazil, where no extant creole variety has been identified, despite features shared by VBP with creoles of Cape Verde and São Tomé (Mello 1996; Holm 2004).

According to an alternative hypothesis put forth by Holm (2004), BVP would be the outcome of a process of partial restructuring that took place in a language contact situation. The languages or language varieties involved were the EP spoken natively by settlers, the creole brought over in the sixteenth century by slaves, and several African languages which "continued to be spoken by large numbers of people . . . during the eighteenth and nineteenth centuries" (Holm 2004:56). According to this view, a morphologically and syntactically partially restructured variety of Portuguese progressively replaced the *Língua Geral* (7.2.2) spoken in sugar plantations located in coastal regions. A similar process took place in the areas touched by the rush for the gold and diamond mines discovered in today's states of Minas Gerais, Mato Grosso, and Goiás, which lasted from the last decade of the seventeenth century through the first half of the eigthteenth (Prado Junior 1945: 33–34).

The mining rush, which fostered an intense, if short-lived, cultural revival in the mining area of Minas Gerais in the late eighteenth century, attracted many EP speakers from Portugal. Mining labor requirements caused caused massive importation of slaves, who likely learned Portuguese, albeit imperfectly. When the mines were exhausted by the middle of the eighteenth century, the region in question,

which corresponds to the whole kernel of today's Brazilian territory, encompassing the states of Minas Gerais, Goiás, part of Mato Grosso, and a portion of Bahia . . . [had] [a]pproximately 600,000 inhabitants, that is a little less than a fifth of the colony's total population occupied this area at the beginning of the nineteenth century. (Prado Junior 1942:50)

According to Holm's hypothesis, assuming that substantial linguistic leveling took place among this population during the decades of the mining rush, a vernacular variety could have developed which, once it had spread outside its region of origin, would have "probably played a key role in spreading a newly leveled variety of Portuguese" which would be the source of today's VBP. This view is compatible with Megenney's hypothesis (2002) that, even if there never was a generalized creole spoken all over colonial Brazil, there may have existed small creole-speaking pockets which, before vanishing completely, had some effect on VBP. This resulting partially restructured variety, neither a creole nor a semi-creole but bearing some creole-like features, would be constantly under presssure from the standard language, made mandatory in education and public administration in 1758 (7.2.2), and reinforced by the arrival of the Portuguese court in 1808.

While these influences likely checked the vernacular from drifting further away from the standard variety, other forces were shaping Brazilian Portuguese. From the nineteenth century on an increasing number of Brazilians underwent a process of first language acquisition characterized by several unique features. First, they acquired Portuguese from Brazil-born parents whose speech already differed markedly from EP. Second, even upper-class children grew up in close contact with speakers of vernacular varieties, be they White, Negro, or ethnically mixed. Throughout the nineteenth century (and in some regions into the twentieth as well) many White children had Negro wet-nurses and played with children of African or mixed ancestry. Even nowadays, in small towns children of all socioeconomic groups attend public schools where the teachers' standard or semi-standard Portuguese coexists with vernacular varieties. It is in such schools that children have traditionally been initiated into the art of switching from "classroom Portuguese," which they come to associate with school, books, and formal learning in general, to the various levels of Brazilian Portuguese spoken at home and in most other situations. For middle-class children with parents keen on language correction as a prestige marker and a step toward a college education, dialect switching becomes natural, although tinged by the ambivalence already referred to (7.1): familiar and comfortable as it may be, the vernacular evokes a vague feeling of guilt for saying something that is not quite "correct," and which, uttered at the wrong time and in the wrong place, may elicit reproach or derision, or worse yet, bar access to desirable jobs or influential positions. Until a solution is found for this dilemma, the relationship between standard and vernacular Brazilian Portuguese will remain conflictive for native speakers and foreign learners alike.

## 7.5    More border talk

A restructuring process may also be involved in certain varieties developed in situations of language contact, particularly when the languages involved are as closely related as Portuguese and Spanish. Along the Brazil–Uruguay border, in areas such as the twin towns of Sacramento (Brazil) and Rivera (Uruguay), there is a variety traditionally called [Sp] *fronterizo*/[Pg] *fronteiriço*, and known to contemporary linguists as DPUs or *dialetos portugueses do Uruguai* 'Uruguay's Portuguese Dialects' (Rona 1965; Hensey 1972, 1982; Elizaincín *et al.* 1987; Elizaincín 1992; Carvalho 1998, 2003).

In fact Portuguese was the language spoken in the northern regions of Uruguay until late in the nineteenth century, when the Uruguayan government began to enforce the use of Spanish in administration and education. Even today, Portuguese is considered a heritage language in some bilingual border areas (Carvalho 2003:125). The basis of DPUs is essentially the popular Portuguese spoken in Brazil. Morphological and syntactic structures are somewhat simplified (although far less so than is the case with pidgins or creoles), and the lexicon, made up of words from both languages, includes many hybrid forms.

Long regarded as unsystematic hybrids, DPUs have been cogently characterized by Carvalho dialects of Portuguese "whose internal variation is the outcome of interference from Spanish, particularly at the lexical level, and the presence of rural Portuguese markers." She further postulates a "continuum of stylistic and social variation" which would include "local forms" and "non-local forms" which would be provided through contact with urban varieties of Brazilian Portuguese through travel, the Brazilian media, and tourism. Rivera speech would thus appear to be "a dialect transition zone" (2003:126–135).

Pronunciation features such as articulation of *lh* as either standard [ʎ] or vernacular [j] (7.3.1.2) are clearly related to social and stylistic factors. The higher a speaker's socioeconomic standard, the higher is the incidence of the standard allophone [ʎ], but the level of formality also plays a role: in all the informants analyzed, there was a rate of 82% of cases of [ʎ] in formal contexts, against only 39% in informal contexts (Carvalho 2003:136).

The everyday lexicon of Rivera Portuguese characteristically includes a large proportion of Spanish loan words, some of which have completely displaced the corresponding Portuguese terms, as shown in examples 52a–52e, all from Carvalho (2003:139):

(52)    a. *Tinha un* juez [Pg juiz] *que trabaiava lá no hotel* . . .
           'There was a judge who worked at the hotel . . .'
        b. *Quando a* patrona [Pg patroa] *vinha pa Rivera* . . .
           'When the boss [f.] came to Rivera . . .'
        c. *Eu vou numa* tienda . . . [Pg loja]
           'I go to a store . . .'
        d. *Eu cheguei na* calle [Pg rua].
           'I came to the street . . .'
        e. *Ela tá trabaiando com a M. na* panadería [Pg padaria]
           'She is working with M. at the bakery . . .'

Another salient characteristic of Rivera Portuguese is codeswitching, that is the practice of alternating languages during the same conversation, as in 53, or even within the same utterance, as in 54, from Carvalho 2003:140:

(53)    [Sp] Trabajaba, trabajaba, no sacaba ni los días, ni los días que dan
        para uno después de cuatro años son cinco días mas yo no sacaba.
        Ah, [Pg] *eu vô deixá de sê boba, vivo tão cansada.* [Sp] Sacaba de
        vez en cuando, sacaba un día para ir a Rivera.

'I worked, worked, I didn't even take off the days they give you after four years, that's five days, but I didn't take them off. Oh, I'm going to quit being silly, I'm always so tired. I'd take a day off every now and then, to go to Rivera.'

(54)    a. [Sp] Yo hablo español, a veces me equivoco y [Pg] *falo brasileiro.*
'I speak Spanish, sometimes I make a mistake and speak Brazilian.'

        b. [Sp] Yo era la limpiadora, fazia todo trabaio, [Pg] *limpava tudo.*
'I was the cleaning woman, I did all the work, I cleaned everything.'

It is anybody's guess to what extent DPU speakers will be able to resist the double pressure to learn official Spanish, taught in schools and used in dealing with the Uruguayan administration, and to bring their own variety of popular Portuguese closer to the prestigious urban model that reaches them from the other side of the border. It would be regrettable if DPUs were to disappear, as they illustrate very vividly the resilience with which a language can survive and adjust itself to a variety of circumstances and yet retain something essential that provides continuity among its varieties.

In border regions as well as all over Brazil, the widespread occurrence of vernacular forms in the unmonitored speech of educated persons presents learners with a difficult – though no means insuperable – problem that can be defined succintly: in order to learn Portuguese to the point of being fully functional in Brazilian society, a degree of mastery of the vernacular is essential. The reason is that functionality requires being able to switch back and forth between the two varieties in order to interact not only with different persons, but also with the same interlocutors, who will effect that switch instinctively, depending on the degree of formality of a given communicative context.

To accomplish that goal learners have to learn to distinguish between what is standard and what is vernacular. This is not necessarily simple, since clues are not always evident, except in the more obvious cases, such as nominal or verbal agreement. Secondly, they have to acquire a feel for how and when a vernacular form should be used to avoid sounding stilted, and when one should switch to the standard form so as not to sound inappropriately casual, or even churlish. Developing such a feel is not made easier by the contradictory views and attitudes toward phenomena of language variation held by many educated native speakers, ranging from strict defense of prescriptive norms to enthusiastic acceptance of vernacular forms – in either case often for ideological reasons that have little to do with language per se.

# 8    Sociolinguistic issues

If languages were uniform and invariable, they might be easier to learn and to use, but their communicative and expressive resources would probably be rather limited. We can only wonder whether such a language would suffice for linguistically creative literary works like João Guimarães Rosa's *Grande Sertão: Veredas*, or António Lobo Antunes's *A Hora dos Lobos,* or Mia Couto's *Terra Sonâmbula.* More likely, a uniform language would be to real language as tic-tac-toe to chess: both games are governed by rules, but chess offers plenty more room for variation.

Language, in fact, is more like a game of chess played by multiple partners who, while abiding by the same general rules, use variants that all along require reinterpretation and accommodation if the game is to proceed. At times the rules in use diverge so sharply – as if some players suddenly decided to try out checker rules – that the game breaks down. More often than not, however, adjustments are made here and there and the match goes on.

It is only by reducing a language to a theoretical construct that we can create the illusion of immutability. Real language varies in time, in geographical space, and in the omnipresent social spectrum. Accordingly, throughout this book we have tried to complement a generic presentation of Portuguese with specific instances of variation. This chapter will take a closer look at how the use of the language relates to social variables.

## 8.1    Attitudes to language variation

One of our most stubborn myths about language is the notion that some forms – words, phrases, or constructions – are intrinsically "better" or "more correct" than others. We are haunted by the nagging suspicion that whenever there are two or more alternate ways of saying something, only one of them can be right, and all the others must be wrong. In fact, as the *Appendix Probi* (5.1) attests, "right vs. wrong" is a model for linguistic thinking which has been in vogue since ancient times. Forms considered correct conform to the norms spelled out in prescriptive grammars and carry a high degree of overt prestige. Forms considered incorrect are relegated to poorly understood and unprestigious categories such as "vulgar speech," "slang," "street language," or worse. What could be simpler than that?

One of the reasons for such misguided beliefs is social differences. As we saw in Chapter 7, Vernacular Brazilian Portuguese (VBP) grew as a popular variety, spoken by a largely illiterate or semi-literate majority of persons of low socio-economic condition. Among those people there were many slaves who, upon being liberated in 1888, found themselves disenfranchised and at the bottom of the social ladder. Another segment of that group was made up of poor peasants, either white or ethnically mixed. Since language is a powerful tool for mark-ing social differences, usage considered correct increasingly became socially prestigious, while the notion of "incorrect Portuguese," equated with popular or vernacular speech, became associated with certain shibboleths regarded as errors to be avoided in proper usage.

A case in point is the use of *ele/ela* as an anaphoric direct object (7.3.2.3), which, although widespread in the colloquial speech of the educated, has tra-ditionally been used in literature to identify ignorant lower-class characters. In the following well-known passage by the Brazilian novelist Machado de Assis (1839–1908), a freed slave's use of *ele* as direct object contrasts with his former master's careful diction, which is marked by the normative use of the verb *perdoar* 'to forgive' with an indirect object represented by the clitic *lhe*. (In all likelihood, the former slave would say instead *eu perdôo ele* 'I forgive him'):

– *É um vadio e um bêbado muito grande. Ainda hoje deixei ele na quitanda, enquanto eu ia lá em baixo na cidade, e ele deixou a quitanda para ir na venda beber.*
– *Está bom, perdoa-lhe, disse eu.* (Machado de Assis, *Memórias Póstumas de Braz Cubas*, Ch. 68)

"He's a great lazybones and drunkard. Even today I left him at the greengrocery while I went downtown, and he left the greengrocery to go and drink at the store."
    "That's all right, forgive him, I said."

Likewise, in the following passage by the Brazilian regionalist author Cornélio Pires (1884–1958), a peasant's speech is marked by several non-standard features:

*Vai pra muitos ano, eu se ajustei cumo arriero de um tropero que ia pro Sur. Eu quiria cunhecê o Brasir e lá se fomo . . . Magine que um dia, no campo aberto, era tanto o friu, que o patrão mandô nóis pará e sortá os alimar.* (Cornélio Pires, *Continuação das Estrambóticas Aventuras do Joaquim Bentinho*. São Paulo: Companhia Editora Nacional, 1929, 82–83.)

(Standard:) *Vai para muitos anos, eu me ajustei como arrieiro de um tropeiro que ia para o Sul. Eu queria conhecer o Brasil e lá nos fomos . . . Imagine que um dia, no campo aberto, era tanto o frio, que o patrão nos mandou parar e soltar os animais.*

Many years ago I got hired as a mule driver by a drover who was going down south. I wanted to know Brazil and there we went . . . Just imagine that one day, out in the open country, it was so cold that the boss told us to stop and release the animals.

Comparing the original with the standard version, we notice several vernacular features. Rhotacism appears in *Brasir (Brasil), Sur (Sur)* and *alimar (animal; alimal* is a regional variant of st. *animal*). There is also diphthongization° of the hiatus° in *frio* ['friu] > *friu* [friw], and diphthongization of the stressed vowel followed by /s/ in *nós* > *nóis* [n js] (7.3.1.1).

Other devices involve instances of "eye dialect," which consists in modifying ordinary spelling to highlight a phonetic feature which, more often than not, corresponds to normal pronunciation, as writing *he sez* or *I wuz* for *he says, I was*. For example, *conhecer* and *queria* appear as *cunhecê* and *quiria*, to show that the pretonic vowels are respectively [u] and [i] rather than [o] and [e] as suggested by the standard spelling. However, the usual pronunciation in BP is precisely with [u] and [i]. Likewise a simple vowel *e* instead of a diphthong is the usual way of pronouncing *ei* in unmonitored speech, as opposed to monitored speech which can have [ej]. Underlying the misspellings *tropero* and *arriero* (for st. *tropeiro, arrieiro*) or *pará* and *soltá* (for st. *parar, soltar*) is the myth that such pronunciation features are found only among speakers of low socioeconomic status, when in fact they are widespread across the social spectrum.

Morphological phenomena involve the shortened form *magine* (for st. *imagine*); in *eu se ajustei*, the clitic *se* has lost its reflexive value and become an extra syllable to the verb. Syntactic features involve lack of nominal agreement: *muitos ano, os alimar* (for *muitos anos, os alimares*) and the pronoun *nós* used as a direct object: *mandô nóis* instead of *nos mandou* or *mandou-nos*.

What is puzzling for the foreign learner, however, is that normative forms tend to be eschewed in informal speech because even educated speakers prefer the less prestigious forms, as in 1a–1b. Both examples come from the same dialogue with a middle-aged male lawyer from São Paulo. In 1a, there was a lot of banter going on while the conversation centered on hunting weapons, but in 1b, where the normative pronoun *lo* occurs, the conversation had taken a slightly more serious turn.

(1)    a. BP *E a doze? Cê já limpou ela?*
          'What about the twelve [-gauge shotgun]? Have you already cleaned it?'
       b. BP *Bom, aquele jipe, eu acho que nós vamos trazê-lo a semana que vem.*
          'Well, that jeep, I think we're going to bring it next week.'

The reason is that using certain normative forms such as *o/a* or its variants *lo/la, no/na* in an informal conversation is considered pedantic, that is, conversationally inappropriate. Use of vernacular forms, though labelled "incorrect" by traditional grammarians, lessens the distance and reinforces solidarity between interlocutors. Such forms carry covert prestige, defined as the positive value ascribed to forms which speakers habitually use even while professing to condemn and avoid them. (Matthews 1997:81). In other words, the relaxed style that includes so many vernacular forms is considered a mode implying more solidarity and is therefore more conducive to effective communication in all but formal contexts. This situation points to a tension between perceptions of grammatical propriety and communicative appropriateness. Such tension is not unusual, but when it interferes with communication – for example, when it makes speakers insecure about the correctness of their speech – then tension is a sign of conflict between the language varieties involved.

## 8.2    Diglossia

Until the first half of the twentieth century the majority of the population of Brazil had limited or no access to formal education and lived in rural environments with little exposure to educated speech. Over the second half century, however, the country became increasingly urbanized: whereas in 1940 some 31% of the population lived in urban areas and 69% in rural areas, by 1996 that proportion was about 78% urban to 22% rural. The 2000 census showed a proportion of 81% urban to 19% rural. Reportedly, since the 1950s increased access to school has reduced illiteracy, from 56% in 1940 to 26% in 1980 (Bortoni-Ricardo 1985:21) and from 22.6% in 1996 to a still high rate of 15.6% in 1999 (IBGE). Nonetheless, such data should be taken with a grain of salt in view of recent reports of widespread functional illiteracy among adolescents (*Correio Braziliense*, 07/01/2003), pegged at a rather high 30.5% (*Almanaque Abril* 2002a:184).

Be that as it may, such data suggest that the traditional distinction between rural and urban speech, which goes back to the ancient Romans (5.1), is no longer as functional as it used to be. Proximity to urban centers and the ubiquitousness of radio and television combine to expose vernacular speakers to educated speech. The result of such changes has been the growth of "non-standard varieties that might be labelled 'rurban'. . . spoken by lower-class illiterate or semi-literate people who live in the cities but who, in most cases, have rural backgrounds, or by the population living in modernized rural areas" (Bortoni-Ricardo 1985:9).

As the number of such speakers has increased from one generation to the next among the majority of the population, the gap between the vernacular and the standard (not to mention the prescriptive norm) has widened. It is useful to look at the contrast between standard and non-standard varieties in terms of the concept of diglossia°, originally defined by Ferguson (1959; see Schiffman

1997 for an update) as a situation in which two or more varieties of a language are used complementarily in the same community in terms of relative prestige and power, so that

in addition to the primary dialects of the language (which may include a standard or regional standards), there is a very divergent, highly codified (often grammatically more complex) superimposed variety, either of an earlier period or in another speech community, which is learned largely by formal education and is used for most written and formal spoken purposes but is not used by any sector of the community for ordinary conversation. (Ferguson 1959:336)

In such a situation the superposed or high variety (H) and the low variety or varieties (L) have different communicative functions and are used in different contexts. In speech, the H variety is required for communication in formal circumstances – such as parliamentary activity, formal addresses, lecturing, news broadcasting – while L is used in casual conversation and informal public contexts such as popular radio and television programs. In writing, the H variety is required for formal written communication, as in drafting administrative reports, parliamentary bills, paperwork involved in making laws and administering justice, news broadcasting, newspaper editorials or major news articles, didactic materials and other publications carrying responsibility, and of course literature regarded as serious. L varieties, if written at all, are used in folk literature, comic books, cartoons, and other forms of light entertainment. Since the H variety has to be acquired through formal schooling, opportunities to learn and practice it regularly are essential for the acquisition of fluency. Because of their low socioeconomic standing, however, most L speakers find themselves doubly jeopardized: on the one hand they cannot accede to certain activities, such as jobs regulated by entrance exams requiring knowledge of the H variety, and on the other they cannot obtain the necessary instruction in H, because either it is too expensive, or too scarce, or both.

The relationship between VBP and the formal prescriptive variety fulfills the basic conditions of Ferguson's definition. Whereas vernacular speakers come from an essentially oral subculture, the formal standard reflects a sophisticated literate culture in which they do not participate. For vernacular speakers, learning the standard is tantamount to learning a code that plays no part in their communicative activities.

In contrast, educated speakers who have acquired the prescriptive norm through formal schooling may use vernacular features in casual conversation with peers or subordinates (Azevedo 1989). It is quite true, as Perini (1997:37) points out, that the two codes

in practice, do not interfere with each other. The vernacular is used in informal speech and in certain written texts, such as theater plays, where realism counts. [Prescriptive] Portuguese is used in formal writing, and is only really spoken in formal situations such as graduation speeches or when being invested of a public function.

The point, however, is that whereas educated speakers can switch between H and L as required by circumstances, vernacular speakers only use the L variety, and thus find themselves at a disadvantage in situations in which H is required.

Considering how intensely vernacular features pervade BP, it makes sense to regard them as part of the language, rather than something to be avoided, corrected or, worse yet, ignored. In fact, considering its importance for effective communication, the role of the vernacular in Brazilian society looms as a crucial sociolinguistic issue with ramifications in possibly every aspect of social life. Even assuming it might be possible to offer effective instruction in the H variety to speakers of the L variety, this might not be a solution. One reason is that the L variety is associated with values of social identity which its speakers may be reluctant to give up, as shown by Bertoni-Ricardo in her landmark study of vernacular speakers who had relocated from rural Minas Gerais to the urban environment of the country's capital, Brasília. Further resistance may come from a reluctance to acquire H features perceived as typical of higher social groups with whom L speakers do not identify (Bortoni-Ricardo 1985; Possenti 2002:317).

## 8.3     Styles and registers

Besides differences like those involving vernacular and standard varieties, the study of social variation takes into account the differences among styles used in speaking and writing. Joos (1967) proposed a simple classification of five styles (in principle for English but applicable, *mutatis mutandis*, to Portuguese as well) ranging along an axis of formality, namely *frozen, formal, consultative, casual*, and *intimate*.

Frozen style, the least spontaneous and most monitored, approaches written language in syntax and lexicon. It is mostly used in solemn speeches, administrative communication, and legal pronouncements and texts. Its syntax and vocabulary may be somewhat archaizing at times (as in legal language), and so require specialized training. It often represents the voice of anonymous authority – hence its impersonality as in announcements or posted notices (2a–2d), even when disguised as requests:

(2)     a. *O Exmo. Sr. Secretário somente receberá com hora marcada.*
           'His Excellency the Secretary will receive only by appointment.'
        b. *Proibida a entrada.*
           'No entry.'
        c. *Pede-se não fumar.*
           'Please do not smoke.'
        d. *Favor usar a outra calçada. Pedimos desculpas pelo incômodo.*
           'Please use the other sidewalk. We regret the inconvenience.'

Formal style allows for some interaction and is a little more relaxed, but it is still closely monitored and stays within recognizable boundaries of prescriptive syntax and vocabulary. In the following passage, from a radio interview, double dashes indicate longer pauses and single dashes mark short pauses:

[1] *Respondendo a sua pergunta – eu diria que essa atividade – embora constituida por um grupo bastante seleto – preparado ao longo de vários anos – ainda é uma coisa muito pequena – quando comparada com o cenário nacional – em pesquisa não só tecnológica mas também científica – –* (42 words)
[2] *O – – o que se faz é muito pouco – em relação ao que se deveria fazer – tendo em vista os objetivos e os benefícios que o país poderia auferir nessa área de pesquisas – –* (32 words)
[3] *A principal razão disso é que a instituição conta somente com umas mil pessoas – das quais quinhentas têm curso superior – e mais de cem têm curso de pós-graduação a nível de mestrado ou doutorado – –* (34 words)
[4] *Ainda assim – isso é pouco – –* (5 words)
[5] *Acontece que o país é carente de recursos humanos qualificados – –* (10 words)
[6] *A ciência no Brasil é uma coisa muito restrita – limitada a grupos pequenos de pesquisadores – –* (15 words) (Radio interview from the late 1980s. Author's files.)

[1] To answer your question – I would say that that activity – although formed by a rather select group – prepared over many years – is still something rather small – when compared with the national scene – not only in technological research but also in scientific research – –
[2] What – – what is done is still very little – compared to what should be done – keeping in mind the goals and the benefits which the country could derive from that research area – –
[3] The main reason for that is that our institution has only some one thousand people – five hundred of whom are university graduates – and more than a thousand have a graduate degree at the masters or doctoral level – –
[4] Even so – that is too little – –
[5] The truth is that in this country there is a shortage of qualified human resources – –
[6] Science is still something very restricted in Brazil – limited to small groups of researchers – –

Despite the fact that this is a spoken text, its syntactic and lexical characteristics, as well as its thematic organization, bring it close to written styles. The longest segments (comparable to sentences if it were a written text) have 42, 34 and 32 words, and the shortest ones 15, 10 and 5. Except for a brief hesitation in segment [2], namely *O – o*, phonetically [o: – o:], speech flows in orderly fashion, suggesting the speaker is used to expounding complex ideas to sophisticated audiences. Other than the simple utterance (4), all others include one or more embedded clauses. The lexicon is standard, showing only one word might be considered a bit uncommon (*auferir* 'garner') and several terms pertaining to higher education (*mestrado, doutorado, curso superior*).

The remaining three styles, *consultative, casual,* and *intimate,* are the natural range of oral interaction. Consultative style ranges between formality and intimacy, and is characterized by an intention of clarity which favors everyday vocabulary, relatively monitored pronunciation and syntax, absence of technical terms or neologisms, and few, if any, slang terms or swear words. Syntax eschews complex constructions with multiple embedded sentences to avoid overloading the interlocutors' memory, thus contributing to intelligibility. These features are apparent in the following segment of a conversation about literature in which there is a clear intention to favor exchange of information:

A: [1] *Porque eu sempre fui muito relaxado para correspondência – – [2] ele não – ele era muito correto – – [3] mas eu tenho uma carta dele muito importante – [4] em que ele desenvolve – [5] em tom epistolar – [6] aquelas mesmas idéias que ele tratou naquela conferência – – [7] que você deve conhecer – – [8] e se não conhece é urgente que conheça – – [9] porque toda a explicação da experiência lingüística dele está lá – sabe?*
B: *sim – sim – eu conheço – – inclusive há poucos dias eu li outra vez para um trabalho que eu estou escrevendo – – ele deve ter sido um sujeito excepcional – –*
A: *aaah – fabuloso – – uma presença que a gente via que era um homem fora do comum – –* (Conversation in Belo Horizonte, 1985. Author's files)

A: [1] Because I have always been too lazy about my correspondence – – [2] he wasn't – he was very correct – – [3] but I have a very important letter from him – [4] in which he develops – [5] in an epistolary tone – [6] those same ideas which he dealt with in that lecture – – [7] which you must know – – [8] and if you don't it's urgent that you get to know it – – [9] because the whole explanation of his linguistic experience is there – you know?
B: yes – yes – I know it – – just a few days ago I read it again for a paper I'm writing – – he must have been an exceptional fellow – –
A: aaah – fabulous – – a presence that you could see he was a man out of the ordinary – –

Although ideas are developed sequentially, there is a sense of improvisation that is absent in the preceding formal radio interview. The utterance begins with a subordinating conjunction ([1] *porque*) unconnected to any preceding matrix clause, just as *mas* [3] seems to function as a milder attention-getter; the short pauses at the beginning of [4], [5], and [6], and particularly the intercalated sentence [8] (*e se não conhece é urgente que conheça*) add to the impression that the utterance is unplanned, as is the last segment, with its anacoluthon° (*uma presença que a gente via que era um homem*).

Interactions in casual or intimate styles frequently favor phatic° communication, promoting a relaxed atmosphere and encouraging banter and humor, as in the following fragment of dialog among three people, introductory to a joke-telling event:

A: *conta uma piada aí – aquela que uma vez você me contou – –*
B: *qual?* [laughter] – –
A: *uma da mamãe – eu não sei ela até hoje – mas eu achei – só o que eu ouvi – cê estava contando para as outras pessoas –* [laughter] *você contou só eu que ouvi – mas achei espetacular –* [laughter] *mas é super-forte também – dessas – –*
C: *mas as piadas dele são de indecentes para cima – –*
A: *ou para baixo* [laughter] – – (Conversation in São Paulo, 1991. Author's archives.)

A: tell a joke – that one you told me once – –
B: which one? [laughter] – –
A: the one about mom – I still don't know it, even today – but I thought – only what I heard – you were telling it to other people – [laughter] you told [it] only I heard – but I loved it – [laughter] but it's too strong too – one of those – –
C: but his jokes are indecent or worse – –
A: or below [laughter] – –

Occurrence of *ela* as direct object (*não sei ela*), clipped phrases (*mas eu achei – só o que eu ouvi, só eu que ouvi*), and information added through coordination (*mas . . . mas . . . mas . . .*) suggest absence of monitoring or planning in a context in which all participants improvise as they go along.

Registers° have been characterized by sociolinguists as "sets of language items associated with discrete occupational or social groups" (Wardhaugh 2002:51). A book like the present one, for example, contains many items from the register of language specialists, which uses a certain vocabulary and a certain argumentation style as a metalanguage for talking about language. In the following text, however, a linguist uses another register combining slang terms and soccer jargon to describe his team's poor performance:

*Os caras fizeram um puta papelão – – o goleiro engoliu um puta frango – o B tentou driblar e acabou pisando na bola – o C tentou uma bicicleta e não conseguiu – o D cobrou mal aquele pênalti – – levaram cinco cartões amarelos e um vermelho – teve erros de passe até não poder mais – só podia acabar do jeito que acabou – – um puta papelão –* (*From a conversation on a soccer game.* (Players' names have been replaced by capitals B, C, D. Author's files.)

The guys were such a damn fiasco – the goalkeeper failed to stop such a damn easy ball – B tried to dribble and ended up stepping on the ball – C tried a bicycle kick but didn't manage it – D did poorly on that penalty shot – they got five yellow cards and a red one – they made made all sorts of mistakes in passing – it could only end up the way it did – a damn fiasco –

Soccer jargon terms include *driblar* 'dribble'; *bicicleta* (lit. 'bicycle'), a move in which a player, with his back to the goal, does a somersault and kicks the ball backward over his head; *engolir frango* (lit. 'to swallow a chicken') describes a goalkeeper's letting an easily defensible ball into the goal; *cobrar pênalti* is to make a direct kick for goal, after a foul; *levar cartão* is to be reprimanded by the referee (by being shown a yellow card) or to be expelled from the field (a red card). Terms like *cara* 'guy' and *papelão* 'fiasco,' or the intensifier *puta* 'big' (from *puta* 'whore;' see section 8.7) are not limited to sports talk, or to any other register for that matter, but rather fall into the generic and somewhat vague category of slang. This is a widely shared non-standard colloquial register that includes many terms originally from the speech of low socioeconomic groups and other marginalized communities.

## 8.4     Forms of address

A different kind of variation concerns pronouns and other forms which speakers must choose from to address each other. It is customary to analyze these choices in terms of a framework proposed by Brown and Gilman (1960), based on two parameters, namely power and solidarity. This framework follows an informal/formal binary contrast represented as T/V, where T stands for the informal pronoun (Fr *tu*, Sp *tú*, Ger *du*, It *tu*) and V for the formal pronoun (Fr *vous*, Sp *usted*, Ger *Sie*, It *Lei*). Generally speaking, relationships based on power entitle the more powerful interlocutor to receive V and to use either T (thus showing power) or V (implying solidarity); the less powerful interlocutor, however, has no such choice and must use V in addressing the more powerful one. In a relationship based on solidarity, the interlocutors use either T or V reciprocally. In Portuguese – and particularly in EP – several other factors intervene to make the choice of a form of address particularly complex.

It will be useful to review the development of the address system. The original pronouns of address inherited by the Romance languages from Latin included two second person forms, namely *tu* ( < Lat TU) for a single addressee and *vós* (Lat VOS) for either a plural addressee or a single addressee entitled to special courtesy. A traditional explanation is that the latter practice developed after the division of the Roman Empire (395 AD) into a Western Empire and an Eastern Empire: use of *vos* was a deferential way to acknowledge that addressing one of the two emperors was equivalent to addressing both of them.

While the criteria of power and solidarity are applicable, not all choices are binary like Fr *tu/vous* or Sp *tú/usted*. EP in particular seems to operate along a rather nuanced gradient from informal to formal. In the singular the informal mode goes from intimate *tu* to a set of informal but non-intimate forms of address in the third person; in all, we can recognize several levels of increasing formality, namely (a) *tu*, (b) third person verb with no pronoun, (c) third person verb with the interlocutor's name preceded by a definite article, and (d) third person verb with definite article + title + noun, as exemplified in 2a–2d. An additional level is represented in 2e, showing the extremely deferential *Vossa Excelência* 'your excellency'; still in use in the 1970s it now seems to be increasingly rare, at least in major urban areas such as Lisbon.

(2)    a. *Tu vais sair?*
          'Are you leaving?'
       b. *Vai sair?*
          'Are you leaving?'
       c. *O João vai sair?*
          'Are you leaving, João?'
       d. *O Sr. João vai sair?*
          'Are you leaving, Mr. João?'
       e. *Será como Vossa Excelência quiser.*
          'It will be as your excellency may wish.'

In EP reciprocal *tu* is reserved for close friends, siblings, same-generation relatives, and, more recently (though not universally), parents. On the other hand, the pronoun *você* – to the surprise of those familiar with its informal connotation in BP – conveys more deference.

Although a large-scale study of the distribution of address forms in EP has yet to be carried out, available data and informal inquiries suggest that educated middle-class Lisbon children and teenagers nowadays are likely to be on a reciprocal *tu* basis with their parents. Some of the latter, however, report using *você* in the traditional manner when addressing their own parents (Hammer Müller 1984:158), who in turn call them *tu*. Thus the trend seems to be for the new generations to use intimate *tu* with their parents, instead of the more formal *você*. A father in his late forties, who insisted he would never dream of calling his own parents anything other than *você*, expressed resignation about this trend: "Times have changed, you have to accept the new ways." Some grandparents who are called *você* by their adult children, however, do not seem to mind being called *tu* by their grandchildren.

Things are actually more complex than the above examples suggest. For many EP speakers, calling someone *você* actually implies not using this pronoun at all, but rather what might be called "zero pronoun address" as in 2b, where a third person verb form is used without an overt subject pronoun. This is the case in 3a, a perfectly normal question in EP which bypasses the issue of having to choose among *você*, *o senhor*, or *article + noun*. In BP, however, 3a could easily be interpreted as a question about a third party, for which reason the quesion would likely be worded as in one of the choices shown in 3b. This is a question of pragmatics: either construction is grammatically possible in either variety, but whereas the pattern in 3a is commonly used in EP, which favors null subjects, in BP the choice falls on the pattern in 3b, with an overt subject.

(3)    a. EP *É brasileiro?*
          'Are you Brazilian?'
       b. BP *O senhor/você é brasileiro?*
          'Are you Brazilian?'

A widespread neutral (that is, neither formal nor intimate) form of address in EP consists in using a noun phrase made up of a definite article combined with the interlocutor's name, as in 2c and 4a. Speakers of BP tend to interpret this construction as referring to a third party, which may lead to non-sequitur replies, as in the dialogue in 4b:

(4)    a. EP A – *A Fernanda aceita vinho?*
          'Will you have some wine, Fernanda?' (lit. 'Does Fernanda accept wine?')
          EP B – *Aceito, muito obrigada.*
          'Yes, thank you.'
       b. EP A – *O Milton pensa assistir ao congresso?*
          'Does Milton [the interlocutor] intend to attend the congress?'
          BP B – *Não sei, vamos ter que perguntar para ele.*
          'I don't know, we'll have to ask him.'

In fact, this construction is simply an extension of the generic construction *article + noun* which has coined the lexicalized° deferential forms *o senhor/a senhora*. This is the usual option in formal contacts between adult strangers, as when asking for information at an office, or dealing with a bank, a travel company, and so on. Other stereotyped formulae include *o doutor/a doutora,* literally 'the doctor,' a courtesy title given to anyone who holds, or seems to hold, a university degree. *O amigo,* literally 'the friend,' helps to establish a relationship of solidarity between men. *A menina,* lit. 'the girl,' is a courteous way of addressing a young woman.

Even within the same setting, such as a university environment, usage varies. While some professors prefer to address their students as *tu,* others feel more comfortable with the more deferential *você.* Students, in turn, may address a professor, in order of increasing deference, as *o professor (a professora), o senhor professor (a senhora professora), o senhor professor doutor (a senhora professora doutora).* Due to reduction or elimination of unstressed vowels in EP (2.3), these formulae are conveniently reduced to a brief whisper: [usjo$^r$pfso$^r$], [usjo$^r$pfso$^r$dto$^r$].

Though non-intimate, *você* is courteous enough to be used with people one calls by name, as in example 5, from a call-in radio program (Lisbon, 2000):

(5)    EP *Manuel, então você acha que . . .*
        'Manuel, so you think that . . .'

In addressing two or more persons, the contrast between *tu, você*, and the other third person choices is neutralized. Although *os senhores* is appropriate in formal address, zero pronoun with a third person plural verb form constitutes a less formal alternative. In this case, corroborating evidence of a reorganization of the pronoun system (Tláskal 1981:39–41), the possessive used is *vosso/a*, as in 6a, said by a university official greeting congress participants (Évora, 2000), or in 6b, said by a man addressing a visiting couple:

(6)    a. EP *Eu queria aproveitar o vosso tempo para cumprimentar os participantes do congresso.*
          'I'd like to take advantage of your time to greet the participants in this congress.'
       b. EP *Onde deixaram o vosso carro?*
          (Cf. BP *Onde vocês deixaram o carro?*)
          'Where did you leave your car?'

In BP the choice is simpler, involving an informal mode with *você* (or, in a few regions, *tu*) and a formal mode that requires *o senhor/a senhora* combined with a third person verb form. Address pronouns also have their corresponding object pronouns and possessives, but selection of these elements shows some variation as well. As in EP, a basic principle in this choice is the tension between the power differential that separates interlocutors and the degree of solidarity that brings them together. In a hierarchical relationship, in BP a superior may call a subordinate *você* and expect to be called *o senhor/a senhora*. Actually, in some hierarchies, like the military, this practice is spelled out by regulations. In the Brazilian military subordinates address their superiors as *o senhor/a senhora* while receiving *você*. In the Portuguese military, in contrast, subordinates address their superiors with a third person formula made up of a definite article and a possessive followed by a rank: BP *O senhor me chamou, capitão?* EP *O meu capitão chamou-me?* 'Did you call me, Captain?'

There may be reasons for a speaker of BP to choose to address a subordinate as *o senhor/a senhora*: to increase the distance (that is, to decrease solidarity) between them, or to show a degree of deference (to an employee's age, for example, implying greater solidarity), or as a differentiating factor, as when a business owner/director gives *o senhor* to a mid-level manager or staff professional such as a senior accountant, while addressing the clerks and secretaries as *você*. If differences of social standing are not great, a superior may initiate reciprocal *você* with subordinates, but a situation in which a superior received *você* while calling subordinates *o senhor/a senhora* would be rather unusual, if possible at all.

Substitution of *você* for *tu* in BP seems to date from the second half of the nineteenth century. It is far from complete, for *tu* is still used in the two southernmost states of Santa Catarina and Rio Grande do Sul, in areas of the north and the northeast, and, due to massive migration from the latter area, it is heard in urban areas such as the cities of São Paulo and Rio. The recessive status of *tu* is underscored by the fact that it alternates with *você* and is often used with third-person verb forms, as in 7a–7b.

(7)      a. BP *Onde é que tu vai* [for *vais*] *agora*?
          'Where are you going now?'
      b. BP *Tu não deve* [for *deves*] *fazer assim que o gerente dana com você* [ko'se].
          'You shouldn't do that or the manager will get mad at you.'

As mentioned earlier (7.3.2.3) clitics and possessives associated with *tu* have continued to be used with *você*. Far from being the "pronoun mixture" purists moan about, this usage corroborates two important points about BP. First, since BP favors using overt subjects, the marked choice for direct address is between formal *o senhor/a senhora* and informal *você*. Beyond that, it is immaterial which clitics are used, provided deference is overtly marked when necessary. For some speakers (Azevedo 1981b), *você* combined with *te/teu* connotes more intimacy than if *o/a/seu/sua* are used instead, but other speakers hardly ever use *o/a* and make no distinction, insofar as intimacy is concerned, between *te/teu* and *seu*. For such speakers *seu/teu* alternate if *você* is chosen, and if *o senhor* is chosen, deference may be indicated by using the possessive construction *do senhor/da senhora* (8a–b), or by combining *seu* and *o senhor/senhora* (8c):

(8)      a. BP *Por favor, o ticket do senhor, por gentileza*?
          'If you please, may I have your ticket, sir?'
      b. BP *Agora ele vai trazer o* [carro] *da senhora.*
          'He's now bringing your car, ma'm.'
      c. BP *O seu passaporte, por gentileza? Obrigado. O senhor faz favor de aguardar um instante*?
          'Your passport, please? Thank you. Would you please wait a minute?'

The rules governing forms of address in BP seem to be in a state of transition, but the general trend is clearly an increase in the use of *você*. Regarding the use of address forms in the family circle, for example, the general picture is as follows. Until the 1960s, approximately, the general norm was that children and youngsters would use *o senhor/a senhora* in addressing their parents, grandparents, uncles, and aunts, who in turn would call them *você*. At primary school students called teachers *o senhor/a senhora* and were called *você* (being called *o senhor/a senhora* spelled trouble). In secondary school and beyond students continued to call teachers *o senhor/a senhora* and received the same treatment, although some teachers used non-reciprocal *você*.

The trend to use reciprocal *você* in the family circle in BP seems have begun among the middle class in large cities and since the 1960s it has increased at rates varying from one region to another. In a landmark study Head (1976) determined that the overall rates of reciprocal informal address (*você*) between middle-class strangers of similar social standing were about 80% in Rio de Janeiro and São Paulo, but under 50% in the cities of Salvador (state of Bahia) and Porto Alegre (state of Rio Grande do Sul, where the informal address form was *tu*). In the family circle, parents and their offspring were somewhat more likely to use intimate reciprocal *você* in the city of Rio de Janeiro (58.3%) than in the city São Paulo (50%), whereas in the interior of the state of São Paulo non-reciprocal *você* vs. *senhor/a senhora* reached 96.7% as used by children and parents, respectively.

Among strangers, unless a clear hierarchical situation or significant differences in age or socioeconomic standing are involved, the general trend seems to be reciprocal *você* as a default mode of address. Otherwise, choice between *você* and *o senhor/a senhora* hinges on a delicate combination of their relative (actual or perceived) socioeconomic standing, age, sex, and the context in which the interaction takes place. A fleeting exchange between adults of the same sex may begin and end with mutual *o senhor/a senhora*, but a more prolonged conversation, particularly if the interlocutors are relatively young, may quickly switch to reciprocal *você*. In certain business places (such as banks or government offices) house rules may direct employees to address customers as *o senhor/a senhora*, and in such cases the customer has a choice whereas the employee does not.

In addressing two or more people, things change somewhat. *Vós*, the historical plural counterpart of *tu*, only occurs in very formal rhetorical styles, and persons addressed individually as *tu* will be called *vocês* if addressed together, just like persons individually addressed as *você*. In all regions studied by Head (1976) the frequency of *vocês* was higher than that of *você*, showing that a significant proportion of speakers who addressed their parents or social superiors individually as *o senhor/a senhora* tended to address them collectively as *vocês*. This suggests that the plural forms *os senhores/as senhoras* are perceived as more formal (and thus more distant or less indicative of solidarity) than their singular counterparts. The possessive form of *vocês* is simply *de vocês*, although in rural areas in São Paulo and Minas Gerais *vosso* can be heard (Azevedo 1981b: 273).

Table 8.1 *Deferential forms of address*

| Abstract quality | Portuguese form | Approximate equivalent |
| --- | --- | --- |
| majesty | Vossa Majestade | Your Majesty |
| highness | Vossa Alteza | Your Highness |
| grace | Vossa Graça | Your Grace |
| excellency | Vossa Excelência | Your Excellency |
| mercy, grace | Vossa Mercê | Your Grace |
| Sanctity, Holiness | Vossa Santidade | Your Holiness |
| honor | – | Your Honor |
| lord/ladyship | Vossa Senhoria | Your Lord/Ladyship |

In early days of Portuguese choice of pronoun was not reciprocal when a social difference was involved. An upper-class person would address a social inferior as *tu* and expect to be addressed as *vós*. Upper class equals would use reciprocal *vós*, while lower-class individuals would address each other as *tu*. Around the beginning of the sixteenth century, however, deference began to be shown by combining the possessive *vossa* with a noun suggestive of an abstract quality supposedly held by the interlocutor, such as highness, grace, or majesty. The same mechanism was at work in other European societies and generated comparable expressions in English, as shown in Table 8.1.

These lexicalized forms share a mechanism of indirectness, whereby the speaker addresses a social superior indirectly by referring to the latter's supposed quality rather than to the individual. Cintra (1972) lists the forms *Vossa Alteza* and *Vossa Excelência* as originally applicable to the king alone; *Vossa Senhoria* was applicable to both the king and the high nobility, while *Vossa Mercê*, which appears in the early fourteenth century as a royal form of address, became generalized to persons of quality in the sixteenth century. Some of these forms (*majestade, alteza*) fell into disuse for lack of suitable interlocutors with the end of monarchy in Brazil (1889) and in Portugal (1910). Other forms subsist, regulated by protocol, in the rarefied glasshouse of ceremonial usage. Thus in Brazil (MRPR 2002) the President, Vice President, Ministers, Governors, Mayors, Representatives, Senators, Ambassadors, and officers with the rank of General are entitled to *Vossa Excelência,* while lesser functionaries, such as consuls, get only *Vossa Senhoria.* This latter form is used in formal parliamentary address and, either in full or abbreviated as *V. Sa.,* in business letters.

Though most speakers never have an opportunity to do so, the Roman Catholic Pope, should he be addressed in Portuguese, is entitled to *Vossa Santidade*, cardinals and bishops to *Vossa Eminência Reverendíssima* or just *Vossa Eminência*, and plain priests to a modest *Vossa Reverência,* although in practice *seu Padre* 'Mr. Priest' or *Padre Fulano* 'Father So-and-So' are more likely to be heard. Judges are formally addressed as *Meritíssimo* (abbreviated *MM.*), coined from Lat *meritissimus* 'most worthy,' which popular pronunciation converts, either by metathesis° or by some convoluted association with *meretriz* 'whore,' into the irreverent *meretríssimo* 'most meretricious.' From the Latin title *Rector Magnificus* (still used for the heads of Germanic universities) was forged *Magnífico Reitor*, used at universities in Portugal and Brazil along with the corresponding address form *Vossa Magnificência* 'Your Magnificence.' A quaintness of epistolary style is the use, before the addressee's name, of the courtesy initials *Ilmo. Sr./Ilma. Sra.*, meaning *Ilustríssimo/a Senhor/a* 'most illustrious Mr./Ms.,' or *Exmo. Sr./Exma. Sra.* for *Excelentíssimo/a Senhor/a* 'Most excellent Mr./Ms.'

Of the profusion of forms patterned after *vossa + noun* only a few have survived. A series of phonetic changes has changed the original *vossa mercê* into the deferential forms *vancê, vassuncê* or *vosmecê* (> *mecê*), which was petering out in the early twentieth century (Amaral 1920:56) and seems to lead a ghostly existence among older speakers in fast-shrinking rural environments. Hammermüller (1984:158) registers *vossemecê* in the speech of a 68-year old Portuguese informant. The true heir of *vossa mercê*, however, is *você*, which in BP is shortened, in casual pronunciation, to *ocê* [o'se] or just *cê* [se].

Names play a major role in direct address. Informal address – what is known as "first-name basis" in English-speaking societies – involves a name, though not necessarily the first or given name, without a title. Formal address, in turn, consists of combining a title (such as *senhor, doutor, professor*) with a name – again, not necessarily the last or family name. A man named *José Ferreira Antunes* may be known as *José* to his family but as either *José*, *Ferreira*, or *Antunes* by his friends. In fact, friends made under some circumstances – at school, for example – may call him *José*, while others may call him *Antunes* or *Ferreira,* or the other way around. Perhaps when he started his military service his company sergeant put down *Ferreira* or *Antunes* to distinguish him from the other recruits named *José*, which is a rather frequent name. Consequently those who served with him may remember him as such and thus address him if they run into him years later. Another recruit named Nelson Silva, on the other hand, might be known as *Nelson* (to distinguish him from the other Silvas in his company). If those men decided to have a career in the army they might become *Cadete Ferreira* or *Cadete Nelson*, and eventually get to be *Coronel Ferreira* or *General Nelson*. If *José Ferreira Antunes* goes into medicine, he will be eventually addressed as *Doutor José* or *Doutor Ferreira*, or *Doutor Antunes*, depending largely on his choice. But on seeing his full name on his shingle or call card, in Brazil people would tend to call him *Doutor José* unless told otherwise. If Nelson Silva does not get a university degree, he will likely be given the courtesy title of *senhor*, which in BP is colloquially shortened to *seu*, thus combining courtesy with a touch of informality, as in example 9:

(9)     a. BP *Seu Nelson, o senhor viu se tem correio pra mim?*
           'Mr. Nelson, have you seen if there's mail for me?' [Female
           condominium owner addressing the janitor]

For women, choices are slightly different. A young woman named *Beatriz Oliveira* will be informallly called *Beatriz*, but when she reaches adult age she will be formally referred to and addressed as *Dona Beatriz* (*Dona Bia* or *Dona Biá* would be intimate but respectful possibilities, particularly in small towns, if she uses a nickname at all). If she is a lawyer, a physician, or a dentist, she will be called and referred to as *Doutora Beatriz*, and if she is a teacher or a professor she will be known as *Doutora/Professora Beatriz* rather than *Doutora/Professora Oliveira*. In recent years, referring to professional women by their last name has become common in some professional journals.

*Dom,* the masculine counterpart of *Dona*, is only used with the first name of Roman Catholic bishops or cardinals (*Dom Hélder, Dom Francisco*) or in referring to former Portuguese kings (*Dom João*) or Brazilian emperors (*Dom Pedro*), although the habit persists in referring to would-be nobility in the hothouse context of social columns. *Senhorita,* once widespread, has fallen into disuse as a title (*Senhorita Maria*), although it is heard in Brazil in contexts where a server–client relationship is involved, as in *A senhorita deseja mais chá?* 'Would you like more tea, miss?' (cf. EP *a menina*, above).

As with pronouns of address, the use of names and titles in EP is more fine-grained than in BP. While both varieties use *dona* + *first name* to address a woman, and in fact this is the only possibility in BP, in EP it used to be that some thirty years ago this form of address, while appropriate for talking to the concierge, was not enough for addressing a middle- or upper-middle-class woman, who would expect to be called *a senhora dona Francisca*, although the latter construction seems to be considered too formal nowadays.

Whereas in BP only one title is used, alone or in combination with a name in direct address (*Senhor/Seu José, Dona Maria, Doutora Joana, Professor Cardoso*), in EP social convention requires combining titles. Thus, whereas *o senhor/a senhora* is the basic formal form, in addressing someone who has a title such as *doutor/doutora* one would say *o senhor doutor/a senhora doutora*, often clipped to *sotor* [stoɾ] or *sotora* [stoɾɐ], respectively. Professional titles or titles indicative of rank are also combined with *senhor/senhora*, and so an engineer is likely to be referred to and addressed as *o senhor engenheiro*, a civil service official as *a senhora directora*, and a military officer *o senhor coronel*, as in example 10.

(10)     a. EP *Se o senhor doutor quiser, pode-se fazer.*
             'If you want it, sir, it can be done.'
         b. EP *O senhor doutor tem reserva?*
             'Do you have a reservation, sir?'
         c. EP *O senhor director ainda não chegou.*
             'The director has not arrived yet.'
         d. EP *Está lá o senhor engenheiro?*
             'Is the engineer there?'

Traditionally, a university instructor who has a doctorate (not all do, given the practice of obtaining it after several years in the profession) would be addressed as *o senhor professor doutor* or *a senhora professora doutora* and referred to as *o senhor professor doutor Cintra* or *a senhora professora doutora Silva*. According to informants from universities in Lisbon and elsewhere, this practice seems to be moving toward a more relaxed *senhor professor/senhora professora* – which, however, would be considered rather formal in BP. Some nuances are reflected in writing: whereas in EP anyone with a university degree (*licenciatura*) receives the courtesy title of *doutor/doutora*, in writing that would appear as *Dr./Dr.ª*, the full form being reserved for those having an actual doctorate. Thus the hierarchy is clearly displayed on name tags on office doors: whereas *Prof.ª Dr.ª Maria Silva* only has the basic *licenciatura*, *Prof.ª Doutora Teresa Silva* has a Ph.D.-level degree.

Such linguistic changes may be the result of social changes that have taken place after the revolution that put an end to the dictatorial regime (1928–1974). Soon after the revolution, there was a noticeable increase in *tuteio* – calling one another *tu* – and although the initial enthusiasm for it has dwindled, some changes are apparent. As mentioned above, among the middle class, whereas in the past parents called their children *tu* and received *você* while siblings used reciprocal *tu,* nowadays reciprocal *tu* is used in both cases, suggesting the relationship between parents and their children has shifted away from a referent of power to one of solidarity (for an updated analysis, see Oliveira, forthcoming). Household servants, on the other hand, continue to address their employers as *o/a senhor/a,* but whereas in the past they used to be called *você,* in some families they are now called *tu,* which again suggests a shift (albeit a unilateral one) toward solidarity. The resulting scene, far from uniform, has yet to be analyzed in detail, as it will probably be as sociolinguistic studies develop in Portugal (Castro 2001:24). At any rate, even informal inquiries suggest there is a great deal of diversity in the contacts outside the circle of family or intimate friends. A middle-aged female professor from Lisbon commented that "nowadays it is difficult to know how to address people, particularly in restaurants and public services." This comment echoed remarkably a remark by a female Brazilian informant in her early fifties:

This matter of forms of address is so confusing nowadays, and the problem has to do with *o senhor/a senhora*. Some of my son's friends call me *D. Maria/a senhora*, others call me *Maria/a senhora*. His girl friend calls me *Maria/você*. He has always called me *você*, but I still say *o senhor/a senhora* to my parents and my uncles and aunts. I don't see how a foreigner can learn to speak in such a confusion.

## 8.5     Influence from other languages

An often polemicized issue involving variation concerns the use of words and phrases borrowed from other languages. Some languages, like English, are quite open to wholesale admission of foreign terms, which are quickly adapted to its phonological patterns, to the point of becoming unrecognizable to the ears of speakers of the donor languages. The beneficial non-existence of regulatory agencies, such as a language academy, allows this process to occur naturally and as a constant source of expressive enrichment for the lexicon.

While speakers of Portuguese seem quite willing to adopt loan words and loan expressions, they have to contend with organized resistance from institutions or individuals who see such borrowing as a deleterious process. This attitude flies in the face of the fact that, as seen in Chapter 5, borrowing has promoted language growth since the time when speakers of Germanic dialects or Arabic started settling in the Iberian Peninsula. French influence, substantial since the early days of Portugal's history, contributed loan words, particularly in the nineteenth century, under the influence of developments in France in areas of literature, social sciences, and experimental science.

French presence was welcome in Brazil, where in 1816 King John VI sponsored the arrival of a group of artists historically known as the *Missão Francesa* 'French Mission,' who founded the Academia de Belas-Artes 'Academy of Fine Arts' in Rio de Janeiro, which for decades set norms for the plastic arts. At the turn of the twentieth century, when French impregnated Brazilian social life (Needell 1987; Azevedo 2003:96–99), dozens of French terms were glibly used in the press and other publications. Lists of gallicisms to be avoided were included in grammars; dictionaries were published (such as Goes 1940); and substitute terms were coined, and although a number of French loan words have been permanently incorporated into the lexicon, most eventually faded into oblivion. Through the first half of the twentieth century French culture was avidly sought after and it left its mark on the University of São Paulo, created in 1934, whose initial faculty included a number of French social scientists. French influence faded after the Second World War as English fast became the international language of business, science, technology, and entertainment. A cursory glance at news, business and technical magazines reveals a variety of English words and expressions that contribute, sometimes as part of larger expressions, to some perceived communication need:

| | | |
|---|---|---|
| armazenamento *on demand* | sistema *push* de vendas | sistema *pull* |
| o papel de *coach* dos líderes | *middle market* | *background* |
| *brainstorming* | bancos de *design* esportivo | *design* exclusivo |

Such loan words are invariably adapted to Brazilian pronunciation, and many items have been orthographically adjusted to Portuguese:

| | | |
|---|---|---|
| *leader > líder* | *check > checar* | *fan > fã* |
| *cartoon > cartún* | *dandy > dândi* | *roastbeef > rosbife* |
| *drink > drinque* | *bluff > blefe* | *knock out > nocaute* |

Others, however, remain in the original:

| | | | |
|---|---|---|---|
| *fanzine* | *freelancer* | *full time* | *boom* |
| *background* | *ferry/ferry boat* | *flashback* | *zoom* |

Some attempts at adapting English terms strike the eye as odd (*layout > leiaute, living > lívingue, scanner > escâner, site > sait, shopping [center] > xópin, show > xou, cheeseburger > X-burger, egg-cheeseburger > egue-X burger*), but there is no telling whether they will eventually be adopted. The point, however, is that borrowing is a perfectly normal process.

Even so, there are those who regard use of foreign terms as a threat to the language and national culture. A recent manifestation of this view has been a bill, cogently criticized by linguists (Faraco 2001), submitted to the Brazilian Congress and intended for the "protection of the Portuguese language against attacks provoked by unnecessary foreign words or expressions" (Rebelo 1999). If passed into law, this bill would make Portuguese mandatory in a variety of situations such as education, the workplace, the law, the media, labeling and reference to consumer goods and services, and advertising. With the exception of loan words already incorporated in the language, "any and every use of a word or expression in a foreign language . . . will be considered harmful to the Brazilian cultural patrimony and punishable as determined by the law" (Article 4).

Top-down approaches to language planning are not new in the Luso-Brazilian tradition. Early instances include the royal decrees (1757, 1758) mandating the use of Portuguese in all official acts and banning Indian languages from education in Brazil (7.2.2). In 1770 a decree mandated the use in schools of Antonio

José dos Reis Lobato's *Arte da Grammatica Portuguesa*, which had more than forty editions in over two hundred years (Assunção 1998, 2000). Brazilian schools are supposed to use an official grammatical terminology issued in 1959 by the Education Ministry (*Portaria* [Executive Order] 36, January 28, 1959). Since 1911, spelling reforms have periodically been the subject of government decision (Estrela 1993).

Attempts to protect a language from perceived foreign threats are usually based on a misconception of how language operates. Most instances of borrowing – as exemplified by English loan words in BP – take place at the lexical level, and very rarely affect the grammatical core that defines a language's structure. If history is any guide, there is reason to think that while some of the loan words currently in use may stay in the language, others will be short-lived and vanish without any need for official regulation. Similar recent campaigns in other countries with a tradition of linguistic protectionism, such as France, suggest that such laws, for all the hot air they generate, tend to quickly turn into dead letter.

## 8.6     Communicative strategies

Outside of elementary textbook dialogs that unfold with the precision of an error-free ping-pong match engaged in by ideal players, real conversation involves false starts, self-correction devices, reiteration, and a great deal of hemming and hawing cast in apparently meaningless phrase fragments which are actually essential to keep the interaction going. To communicate with a maximum of efficiency and a minimum of friction we resort to an arsenal of socially accepted strategies to greet, make requests, issue commands, express assent or negation, clarify, negotiate, and eventually bring the interaction to a close by indicating we have nothing to add, at which point interlocutors take leave of each other, hopefully without loss of face to anyone. Some such communicative strategies, which are the concern of the still poorly explored field of pragmatics, will be dealt with in the following sections.

### 8.6.1    Greetings

A greeting is a formula for acknowledging someone's presence or arrival and it may involve a single word (*Olá!* 'hello' or BP *Oi!* 'hi'); a set phrase (*boa tarde* 'good afternoon'); or a ritualized combination thereof. Deference usually requires acknowledging the interlocutor's identity by mentioning his or her name or title, or title and name, as the case may be. In cases (as at a restaurant or store) when the newly arrived customer's name is not known, a courtesy title (*senhor, senhora, doutor*) is used as in 11a–11b. Except in situations of power differences, greetings tend to be reciprocated at the same level of courtesy, as

in 12 and 13. In 14 we have a banter exchange of extremely formal greetings
between two academic friends, but the point is that B uses the same level of
mock formality to signal willingness to participate in the word play.

(11)    a. BP – *Boa tarde, senhor.*
        'Good afternoon, sir.' (Clerk at a store in São Paulo)
        b. EP – *Bom dia, senhora professora doutora.*
        'Good morning, (lit.) Ms. Professor Doctor (f.)' (Young professor
        greeting a senior colleague at a university in Viseu)

(12)    BP (Resident) – *Bom dia, seu Tonho. Tudo bem?*
        (Janitor) – *Bom dia, Dona Maria. Tudo jóia.*
        'Good morning, Mr. Tonho. Everything all right?'
        'Good morning, Ms. Maria. Everything ok.' (At a condominium in
        São Paulo)

(13)    BP (Woman A) – *Oi querida, tudo bem?*
        (Woman B) – *Oi meu amor, tudo. E ocê, tá boa?*
        'Hi darling, everything ok?'
        'Hi love, everything. What about you, are you ok?' (At a smart
        restaurant in São Paulo)

(14)    BP A – *Excelentíssimo professor, como vai vossa senhoria?*
        B – *Minha senhoria vai muito bem, prezado colega. E a vossa?*
        'Most honorable professor, how is your lordship?'
        'My lordship is fine, my dear colleague. What about yours?'
        (Two male professors in São Paulo, using a mock-formal style)

### 8.6.2    Requests, orders, assent, and negation

Except when exchanged in passing, greetings signal the opening of a longer
exchange. If this involves an attempt to get the other person to do something,
some sort of verbal negotiation takes place. It may be minimal in situations
involving patterned behavior, as in a fast-food place where verbal exchanges
are very brief and impersonal. In 15 the server at a bar counter uses the formula
*pois não?* ('may I help you?') to acknowlege a customer's presence and to
indicate readiness to take an order. In 16, where the customer is sitting at a
table, the exchange is likely to be somewhat longer, which justifies the reciprocal
greeting *boa tarde*, followed immediately by the question and answer, *O senhor
deseja?/Pode ser um bauru e um chopinho?* Although neither customer used the
formula *por favor* 'please,' in both cases the request was appropriately polite
by being worded as a question. Furthermore, in 16 the request is signaled by
the courtesy form *pode ser . . .?*, roughly equivalent to *what about . . .?*.

(15) BP A (Server, at counter) – *Pois não?*
B (Customer) – *Me dá uma garapa e um pastel?*
'Can I help you?'
'May I have a glass of sugar cane juice and an empanada?' (At a bar counter in São Paulo)

(16) BP A (Waiter, standing by the table) – *Boa tarde, senhor. O senhor deseja?*
B (Customer) – *Boa tarde. Pode ser um bauru e um chopinho?*
A – *Pois não, agora mesmo.*
'Good afternoon, sir. What would you like?'
'Good afternoon. What about a hot ham and tomato sandwich and a draft?'
"Sure, right away." (At a snack bar in São Paulo)

Directives, that is verbal attempts at influencing an addressee's behavior, may take various shapes, such as orders, assertions and suggestions, requests, hints, or avoidance of the directive or the issue at hand (Koike 1992:36–43). Choosing among these strategies is influenced by a variety of factors and, except in the case of direct orders (which require a degree of authority and power), involves politeness markers (Koike 1992:29). These may be set forms such as (*por favor,* BP *faz favor, por obséquio,* EP *se faz favor, por gentileza,* 'please') or constructions with *poder* or *dar,* as in 16 above or 17a–17c:

(17) a. BP *Podia me emprestar o lápis, por favor?*
'Could you lend me the pencil, please?'
b. BP *Daria para vocês chegarem às sete?*
'Could you arrive at seven?'
c. BP *Será que dava para você me emprestar cinco reais?*
'Would it be possible for you to lend me five *reais*?'

Depending on circumstances and the participants involved, the same wording may be polite or not. As Stewart (1999:170) points out, the concept of politeness refers "to the ways in which speakers use language to create, maintain, or modify interpersonal relationships." Politeness norms are closely related to the notion of *face wants* (Yule 1996:61), that is an individual's need to be free of injunctions from others (negative face) and to be accepted by others (positive face).

Since face wants are relative, the degree of politeness required at a fast-food place is considerably less than that expected at a restaurant where customer–server interaction will likely involve several exchanges over a longer period of time. In 18 there is a clear power difference, since B addresses A by a combination of title + name and *o senhor,* while being called by his name and *você* in return. A's initial question is a purely rhetorical way of announcing his presence, since he had been told to report to B's office. B's question, in turn, is a command disguised as a question (B had ordered A to write a report and now he expected to receive it). Furthermore, A apparently knew why he had been summoned, and consequently had brought the report along.

(18)     BP A – *O senhor chamou, Doutor Paulo?*
           'Did you call, Mr. Paulo?'
        B – *Ô Marcos, você aprontou aquele relatório pro* [= *para o*]
        *Banco?*
        'Marcos, have you prepared that report for the Bank?'
        A – *Ah sim, está pronto. Olha ele aqui, Doutor.*
        'Yes, it's ready. Here it is, sir.'

Politeness norms function as *face-saving acts* – more or less ritualized formulae for protecting the interlocutors' "face." In a situation where someone's job is to serve, use of polite forms such as question intonation, expressions such as *por favor*, EP *se faz favor*, or indirect requests couched as questions introduced by expressions like *Pode ser . . .?* function as face-saving acts by creating the purely linguistic fiction that one is requesting as a favor what one is entitled to on account of a business deal, or an employer–employee relationship, or the like.

### 8.6.3     Closures

Bringing a conversation to an end is signaled by indicators that precede farewell terms. Terms like *então, então é isso, então ficamos assim, pois é isso, pois então*, BP *é isso aí*, EP *pois*, indicate that a measure of agreement has been reached and are usually replied to by an echo response which prepares the ground for a farewell formula, as in the closure of a telephone conversation between two Brazilian men (19):

(19)     A – *então é isso – amanhã à noite lá em casa*
        'so that's it – tomorrow evening at our place'
      B – *certo – amanhã a gente se vê*
        'right – tomorrow we'll see each other'
      A – *e lembra – pode estacionar em frente – hem.*
        'and remember – you can park in front – huh.'
      B – *tá – pode deixar – até amanhã – um abraço –*
        'yeah – don't worry – until tomorrow – so long [lit. 'a hug'] –'
      A – *outro – até amanhã então – ciao!*
        'same to you – until tomorrow then – ciao!'
      B – *ciao – até amanhã*
        'ciao – until tomorrow.'
     (Author's files.)

While closures can be shorter or far more elaborate than this example, the exchange in example 19 includes several elements usually found in closures, to wit:

(a) an indication of intention to bring the conversation to an end (*então é isso*),
(b) a signal of agreement from the interlocutor (*certo*)
(c) a recap of the agreement reached (*amanhã à noite lá em casa, amanhã a gente se vê*)
(d) some reiteration of an important item in the conversation (*pode estacionar em frente*), usually preceded by a warning (*e lembra*) and followed by a tag (*hem* [ẽj])
(e) an exchange of farewells: *ciao* (an Italian loan word), *até amanhã, até amanhã, um abraço, outro*)

### 8.6.4 Discourse markers

The term "discourse marker" does not refer to a specific morphological category but rather serves as an umbrella label for a variety of elements that regulate the interaction between the interlocutors in a dialog by performing several pragmatic functions. They provide sequencing, request or offer feedback, indicate hesitation, signal the end or beginning of a conversation turn, and highlight the relative import of the different parts of an utterance, emphasizing certain elements and providing clues about their contribution to the message. Discourse markers are typical of oral language, and in informal styles in BP they may make up as much as 25% of the words (Marcuschi 1989:281); nevertheless, they have received little attention from traditional grammars (Silva and Macedo 1991:235).

Regarding form, discourse markers range from single words to phrasal compounds of varying degrees of lexicalization, as shown in 20 and 21:

(20)  A – *Me diga uma coisa* – **bom** – *que você é paulista eu já sei* – **mas** – *você é paulistana mesmo?*
    B – **Olha** – *sou quase / eu nasci em Jundiaí* – **né?** / *e* **aí** *eu vim pra São Paulo aos seis meses.*
    A – *Aos seis meses?* **Então** – **muito bem** – *e você sempre viveu aqui?*
    B – *Sempre.*[1]

    A – Tell me something – **well** – that you are from São Paulo I already know – **but** – are you really from the city of São Paulo?
    B – **Look** – I'm almost / I was born in – **you know?** / and **then** I came to São Paulo when I was six months old.
    A – Six months? **Then** – **all right** – and have you always lived here?
    B – Always.
    (Recorded interview, ca. 1985)

(21)     *Você sobe a rua Bahia – ela é Bahia até Contorno – **sabe como é?***
         [saku'mɛ] – *aí de Contorno em diante ela tem o nome de Carangola
         – compreende?*

You go up Bahia street – it's called Bahia as far as Contorno
(Avenue) – **you know how it is?** – **then** from Contorno on it's called
Carangola – **understand?** (Recorded interview, ca. 1985)

In the first line of example 20, the discourse markers *bom* and *mas* ensure
sequencing, by providing a brief pause that informs B that something is to
follow. In the reply, *olha* is an attention-getter, whereas *né? (< não é?)* is a
generic request for positive feedback. *Aí*, in turn, provides sequencing, in this
instance of a temporal kind, connecting the two narrated events *eu nasci em
Jundiaí* and *eu vim para São Paulo.* In the next line, *então* and *muito bem*
are basically place holders, announcing that A has something to add, which
A in fact does by asking another question (*e você sempre viveu aqui?*). In 21
the questions *sabe como é?* [saku'mɛ] and *compreende?* are purely rhetorical
requests for feedback which need not be more elaborate than a one-syllable
discourse marker such as *sei,* or even a nod with the head, since the speaker is
not really requesting a reply but only making sure he has the listener's attention.

Prosodic discourse markers (Travaglia 1999:76–130) are formed by certain
variations in intonation or pitch or by pauses interpreted as signalling hesitation. Although there is no standardized way of representing prosodic discourse
markers in writing, linguists tend to use combinations of larger type and boldface to suggest higher pitch, repeated letters to show vowel length, hyphens
for emphatic syllabification and short pauses, and slashes for longer pauses, as
in 22:

(22)     BP . . . *bom / **E-**la disse que queria . . . mas **NÓS** acabamos /
         achando / bom / **RE-**solvendo que não **DA**va **MEEESMO** para a
         gente vir / de **JEI-**to nenhum, sabe?*

         . . . well / she said she wanted – but we ended up / thinking / it was
         ok / decided there was no way we could come / no way, you know?
         (Recorded interview, ca. 1985)

Discourse markers perform the crucial phatic function of creating or strength-
ening links between the participants in a conversation. A passage like the following, if delivered orally as written, might be perceived as a short lecture, in
which the speaker gives information without interacting with his listeners.

(BP) *É a festa da imagem milagrosa, o Bom Jesus. O pessoal vem nessa ocasião cumprir
promessa, visitar, dar esmola aos pobres. Nessa ocasião vêm muitos pobres de fora para
aqui, para ganhar esmola. Ou se aproveita para fazer compras. É uma boa época de
fazer compras, porque essa rua aqui, daqui até lá em baixo, fica cheia de comerciantes,
vem muita gente do Rio, São Paulo, Belo Horizonte, diversos lugares, vem muita gente.*

It is the festival of the miraculous image, the Holy Jesus. At that time people come to keep their promises, to visit, to give alms to the poor. At that time many poor people come here from other places, to get their alms. Or then they just go shopping. It's a good time to go shopping, because this street, from here all the way down there, is full of tradesmen, many people come from Rio, São Paulo, Belo Horizonte, from several places, many people come here.

This passage, however, is an edited version of a recording in which a man explains the significance of a holy feast and pilgrimage in honor of the image of Christ named *Bom Jesus*. A transcription of the recording, with hyphens and slashes indicating short and long pauses respectively, is given in the following passage:

*É – é – é festa da imagem milagrosa – o Bom Jesus – **né?** / que é a imagem milagrosa / **e então** – o pessoal vem nessa ocasião cumprir promessa – **né?** / visitar – dar esmola aos pobres – nessa ocasião vêm muito pobre de fora pra aqui pra ganhar esmola – e vêm – ou se aproveita pra – fazer compras – **né?** / é uma boa época de fazer compra porque essa rua – aqui / daqui até lá em baixo – fica cheia de comerciantes – **né?** / vem muita gente do Rio – São Paulo – Belo Horizonte – diversos lugares – vem muita gente –* (Recording in Congonhas do Campo, state of Minas Gerais, ca. 1991. Author's archive)

It's – it's – it's the festival of the miraculous image – the Holy Jesus – **you know?** / which is the miraculous image – **and so** / people come on that occasion to pay their vows – **you know?** / to visit / to give alms to the poor – on that occasion many poor people come from other places to get alms – and they come – or one just – goes shopping / **you know?** / it's a good time to go shopping because you see this street – here – from here all the way down there – it gets crowded with merchants – **you know?** / lots of people come from Rio – São Paulo – Belo Horizonte – several places – lots of people come –

In this brief passage there are five discourse markers, strategically distributed to create four opportunities for asking the rhetorical question *né?* (< *não é?*) and one for the rejoinder *e então*, thus providing five occasions for addressing the listener and thus creating the impression that what was actually a description – one might say a miniclass – was a dialog.

As interlocutors take turns in the roles of speaker and listener during a conversation, discourse markers perform a variety of functions. Listener-produced discourse markers tend to be brief and typically provide positive feedback in the form of agreement or encouraging the speaker to go on talking (23), or negative feedback in the form of disagreement (24):

(23) a. BP A – *eu disse para ele que isso não era possível*
         'I told him that wasn't possible'
    B – *claro* –
        'sure'
    A – *porque não estava previsto no orçamento*
        'because it was not included in the budget'

B – é –
'yeah'
A – *e então não tinha jeito mesmo.*
'and so there was really no way.'

b.  BP A – *sabe, eu queria deixar para entregar semana que vem –*
'you know, I wanted to put off submitting [my paper]
next week'
B – *sim mas –*
'yes but'
A – *por que esta não vai dar tempo mesmo sabe?*
'because this [week] there won't be any time you
know?'

Speaker-generated discourse markers can be more abundant, since the speaker holds the floor, and perform a variety of functions, e.g. statement openers (24), attention-getters (25), reiterators (26).

(24)    BP a. A – *Você entende de computador?*
'Do you know about computers?'
B – *Muito não, **sabe como é** [saku'mε], mas dá para quebrar o galho, **né?***
'Not much, you know how it is, but enough to get by, you know?'
BP b. A – *Quando é que você me entrega?*
'when will you return [it]?'
B – ***Bom**, lá por quarta ou quinta?*
'Well, around Wednesday or Thursday?'

(25)    A – *Você quer alguma coisa de lá?*
'Do you want something from there?'
B – ***Olha**, tem um livro que eu estou precisando dele.*
'Look, there's a book I need'

(26)    . . . *eu tenho que entregar o trabalho que eu ainda nem comecei – **e tem mais** – ainda nem não fiz as malas – sabe? – de modo que não vai dar para ir na tua festa não – sinto muito –*

'I need to hand in the paper which I haven't even started – and there's more – I haven't even packed – you know? – and so I won't be able to come to your party – I'm sorry.'

Interrogative discourse markers often have the phatic function (Urbano 1999) of eliciting feedback, agreement, or support, or simply ensuring the listener's attention, as in (27):

Table 8.2 *Discourse markers*

| Simple | Compound | Phrase/Sentence |
|---|---|---|
| *ah* 'ah' | *sim mas* 'yes but' | *acontece que* 'what happens is' |
| *mas* 'but' | *mas isso* 'but that' | *o problema é que* 'the problem is that' |
| *claro* 'of course' | *pois então* 'well then' | BP *sabe como é* [saku'mɛ] 'you know what it's like' |
| *agora* 'now' | *por exemplo* 'for example' | *vamos dizer* 'let's say' |
| *então* 'then, so' | *ou seja* 'in other words' | *vamos ver* 'let's see' |
| *assim* 'so' | *quer dizer* 'that is' | *sabe? não sabe?* 'you know? don't you know?' |
| *bom/bem* 'well' | EP *pois pois* 'so' | EP *percebe?* 'you get it?' |
| *olha/olhe* 'look' | | BP *(es)tá bom mas* 'all right but' |
| *agora* 'now' | | *é isso* 'that's it' |
| | | BP *não sabe não?* 'don't you know?' |

(27)    *eu – eu tenho tomado muito remédio – **ainda mais** quando eu tomo
        remédio não tomo nada de álcool – **não é?** – porque senão perde o
        efeito – **não é então?** – então eu – **olha** – eu fiquei duas semanas sem
        tomar nada nada – **sabe como é?** – tomei umas injeções de – dum
        antibiótico e –*

   'I – I have been taking a lot of medicine – **even so** when I take
   medicine I don't drink any alcohol – **isn't it?** – because otherwise it
   doesn't work – **isn't that so?** – so I – **look** – I went for two weeks
   without taking anything – **you know how it is?** – I took some
   injections of – of an antibiotic and –'

As these examples reveal, the same discourse marker can perform different
functions, as listed in Table 8.2.

## 8.7    Profane language: Swearing and insults

The last text transcribed in section 8.3 includes the intensifier *puta* 'damn,'
sometimes thinly disguised as *puxa*, derived from the vernacular noun *puta*
'whore.' In recent decades, this and many other off-color terms have become
more frequent in public discourse – in conversation as well as in print and on
television and radio – following what seems to be a common trend in the western
world (Hughes 1998:188). Eschewed by some, and used by many, profanity,
in all of its forms, pervades the language, and consequently serious learners,
whether or not they intend to use it, would be well advised to learn to navigate
its murky waters.

   Profanity includes off-color words used as expletives or intensifiers, often
intended to vent anger or to signal annoyance, impatience, or even enthusiasm,

again depending on one's frame of mind and context, as in 28a–28d. Some off-color words do double duty, e.g. the expletive *porra*, which from its former meaning of 'cudgel, nightstick' (which it still has in Spanish) has acquired the slang meaning of 'sperm' and is otherwise used as an emphasizer, as in 28c and 28d. Particularly, though not only among men, *porra* is widely used (often reduced to *pô*, or, slightly diphthongized, *pôa* [poɐ]), as a marker of masculine "tough talk," though overuse tends to make it no stronger than *damn* or *blooming,* as in the following passage from a conversation between two Brazilian friends (28e):

(28)  a. Merda! *Esse gravador está quebrado!*
           'Shit! This tape-recorder is broken!'
      b. *Comprei uma coleção de CD* do caralho!
           'I've bought a damn good [lit. 'of the prick'] CD collection.'
      c. *Essa* porra *de laptop quebrou de novo!*
           'This shitty laptop broke down again!'
      d. *Ele não fez* porra *nenhuma.*
           'He didn't do shit.'
      e. Pô, *cê ainda tá escrevinhando essa* porra *desse livro? E aquela* porra *do nosso projeto, como é que fica?* Pôa, *nêgo, vê se acaba com essa* porra *logo. Cê já está nisso tem não sei quanto tempo,* porra!¹

           'Dammit, you're still scribbling that damn book? And what about our damn project, what's gonna become of it? Dammit man, see you finish that damn thing fast. You've been at it I don't know how long, damn it!'

The pattern *preposition + NP* in 28b–28c, in which NP is a swear noun, is also very productive to generate insults directed against persons or institutions (29a–29b):

(29)  a. *Mas o que esse* filho da puta *quer de mim a essa hora?*
           'But what does this son of a bitch want from me at this hour?'
      b. *Esse governo* do cacete *vai foder o país de uma vez.*
           'This damn government [lit. 'government of the prick'] is going to fuck up the country once and for all.'

Taboo language arises from restrictions a community imposes on certain words or expressions, usually related to topics deemed inappropriate in certain conversational contexts. A major difference between English and Portuguese-speaking societies has to do with blasphemy, which involves religious terms and concepts. In Anglo-Saxon tradition, using names such as God, Devil, or Hell used to be – and in certain circles still is – considered blasphemous, whereas in Portuguese (and other Romance languages) uttering the equivalent terms is often regarded as pious. Thus, whereas "My God!," "Jesus Christ!," or "Holy Mary!" may be frowned upon, *Meu Deus!*, *Jesus!*, *Minha Nossa Senhora!* are routinely uttered by the most devout church-goers. Likewise, whereas asking "What the devil is that?" may be regarded in poor taste, the question *Que diabo é isso?*, while colloquial, will hardly raise an eyebrow, and if a sweet old lady says her granddaughter *é uma menina levada do diabo* (lit. 'is a girl carried by the devil') she probably means simply the young woman is a bit too lively, but by no means possessed.

As a word acquires a profane meaning, it is usually removed, partially or totally, from its former use. Thus in BP the word *veado* 'deer' is a slang (and derogatory) term for 'homosexual' and consequently is often replaced by *cervo* 'deer' (Taylor 1963:635), though it persists in compounds like *veado-campeiro* 'pampas deer' or *veado-galheiro* 'marsh deer.' Some fifty years ago, *bicha* meant a line of people, but as it became a derogatory term for 'homosexual' in Brazil it was replaced by *fila*. The word *boceta*, which originally meant 'a small box' (as in *boceta de rapé* 'snuff box') and was still used with that meaning (which it retains in EP) in Brazilian literary works at the turn of the twentieth century, has become a coarse term for 'vagina,' and consequently it has been dropped in its original meaning, and the expression *boceta de Pandora* 'Pandora's box' was replaced by *caixa de Pandora*. *Porra*, already mentioned, retains its original meaning in derived nouns like *porrada* 'a blow with a stick; a punch' or *porrete* 'a cudgel.' Likewise, while *pau* 'stick, any piece of wood' and *cacete* 'stick, cudgel' have become generic slang terms for 'penis,' the derived forms *paulada* and *cacetada* are still used to mean 'a blow with a stick.'

As we move from one variety of Portuguese to another, we have to deal with the fact that a perfectly innocent term in one variety may connote profanity in the other, just like *bloody*, which is a swear word in Britain but not in America, or *faggot*, which is a slang (and derogatory) term for 'male homosexual' in the United States but the name of a baked or fried ball of chopped liver in Britain. Table 8.3 gives a sample of terms that fall in the range of sexual taboo words in one variety but not in the other.

Social as well as regional variables should be taken into account when dealing with profanity, and not only across the Atlantic. A female Portuguese linguist (who prefers to remain anonymous) indicated that generally speaking, swearing is far more used and acceptable in everyday conversation in the north of Portugal than in the south. That colleague submitted that an utterance like 30a, using the noun *foda* 'fuck,' or 30b, with the verb *foder* 'to fuck,' would be acceptable in at least certain circles of "polite company" in Minho, though not in Lisbon, where 30c, with the noun *seca* 'bore' and 30d, with the verb *chatear* 'to annoy,' would be far preferable:

Table 8.3 *Slang and non-slang meanings of some words in European and Brazilian Portuguese*

|  | Slang EP meaning | Non slang BP meaning |
|---|---|---|
| *breque* | 'fart' | 'brake' (< Eng. brake) |
| *broche* | 'fellatio' | 'brooch, clasp' |
| *paneleiro* | 'male homosexual' | 'pan maker/seller' |
| *paninho* | 'effeminate man' | 'small rag' |
|  | **Slang BP meaning** | **Non slang EP meaning** |
| *bicha* | 'male homosexual' | 'line, que' |
| *cacete* | 'penis' | 'small loaf of bread' |
| *fresco* | 'male homosexual' | 'fresh' (adj.) |
| *pica* | 'penis' | 'injection' |
| *puto* | 'male prostitute' | 'child' |
| *saco* | 'scrotum' | 'handbag' |
| *veado* | 'male homosexual' | 'deer' |

(30)    a. EP *O discurso foi uma foda!*
            'The speech was damn boring!'
            (lit. 'the speech was a fuck!')
        b. EP *Não me fodas a cabeça!*
            'Don't bother me!'
            (lit. 'don't fuck my head!')
        c. EP *O discurso foi uma seca!*
            'The speech was dreadfully boring.'
        d. EP *Não me chateies!*
            'Don't annoy me!'

Even in tolerant environments, learners would do well to put off using swear words until they have developed full proficiency, for swearing, like telling jokes, requires native-like ability to be effective. They would do well, on the other hand, to systematically observe the various ways in which words with unpleasant connotations are replaced by neutral synonyms or euphemisms. Instead of saying that someone *morreu* 'died,' it may be socially preferable to use a verb like *falecer* 'to pass away,' or, more piously, *descansar* 'to rest.' Delicacy, or perhaps a lingering belief in word magic, prevents some people mentioning certain diseases by name, and so it may take discreet research to understand that EP *Fulano tem uma fraqueza pulmonar* 'So-and-so has a lung weakness' means he is suffering from tuberculosis, or that EP *Ela faleceu de uma coisinha má* 'She passed away from a little bad thing' is a reference to a death from cancer. Table 8.4 provides a thumbnail comparison of standard terms, their slang equivalents, and related euphemisms.

Table 8.4 *Euphemisms and slang terms*

|  | **Standard** | **Colloquial**[1] | **Euphemism** |
|---|---|---|---|
| to have sexual relations | *ter relações sexuais* | *Foder*[+] BP *transar,* BP *trepar,*[+] BP *tirar o atraso,* BP *dar uma bimbada* | *fazer amor, ficar junto(s) ter relações* |
| to defecate | *defecar* | *cagar,*[+] BP *fazer cocô,* EP *fazer cocó* | BP *ir ao banheiro, fazer um barro,* BP *passar um telegrama, fazer necessidades* |
| to urinate | *urinar* | *mijar,*[+] *fazer xixi* | BP *trocar a água do canário,* EP *verter águas* |
| to masturbate | *masturbar-se* | BP *pelar o galo,* EP *bater uma pívia*[+] *bater punheta,*[+] BP *afogar o ganso* | *praticar o onanismo* |
| to pass gas | *soltar gases* | BP *soltar um pum,* EP *dar um pum, peidar*[+] | BP *soltar gás,* EP *descuidar-se* |
| to menstruate | *menstruar* | *estar com o chico* | BP *estar incomodada,* EP *estar com as regras* |
| buttocks | *a(s) nádega(s)* | BP *bumbum, bunda,* EP *cu* | *traseiro* |
| anus | *o ânus* | BP *cu,*[+] *rabo,*[+] *olho do cu*[+] | *olho (do cu)* [+] |
| penis | *o pênis* | BP *pinto,* BP *pica,*[+] EP *pixota, caralho*[+] | *o órgão sexual masculino* |
| vagina | *a vagina* | BP *xoxota, boceta*[+] *racha*[+] EP *cona*[+] | *o órgão sexual feminino* |
| to get drunk | *embriagar-se* | BP *encher a cara, tomar um fogo* | BP *ficar alto, ficar alegre* |
| to meddle | *intrometer-se* | BP *meter o bedelho* | BP *ir onde não é chamado* |
| unintelligent | *pouco inteligente* | *burro* | BP *(ser) sem noção* |
| drugged | *drogado* | BP *chapado* | BP *meio doido* |
| senile | *senil* | *caduco* | BP *(estar) esquecido* |
| to die | *morrer, falecer* | BP *bater as botas*[+] | BP *descansar* |

[1] Items marked [+] are considered inappropriate in polite conversation by many speakers.

Less innocent than expletives are everyday words and expressions whose origin contains a derogatory element. A case in point is the verb *judiar* (from *judeu* 'Jew, Jewish' plus the verb-forming suffix *-iar*), which, from the original meaning 'to adopt Jewish practices' (in which case it was synonymous with *judaizar*), acquired the meanings of 'to mock' or 'to mistreat physically or morally, to torment' (Houaiss 2001, s.v. *judiar*). Nevertheless, a significant degree of ambivalence pervades the use of such terms, which to most speakers are so lexicalized as to be devoid of ethnic connotations, as in 31a, where *judiar* means simply *to mistreat*, or in 31b, where the derived noun *judiação* is no more than a pious expression of sympathy:

(31)    a. BP *Uma vez o meu velho me pegou judiando do gato e deu uma*
          *puta coça em mim pra eu aprender.*
          'Once my old man caught me mistreating the cat and he beat the
          crap out of me to teach me a lesson.'
       b. BP *Que judiação, a Fátima não passou no vestibular.*[1]
          'What a shame, Fátima hasn't passed her college-entrance exam.'

Ethnic prejudice is also at the root of derogatory nouns derived from *negro* (n./adj.) 'black, negro,' such as *negrice* 'action supposedly typical of a black person' or *negrão/negão* '(big) black man' and its feminine counterpart *negrona/negona* '(big) black woman,' recurring protagonists of a genre of ethnic jokes significantly known as *piada de negão* 'black man jokes.' Even such terms, however, can be employed without ethnic connotations: both *negão* and the shortened variants *nêgo/nêga* and their diminutives *neguinho/neguinha* are widely used as terms of endearment, irrespective of the interlocutors' ethnicity, with the approximate meaning of 'honey' or 'buddy,' as in 32a, where a man thanks his wife for a surprise gift, or in 32b, where a man addresses a close friend:

(32)    BP a. *Ô neguinha, que que é isso? Não precisava, muito obrigado.*
           'Hey honey, what's that? There was no need, thank you very
           much.'
        BP b. *Como é, negão? Vai mais um uísque aí?*
           'How about it, pal? Can I pour you another whisky?'

Speakers' reactions to such controversial matters as swearing and so-called bad language cover an ample gamut, from offended rejection to amused tolerance, passing through benign indifference or enthusiastic acceptance. Clearly, it is not the words in themselves that are good or bad, but the intention with which they are uttered and the effect they may have on those the receiving end. Research on negative language (Preti 1984; Stephens 1999, 2002) has led some scholars to make a case for intentional use of positive language as a strategy to improve communication, and ultimately, one would hope, human relations (Gomes de Matos 1996, 2002). Whether such efforts can be effective as a tool for social change is an open empirical question.

On the other hand, tolerance for actual ethnic-based insults seems to be decreasing, albeit slowly. In January 2004 a news item on an electronic bulletin (*Migalhas* 2004) reported that a court of law had sentenced a building company in the interior of the state of São Paulo to pay a former employee 50,000 *reais* (ca. US$17,000) moral damages, as a result of his complaint that for six months his foreman had insisted on calling him *nego burro* 'dumb blackie' and *nego fedido* 'stinking blackie.' According to the report, "the Court did not accept the company's argument that the verbal attacks took place between the two employees, without the company's knowledge." Maybe that is a sign of an overdue change.

Attitudes towards so-called bad language can be seen as just one piece in an ample mosaic of attitudes towards diversity in language. Maybe in an ideal world language variation would be regarded with tolerance, regional or social dialect differences would be accepted as the natural things they are, no accent would be considered more or less prestigious than any other, and – one might add to the wish list – insults and swear words would be unnecessary. Such a world, unfortunately, neither exists nor seems likely to come about in the foreseeable future. Every speech community possesses a body of opinions – most of them preconceived and completely lacking any objective foundation – about language in general and its own language in particular. Such opinions are actually part of the language, in the sense that they cover not only the lexicon and the grammar, but also a multidimensional cultural complex that pervades every aspect of the life of people who speak it. By shaping the culture and giving it a synchronic voice and a diachronic projection, the language, in a broad sense, *is* the culture, and opinions about language are part of that culture. Whilst native speakers can – some more successfully than others – navigate such largely uncharted waters, non-native learners, in order to communicate successfully within a cultural context, need to take those opinions into account and develop the instinct that will enable them to automatically decide, at any given moment, which of two or more options is pragmatically more appropriate for their communicative goals.

Acquiring such a feel requires both accepting language variation as something natural and acquiring the habit of relating apparently competing linguistic forms to the various communicative contexts appropriate to them. This book has attempted to contribute to the development of such a feel not by looking at the language as a homogeneous object but rather from a perspective in which variation appears as a constant reminder that Portuguese is a plural entity. With some practice, this approach can lead to a heightened awareness of such variation and an understanding that, far from being a cause for concern, it is a sure sign of the language's vitality. At a time when diversity, linguistic or otherwise, is praised as something positive, it would seem that understanding, appreciating, and celebrating such vitality is a goal worth pursuing.

# Suggestions for further reading

Besides the works mentioned in the text, several others of a general character which provided background information for one or more chapters have been added to the list below. An asterisk indicates that an item requires some familiarity with linguistic theory.

## REFERENCE WORKS AND MANUALS

### (A) INTRODUCTION TO LINGUISTICS IN PORTUGUESE

Faria, Isabel Hub, Emília Ribeiro Pedro, Inês Duarte, and Carlos A. M. Gouveia. 1996. *Introdução à Linguística Geral e Portuguesa*. Lisboa: Editorial Caminho.
Mussalim, Fernanda and Anna Christina Bentes, eds. 2001. *Introdução à Linguística. Domínios e Fronteiras*, 2 vols. 2nd edition. São Paulo: Cortez Editora.

### (B) INTRODUCTION TO PORTUGUESE LINGUISTICS

* Câmara, Joaquim Mattoso, Jr. 1972. *The Portuguese Language*, trans. Anthony J. Naro. Chicago: University of Chicago Press.

### (C) LINGUISTICALLY ORIENTED GRAMMARS

Luft, Celso Pedro. 1996. *Moderna Gramática Brasileira*. São Paulo: Editora Globo.
Neves, Maria Helena de Moura, 2000. *Gramática de Usos do Português*. São Paulo: Editora UNESP.
Neves, Maria Helena de Moura, 2003. *Guia de Uso do Português: Confrontando Regras e Usos*. São Paulo: Editora UNESP.

### (D) PRESCRIPTIVE GRAMMARS BASED ON LITERARY USAGE

Bechara, Evanildo. 1999. *Moderna Gramática Portuguesa*. 37th edition. Rio de Janeiro: Editora Lucerna.
Cunha, Celso and Luís Filipe Lindley Cintra. 1985. *Nova Gramática do Português Contemporâneo*. 2nd edition. Rio de Janeiro: Editora Nova Fronteira.

### (E) COMPARATIVE GRAMMARS

Vázquez-Cuesta, Pilar and Maria Albertina Mendes da Luz. 1987. *Gramática portuguesa*, 2 vols. 3rd edition. Madrid: Gredos (in Spanish).

(F) DICTIONARIES

Biderman, Maria Tereza Camargo. 1998. *Dicionário Didático de Português*. São Paulo: Editora Ática.

Borba, Francisco da Silva, ed. 1990. *Dicionário Gramatical de Verbos do Português Contemporâneo do Brasil*. São Paulo: Editora da UNESP.

Borba, Francisco S. 2002. *Dicionário de Usos do Português do Brasil*. São Paulo: Editora Ática.

Ferreira, Aurélio Buarque de Holanda. 1986. *Novo Dicionário Aurélio da Língua Portuguesa*. Rio de Janeiro: Nova Fronteira.

Houaiss, Antônio. 2001. *Dicionário Houaiss da Língua Portuguesa*. Rio de Janeiro: Editora Objetiva.

Houaiss, Antônio. 1982. *Dicionário Inglês–Português*. Rio de Janeiro: Editora Record.

Taylor, James L. 1970. *Portuguese–English Dictionary*. Rio de Janeiro: Editora Record.


(G) SPELLING

Bergström, Magnus and Neves Reis. 1999. *Prontuário Ortográfico e Guia da Língua Portuguesa*. Lisboa: Notícias Editorial (European Portuguese).

Estrela, Edite. 1993. *A Questão Ortográfica. Reforma e Acordos da Língua Portuguesa*. Lisbon: Editorial Notícias.

Luft, Celso Pedro. 2003. *Novo Guia Ortográfico*. Rio de Janeiro: Editora Globo (Brazilian Portuguese).


THEMATIC READINGS

(A) GENERAL WORKS

Ferronha, António Luís, ed. 1992. *Atlas da Língua Portuguesa na História e no Mundo*. Lisbon: Imprensa Nacional – Casa da Moeda.

Fonseca, Fernando Venâncio Peixoto. 1985. *O Português entre as Línguas do Mundo*. Coimbra: Livraria Almedina.

Lopes, David. 1969. *A Expansão da Língua Portuguesa no Oriente durante os Séculos XVI, XVII e XVIII*. 2nd edition revised by Luís de Matos. Lisbon: Portucalense Editora.


(B) PHONETICS AND PHONOLOGY

*Bisol, Leda, ed. 1996. *Introdução a Estudos de Fonologia do Português Brasileiro*. Porto Alegre: EDIPUCRS.

*Ferreira Netto, Waldemar. 2001. *Introdução à Fonologia da Língua Portuguesa*. São Paulo: Editora Hedra.

Leite, Yonne and Dinah Callou. 2002. *Como Falam os Brasileiros*. Rio de Janeiro: Jorge Zahar Editor.

Perini, Mário A. 2004. *Talking Brazilian. A Brazilian Portuguese Pronunciation Workbook*. New Haven: Yale University Press.

Silva, Thaïs Cristófaro. 1998. *Fonética e Fonologia do Português: Roteiro de Estudos e Guia de Exercícios*. São Paulo: Editora Contexto.

(C) MORPHOLOGY AND SYNTAX

*Costa, João, ed. 2000. *Portuguese Syntax. New Comparative Studies*. Oxford University Press.
* Mira Mateus, Maria Helena, Ana Maria Brito, Inês Silva Duarte, and Isabel Hub Faria. 1983. *Gramática da Língua Portuguesa*. Coimbra: Livraria Almedina.
*Modesto, Marcello. 2001. *As Construções Clivadas no Português do Brasil: Relações entre Interpretação Focal, Movimento Sintático e Prosódia*. São Paulo: Humanitas–FFLCH/USP.
Monteiro, José Lemos. 1991. *Morfologia Portuguesa*. Campinas: Pontes Editores.
Perini, Mário A. 2002a. *Modern Portuguese. A Reference Grammar*. New Haven: Yale University Press.
*Perini, Mário A. 1998a. *Gramática Descritiva do Português*. 3rd edition. São Paulo: Editora Ática.
*Perini, Mário A. 1998b. *Sintaxe Portuguesa. Metodologia e Funções*. São Paulo: Editora Ática.
Sandalo, Maria Filomena Spatti. 2000. "Morfologia." In *Introdução à Lingüística. Domínios e Fronteiras*, vol. 1, ed. Fernanda Mussalim and Anna Christina Bentes. São Paulo: Cortez Editora, 181–206.
Sandmann, Antônio José. 1996. *Formação de Palavras no Português Brasileiro Contemporâneo*. 2nd. edition. Curitiba: Editora da UFPR.


(D) HISTORY OF THE LANGUAGE

*Ali, Manuel Said. 2001 [1921]. *Gramática Histórica da Língua Portuguesa*. 8th edition, revised by Mário Eduardo Viaro. São Paulo: Companhia Melhoramentos and Brasília: Editora Universidade de Brasília.
*Castilho, Ataliba Teixeira de, ed. 1998. *Para a História do Português Brasileiro*, vol. 1: *Primeiras Idéias*. São Paulo: Humanitas–FFLCH/USP.
*Duarte, Maria Eugênia Lat and Dinah Callou, eds. 2002. *Para a História do Português Brasileiro*, vol. 4: *Notícias de Corpora e Outros Estudos*. Rio de Janeiro: UFRJ/Letras, FAPERJ.
*Ilari, Rodolfo, 1992. *Lingüística Românica*. São Paulo: Editora Ática.
*Silva, Rosa Virginia Mattos e, ed. 2001. *Para a História do Português Brasileiro*, vols. 2 and 3: *Primeiros Estudos*. São Paulo: Humanitas–FFLCH/USP.
Tarallo, Fernando. 1990. *Tempos Lingüísticos. Itinerário Histórico da Língua Portuguesa*. São Paulo: Editora Ática.
Teyssier, Paul. 1994. *História da Língua Portuguesa*, trans. Celso Cunha. Lisbon: Livraria Sá da Costa.
*Williams, Edwin B. 1968. *From Latin to Portuguese*. 2nd edition. Philadelphia: University of Pennsylvania Press.


(E) PIDGINS AND CREOLES

Holm, John. 2000. *An Introduction to Pidgins and Creoles*. Cambridge University Press.
*Holm, John. 2004. *Languages in Contact. The Partial Restructuring of Vernaculars*. Cambridge University Press.
Tarallo, Fernando and Tania Alkmin. 1987. *Falares Crioulos. Línguas em contato*. São Paulo: Editora Ática.

(F) BRAZILIAN PORTUGUESE

Amaral, Amadeu. 1920. *O Dialecto Caipira*. São Paulo, Casa Editora "O Livro."
Bagno, Marcos. 1999. *Preconceito Lingüístico. O que é, como se faz*. São Paulo: Edições Loyola.
*Bagno, Marcos. 2000. *Dramática da Língua Portuguesa. Tradição Gramatical, Mídia e Exclusão Social*. São Paulo: Edições Loyola.
Bagno, Marcos, ed. 2002. *Lingüística da Norma*. São Paulo: Edições Loyola.
*Bortoni-Ricardo, Stella Maris. 1985. *The Urbanization of Rural Dialect Speakers: A Sociolinguistic Study in Brazil*. Cambridge University Press.
Cardoso, Suzana Alice Marcelino. 1999. "A Dialectologia no Brasil: Perspectivas." *DELTA: Documentação de Estudos em Lingüística Teórica e Aplicada*, 15, special number, 233–255.
Cardoso, Suzana Alice Marcelino. 2001. "Dialectologia: Trilhas Seguidas, Caminhos a Perseguir" *DELTA: Documentação de Estudos em Lingüística Teórica e Aplicada*, 17, special number, 25–44.
*Cardoso, Suzana and Carlota Ferreira. 1994. *A Dialetologia no Brasil*. São Paulo: Editora Contexto.
Castilho, Ataliba Teixeira de. 1992. "O Português do Brasil." In Ilari 1992, 237–272.
Castilho, Ataliba Teixeira de. 2000. *A Língua Falada no Ensino de Português*. São Paulo: Editora Contexto.
*Castilho, Ataliba Teixeira de, ed. 1989b. *Português Culto Falado no Brasil*. Campinas: Editora da Unicamp.
*Castilho, Ataliba Teixeira de, ed. 1990a. *Gramática do Português Falado*, vol. 1: *A Ordem*. Campinas: Editora da Unicamp; São Paulo: FAPESP.
*Castilho, Ataliba Teixeira de and Margarida Basilio, eds. 1996. *Gramática do Português Falado*, vol. 4: *Estudos Descritivos*. Campinas: Editora da Unicamp; São Paulo: FAPESP.
Fiorin, Jusé Luiz. 1998. *Linguagem e Ideologia*. 6th edition. São Paulo: Editora Ática.
Leite, Yonne and Dinah Callou. 2002. *Como Falam os Brasileiros*. Rio de Janeiro: Jorge Zahar Editor.
Paiva, Maria da Conceição de and Maria Marta Pereira Scherre. 1999. "Retrospectiva Sociolingüística: Contribuições do Peul." *DELTA Documentação de Estudos em Lingüística Teórica e Aplicada*, 15, special number, 201–232.
Perini, Mário A. 1997. *Sofrendo a Gramática. Ensaios sobre a Linguagem*. São Paulo: Editora Ática.
Preti, Dino. 1984. *A Linguagem Proibida. Um Estudo sobre a Linguagem Erótica*. São Paulo: T. A. Queiroz, Editor.
Preti, Dino. 1994. *Sociolingüística. Os Níveis da Fala*. 7th edition. São Paulo: EDUSP.
Preti, Dino, ed. 1997. *O Discurso Oral Culto*. São Paulo: Humanitas–FFLCH/USP.
*Roberts, Ian and Mary A. Kato, eds. 1993. *Português Brasileiro. Uma Viagem Diacrônica*. Campinas: Editora da Unicamp.
Thomas, Earl. 1969. *The Syntax of Spoken Brazilian Portuguese*. Nashville: Vanderbilt University Press.

# Glossary

A star (*) indicates of a cross-reference to another term that appears as an entry in this glossary.

**Accent**    A term used to refer to pronunciation features that identify a speech variety as typical of a given region, social group, or the like. Cf. *dialect.

**Accusative**    In Latin, a *case related to *direct object complements.

**Actor**    The semantic component of a sentence which refers to the entity that performs an action expressed by a verb. Syntactically, the formant of a passive construction (usually introduced by *por* 'by') that refers to the semantic actor (*esse quadro foi pintado por João* 'that picture was painted by John').

**Affix**    A bound *morpheme attached at the beginning (*prefix) or at the end (*suffix) of a word to form a new word, as in *pré-história* 'pre-history' or *social + ista > socialista* 'socialist.'

**Agreement**    A morphosyntactic process whereby features of a sentence component, such as a noun, are replicated in other elements, such as articles or adjectives. Agreement in person and number also takes place between a *subject and its verb.

**Allomorph**    An actual manifestation of a *morpheme, e.g. -s in *canetas* 'pens,' or -*es* in *senhores* 'gentlemen,' both representing the morpheme 'plural.'

**Allophone**    An actual manifestation of a *phoneme through a *phone. Thus in Portuguese [t] and [ʧ] are allophones of the phoneme /t/ as in *tia* /ˈtiɐ/ or /ˈʧiɐ/ 'aunt.' See also *phone, *phoneme.

**Anacoluthon**    A syntactic switch in midsentence, as in *Ela telefonou, e será que eu podia ir ao aeroporto?* 'She called up, and would it be possible for me to go to the airport?'

**Anaphora, anaphoric**    A reference to something already mentioned, as *ela* in *Minha prima chegou ontem e ela vai ficar até a semana que vem* 'My cousin arrived yesterday and she's going to stay until next week.'

**Aspect**    A verbal category related to the speaker's perception of the manner in which a verbal action is carried out. Aspect is manifested in contrasts between the preterit (a past action seen as finished, as in *Maria serviu o café às oito ontem* 'Maria served coffee at eight yesterday') and the imperfect (a past action seen as going on as in *Cheguei quando fechavam o bar* 'I arrived as they were closing the bar,' or as habitual, as in

*Naquele tempo fechavam o bar à meia noite* 'In those days they used to close the bar at midnight').

**Assimilation**    A phonological process whereby a sound becomes more like a neighboring sound by acquiring one or more of its features.

**Auxiliary verb**    A verb such as *ter* or *haver* which combines with another (called the *main verb*) to form a compound tense, as in *eu tinha/havia falado* 'I had spoken.'

**Benefactive**    A semantic component of a sentence referring to someone or something who/that receives something (whether or not a real benefit is involved). In *Dei o dinheiro a Daniel* 'I gave the money to Daniel,' the noun *Daniel* stands for the semantic benefactive, which in this case is the syntactic *indirect object.

**Borrowing**    A process whereby a language adopts elements from another language, e.g. Eng *stress* > Pg *estresse*.

**Caipira**    Of, or pertaining to, a rural subculture associated with the hinterland of the state of São Paulo and part of the state of Minas Gerais in Brazil as in *dialeto caipira* 'Caipira dialect.'

**Carioca**    Referring to (adj.) or a native of (n.) Rio de Janeiro.

**Case**    A category related to syntactic functions which in languages like Latin are overtly signaled by a specific ending that characterizes a noun as being the *subject (nominative case), the *direct object (accusative case), or the *indirect object (dative case), and so on.

**Clitic**    A morphologically unstressed free *morpheme that only occurs linked to another word, with which it forms a phonological unit. Said particularly of Portuguese unstressed pronouns such as *o, a, os, as, se*: – *E essa garrafa? – Eu a trouxe de Minas. – Quer vendê-la?* "What about this bottle?" "I brought it from Minas." "Do you want to sell it?"

**Code-switching**    The habit of switching in conversation from one language to another, or from one variety of the same language to another.

**Commentary**    That part of a statement which completes the *topic. Thus in *O que eu quero é que chova* 'What I want is for it to rain,' the segment *é que chova* serves as a commentary to the topic *o que eu quero*.

**Conjugation**    (1) Changes in a verb form to show tense, voice, mood etc. (2) The class to which a particulars verb belongs. Portuguese has three conjugations, *ar, er,* and *ir*.

**Conjugation vowel**    See *theme vowel.

**Creole**    A full-fledged language that originates from a *pidgin when it becomes the first language of the offspring of pidgin-speaking parents.

**Declension**    A morphological category found in Latin (and other inflected languages) consisting of a set of *case endings for nouns, adjectives, pronouns, and determinants, which change them according to their syntactic function in a sentence. A declension is also a morphological class to which belong the names and other words sharing the same set of case endings. Latin had five declensions, which disappeared in the formation of the Romance languages.

**Deictic**    From *deixis* (n.), a signaling process whereby a term (such as a demonstrative) indicates the position of something in relation to the speaker: *este livro* 'this book' vs. *aquele livro* 'that book.'

**Devoicing**    Loss of the phonetic feature *voicing, caused by a cessation of the vibration of the vocal cords.

**Diachronic**    Relating to or taking into account the passing of time, as in *diachronic linguistics*, which considers language forms from the viewpoint of the changes suffered by them through time. Cf. *synchronic.

**Diacritic**    An extra sign placed over a letter, such as an accent (á, à, ã, â), or below, such as the cedilla (ç), to represent a specific sound.

**Dialect**    A term designating a distinct variety of a language, often one contrasting with that taken as the standard (which technically is also a dialect). As used since the end of the nineteenth century, the term "dialect" tends to designate a geographically or regionally defined variety. When social variables intervene, *social dialect* or *sociolect* is used. The more generic term *language variety* covers both kinds. In common parlance, the term "dialect" often has negative connotations, which are totally absent from its use in linguistics. Cf. *lect, *sociolect.

**Dialect leveling**    A process whereby the contrast between features from two or more language varieties represented in the same community is ironed out.

**Diglossia, diglossic**    A situation in which two forms of the same language, or two different languages, are used in the same community for different purposes. One form, characterized as "high" or H (e.g.: Classical Arabic in Arab countries, Standard German in Switzerland, Spanish in Paraguay) is learned at school and used in formal situations, public administration, and the more formal sectors of the media, while the other form, characterized as "low" or L (e.g. popular spoken Arabic, Swiss German, Guaraní) is learned informally and used in ordinary conversation, popular literature, and other such informal situations.

**Digraph**    A combination of letters that stands for a single sound, e.g. *ch* in English (*cheap*) or in Portuguese (*chato* 'boring').

**Diphthong**    Phonetically, a combination of a vowel and a glide, or a glide and a vowel, standing together in the same syllable, e.g. Pg *ai* [aj] 'ouch' or *ua* [wa] in *quatro* 'four.'

**Diphthongization**    A phonological process whereby a vowel develops into a diphthong by adding a glide, as in BP *mas* 'but' (phonologically /mas/ and phonetically [majs]), rhyming with *mais* (phonologically /majs/ and phonetically [majs]) 'more.'

**Direct object**    The direct object (DO) is the syntactic complement of a *transitive verb, e.g. *um carro* in *Daniel comprou um carro* 'Daniel bought a car.'

**Ditransitive verb**    A verb requiring both a direct object and an indirect object, e.g. *dar* 'to give,' *oferecer* 'to offer,' *entregar* 'to deliver,' e.g. *Ele ofereceu as flores à enfermeira* 'He offered the flowers (DO) to the nurse (IO).'

**Embedding**    A syntactic process whereby one sentence is inserted into another by means of a connector such as the relative pronoun *que* 'that, who': *Aquele homem veio ontem. Aquele homem é encanador. > Aquele homem que veio ontem é encanador* 'That man who came yesterday is a plumber.' Also referred to as *\*subordination*.

**Enclitic**    An unstressed pronoun or \*clitic placed after a verb, as in *chamou-me* 'he called me.' Cf. \*proclitic.

**Form**    A generic term (as in *linguistic form*) referring to any \*morpheme, word, phrase, sentence, and the like.

**Gentile**    Said of a noun or adjective referring to a nation, country, or region, such as *brasileiro, português, americano*, etc.

**Hiatus**    A sequence of two contiguous vowels in different syllables, as in *álcool* (ál-co-ol) 'alcohol' or *viúva* (vi-ú-va) 'widow.' Cf. *\*diphthong*.

**Inpersonal verb**    A verb that occurs only in the third person singular, such as verbs referring to atmospheric events: *Quando não neva, chove* 'When it doesn't snow, it rains.'

**Indirect object**    The indirect object (IO) is one of the syntactic complements of a \*ditransitive verb, e.g. *ao vizinho* in *Daniel deu um presente ao vizinho* 'Daniel gave a gift to the neighbor.' It usually corresponds to the semantia \*benefactive.

**Indirect transitive verb**    A verb requiring an \*indirect object (IO) but not a \*direct object (DO), such as *assistir* in the sense of 'attend,' as in *Assistimos ao concerto* 'We attended the concert.'

**Intervocalic**    Said of a sound between two vowels, e.g. r [r] in *cara* 'face.'

**Intransitive verb**    A verb that requires no complement, e.g. *nascer, viver, morrer: João nasceu, viveu e morreu sem pena nem glória* 'João was born, lived, and died without suffering or glory.'

**Koine**    A spoken variety of a given region that is used as a \*lingua franca or a standard among related varieties, usually as the result of leveling differences among them.

**Lect**    A generic term designating any language variety, whether defined regionally, socially, or otherwise.

**Lenition**    A phonological process causing a softening of the articulatory effort.

**Leveling**    A process whereby in a situation where speakers of several dialects are in constant contact with one another, dialectal differences tend to be reduced, thus fostering a more homogeneous speech in phonology, morphology, syntax, and the lexicon.

**Lexical**    Having to do with the lexicon, that is the set of words of a language.

**Lexicalized form**    See *lexicalization.

**Lexicalization**    A process whereby a linguistic form, usually a construction of two or more words, functions very much like a single word, e.g. *o senhor* 'you (sg., formal).'

**Lingua franca**    Generic name for a language used for purposes of communication among individuals or communities that do not share another language, as with as the use of English worldwide. The original *Lingua Franca* ('language of the Franks, meaning Europeans, as opposed to other ethnic groups') was a *Romance-based *pidgin, also known as *Sabir* (from Pg/Sp *saber* 'to know') used around the Mediterranean in the Middle Ages.

**Loan word**    A word taken from another language by a process called *borrowing, as Pg *futebol* (from Eng *football*).

**Macrodialect**    A generic term for a language variety which encompasses several other subvarieties, such as Brazilian Portuguese.

**Marked**    See *unmarked.

**Metaphony**    A phonological process involving a change in the phonetic features of a vowel, as in the formation of certain plurals such as *corvo* ['koɾvu] /*corvos* ['kɔɾvus].

**Metathesis**    A phonological process involving changing the normal order of sounds, as in *estrupo* for *estupro* 'rape', or *fletro* for *feltro* 'felt', in popular Brazilian Portuguese.

**Mineiro**    Relative to or pertaining to the state of Minas Gerais, Brazil; the variety of Brazilian Portuguese spoken in that region.

**Minimal pairs**    Sound sequences that differ by a single *phone which signals a difference in meaning, e.g. *pato* ['patu] 'duck vs. *gato* ['gatu] 'cat.' In such pairs the contrasting phones are said to represent different *phonemes.

**Modal verb**    Traditionally the term for verbs like *can, may, must, ought to*, which express an attitude of the speaker (possibility, permission, necessity) toward the action represented by an accompanying verb; by extension the label is applied to similar verbs in other languages, e.g. Pg *dever, querer, poder*, which combine with another verb (typically in the infinitive form), e.g. *Ele queria comprar o carro mas não podia pagar o preço* 'He wanted to buy the car but could not pay the price.'

**Monophthongization**    A phonological process consisting in the reduction of a diphthong to a vowel, as in /ei/ > [e], e.g., *madeira* [ma'deɾɐ] instead of [ma'dej ɾɐ].

**Moor**    N. and adj. derived from *Mauri*, the name of the inhabitants of Mauritania in Roman North Africa; traditionally used to designate the Islamic peoples who invaded the Iberian Peninsula in 711. Though the invaders included more Berbers than Arabs, expressions like "Arab invasion" and "Arab domination" are used.

**Morpheme**    The basic distinctive form, smaller than a word, which cannot be further subdivided without losing its meaning. Morphemes are the building blocks of words; a word may have a single morpheme, e.g. *eu* 'I,' but a morpheme need not be a full word, e.g. *compr-* in *comprar* 'to buy.'

**Mozarabic**   (from Ar *musta'rib* 'Arab-like'). There is very little consensus about the actual form of Mozarabic dialects, and some scholars question whether they existed as an individualized form of Romance. As Islamic-held lands were reconquered, surviving Mozarab groups eventually became integrated in the newly formed communities.

**Nominalization**   A process whereby a word (such as an adjective or a verb) is **nominalized,** that is, made into a noun, usually by using it in a noun phrase preceded by the article *o* 'the': *O bom dessa greve é que amanhã não temos aula* 'The good thing about this strike is that tomorrow we won't have classes'; *O muito falar e o pouco dormir fazem mal à saúde* 'Too much talking and too little sleeping are bad for your health.'

**Normative**   Having to do with norms or rules. Said of grammars that provide norms for language use instead of describing language as it actually occurs. Synonym: *prescriptive.*

**Object pronouns**   Pronouns such as *me, te, se, o, a,* etc., which stand for a *direct object or an *indirect object.

**Oxytone**   A word stressed on the last syllable, e.g., *falarei* 'I will talk.'

**Paroxytone**   A word stressed on the penult or next-to-last syllable, e.g. *casa* 'house.'

**Patient**   A semantic component of a sentence that refers to the entity which receives the action of the verb, as *carta* 'letter' in either *Maria queimou a carta* or *A carta foi queimada por Maria.*

**Patronymic**   Term used to indicate names derived from the name of one's father or ancestor; also, a word or part of a word, such as a *suffix, that indicates such derivation, e.g. Pg *-es* (Rodrigues = son of Rodrigo) or Eng *-son* (Peterson = son of Peter), or a *prefix such as Eng *Fitz* (Fitzgerald = son of Gerald) or Irish *O'* (O'Connor = son (originally grandson) of Connor).

**Paulista**   Relative to or pertaining to the state of São Paulo, Brazil; the variety of Brazilian Portuguese spoken in that region.

**Periphrasis** (Also **periphrastic construction**)   A verbal construction functioning as a single verb tense and made up of an *auxiliary verb and a main verb, e.g. *tenho falado* 'I have spoken,' *terei falado* 'I will have spoken.'

**Phatic**   Relative to language used for sociability and banter rather than factual communication.

**Phone**   Any speech sound, as opposed to other sounds made by the vocal apparatus which do not participate in speech.

**Phoneme**   A basic element in the sound system of a language, represented by a sign of the phonetic alphabet between slashes (e.g. /b/) and capable of signaling a difference in meaning, as in /b/ in *bala* 'bullet' vs. /m/ in *mala* 'suitcase. See also *allophone, *phone.

**Phonetic alphabet**   A system of letters and other signs for representing phones in writing. E.g. the International Phonetic Alphabet (I.P.A. or IPA).

**Phonological phrase**   A group of words pronounced in the same breath group.

**Phonotactics**    The set of language-specific rules describing how the phonemes of a language can organize to form syllables and words.

**Phrase**    A coherent syntactic unit less complex than a sentence, such as *Proibida a entrada* 'Entry forbidden' or *Para levar* 'To take home.'

**Pidgin**    A simplified hybrid language developed when speakers of two or more languages try to communicate (as in trade situations) using elements from their respective languages. Portuguese-based pidgins were widespread in coastal regions of Africa and Asia in the fifteenth and sixteenth centuries. A pidgin is not anyone's native language, but when the young of a pidgin-speaking community grow up speaking it as their first language, it becomes a *creole (See also *lingua franca.)

**Post-vocalic**    Said of a speech sound or a phoneme occurring after a vowel, e.g. /r/ in *quarto* 'room.' Cf. *pre-vocalic.

**Predicate**    The segment of a sentence that stands for what is stated, or predicated, of the *subject, e.g. *morreram* 'died' in as *árvores morreram* 'the trees died.'

**Prefix**    See *affix.

**Prescriptive**    See *normative.

**Pre-vocalic**    Said of a speech sound or a phoneme occurring before a vowel, like /l/ in *lado* 'side.' Cf. *post-vocalic.

**Proclitic**    An unstressed pronoun or *clitic placed before a verb, as in *me chamou* 'he called me.' Cf. *enclitic.

**Proparoxytone**    A word stressed on the antepenult or second-from-last syllable, e.g. *lâmpada* 'lamp.'

**Raising**    A phonological process that causes a vowel to be articulated one level higher on the scale represented by the vowel phoneme (see Table 2.4).

**Referent**    The non-linguistic entity to which a linguistic form or expression refers. *Reference*, or *referential meaning*, is the relationship between e.g. the linguistic form *Daniel* and the referent, that is the individual so named.

**Register**    A language variety (or the set of linguistic elements that comprise it) defined in terms of social parameters, such as a trade, occupation, profession, hobby, and so on.

**Relexified, Relexification**    The process of replacing the lexicon of a language variety by the lexicon of another.

**Resumptive**    Said of a word, such as a pronoun, that repeats the information contained earlier in the same sentence, as in *ele* in VBP *a moça que eu saí com ela* 'the young woman that I went out with (her),' used for st. *a moça com quem eu saí* 'the young woman with whom I went out.'

**Romance** (or **Neo-Latin**) **languages.**    A family of languages derived from Latin. Romance languages with national official status include Catalan (in Andorra), French, Italian, Portuguese, Rumanian, Rumansh (in Switzerland), and Spanish. Catalan and Galician enjoy regional coofficial status in their respective regions in Spain. Other Romance languages that have limited or no official recognition include Aragonese, Asturian, Corsican, Occitan, Piedmontese, Sardinian, and Sicilian.

**Semantic actor**   See *actor.

**Sociolect**   A language variety, or dialect, defined in terms of social features, such as the sex, age, or social class of the speaker. See also *dialect, *lect.

**Stem**   That part of a word which carries its lexical meaning, e.g. *cas-* in *casa* 'house' and *casas* 'houses'; *fal-* in *falarei* 'I'll speak,' *falei* 'I spoke.'

**Subject**   A syntactic component of a sentence of which something is predicated, as in *Pedro saiu* 'Peter went out,' where the verb form *saiu* 'went out' constitutes a statement about *Pedro*. The subject is said to govern the verb of the sentence, which must agree with it in person and number, e.g. *eu saí* 'I went out' but *nós saímos* 'we went out.' Cf. *predicate.

**Subordination**   The process of inserting one sentence (called the subordinate clause) into another (called the main clause, or matrix) by means of a relative pronoun or a subordinating conjunction. Cf. *embedding.

**Suffix**   See *affix.

**Syllable**   A sequence of *phones forming a phonological unit and made up of a nucleus, which in Portuguese may be a vowel or a diphthong. This nucleus may be preceded by an onset (a consonant or a cluster of consonants such as /pl/, /br/, etc.) and followed by a coda (a consonant). An open syllable ends in the nucleus vowel: *ba-ta-ta* 'potato,' while a closed syllable ends in a consonant: *par-tes* 'you leave.'

**Synchronic**   Said of a linguistic analysis that considers language forms from the viewpoint of their structure but takes into account neither the passing of time nor considerations of a historical nature. Cf. *diachronic.

**Theme vowel**   (1) A vowel used as a noun-forming element, e.g. *-a, -o, -e* in *cas-* + *-a> casa* 'house,' *cas-* + *- o> caso* 'case,' *gent-* + *e> gente* 'people.' (2) A vowel added to a verb stem which indicates the class or *conjugation to which the verb belongs, e.g. *-a, -e, -i* in *falar* 'to speak,' *comer* 'to eat,' *partir* 'to leave.'

**Topic**   That part of a statement, whether a phrase or a full sentence, that contains information on what the statement is all about. Thus in *lá em casa não tem dessas coisas* 'at home they don't have those things' *lá em casa* may be seen as the topic, wheras *não tem dessas coisas* is the *commentary.

**Topicalization**   A syntactic process consisting in placing a sentence element in a position, usually at the beginning, where it may serve as its *topic, as in *verbos, eu detesto ter que estudar,* 'verbs, I hate having to study.'

**Transitive verb**   A verb requiring a *direct object (DO), such as *comprar* 'to buy'or *fazer* 'to make,' e.g. *Ele compra farinha e faz pão* 'He buys flour (DO) and makes bread (DO).'

**Unmarked**   A term used to designate the generic member of a pair or series of linguistic items. The word order subject – verb – direct object (as in *Eu comi o hambúrger* 'I ate the hamburger') is considered unmarked and thus unexceptional. The order verb – subject – direct object (*Comi eu o hambúrger*) or direct object – subject – verb (*O hambúrger eu comi*), in turn, are considered marked, since they present a less common distribution of information.

**Vernacular**    (from Lat *vernaculus* 'native, domestic') The native language of a community, in contrast to a language acquired through instruction, formal or otherwise. The *Romance languages, which developed from spoken Latin in the Middle Ages, are considered vernaculars in relation to Classical Latin, which required formal training.

**Voicing**    A quality imparted to a speech sound by the vibration of the vocal cords.

**Vowel harmony**    A phonological process whereby a vowel displays a feature that approximates it to another vowel in the same word, as when the first vowel of a word like *menino* is pronounced as [i], like the stressed vowel in the syllable *ni*.

# Bibliography

This bibliography includes some reference works consulted, but not directly cited in the text.

Abaurre, Maria Bernadete M. and Angela C. S. Rodrigues, eds. 2002. *Gramática do Português Falado*, vol. 8: *Novos Estudos Descritivos*. Campinas: Editora da Unicamp.

Abreu, Maria Isabel and Clea Rameh. 1972. *Português Contemporâneo 1*. Washington, DC: Georgetown University Press.

Abreu, Maria Isabel and Cléa Rameh. 1973. *Português Contemporâneo 2*. Washington, DC: Georgetown University Press.

Afonso, Elisabete Vaz. 1998. "Problemas de Reintegração Linguística e Social de Emigrantes de Segunda Geracão." In *Linguística e Educação. Actas do Encontro da Associação Portuguesa de Linguística*, ed. Rui Vieira de Castro and Maria de Lourdes Sousa. Lisbon: Edições Colibri, 6–13.

Aguilera, Vanderci de Andrade. 1994. *Atlas Lingüístico do Paraná*. Curitiba, PR: Imprensa Oficial do Paraná.

Ali, Manuel Said. 2001 [1921]. *Gramática Histórica da Língua Portuguesa*. 8th edition, revised by Mário Eduardo Viaro. São Paulo: Companhia Melhoramentos and Brasília: Editora Universidade de Brasília.

Alkmin, Tania Maria, ed. 2002. *Para a História do Português Brasileiro*, vol. 3: *Novos Estudos*. São Paulo: Humanitas–FFLCH/USP.

Allen, Joseph H. D. 1941. *Portuguese Word-Formation with Suffixes*. Baltimore: Linguistic Society of America.

Almanaque Abril. 2002a. *Brasil*. São Paulo: Editora Abril.

Almanaque Abril. 2002b. *Mundo*. São Paulo: Editora Abril.

Almeida, Napoleão Mendes de. 1967. *Gramática Metódica da Língua Portuguesa*. São Paulo: Edições Saraiva.

Almeida, Onésimo T. 2001. "Two Decades of Luso-American Literature: An Overview." In *Global Impact of the Portuguese Language*, ed. Asela Rodriguez de Laguna. New Brunswick and London: Transaction Publishers, 231–254.

Altman, Cristina. 1998. *A Pesquisa Lingüística no Brasil (1968–1988)*. São Paulo: Humanitas–FFLCH/USP.

Alves, António Bárbolo, ed. 1999. *Lhiteratura Oral Mirandesa. Recuôlha de Textos an Mirandés*. Porto: Granito Editores e Livreiros.

Alves, Francisco. n/d. *Revivendo Francisco Alves*, CD-001. Rio de Janeiro: Revivendo Músicas Comércio de Discos Ltda.

Amaral, Amadeu. 1920. *O Dialecto Caipira*. São Paulo, Casa Editora "O Livro."

Andrade, Mario de. [1928] 1978. *Macunaíma (O Herói sem Nenhum Caráter)*. São Paulo: Livraria Martins Editora.

Aragão, Maria do Socorro and Cleusa Menezes. 1984. *Atlas Lingüístico da Paraíba. Cartas Léxicas e Fonéticas*. Brasília: Universidade Federal da Paraíba, Conselho Nacional de Pesquisas.

Araujo, Antonio Martins de. 1995. "Breve Notícia da Ortografia Portuguesa." In *Miscelânea de Estudos Lingüísticos, Filológicos e Literários in Memoriam Celso Cunha*, ed. Cilene da Cunha Pereira and Paulo Roberto Dias Pereira. Rio de Janeiro: Editora Nova Fronteira, 431–448.

Assunção, Carlos Costa. 1998. "O Poder e a Gramática com Base num Exemplo." In *Linguística e Educação. Actas do Encontro da Associação Portuguesa de Linguística*, ed. Rui Vieira de Castro and Maria de Lourdes Sousa. Lisbon: Edições Colibri, 15–34.

Assunção, Carlos Costa. 2000. *"A Arte da Grammatica da Língua Portugueza" de António José dos Reis Lobato*. Critical edition and study. Lisbon: Academia de Ciências.

Augel, Moema Parente. 1998. "O Crioulo como Língua Literária?" *A Nova Literatura da Guiné-Bissau*. Bissau: Instituto Nacional de Estudos e Pesquisa, 27–53.

Azevedo, Milton M. 1974. "On the Semantics of *estar* + participle Sentences in Portuguese." *Linguistics* 135, 25–33.

Azevedo, Milton M. 1976. "Thematic Meaning, Word Order, and Indefinite Actor Sentences in Portuguese." In *Georgetown University Round Table on Language and Linguistics* ed. Cléa Rameh. Washington, DC: Georgetown University Press, 217–235.

Azevedo, Milton M. 1980. *Passive Sentences in English and Portuguese*. Washington, DC: Georgetown University Press.

Azevedo, Milton M. 1981a. *A Contrastive Phonology of Portuguese and English*. Washington, DC: Georgetown University Press.

Azevedo, Milton M. 1981b. "Sobre o Emprego de *você* no Português Brasileiro Atual." *Hispania* 64: 273–278.

Azevedo, Milton M. 1989. "Vernacular Features in Educated Speech in Brazilian Portuguese." *Hispania* 72:4, 862–872.

Azevedo, Milton M. 2003. *Vozes em Branco e Preto. A Representação Literária da Fala Não–Padrão*. São Paulo: Editora da Universidade de São Paulo.

Azevedo Maia, Clarinda de. 1975. *Os Falares do Algarve. Inovação e Conservação*. Coimbra: Separata da Revista Portuguesa de Filologia, Vol. 17, 1–2.

Bagno, Marcos. 1999. *Preconceito lingüístico. O que é, como se faz*. São Paulo: Edições Loyola.

Bagno, Marcos. 2000. *Dramática da Língua Portuguesa. Tradição Gramatical, Mídia a Exclusão Social*. São Paulo: Edições Loyola.

Bagno, Marcos, ed. 2002. *Lingüística da Norma*. São Paulo: Edições Loyola.

Barbadinho Neto, Raimundo. 1972. *Tendências e Constâncias da Língua do Modernismo*. Rio de Janeiro: Livraria Acadêmica.

Barbadinho Neto, Raimundo. 1977. *Sobre a Norma Literária do Modernismo. Subsídos para uma Revisão da Gramática Portuguesa*. Rio de Janeiro: Ao Livro Técnico.

Barbeitos, Arlindo. 1985. "2a. Mesa-Redonda." In *Actas do Congresso sobre a Situação Actual da Língua Portuguesa no Mundo (1983)*. Lisbon: Instituto de Cultura e Língua Portuguesa, 421–422.

Barros, Agnela. 2002. "A Situação do Português em Angola." In *Uma Política de Língua para o Português*, ed. Maria Helena Mira Mateus. Lisbon: Edições Colibri, 35–44.

Barros Ferreira, Mário de. 1988. "Vacanças, Retrete e Companhia Ilimitada. O Frantuguês Tal Qual o Falamos." *Peregrinação. Artes e Letras da Diáspora Portuguesa* 19, 16–29.

Batalha, Graciette. 1985. "Situação e Perspectivas do Português e dos Crioulos de Origem Portuguesa na Ásia Oriental (Macau, Hong Kong, Malaca, Singapura, Indonésia." In *Actas do Congresso sobre a Situação Actual da Língua Portuguesa no Mundo (1983)*. Lisbon: Instituto de Cultura e Língua Portuguesa, 287–303.

Baxter, Alan N. 1988. *A Grammar of Kristang (Malacca Creole Portuguese)*. Canberra: Research School of Pacific Studies, The Australian National University.

Baxter, Alan. 1990. "Some Observations on Verb Serialization in Malacca Creole Portuguese." *Boletim de Filologia* 31 [1986–1987], 161–184.

Baxter, Alan N. 1998. "Morfossintaxe." In *América negra: panorámica actual de los estudios lingüísticos sobre variedades hispanas, portuguesas y criollas*, ed. Mattias Perl and Arnim Schwegler. Lengua y Sociedad en el Mundo Hispánico, 97–137.

Baxter, Alan N. and Dante Lucchesi. 1997. "A Relevância dos Processos de Pidginização e Crioulização na Formação da Língua Portuguesa no Brasil." *Estudos Lingüísticos e Literários* 19, 65–84. Salvador: Universidade Federal da Bahia, Programa de Pósgraduação em Letras e Lingüística.

Bechara, Evanildo. 1999. *Moderna Gramática Portuguesa*. 37th edition. Rio de Janeiro: Editora Lucerna.

Bendiha, Urbana Pereira. 1998. "Língua(s), Emigração e Retorno." In *Linguística e Educação. Actas do Encontro da Associação Portuguesa de Linguística*, ed. Rui Vieira de Castro and Maria de Lourdes Sousa. Lisbon: Edições Colibri, 35–41.

Bento, Pedro 1998. "Para onde caminha o Português?" *Portuguese Post* (New Jersey), http://portal.com.pt/lusofore/4.htm.

Biderman, Maria Tereza Camargo. 1972–1973. "Formas de Tratamento e Estruturas Sociais." *ALFA* 18/19, 339–382.

Bisol, Leda. 1992. "Sândi Vocálico Externo: Degeminação e Elisão." *Cadernos de Estudos Lingüísticos* 23, 83–101.

Bisol, Leda. 1996. "O Sândi e a Ressilabação.' *Letras de Hoje* 104, 159–168.

Bisol, Leda, ed. 1996. *Introdução a Estudos de Fonologia do Português Brasileiro*. Porto Alegre: EDIPUCRS.

Bloemraad, Irene. 1999. "Portuguese Immigrants and Citizenship in North America." In *Lusotopie. Enjeux contemporains dans les espaces lusophones*. Paris: Editions Karthala, 103–120.

Borba, Francisco da Silva, ed. 1990. *Dicionário Gramatical de Verbos do Português Contemporâneo do Brasil*. São Paulo: Editora da Unesp.

Borba, Francisco S. 2002. *Dicionário de Usos do Português do Brasil*. São Paulo: Editora Ática.

Borges, Diniz. 2001. "Falar Português, na Califórnia." *Portal da Lusofonia* (www.portal.com)

Borges, Nair Odete da Câmara. 1960. *Influência Anglo-Americana no Falar da Ilha de S. Miguel (Açores)*. Suplemento II da *Revista Portuguesa de Filologia*. Coimbra: Universidade de Coimbra. Instituto de Estudos Románicos.

Bortoni-Ricardo, Stella Maris. 1985. *The Urbanization of Rural Dialect Speakers: A Sociolinguistic Study in Brazil*. Cambridge University Press.

Bortoni-Ricardo, Stella Maris. 2002. "Um Modelo para a Análise Sociolingüística do Português do Brasil." In Bagno 2002, 333–350.

Brandão, Cláudio. 1963. *Sintaxe Clássica Portuguesa*. Belo Horizonte: Imprensa da Universidade de Minas Gerais.

*Brasilians, The*. 2003. Monthly newspaper. 21 West 46th Street, Suite 203, New York, NY 10036. www.thebrasiliansonline.com.

Brito, Ana Maria. 1999. "Concordância, Estrutura de Frase e Movimento do Verbo no Português Europeu, no Português Brasileiro e no Português de Moçambique." In *Lindley Cintra. Homenagem ao Homem, ao Mestre e ao Cidadão*, ed. Isabel Hub Faria. Lisbon: Edições Cosmos, 333–365.

Britto, Luiz Percival Leme. 2002. "Língua e Ideologia. A Reprodução do Preconceito." In Bagno 2002, 135–154.

Brittos, Valério Cruz. 2001. "A Influência da Globo na Televisão Portuguesa." www.iuperj.br/Lusofonia/papers/valerio.

Brown, Roger and Albert Gilman. 1960. "The Pronouns of Power and Solidarity." In *Style in Language*, ed. Thomas A. Sebeok. New York: John Wiley, 253–276.

Bueno, Francisco da Silveira. 1951. *Tratado de Semântica Geral Aplicada à Língua Portuguesa do Brasil. Segunda Edição Aumentada com a Polêmica*. São Paulo: Edição Saraiva.

Bueno, Francisco da Silveira. 1955. *A Formação Histórica da Língua Portuguesa*. Rio de Janeiro: Livraria Acadêmica.

Bueno, Francisco da Silveira. 1965. *Tratado de Semântica Brasileira*. 4th edition. São Paulo: Edição Saraiva.

Burns, Anne and Caroline Coffin. 2001. *Analysing English in a Global Context. A Reader*. London and New York: Routledge.

Cagliari, Luiz Carlos. 1999. *Acento em Português*. Campinas: Edição do Autor.

Cagliari, Luiz Carlos and M. B. M. Abaurre. 1986. "Elementos para uma Investigação Instrumental das Relações entre Padrões Rítmicos e Processos Fonológicos no Português Brasileiro." *Cadernos de Estudos Lingüísticos*, 10. Campinas. Unicamp/ IEL.

Cahen, Michel. 1994. "Mozambique, histoire géopolitique d'un pays sans nation." *Lusotopie. Enjeux Contemporains dans les Espaces Lusophones* 1-2, 213–266.

Cahen, Michel, Déjanirah Couto, Peter Ronald Desouza, Louis Marrou, and Alito Siqueira. 2000. "Problématiques des lusophonies et *lusotopies* asiatiques." In *Lusotopie 2000. Lusophonies asiatiques, Asiatiques en lusophonies*. Paris: Editions Karthala, 137–158.

Callou, Dinah and Juanito Avelar. 2002. 'Estruturas com *ter* e *haver* em Anúncios do Século xix." In *Para a História do Português Brasileiro*, vol. 3: *Novos Estudos*, ed. Tania Maria Alkmin. São Paulo: Humanitas–FFLCH/USP, 47–67.

Câmara Jr., Joaquim Mattoso. [1963] 1975. "Línguas Européias de Ultramar: O Português do Brasil." In *Dispersos*. Rio de Janeiro: Fundação Getúlio Vargas, 71–87.

Câmara Jr., Joaquim Mattoso, 1972. *The Portuguese Language*, trans. Anthony J. Naro. Chicago: University of Chicago Press.

Campos, Odette G. L. A. de S. and Ângela C. S. Rodrigues. 1992. "Flexão Nominal: Indicação de Pluralidade no Sintagma Nominal." In *Gramática do Português Falado*, vol. 2: *Níveis de Análise Lingüística*, ed. Rodolfo Ilari. Campinas: Editora da Unicamp, 111–134.

Cardoso, Suzana Alice Marcelino. 1999. "A Dialectologia no Brasil: Perspectivas." *DELTA: Documentação de Estudos em Lingüística Teórica e Aplicada*, 15, special number, 233–255.

Cardoso, Suzana Alice Marcelino. 2001. "Dialectologia: Trilhas Seguidas, Caminhos a Perseguir." *DELTA: Documentação de Estudos em Lingüística Teórica e Aplicada*, 17, special number, 25–44.

Cardoso, Suzana and Carlota Ferreira, 1994. *A Dialetologia no Brasil*. São Paulo: Editora Contexto.

Carreira, Maria Helena de Araújo. 1995. "Contribuição para o Estudo das 'Formas de Tratamento' em Português: Uma Abordagem da Expressão Linguística da Área Nocional de 'Proximidade.'" In *O Amor das Letras e das Gentes. In Honor of Maria de Lourdes Belchior Pontes*, ed. João Camilo dos Santos and Frederick G. Williams. Santa Barbara: Center for Portuguese Studies, 447–454.

Carvalho, Ana Maria. 1998. "The Social Distribution of Spanish and Portuguese Dialects in the Bilingual Town of Rivera, Uruguay." Ph.D. dissertation, University of California, Berkeley.

Carvalho, Ana Maria. 2003. "Rumo a uma Definição do Português Uruguaio." *Revista Internacional de Lingüística Iberoamericana*, 1/2, 125–149.

Castilho, Ataliba Teixeira de. 1989a. In Castilho 1989b, 57–63.

Castilho, Ataliba Teixeira de, ed. 1989b. *Português Culto Falado no Brasil*. Campinas: Editora da Unicamp.

Castilho, Ataliba Teixeira de, ed. 1990a. *Gramática do Português Falado*, vol. 1: *A Ordem*. Campinas: Editora da Unicamp/FAPESP.

Castilho, Ataliba Teixeira de. 1990b. "Apresentação do Projeto de Gramática do Português Falado." In Castilho 1990a, 7–27.

Castilho, Ataliba Teixeira de. 1990c. "Português Culto Falado no Brasil: história do Projeto NURC/BR." In *A Linguagem Falada Culta na Cidade de São Paulo*, vol. 3, ed. Dino Preti and Hudinilson Urbano. São Paulo: TAQ/FAPESP, 141–202.

Castilho, Ataliba Teixeira de. 1992. "O Português do Brasil." In Ilari 1992, 237–272.

Castilho, Ataliba Teixeira de. 1995. "Para uma Gramática do Português Falado." In *Miscelânea de Estudos Lingüísticos, Filológicos e Literários in Memoriam Celso Cunha*, ed. Cilene da Cunha Pereira and Paulo Roberto Dias Pereira. Rio de Janeiro: Editora Nova Fronteira, 79–101.

Castilho, Ataliba Teixeira de, ed. 1998. *Para a História do Português Brasileiro*, vol. 1: *Primeiras Idéias*. São Paulo: Humanitas–FFLCH/USP.

Castilho, Ataliba Teixeira de. 2001. "Proposta de Agenda para uma Poítica Lingüística." In *As Línguas da Península Ibérica*, ed. Maria Helena Mira Mateus. Lisbon: Edições Colibri, 119–133.

Castilho, Ataliba Teixeira de and Margarida Basilio, eds. 1996. *Gramática do Português Falado*, vol. 4: *Estudos Descritivos*. Campinas: Editora da Unicamp; São Paulo: FAPESP.

Castilho, Ataliba Teixeira de and Dino Preti, eds. 1987. *A Linguagem Falada Culta na Cidade de São Paulo*, vol. 2: *Diálogos Entre Dois Informantes*. São Paulo: FAPESP.

Castro, Ivo, 1991a. *Curso de História da Língua Portuguesa*. Lisbon: Universidade Aberta.

Castro, Ivo, ed. 1991b. *Curso de História da Língua Portuguesa. Leituras Complementares*. Lisbon: Universidade Aberta.

Castro, Ivo. 1999. "O Português Médio segundo Cintra (Nuga Bibliográfica)." In *Lindley Cintra. Homenagem ao Homem, ao Mestre e ao Cidadão*, ed. Isabel Hub Faria. Lisbon: Edições Cosmos.

Castro, Ivo. 2001. "Diversidade Lingüística." In *Mais Línguas, Mais Europa: Celebrar a Diversidade Linguística e Cultural da Europa*, ed. Maria Helena Mira Mateus. Lisbon: Edições Colibri, 23–25.

Castro, Rui Vieira, Maria de Lourdes Dionísio, and Orlanda Gomane. 2001. "O Ensino do Português em Moçambique. Contexto Linguístico, Políticas de Língua e Orientações Curriculares." *Revista Portuguesa de Humanidades*, 5, 233–253.

Castro, Yeda Pessoa de. 1980. *Os Falares Africanos na Interação Social do Brasil Colônia*. Salvador: Universidade Federal da Bahia.

Castro, Yeda Pessoa de. 1983. "Das Línguas Africanas ao Português Brasileiro." *Afro-Ásia*, 14, 81–106.

Castro, Yeda Pessoa de. 1997. "Línguas Africanas como Objeto de Estudo no Brasil." *Lusorama*, 34, 52–60.

Charpentier, Jean Michel. 1992. "La survivance du créole portugais 'makaista' en Extrème-Orient." In *Actas do Colóquio sobre Crioulos de Base Lexical Portuguesa*, ed. Ernesto d'Andrade and Alain Kihm. Lisbon: Edições Colibri, 81–95.

Cintra, Geraldo. 1983. "Mente: Sufixo adverbial?" *Cadernos de Estudos Lingüísticos*, 5, 73–83.

Cintra, Luís Filipe Lindley. 1971. "Nova Proposta de Classificação dos Dialectos Galego-Portugueses." *Boletim de Filologia*, 22, 81–116. Reprinted in Cintra 1995, 117–163.

Cintra, Luís Filipe Lindley. 1972. *Sobre 'Formas de Tratamento' na Língua Portuguesa*. Lisbon: Livros Horizonte.

Cintra, Luís F. Lindley. 1986/1987 (publ. 1990). "Sobre o Mais Antigo Texto Não-literário Português: A Notícia de Torto (Leitura Crítica, Data, Lugar de Redacção e Comentário Linguístico)." *Boletim de Filologia*, 31, 21–77.

Cintra, Luís Filipe Lindley. 1995. *Estudos de Dialectologia Portuguesa*. 2nd edition. Lisbon: Livraria Sá da Costa Editora.

Cintra, Luís Filipe Lindley. 1999a [1981]. "Situação Actual da Língua Portuguesa no Mundo." In *Lindley Cintra. Homenagem ao Homem, ao Mestre e ao Cidadão*, ed. Isabel Hub Faria. Lisbon: Edições Cosmos, 289–300.

Cintra, Luís Filipe Lindley. 1999b [1971]. "*Tu e vós*, como Formas de Tratamento de Deus, em Orações e na Poesia em Língua Portuguesa." In *Lindley Cintra. Homenagem ao Homem, ao Mestre e ao Cidadão*, ed. Isabel Hub Faria. Lisbon: Edições Cosmos, 241–268.

Cintra, Luís Filipe Lindley. Forthcoming. "Os Dialectos da Ilha da Madeira no Quadro Geral dos Dialectos Galego-Portugueses." Paper given at the II Congresso da Cultura Madeirense (1990). *Boletim de Filologia* 30 (cited in Cruz and Saramago 1999).

Clements, J. Clancy. 1992. "Foreigner Talk and the Origins of Pidgin Portuguese." *Journal of Pidgin and Creole Languages*, 7:1, 75–92.

Clements, J. Clancy. 2000. "Evidência para a Existência de um Pidgin Português Asiático." In *Crioulos de Base Portuguesa*, ed. Ernesto d'Andrade, Dulce Pereira, and Maria Antónia Mota. Lisbon: Associação Portuguesa de Linguística, 185–200.

Coelho, F. Adolpho. 1880–1886. "Os Dialectos Românicos ou Neolatinos na Africa, Asia e América." *Boletim da Sociedade de Geographia de Lisboa*. Reprinted 1967 in *Estudos Linguísticos Crioulos*, ed. J. Morais Barbosa. Lisbon: Academia Internacional de Cultura Portuguesa.

*Correio Braziliense*. 2003. "Mais da metade dos estudantes brasileiros não compreende o que lê." www.theworldpress.com July/1st.

Costa, Lluís. 1995. "O Português em Timor e o Português de Timor." *Revista Internacional de Língua Portuguesa*, 14, 5–6.

Coutinho, Ismael de Lima. 1962. *Gramática Histórica*. 5th edition. Rio de Janeiro: Livraria Acadêmica.

Couto, Hildo Honório do. 1991. "A Situação da Língua Portuguesa na Guiné-Bissau." *Revista Internacional de Língua Portuguesa*, 5/6, 114–124.

Couto, Hildo Honório do. 1994. *O Crioulo Português da Guiné-Bissau*. Hamburg: Helmut Buske Verlag.

Couto, Hildo Honório do. 1999. "A Reduplicação em Português." *Lusorama*, 40, 29–49.

Cruz, Maria Luísa Segura da and João Saramago. 1999. "Açores e Madeira: Autonomia e Coesão Dialectais." In *Lindley Cintra. Homenagem ao Homem, ao Mestre e ao Cidadão*, ed. Isabel Hub Faria. Lisbon: Edições Cosmos, 707–738.

Cruz, Maria Luísa Segura da, João Saramago, and Gabriela Vitorino. 1994. "Os Dialectos Leoneses em Território Português: Coesão e Diversidade." In *Variação Linguística no Espaço, no Tempo e na Sociedade*. Lisbon: Associação Portuguesa de Linguística/Edições Colibri, 281–293.

Cruz-Ferreira, Madalena. 1999. "Portuguese (European)." In *Handbook of the International Phonetic Association. A Guide to the Use of the International Phonetic Alphabet*. Cambridge University Press, pp. 126–130.

Crystal, David. 1994. *An Encyclopedic Dictionary of Language and Languages*. London: Penguin Books.

Crystal, David. 1997. *The Cambridge Encyclopedia of Language*, 2nd edn. Cambridge University Press.

Crystal, David. 1998. *The Cambridge Encyclopedia of The English Language*. Cambridge University Press.

Cunha, Antônio Geraldo da. 1998. *Dicionário Histórico das Palavras Portuguesas de Origem Tupi*. São Paulo: Companhia Melhoramentos.

Cunha, Celso. 1985. *A Questão da Norma Culta Brasileira*. Rio de Janeiro: Tempo Brasileiro.

Cunha, Celso and Luís Filipe Lindley Cintra. 1985. *Nova Gramática do Português Contemporâneo*. 2nd edition. Rio de Janeiro: Editora Nova Fronteira.

Cunha, Isabel Ferin. 2002. "As telenovelas brasileiras em Portugal." http://www.bocc.ubi.pt/pag/cunha-isabel-ferin-telenovelas-brasileiras.pdf.

Cyrino, Sonia Maria L. 1999. "Elementos Nulos Pós-verbais no Português Brasileiro Oral Contemporâneo." In *Gramática do Português Falado*, vol. 7: *Estudos Descritivos*, ed. Maria Helena de Moura Neves. Campinas: FAPESP/Unicamp/Humanitas; São Paulo: FAPESP, 595–625.

Daneš, František. 1966. "A Three-Level Approach to Syntax." *Travaux Linguistiques de Prague*, 1, 225–240.

Demasi, Maria do Socorro. 1995. "O -*l*- Pos-vocálico na Fala Culta do Rio de Janeiro." In *Miscelânea de Estudos Lingüísticos, Filológicos e Literários in Memoriam Celso Cunha*, ed. Cilene da Cunha Pereira and Paulo Roberto Dias Pereira. Rio de Janeiro: Editora Nova Fronteira, 115–143.

*Diálogo com as Ilhas. Sobre Cultura e Literatura de São Tomé e Príncipe*. Lisbon: Edições Colibri, 33–34.

Dias, Eduardo Mayone. 1989. *Falares Emigreses. Uma Abordagem ao Seu Estudo*. Lisbon: Instituto de Cultura e Língua Portuguesa.

Dias-Tatilon, Manuela. 2000. "Influences on Portuguese Spoken in Montreal." In Teixeira and da Rosa 2000, 145–157.

Dietrich, Wolf. 1980. *Bibliografia da Língua Portuguesa do Brasil*. Tübingen: Gunter Narr Verlag.

Duarte, Inês. 1996. "A Topicalização em Português Europeu: Uma Análise Comparativa." In *Actas do Congresso Internacional sobre o Português*, vol. 1, ed. Inês Duarte and Isabel Leiria. Lisbon: Edições Colibri, 327–360.

Duarte, Inês. 2002. "Português Europeu. A Língua Portuguesea e a Sua Variedade Europeia." In *As Línguas da Península Ibérica*, ed. Maria Helena Mira Mateus. Lisbon: Edições Colibri, 101–118.

Duarte, Maria Eugênia L. and Dinah Callou, eds. 2002. *Para a História do Português Brasileiro*, vol. 4: *Notícias de* Corpora *e Outros Estudos*. Rio de Janeiro: UFRJ/Letras, FAPERJ.

Elcock, W. D. 1940. *The Romance Languages*. London: Faber & Faber.

Elizaincín, Adolfo. 1992. *Dialectos en contacto. Español y portugués en España y América*. Montevideo: Arca Editorial.

Elizaincín, Adolfo, Luis Behares, and Graciela Barrios. 1987. *Nos Falemo Brasilero*. Montevideo: Editorial Amesur.

Ellison, Fred P., Francisco Gomes de Matos, *et al*. 1971. *Modern Portuguese*. New York: Alfred A. Knopf.

Endruschat, Annette. 1995. "Acerca da Colocação dos Pronomes Clíticos no Português de Angolanos e Moçambicanos, Sua Problemática no Contexto dos Diferentes Registos e na Aquisição da Linguagem." In *Actas do 4° Congresso da Associação Internacional de Lusitanistas*. Lisbon: Lidel, 95–102.

Endruschat, Annette. 2001. "Lusitanistisches Lehrangebot deutschsprachiger Universitäten im Sommersemester 2001." *Lusorama*, 46, 95–119.

Eslava-Galán, Juan. 1995. *La historia de España contada para escépticos*. Barcelona: Editorial Planeta.

Esling, John H. 1998. "Everyone Has an Accent Except Me." In *Language Myths*, ed. Laurie Bauer and Peter Trudgill. London: Penguin Books.

Espírito Santo, Carlos. 1985. "Situação Actual da Língua Portuguesa nas Ilhas de S. Tomé e Príncipe." In *Actas do Congresso sobre a Situação Actual da Língua Portuguesa no Mundo (1983)*. Lisbon: Instituto de Cultura e Língua Portuguesa, 253–263.

Estrela, Edite. 1993. *A Questão Ortográfica. Reforma e Acordos da Língua Portuguesa*. Lisbon: Editorial Notícias.

Faraco, Carlos Alberto. 2002. "Norma-Padrão Brasileira. Desembaraçando Alguns Nós." In Bagno 2002, 37–61.

Faraco, Carlos Alberto, ed. 2001. *Estrangeirismos. Guerras em Torno da Língua.* São Paulo: Parábola Editorial.

Faria, Isabel Hub, Emília Ribeiro Pedro, Inês Duarte, and Carlos A. M. Gouveia. 1996. *Introdução à Linguística Geral e Portuguesa.* Lisbon: Editorial Caminho.

Ferguson, Charles A. 1959. "Diglossia." *Word*, 15, 325–340.

Fernández Rodríguez, M. A. *et al.* 1996. *Lingua Inicial e Competencia Lingüística en Galicia.* Vigo: Seminario de Sociolingüística, Real Academia Galega.

Ferreira, Carlota. 1995. "Um Panorama da Dialectologia no Brasil." *Revista Internacional de Língua Portuguesa*, 14, 91–105.

Ferreira, Carlota et al. 1987. *Atlas lingüístico de Sergipe*, vol. 1. UFBA/Fundação Estadual de Cultura do Estado de Sergipe.

Ferreira, Manuel. 1988. *Que Futuro para a Língua Portuguesa em África? Uma Perspectiva Sociocultural.* Linda-a-Velha: ALAC, África–Literatura, Arte e Cultura Ltda.

Ferreira, Manuela Barros. 1992. "Dialectologia da Área Galego-Portuguesa." In Ferronha *et al.* 1992, 30–37.

Ferreira, Manuela Barros. 1994. "A Limitrofia do Sendinês." In *Variação Linguística no Espaço, no Tempo e na Sociedade.* Lisbon: Associação Portuguesa de Linguística/Edições Colibri, 35–42.

Ferreira, Manuela Barros. 2002. "O Mirandês, Língua Minoritária." In *Uma Política de Língua para o Português*, ed. Maria Helena Mira Mateus. Lisbon: Edições Colibri, 137–145.

Ferreira Netto, Waldemar. 2001. *Introdução à Fonologia da Língua Portuguesa.* São Paulo: Editora Hedra.

Ferronha, António Luís *et al.* 1992. *Atlas da Língua Portuguesa na História e no Mundo.* Lisbon: Imprensa Nacional–Casa da Moeda.

Firmino, Gregório. 1995a. "Revisiting the 'Language Question' in Post-Colonial Africa: the Case of Portuguese and Indigenous Languages in Mozambique." Ph.D. dissertation, University of California, Berkeley.

Firmino, Gregório. 1995b. "O Caso do Português e das Línguas Indígenas de Moçambique (Subsídios para uma Política Linguística)." *Revista Internacional de Lingua Portuguesa*, 13, 33–41.

Freitas, Judith. 1995. "*Nós* e *a gente* em elocuções formais." In *Miscelânea de Estudos Lingüísticos, Filológicos e Literários in Memoriam Celso Cunha*, ed. Cilene da Cunha Pereira and Paulo Roberto Dias Pereira. Rio de Janeiro: Editora Nova Fronteira, 155–163.

Gadet, Françoise. 1997. *Le français populaire.* Deuxième édition corrigée. Paris: Presses Universitaires de France.

Galves, Charlotte C. 1993. "O Enfraquecimento da Concordância no Português Brasileiro." In Roberts and Kato 1993, 387–408.

Galves, Charlotte and Maria Bernadete Marques Abaurre. 1996. "Os Clíticos no Português Brasileiro: Elementos para uma Abordagem Sintático-Fonológica." In Castilho and Basilio 1996, 273–319.

Goes, Carlos. 1940. *Dicionário de Galicismos.*

Gomes de Matos, Francisco. 1996. *Pedagogia da Positividade.* Recife: Editora da Universidade Federal de Pernambuco.

Gomes de Matos, Francisco. 2002. *Comunicar para o Bem. Rumo à Paz Comunicativa.* São Paulo: Editora Ave Maria.

Gonçalves, Perpétua. 1985. "Situação Actual da Língua Portuguesa em Moçambique." In *Actas do Congresso sobre a Situação Actual da Língua Portuguesa no Mundo. Lisboa 1983*, vol. 1, 243–252.

Gonçalves, Perpétua. 1996. *Português de Moçambique. Uma Variedade em Formação.* Maputo: Livraria Universitária e Faculdade de Letras da Universidade Eduardo Mondlane.

Greenough, J. B. *et al.* 1903. *New Latin Grammar.* Boston: Ginn & Company.

Guy, Gregory R. 1981. "Linguistic Variation in Brazilian Portuguese: Aspects of the Phonology, Syntax, and Language History." Ph.D. dissertation, University of Pennsylvania.

Guy, Gregory R. 1989. "On the Nature and Origins of Popular Brazilian Portuguese." In *Estudios sobre Español de América y Lingüística Afroamericana.* Bogotá: Instituto Caro y Cuervo, 226–244.

Hammermüller, Gunther. 1984. " 'Tu, é cachorro'?–Bemerkungen zum Duzen in Portugal." In *Umgangssprache in der Iberoromania*, ed. Günter Holtus and Edgar Radtke. Tübingen: Gunter Narr Verlag, 153–164.

Head, Brian F. 1973. "O Estudo do 'r-caipira' no Contexto Social." *Revista Vozes*, 67:8, 43–49.

Head, Brian F. 1976. "Social Factors in the Use of Pronouns for the Addressee in Brazilian Portuguese." In *Readings in Portuguese Linguistics*, ed. J. Schmidt-Radefeldt. Amsterdam: North-Holland Publishing Company, 289–348.

Head, Brian F. 1994. "O 'Dialecto Brasileiro' segundo Leite de Vasconcellos." In *Variação linguística no espaço, no tempo e na sociedade.* Lisbon: Associação Portuguesa de Linguística/Colibri–Artes Gráficas, 297–315.

Head, Brian F. 1996. "Os Parâmetros da Variação Dialectal no Português do Brasil." In *Actas do Congresso Internacional sobre o Português*, vol. 3, ed. Inês Duarte and Isabel Leiria. Lisbon: Edições Colibri, 141–165.

Helms-Park, Rena. 2000. "Two Decades of Heritage Language Education." In Teixeira and da Rosa 2000, 127–144.

Henriques, Maria Augusta. 1985. "Situação e Perspectivas do Português na Guiné-Bissau." In *Actas do Congresso sobre a Situação Actual da Língua Portuguesa no Mundo (1983).* Lisbon: Instituto de Cultura e Língua Portuguesa, 234–241.

Hensey, Frederick. 1972. *The Sociolinguistics of the Brazilian-Uruguayan Border.* The Hague, Mouton.

Hensey, Frederick. 1982. "Spanish, Portuguese and Fronteiriço: Languages in Contact in Northern Uruguay." *International Journal of the Sociology of Language*, 34, 9–23.

Holm, John. 1987. "Creole Influence on Popular Brazilian Portuguese." *Pidgin and Creole Languages: Essays in Memory of John E. Reinecke.* Honolulu: University Press of Hawaii, 406–430.

Holm, John. 1989. *Pidgins and Creoles*, 2 vols. Cambridge University Press.

Holm, John. 1992. "Vernacular Brazilian Portuguese: A Semi-Creole." In *Actas do Colóquio sobre "Crioulos de Base Lexical Portuguesa,"* ed. Ernesto d'Andrade and A. Kihm. Lisbon: Colibri, 37–66.

Holm, John. 2000. *An Introduction to Pidgins and Creoles.* Cambridge University Press.

Holm, John. 2004. *Languages in Contact. The Partial Restructuring of Vernaculars.* Cambridge University Press.

Houaiss, Antônio. 1960. *Sugestões para uma Política da Língua.* Rio de Janeiro: Ministério da Educação e Cultura, Instituto Nacional do Livro.

Houaiss, Antônio. 1985. *O Português no Brasil.* Rio de Janeiro: Unibrade.

Houaiss, Antônio. 2001. *Dicionário Houaiss da Língua Portuguesa.* Rio de Janeiro: Editora Objetiva.

Huber, Joseph [1933] 1986. *Gramática do Português Antigo,* trans. Maria Manuela Gouveia Delille. Lisbon: Fundação Calouste Gulbenkian.

Hughes, Geoffrey. 1998. *Swearing. A Social History of Foul Language, Oaths, and Profanity in English.* London: Penguin Books.

Hutchins, John A. 1975. "Use and Frequency of Occurrence of Verb Forms in Spoken Brazilian Portuguese." *Hispania,* 58:1, 59–67.

IBGE–Instituto Brasileiro de Geografia e Estatística. www.ibge.gov.br.

IBGE (Instituto Brasileiro de Geografia e Estatística) 2000. *Brasil: 500 Anos de Povoamento.* Rio de Janeiro.

Ilari, Rodolfo, 1992. *Lingüística Românica.* São Paulo: Editora Ática.

Ilari, Rodolfo. 1996. "A Categoria Advérbio na Gramática do Português Falado." In *Actas do Congresso Internacional sobre o Português,* vol. 1, ed. Inês Duarte and Isabel Leiria. Lisbon: Edições Colibri, 107–139.

Ilari, Rodolfo, Carlos Franchi, Maria Helena de Moura Neves, and Sirio Possenti. 1996. "Os Pronomes Pessoais do Português Falado: Roteiro para a Análise." In Castilho and Basilio 1996, 79–166.

IPA. 1999. *Handbook of the International Phonetic Association. A Guide to the Use of the International Phonetic Alphabet.* Cambridge University Press.

Jensen, John B. 1981. "Forms of Address in Brazilian Portuguese: Standard European or Oriental Honorifics?" In *From Linguistics to Literature. Romance Studies Offered to Francis M. Rogers,* ed. Bernmard H. Bichakjian. Amsterdam: John Benjamins, 45–61.

Jensen, John B. 1977. "A Investigação de Formas de Tratamento e a Telenovela: *A Escalada,* parte I." *Revista Brasileira de Lingüística,* 4:2, 45–73.

Jensen, John B. n.d. *Não Me Chame de Senhor: Aspectos de Formas de Tratamento no Português do Brasil.* Printout.

Jeroslow [McKinney], Elizabeth Helen. 1974. "Rural Cearense Portuguese: A Study of One Variety of Nonstandard Brazilian Speech." Doctoral dissertation, Cornell University.

Joel, António Augusto. 2000. "Literature of Portuguese Background in Canada." In Teixeira and da Rosa 2000, 223–235.

Joos, Martin. 1967 [1961]. *The Five Clocks. A Linguistic Excursion Into The Five Styles of English Usage.* New York: Harcourt, Brace & World.

Katamba, Francis. 1993. *Morphology.* New York: St. Martin's Press.

Kato, Mary. 1993. "Recontando a História das Relativas em uma Perspectiva Paramétrica." In Roberts and Kato 1993, 223–261.

Katupha, J. M. M. 1994. "The Language Situation and Language Use in Mozambique" In *African Languages, Development and the State,* ed. Richard Fardon and Graham Furniss. London: Routledge, 89–96.

Kehdi, Valter. 1990. *Morfemas do Português.* São Paulo: Editora Ática.

King, Brian. 2001. "Na Kal Língua Ke Bu Na Skirbi Nel? Linguistic Conflict and Narrating the Nation in Guinea-Bissau." Graduate paper, University of California, Berkeley. Published as King 2004.

King, Brian. 2004. "Conflicto Linguístico e Narrativa da Nação." *Soronda. Revista de Estudos Guineenses. Nova Série*, 7, 113–172.

Koike, Dale A. 1992. *Language and Social Relationship in Brazilian Portuguese. The Pragmatics of Politeness.* Austin: University of Texas Press.

Ladefoged, Peter. 2001. *A Course in Phonetics.* 4th edition. Fort Worth: Harcourt College Publishers.

Larsen, Ingmar. 2003. "O império português responde por escrito ou *estamos numa nice*– sobre situaçao luso-africana na perspectiva dos estudos de pós-colonialismo." Unpublished ms.

Lee, Seung-Hwa. 2000. "Sobre os Compostos do PB." *DELTA: Documentação de Estudos em Lingüística Teórica e Aplicada*, 13:1, 1–15.

Leite, Yonne and Dinah Callou. 2002. *Como Falam os Brasileiros.* Rio de Janeiro: Jorge Zahar Editor.

Le Page, R. and David De Camp. 1960. *Jamaican Creole.* London: Macmillan.

Lessa, Luiz Carlos. 1966. *O Modernismo Brasileiro e a Língua Portuguesa.* Rio de Janeiro: Fundação Getúlio Vargas. 1976. 2nd edition. Rio de Janeiro: Grifo.

Lipski, John. 1975. "Vowel Nasalization in Brazilian Portuguese." *Canadian Journal of Linguistics*, 20, 58–67.

Lopes, Armando Jorge. 1997a. *Language Policy. Principles and Problems.* Maputo: Universidade Eduardo Mondlane.

Lopes, Armando Jorge. 1997b. "Language Policy in Mozambique: A Taboo?" In *African Linguistics at the Crossroads: Papers from Kwaluseni*, ed. R. K. Herbert. Cologne: Rüdiger Köppe, 485–500.

Lopes, Armando Jorge. 2002a. "Em Direcção ao Primeiro Léxico de Usos do Português Moçambicano." www.fortunecity.com.

Lopes, Armando Jorge. 2002b. "O Português Como Língua Segunda em África: Problemáticas de Planificação e Política Linguística." In *Uma Política de Língua para o Português*, ed. Maria Helena Mira Mateus. Lisbon: Edições Colibri, 15–31.

Lopes, Armando Jorge. 2002c. "Alguns Dados sobre a Situação do Português em Moçambique." In *Uma Política de Língua para o Português*, ed. Maria Helena Mira Mateus. Lisbon: Edições Colibri, 51–54.

Lopes, Armando Jorge, Salvador Júlio Sitoe, and Paulinho José Nhamuende. 2002. *Moçambicanismos: Para um Léxico de Usos do Português Moçambicano.* Maputo: Livraria Universitária, Universidade Eduardo Mondlane.

Lopes, Célia Regina dos Santos. 2002. "De *gente* para *a gente*: O Século XIX como Fase de Transição." In *Para a História do Português Brasileiro*, vol. 3: *Novos Estudos*, ed. Tania Maria Alkmin. São Paulo: Humanitas–FFLCH/USP, 25–46.

Lopes, David. 1969. *A Expansão da Língua Portuguesa no Oriente Durante os Séculos XVI, XVII e XVII.* 2nd edition revised by Luís de Matos. Porto: Portucalense Editora.

Lorenzino, Gerardo Augusto. 2000. "Uma Avaliação Socio-linguística sobre São Tomé e Príncipe." In *Crioulos de Base Portuguesa*, ed. Ernesto d'Andrade, Dulce Pereira, and Maria Antónia Mota. Lisbon: Associação Portuguesa de Linguística, 435–451.

Lucchesi, Dante. 2002. "Norma Lingüística e Realidade Social." In Bagno 2002, 63–92.

Machado, Aires da Mata, Filho. 1940. *O Negro e o Garimpo em Minas Gerais.* Published as offprint (*separata*) of *Revista do Arquivo Municipal* (São Paulo). 1964 2nd edition, Rio de Janeiro: Editora Civilização Brasileira.

Magalhães, Erasmo D'Almeida. 1983. "Notas aos Estudos sobre o Português Falado no Brasil." In *III Encontro de Professores de Língua Portuguesa. O Português falado no Brasil. Contribuição para Seu Estudo.* Taubaté: Universidade de Taubaté, 5–42.

Magalhães, Erasmo D'Almeida and Maria Resende San-Martin. 1983. "Seleção Bibliográfica e Comentários sobre o Português Falado no Brasil." In *III Encontro de Professores de Língua Portuguesa. O Português Falado no Brasil. Contribuição para Seu Estudo.* Taubaté: Universidade de Taubaté, 43–105.

Mann, Charles and Gabriella Wong. 1999. "Issues in Language Planning and Language Education: A Survey from Macao on Its Return to Chinese Sovereignty." *Language Problems & Language Planning*, 23:1, 17–36.

Marcos Marín, Francisco A. 2002. "El Español: Variantes Europea y Americana." In *As Línguas da Península Ibérica*, ed. Mira Mateus. Lisbon: Edições Colibri, 35–48.

Marcuschi, Luiz Antônio. 1989. "Marcadores Conversacionais do Português Brasileiro: Formas, Posições e Funções." In Castilho 1989b, 281–321.

Marques, Maria Helena Duarte. 1995. "Subordinação e Complexidade Sintática." In *Miscelânea de Estudos Lingüísticos, Filológicos e Literários in Memoriam Celso Cunha*, ed. Cilene da Cunha Pereira and Paulo Roberto Dias Pereira. Rio de Janeiro: Editora Nova Fronteira, 277–287.

Marques, Irene Guerra. 1985. "Algumas Considerações sobre a Problemática Linguística em Angola." In *Actas do Congresso sobre a Situação Actual da Língua Portuguesa no Mundo. Lisboa 1983*, vol. 1, 204–224.

Marroquim, Mário. 1934. *A Língua do Nordeste (Alagoas e Pernambuco).* São Paulo: Companhia Editora Nacional.

Martin, John. 1976. "Tense, Mood, and the 'Inflected Infinitive' in Portuguese." In *Readings in Portuguese Linguistics*, ed. Jürgen Schmidt-Radefeldt. Amsterdam: North Holland.

Martinho, Ana Maria. 1991. "Notas sobre o Ensino do Português em Angola–Rumos e Desvios." *Revista Internacional de Língua Portuguesa*, 5/6, 165–168.

Martins, Ana Maria. 1999. "Ainda 'os mais antigos textos escritos em português.' Documentos de 1175 a 1252." In *Lindley Cintra. Homenagem ao Homem, ao Mestre e ao Cidadão*, ed. Isabel Hub Faria. Lisbon: Edições Cosmos, 491–534.

Martins, Cristina. 1995. "O Desaparecimento do Mirandês na Cidade de Miranda do Douro: Uma Leitura dos *Estudos de Filologia Mirandesa* de José Leite de Vasconcelos." In *Variação Linguística no Espaço, no Tempo e na Sociedade.* Lisbon: Associação Portuguesa de Linguística/Edições Colibri, 95–105.

Martins, Eleni Jacques. 1989. "Pronomes Pessoais Complementos de 3ª Pessoa: Uma Revisão de Conceitos e Normas." In Castilho 1989b, 103–118.

Martins, Helena and Vanise Medeiros. 1998. "Considerações Sobre a Flutuação no Emprego do Subjuntivo no Português do Brasil e Seu Impacto no Ensino de Alunos de Português como Segunda Língua." In *Actas do Quinto Congresso da Associação Internacional de Lusitanistas*, ed. T. F. Earle. Oxford/Coimbra: Edições Técnicas, 169–175.

Mascherpe, Mário. 1970. *Análise Comparativa dos Sistemas Fonológicos do Inglês e do Português.* Assis: Faculdade de Filosofia, Ciências e Letras de Assis.

Massini-Cagliari, Gladis. 1992. *Acento e Ritmo*. São Paulo: Editora Contexto.

Mata, Inocência. 1998. "Um Olhar sobre Duas Línguas Minoritárias." In *Diálogo com as Ilhas. Sobre Cultura e Literatura de São Tomé e Príncipe*. Lisbon: Edições Colibri, 33–34.

Matos, I. A. 1991. "Le bilinguisme des jeunes issus de l'immigration portuguaise en France." Doctoral dissertation. C.D.L, Université Stendhal, Grenoble III.

Matthews, Peter. 1997. *The Concise Oxford Dictionary of Linguistics*. New York: Oxford University Press.

Matusse, Renato. 1997. "The Future of Portuguese in Mozambique." In *African Linguistics at the Crossroads: Papers from Kwaluseni*, ed. R. K. Herbert. Cologne: Rüdiger Köppe, 541–554.

McArthur, Tom. 1992. *The Oxford Companion to the English Language*. Oxford University Press.

McWhorter, John H. 2000. *The Missing Spanish Creoles: Recovering the Birth of Plantation Contact Languages*. Berkeley: University of California Press.

Megenney, William W. 1986. *El palenquero: un lenguaje post-criollo de Colombia*. Bogotá: Instituto Caro y Cuervo.

Megenney, William W. 2001. "A Penetração de Influências Africanas no Brasil." *Lusorama*, 47–48, 94–105.

Megenney, William W. 2002. "(H)ouve um Linguajar Crioulo Panbrasileiro?" *Hispania*, 85:3, 587–596.

Mello, Heliana Ribeiro de. 1996. "Contato Linguístico na Formação do Português Vernáculo do Brasil." In *Actas do Congresso Internacional sobre o Português*, vol. 3, ed. Inês Duarte and Isabel Leiria. Lisbon: Edições Colibri, 353–367.

Melo, Gladstone Chaves de. 1971. *A Língua do Brasil*. 2nd edition. Rio de Janeiro: Fundação Getúlio Vargas.

Mendonça, Luís. 2000. *História dos Açores. Visão Geral (sécs. XV–XX)*. São Miguel: Nova Gráfica.

Mesquita, A. 1986. "Educação Bilingue para Filhos de Emigrantes," *Jornal de Psicologia*, 5/2, 12–16.

MICS (Multiple Indicator Cluster Surveys) 1997. Inquérito de Indicadores Múltiplos. Luanda: INE/Unicef.

*Migalhas* (migalhas.migalhas@uol.com.br). 2004. "Racismo." January 16, # 844.

Mingas, Amélia. 2000. *Interferência do Kimbundo no Português Falado em Lwanda*. Oporto: Campodas Letras Editores.

Mingas, Amélia. 2002. "Ensino da Língua Portuguesa no Contexto Angolano." In *Uma Política de Língua para o Português*, ed. Maria Helena Mira Mateus. Lisbon: Edições Colibri, 45–50.

Morais, Maria Aparecida C. R. Torres. 2003. "EPP Generalizado, Sujeito Nulo e Línguas de Configuração Discursiva," *Letras de Hoje*, 38:1, 71–98.

Mota, Maria Antónia. 2001. "Variação e Diversidade Linguística em Portugal." In *Mais Línguas, Mais Europa: Celebrar a Diversidade Linguística e Cultural da Europa*, ed. Maria Helena Mira Mateus. Lisboa: Edições Colibri, 27–34.

MRPR, 2002. *Manual de Redação da Presidência da República*. 2nd edition. Brasília: Presidência da República, Casa Civil, Subchefia para Assuntos Jurídicos.

Naro, Anthony J. 1978. "A Study on the Origins of Pidginization," *Language*, 54:2, 315–347.

Naro, Anthony J. 1981. "Portuguese in Brazil." In *Trends in Romance Linguistics and Philology*, vol. 1: *Romance Comparative and Historical Linguistics*, ed. Rebecca Posner and John N. Green. The Hague: Mouton Publishers, 413–462.

Naro, Anthony J., ed. 1976. *Tendências Atuais da Lingüística e da Filologia no Brasil*. Trans. Maria Candida J. Bardenave and Marilda Winkler Averbug. Rio de Janeira: Livraria Francisco Alves Editora.

Naro, Anthony J. and Miriam Lemle. 1976. "Syntactic Diffusion." In *Papers from the Parasession on Diachronic Syntax*. Chicago: Chicago Linguistic Society, 221–140.

Naro, Anthony J. and Maria Marta Pereira Scherre. 1991. "Variação e Mudança Lingüística: Fluxos e Contrafluxos na Comunidade de Fala," *Cadernos de Estudos Lingüísticos*, 20, 9–16.

Naro, Anthony J. and Maria Marta Pereira Scherre. 1993. "Sobre as Origens do Português Popular do Brasil," *DELTA Revista de Documentação de Estudos em Lingüística Teórica e Aplicada* 9, special number, 437–454.

Naro, Anthony J. and Maria Marta Pereira Scherre. 2000. "Variable Concord in Portuguese: The Situation in Brazil and Portugal." In *Language Change and Language Contact in Pidgins and Creoles*. ed. John McWhorter. Amsterdam: Benjamins, 235–255.

Nascentes, Antenor. 1922. *O Linguajar Carioca*. Rio de Janeiro: Sussekind de Mendonça. 2nd edition 1953. Rio de Janairo: Organização Simões.

Needell, Jeffrey D. 1987. *A Tropical Belle Epoque. Elite Culture and Society in Turn-of-the-Century Rio de Janeiro*. Cambridge University Press.

Neves, Maria Helena de Moura, 2000. *Gramática de Usos do Português*. São Paulo: Editora UNESP.

Neves, Maria Helena de Moura, 2003. *Guia de Uso do Português: Confrontando Regras e Usos*. São Paulo: Editora UNESP.

Neves, Maria Helena de Moura, ed. 1999. *Gramática do Português Falado, vol. 7: Novos estudos*. São Paulo: Humanitas/FFLCH/USP; Campinas: Editora da Unicamp.

Noivo, Edite. 2000. "Diasporic Identities at Century's End." In Teixeira and da Rosa 2000, 158–171.

Nooteboom, Sieb. 1997. "The Prosody of Speech: Melody and Rhythm." In *The Handbook of Phonetic Sciences*, ed. William J. Hardcastle and John Laver. London: Blackwell Publishers, pp. 640–673.

Nunes, Fernando. 1998. *Portuguese-Canadians from Sea to Sea. A National Needs Assessment*. Toronto: Portuguese-Canadian National Congress.

Oliveira, Fernão de. [1536] 2000. *Gramática da Linguagem Portuguesa*, ed. Amadeu Torres and Carlos Assunção. Lisbon: Academia das Ciências de Lisboa.

Oliveira, Gilvan Müller de. 2003. "Lei de Co-oficialização de Línguas Indígenas." E-mail message to the Comunidade Virtual da Linguagem (CVL), http://groups. yahoo.com/group/CVL, dated November 3, 2003. Also in Informe 2003/01, "Lei de Co-oficialização de Línguas Indígenas," IPOL–Instituto de Investigação e Desenvolvimento em Política Lingüística (www.ipol.org.br).

Oliveira, M. António F. de. 1991. "Quimbundismos no Português Literário do Século XVIII nas Áreas Angolana e Brasileira," *Revista Internacional de Língua Portuguesa*, 5/6, 148–160.

Oliveira, Mário de. "Fórmula 1." *Minas Gerais, Suplemento Literário* 519, August 28, 1976, p. 4.

Oliveira, Sandi Michele de. Forthcoming. "A Retrospective on Address in Portugal (1982–2002)."

Paiva, Maria da Conceição de and Maria Marta Pereira Scherre. 1999. "Retrospectiva Sociolingüística: Contribuições do Peul." *DELTA Documentação de Estudos em Lingüística Teórica e Aplicada*, 15, special issue, 201–232.

Pap, Leo. 1949. *Portuguese-American Speech*. New York: King's Crown Press.

Penny, Ralph. 1991. *A History of the Spanish Language*. Cambridge University Press.

Pereira, Dulce. 2000. "Um Crioulo de Outro Planeta." In *Crioulos de Base Portuguesa*, ed. Ernesto d'Andrade *et al*. Lisbon: Associação Portuguesa de Lingüística, 27–46.

Pereira, Zélia. 2000. "Os Jesuítas em Moçambique." In *Lusotopie 2000. Lusophnies asiatiques, Asiatiques en lusophonies*. Paris: Editions Karthala, 81–105.

Peres, João Andrade and Telmo Móia. 1995. *Áreas Críticas da Língua Portuguesa*. Lisboa: Editorial Caminho.

Perini, Mário A. 1997. *Sofrendo a Gramática. Ensaios Sobre a Linguagem*. São Paulo: Editora Ática.

Perini, Mário A. 1998. *Gramática Descritiva do Português*. 3rd edition. São Paulo: Editora Ática.

Perini, Mário A. 2002a. *Modern Portuguese. A Reference Grammar*. New Haven: Yale University Press.

Perini, Mário A. 2002b. "A Língua do Brasil Amanhã." (www.linguanet.hpg.com.br).

Perini, Mário A. 2004. *Talking Brazilian. A Brazilian Portuguese Pronunciation Workbook*. New Haven: Yale University Press.

Pessoa, Marlos de Barros. 1998. "Proposta de Periodização para a História do Português Brasileiro." In *Actas do Quinto Congresso da Associação Internacional de Lusitanistas*, ed. T. F. Earle. Oxford/Coimbra: Edições Técnicas, 229–245.

Pinto, Edith Pimentel, ed. 1978. *O Português do Brasil. Textos Críticos e Teóricos*, vol. 1: *1820/1920. Fontes para a teoria e a história*. Rio de Janeiro: Livros Técnicos e Científicos.

Pinto, Edith Pimentel, ed. 1981. *O Português do Brasil. Textos Críticos e Teóricos*, vol. 2: *1920/1945. Fontes para a teoria e a história*. Rio de Janeiro: Livros Técnicos e Científicos.

Ploae-Hanganu, Mariana. 1998. "A Dinâmica Lexical do Crioulo Português da África." In *Actas do Quinto Congresso da Associação Internacional de Lusitanistas*, ed. T. F. Earle. Oxford/Coimbra: Edições Técnicas, 255–265.

Pontes, Eunice Souza Lima. 1973. *Estrutura do Verbo no Português Coloquial*. 2nd edition. Petrópolis: Editora Vozes.

Pontes, Eunice Souza Lima. 1987. *O Tópico no Português do Brasil*. Campinas: Pontes Editores.

Pontífice, Fernanda. 1991. "A Língua Portuguesa no Ensino," *Revista Internacional de Língua Portuguesa*, 4, 86–90.

Pontífice, Fernanda. 2002. "S. Tomé e Príncipe: Breve Caracterização do Quadro Linguístico." In *Em Uma Política de Língua para o Português*, ed. Maria Helena Mira Mateus. Lisbon: Edições Colibri, 55–60.

Possenti, Sírio. 2002. "Um Programa Mínimo." In Bagno 2002, 317–332.

Prado Junior, Caio. 1942. *Formação do Brasil Contemporâneo*. São Paulo: Livraria Martins Editora.

Prata, Mario. 1994. *Dicionário de Português: Schifaizfavoire. Crônicas Lusitanas.* Rio de Janeiro: Editora Globo.

Preti, Dino. 1984. *A Linguagem Proibida. Um Estudo sobre a Linguagem Erótica.* São Paulo: T. A. Queiroz, Editor.

Preti, Dino, ed. 1997. *O Discurso Oral Culto.* São Paulo: Humanitas–FFLCH/USP.

*Público.* 2000. " 'Portunhol' Será a Língua Brasileira dentro de 300 Anos." April 4, 7.

Rameh, Clea A. S. 1962. "Contrastive Analysis of English and Portuguese Intonation." M.S. Dissertation No. 2118. Georgetown University.

Ramos, Belmiro. 1985. "Situação Actual da Língua Portuguesa em Cabo Verde." In *Actas do Congresso sobre a Situação Actual da Língua Portuguesa no Mundo (1983).* Lisbon: Instituto de Cultura e Língua Portuguesa, 225–232.

Raposo, Eduardo. 1986. "On the Null Object in European Portuguese." In *Studies in Romance Linguistics,* ed. Osvaldo Jaeggli and Carmen Silva-Corvalán. Dordrecht: Foris, 373–390.

Raposo, Eduardo. 1995. "Próclise, Ênclise, e a Posição do Verbo em Português Europeu." In *O Amor das Letras e das Gentes. In Honor of Maria de Lourdes Belchior Pontes,* ed. João Camilo dos Santos and Frederick G. Williams. Santa Barbara: Center for Portuguese Studies, 455–481.

Rebelo, Aldo. 1999. *Projeto de Lei 1676/1999.* http://www.camara.gov.br/aldorebelo.

Ribeiro, Ilza. 1993. "A Formação dos Tempos Compostos: A Evolução Histórica das Formas *ter, haver* e *ser.*" In Roberts and Kato 1993, 343–386.

Ribeiro, João. 1921. *A Língua Nacional. Notas Aproveitáveis.* São Paulo: Editora da Revista do Brasil.

Ribeiro, José *et al.* 1977. *Esboço de um Atlas Lingüístico de Minas Gerais* vol. 1. Rio de Janeiro: MEC/Fundação Casa de Rui Barbosa, Universidade de Juiz de Fora.

Rïïho, Timo. 1999 [1990]. "Entrevista com Luís Filipe Lindley Cintra." In *Lindley Cintra. Homenagem ao Homem, ao Mestre e ao Cidadão,* ed. Isabel Hub Faria. Lisbon: Edições Cosmos, 57–71.

Risso, Mercedes Sanfelice. 1996. "O Articulador Discursivo 'então.'" In Castilho and Basilio 1996, 423–451.

Risso, Mercedes Sanfelice. 1999. "Aspectos Textuais-Interativos fos Marcadores Discursivos de Abertura *bom, bem, olha, ah,* no Português Culto Falado." In *Gramática do Português Falado,* vol. 7: *Novos Estudos,* ed. Maria Helena de Moura Neves. Campinas: Humanitas FFLCH/USP, 259–296.

Roberts, Ian. 1993. "O português brasileiro no contexto das línguas românicas," In Roberts and Kato 1993, 409–425.

Roberts, Ian and Mary A. Kato. 1993. *Português Brasileiro. Uma Viagem Diacrônica.* Campinas: Editora da Unicamp.

Rocha-Trindade, Maria Beatriz. 2000a. "The Portuguese Diaspora." In Teixeira and da Rosa 2000, 15–33.

Rocha-Trindade, Maria Beatriz. 2000b. "Uma imigração retribuída. A presença dos brasileiros em Portugal." *Camões – Revista de Letras e Culturas Lusófonas* (October–November), 120–127.

Rodrigues, Ada Natal. 1974. *O Dialeto Caipira na Região de Piracicaba.* São Paulo: Editorial Ática S.A.

Rodrigues, Aryon D. 1986. *Línguas Brasileiras: para o Conhecimento das Línguas Indígenas.* São Paulo: Loyola.

Rodrigues, Aryon D. 2001. "As Línguas Gerais Sul-Americanas." www.unb.br/il/lali/lingerais.htm.

Rodrigues, Maria de Lourdes Bravo da Costa. 2000. "The Status of Portuguese Language and Some Cultural Aspects in Goa." In *Lusotopie 2000. Lusophonies asiatiques, Asiatiques en lusophonies*. Paris: Editions Karthala 597–609.

Rogers, Francis M. 1946. "Insular Portuguese Pronunciation: Madeira," *Hispanic Review*, 14: 235–253.

Rogers, Francis M. 1948. "Insular Portuguese Pronunciation: Porto Santo and Eastern Azores," *Hispanic Review*, 16: 1–23.

Rogers, Francis M. 1949. "Insular Portuguese Pronunciation: Central and Western Azores," *Hispanic Review*, 17: 47–70.

Rogers, Francis M. 1979. *Atlantic Islanders of the Azores and Madeiras*. North Quincy, MA: The Christopher Publishing House.

Rohlfs Gerhard. 1960. *La diferenciación léxica de las lenguas románicas*. Publicaciones de la *Revista de Filologia Española*, 14. Madrid: CSIC.

Rona, Pedro. 1965. *El dialecto fronterizo del Norte del Uruguay*. Montevideo: Adolfo Linardi.

Rosa, João Guimarães. 1987. *Grande Sertão. Aus dem brasilianischen Portugiesisch von Curt Meyer-Clason*. Cologne: Verlag Kiepenheuer & Witsch.

Rosa, João Guimarães. 1990. *Grande Sertão. Traduzione dal brasiliano e glossario di Edoardo Bizzarri*. 4th edition. Milan: Feltrinelli.

Rosa, João Guimarães. 1991. *Diadorim.* [*Grande Sertão: Veredas.*] *Traduit du brésilien par Maryvonne Lapouge-Pettorelli*. Paris: Albin Michel.

Rossi, Nelson *et al.* 1963. *Atlas Prévio dos Falares Baianos*. Rio de Janeiro: MEC/INL.

Sampaio, Mário Arnaud. 1995. *Palavras Indígenas no Linguajar Brasileiro*. Porto Alegre: Sagra–D. C. Luzzatto.

Sandalo, Maria Filomena Spatti. 2000. "Morfologia." In *Introdução à Lingüística. Domínios e Fronteiras*, vol. 1, ed. Fernanda Mussalim and Anna Christina Bentes. São Paulo: Cortez Editora, 181–206.

Sandemann, Antônio José. 1986. *Wortbildung im heutigen brasilianischen Portugiesisch*. Bonn: Romanistischer Verlag.

Sandemann, Antônio José. 1995. "A Composição no Português Falado." In *Gramática do Português Falado*, vol. 3: *As Abordagens*, ed. Ataliba Teixeira de Castilho. Campinas: Editora da Unicamp/FAPESP, 398–404.

Santos, Maria José de Moura. 1964–1965. "Os Falares Fronteiriços de Trás-os-Montes," *Revista Portuguesa de Filologia*, 13, 1–2, 57–253.

Santos, Valdete Pinheiro. 1991. "Os Vocábulos de Origem Africana no Espaço Literário de Língua Portuguesa: Expresão de Variantes," *Revista Internacional de Língua Portuguesa*, 5/6, 136–147.

Sapir, Edward. 1921. *Language. An Introduction to the Study of Speech*. Nova York, Harcourt, Brace.

Saraiva, José Hermano. 1997. *Portugal: A Companion History*. Edited and expanded by Ian Robertson and Lat C. Taylor. Manchester: Carcanet Press Limited.

Schei, Ane. 2003. "Algumas observações sobre a colocação dos pronomes clíticos no português brasileiro falado." *Studia Neophilologica* 75: 58–70.

Scherre, Maria Marta Pereira and Anthony J. Naro. 1993. "Duas Dimensões do Paralelismo Formal na Concordância Verbal no Português Popular do Brasil." *DELTA*

*Revista de Documentação de Estudos em Lingüística Teórica e Aplicada* 9:1, 1–14.

Scherre, Maria Marta Pereira and Anthony J. Naro. 2000. "Garimpando as Origens Estruturais do Português Brasileiro." Paper presented at the International Congress on 500 Years of the Portuguese Language in Brazil (May 2000). Universidade de Évora, Portugal (www.linguanet.hpg.com.br).

Schiffman, Harold F. 1997. "Diglossia as a Sociolinguistic Situation." *The Handbook of Sociolinguistics*, ed. Florian Coulmas. Oxford: Blackwell.

Schwegler, Armin and John Lipski. 1993. "Creole Spanish and Afro-Hispanic." In *Bilingualism and Linguistic Conflict in Romance*. Trends in Romance Linguistics and Philology, 5, ed. John N. Green and Rebecca Posner. Berlin: Mouton de Gruyer, 407–432.

Schwenter, Scott A. and Gláucia Silva. 2002. "Overt vs. Null Direct Objects in Spoken Brazilian Portuguese: A Semantic/Pragmatic Account," *Hispania*, 853: 577–586.

Silva, David. 1988. "The Sociolinguistic Variance of Low Vowels in Azorean Portuguese." In *Linguistic Change and Contact*. Proceedings of the 16th Annual Conference on New Ways of Analyzing Variation in Language, ed. Kathleen Ferrara *et al*. Austin, TX: University of Texas, Department of Linguistics, 336–344.

Silva, Giselle M. de Oliveira e and Alzira Tavares de Macedo. 1991. "Discourse Markers in the Spoken Portuguese of Rio de Janeiro," *Language Variation and Change*, 4, 235–249.

Silva, João Gomes da. 1991. "Interferência e Variante Linguística. Algumas Considerações Sociolinguísticas sobre o Português Falado em Moçambique," *Revista Internacional de Língua Portuguesa*, 5/6, 101–105.

Silva, Myriam Barbosa da and Rosa Virgínia Mattos e Silva. 1980/81. "Manifestações do Processo de Simplificação em um Dialecto de Contacto," *Boletim de Filologia*, 26, 125–137.

Silva, Rosa Virgínia Mattos e. 1995. "Variação e Mudança no Português Arcaico: *ter* ou *haver* em Estruturas de Posse." In *Miscelânea de Estudos Lingüísticos Filológicos e Literários in memoriam Celso Cunha*, ed. Cilene da Cunha Pereira and Paulo Roberto Dias Pereira. Rio de Janeiro: Editora Nova Fronteira, 299–311.

Silva, Rosa Virginia Mattos e. 1996. "O Português São Dois (Variação, Mudança, Norma e Questão do Ensino do Português no Brasil)." In *Actas do Congresso Internacional sobre o Português*, vol. 2, ed. Inês Duarte and Isabel Leiria. Lisbon: Edições Colibri, 375–401.

Silva, Rosa Virginia Mattos e, ed. 2001. *Para a História do Português Brasileiro*, vols. 2 and 3: *Primeiros Estudos*. São Paulo: Humanitas–FFLCH/USP.

Silva, Thaïs Cristófaro. 1998. *Fonética e Fonologia do Português: Roteiro de Estudos e Guia de Exercícios*. São Paulo: Editora Contexto.

Silva-Corvalán, Carmen. 2001. *Sociolingüística y pragmática del español*. Washington, DC: Georgetown University Press.

Silva Neto, Serafim da. 1970. *História da Língua Portuguesa*. 2nd augmented edition. Rio de Janeiro: Livros de Portugal.

Silva Neto, Serafim da. 1976. *Introdução ao Estudo da Língua Portuguesa no Brasil*. 3rd edition. Rio de Janeiro: Presença.

Silveira [Álvaro F.], Sousa da. [1923] 1952 [issued in 1958]. *Lições de Português*. 5th edition. Coimbra: Atlântida / Rio de Janeiro: Livros de Portugal.

Sitoe, Bento. 1991. "Empréstimos Lexicais do Português no Tsonga," *Revista Internacional de Língua Portuguesa*, 5/6, 106–113.

Smith, Ian R. 1978. *Sri Lanka Creole Portuguese Phonology*. Vanchiyoor, Trivandrum (India): Dravidian Linguistics Association.

Sousa-Möckel, Filomena de. 1995. "O Comportamento Linguístico dos Portugueses Residentes na Alemanha." In *Actas do 4° Congresso da Associação Internacional de Lusitanistas*. Lisbon: Lidel, 257–264.

Souza, Constância Maria Borges de. 1989. "A Concordância Sujeito/Verbo num Dialeto Baiano." In Castilho 1989b, 89–101.

Staub, Augustine. 1956. "Comparative Study of English and Portuguese Intonation." M.S. Dissertation No. 1354. Georgetown University.

Stefanova-Gueorguiev, Irena. 2000. "Español y portugués en la Península Ibérica y en América Latina: dos situaciones de contacto lingüístico." MA dissertation, Simon Fraser University (www.analitica.com/bitbliotteca/irena_stefanova/tesis.pdfeca).

Stephens, Thomas M. 1989. "Language Maintenance and Ethnic Survival: The Portuguese in New Jersey," *Hispania*, 72/3, 716–720.

Stephens, Thomas M. 1999. *Dictionary of Latin American Racial and Ethnic Terminology*. 2nd edition. Gainesville: University Press of Florida.

Stephens, Thomas M. 2002. *A Game of Mirrors. The Changing Face of Ethno-Racial Constructs and Language in the Americas*. New York: University Press of America.

Stewart, Miranda. 1999. *The Spanish Language Today*. London and New York: Routledge.

Stroud, Christopher and Perpétua Gonçalves, eds. 1997–1998. *Panorama do Português Oral de Maputo*, vol. 1, *Objectivos e Métodos*; vol. 2, *A Construção de Um Banco de 'Erros.'* Maputo: Instituto Nacional do Desenvolvimento da Educação.

Tarallo, Fernando. 1983. "Relativization Strategies in Brazilian Portuguese." Doctoral dissertation, University of Pennsylvania.

Tarallo, Fernando. 1993. [1986] "Sobre a Alegada Origem Crioula do Português Brasileiro." In Roberts and Kato 1993, 35–68.

Taylor, James L. 1963. *Portuguese–English Dictionary*. Rio de Janeiro: Distribuidora Record.

Teixeira, Carlos and Victor M. P. da Rosa, eds. 2000. *The Portuguese in Canada. From the Sea to the City*. Toronto: University of Toronto Press.

Teyssier, Paul. 1959. *La langue de Gil Vicente*. Paris: Librairie C. Klincksieck, 1959.

Teyssier, Paul. 1985. "Lição final." In *Actas do Congresso sobre a Situação Actual da Língua Portuguesa no Mundo*, vol. 3. Lisbon: Instituto de Cultura e Língua Portuguesa, 45–55.

Teyssier, Paul. 1994. *História da Língua Portuguesa*, trans. Celso Cunha. Lisbon: Livraria Sá da Costa.

Theban, Laurentiu. 1985. "Situação e Perspectivas do Português e dos Crioulos de Origem Portuguesa na Índia e no Sri-Lanka." In *Actas do Congresso sobre a Situação Actual da Língua Portuguesa no Mundo (1983)*. Lisbon: Instituto de Cultura e Língua Portuguesa, 269–285.

Thomas, Earl. 1969. *The Syntax of Spoken Brazilian Portuguese*. Nashville: Vanderbilt University Press.

Tláskal, Jaromír. 1981 "Dynamique du système du portugais parlé au Brésil," *Boletim de Filologia* (Lisbon), 26/1, 29–37.

Tolman, Jon M., Ricardo M. Paiva, John B. Jensen, and Nivea P. Parsons. 1988. *Travessia 1. A Portuguese Language Textbook Program.* Textbook, Workbook, and Laboratory Manual. Washington, DC: Georgetown University Press.

Tolman, Jon M., Ricardo M. Paiva, John B. Jensen, and Nivea P. Parsons. 1989. *Travessia 2. A Portuguese Language Textbook Program.* Textbook, Workbook, and Laboratory Manual. Washington, DC: Georgetown University Press.

Tomás, Maria Isabel. 1992. "A Presença Africana nos Crioulos Portugueses do Oriente: O Crioulo de Damão." In *Actas do Colóquio sobre Crioulos de Base Lexical Portuguesa*, ed. Ernesto d'Andrade and Alain Kihm. Lisbon: Edições Colibri, 97–107.

Trask, R. L. 1999. *Key Concepts in Language and Linguistics.* London and New York: Routledge.

Travaglia, Luiz Carlos. 1999. "O Relevo no Português Falado: Tipos e Estratégias, Processos e Recursos." In *Gramática do Português Falado*, vol. 7: *Novos Estudos*, ed. Maria Helena de Moura Neves. Campinas: Humanitas–FFLCH/USP, 76–130.

Trudgill, Peter and Jean Hannah. 2002. *International English. A Guide to the Varieties of Standard English.* 4th edition. London: Arnold.

Urbano, Hudinilson. 1999. "Aspectos Basicamente Interacionais dos Marcadores Discursivos." In *Gramática do Português Falado*, vol. 7: *Novos Estudos*, ed. Maria Helena de Moura Neves. Campinas: Humanitas–FFLCH/USP, 194–258.

Väänänen, Veikko. 1966. *Le latin vulgaire des inscriptions pompéiennes.* 3rd edition. Berlin: Akademie-Verlag.

Väänänen, Veikko. 1981. *Introduction au latin vulgaire.* 3rd edition. Paris: Editions Klincksieck.

Vasconcellos, J. Leite de. [1901] 1970. *Esquisse d'une dialectologie portugaise. Thèse pour le Doctorat de l'Université de Paris.* 2nd edition ed. Maria Adelaide Valle Cintra. Lisbon: Centro de Estudos Filológicos.

Vaz, Katherine. 2001. "Songs of Fate: Portuguese Writing in America." In *Global Impact of the Portuguese Language*, ed. Asela Rodriguez de Laguna. New Brunswick and London: Transaction Publishers, 221–230.

Vázquez-Cuesta, Pilar and Maria Albertina Mendes da Luz. 1987. *Gramática portuguesa*, 2 vols. 3rd edition. Madrid: Gredos.

Veado, Rosa Maria Assis. 1982. *Comportamento Lingüístico do Dialeto Rural – MG.* Belo Horizonte: Universidade Federal de Minas Gerais.

Vilhena, Maria da Conceição. 1995. "Falares Portugueses em Território Castelhano: Herrera de Alcântara." In *Miscelânea de Estudos Lingüísticos, Filológicos e Literários in Memoriam Celso Cunha*, ed. Cilene da Cunha Pereira and Paulo Roberto Dias Pereira. Rio de Janeiro: Editora Nova Fronteira, 417–428.

Villar, Mauro. 1989. *Dicionário Contrastivo Luso-Brasileiro.* Rio de Janeiro: Editora Guanabara.

Viudas Camarasa, Antonio. 2001. "A fala, habla fronteriza con Portugal." *Hablas de Extremadura en la Red.* http://www.galeon.com/habla-fronteriza.

Vogt, Carlos and Peter Fry. 1996. *Cafundó: A África no Brasil. Linguagem e Sociedade.* São Paulo: Companhia das Letras.

Vogt, Carlos and Peter Fry. 2000. "A descoberta do Cafundó e o Kafundó descoberto." http://www.comciencia.br.

Wardhaugh, Ronald. 2002. *An Introduction to Sociolinguistics*. 4th edition. Malden, MA: Blackwell Publishers.

Weinberg, Monica. 2003. "A Média Foi só 3,6," *Veja* 36/50 (December 17), 74.

Whinnom, Keith. 1965. "Contacts de langues et emprunts lexicaux," *Orbis*, 14/1, 509–517.

Whitley, M. Stanley. 2002. *Spanish/English Contrasts. A Course in Spanish Linguistics*. 2nd edition, Washington, D.C.: Georgetown University Press.

Williams, Edwin B. 1968. *From Latin to Portuguese*. 2nd edition. Philadelphia: University of Pennsylvania Press.

Yule, George. 1996. *Pragmatics*. Oxford University Press.

# Index

Asterisked page entries refer to terms explained in the glossary. Emboldened page references refer to main sources of information within a run of several page references. Under the heading 'Portuguese,' entries from *Latin source* to *future prospects* referring to the history of the language are arranged in chronological order and entries from *Brazilian* to *varieties* are arranged in alphabetical order.

.

CPSIA information can be obtained at www.ICGtesting.com
Printed in the USA
BVOW020805171211

278594BV00005B/164/P